RELATIONAL AUTONOMY

RELATIONAL AUTONOMY

Feminist Perspectives on Autonomy, Agency, and the Social Self

Edited by
Catriona Mackenzie and Natalie Stoljar

New York   Oxford

Oxford University Press

2000

Oxford University Press

Oxford   New   York

Athens   Auckland   Bangkok   Bogotá   Buenos Aires   Calcutta
Cape Town   Chennai   Dar es Salaam   Delhi   Florence   Hong Kong   Istanbul
Karachi   Kuala Lumpur   Madrid   Melbourne   Mexico City   Mumbai
Nairobi   Paris   São Paulo   Singapore   Taipei   Tokyo   Toronto   Warsaw

and associated companies in
Berlin   Ibadan

Published by Oxford University Press
198 Madison Avenue, New York, New York 10016

Oxford is a registered trademark of Oxford University Press.

Library of Congress Cataloging-in-Publication Data
Relational autonomy : feminist perspective on autonomy, agency, and the social self / edited by
Catriona Mackenzie and Natalie Stoljar.
p.   cm.
ISBN 0-19-512333-6; ISBN 0-19-512334-4 (pbk.)
1. Feminist theory.   2. Autonomy.   3. Agent (Philosophy)   4. Self (Philosophy)
I. Mackenzie, Catriona.   II. Stoljar, Natalie.
HQ1190.R45   1999
305.42—DC21   99-12792

1 3 5 7 9 8 6 4 2
Printed in the United States of America
on acid-free paper

ACKNOWLEDGMENTS

We wish to express our gratitude to the contributors to this volume for their enthusiasm for the project and the generosity with which they responded to editorial comments and suggestions. Diana Meyers also provided encouragement and invaluable advice at various stages of the project.

Some of the articles in the volume were originally presented at the Conference on Feminist Perspectives on Autonomy and Agency, held at the Australian National University in June 1996. We are grateful to Fiona Webster for conference organization and to all the participants at the conference, especially to Susan Brison, Lorraine Code, Marilyn Friedman, and Diana Meyers, who traveled from North America to present their papers.

For financial assistance in hosting the conference, we are indebted to the Philosophy Program, Research School of Social Sciences, ANU; the Social and Political Theory Group, Research School of Social Sciences, ANU; the Department of Philosophy, Faculty of Arts, ANU; and the Australia Foundation for Culture and the Humanities. Financial support for the project as a whole was provided by an Australian Research Council Small Grant and a Macquarie University Visiting Scholar Research Grant.

We received invaluable research assistance from Fiona Webster in the intial stages of the project and from Sarah Bachelard in the final stages. Special thanks are due to Ian Gold, Peter Menzies, and our families.

Sydney, Australia   C. M.
May 1999
Canberra, Australia   N. S.
May 1999

CONTENTS

CONTRIBUTORS

LINDA BARCLAY is a lecturer in ethics at La Trobe University. Her main research is in applied ethics, including professional ethics and political philosophy.

PAUL BENSON is associate professor of philosophy at the University of Dayton. He works primarily in the areas of action theory, moral psychology, and social philosophy and is currently writing a book about the social and normative dimensions of free agency.

SUSAN J. BRISON is associate professor of philosophy at Dartmouth College, where she also teaches in the women's studies program. She has published articles on feminist ethics, philosophy of law, and social and political philosophy in anthologies and in journals including *Ethics, Legal Theory,* and *Nomos.* Coeditor of *Contemporary Perspectives on Constitutional Interpretation* (Westview, 1993), she is author of *Speech, Harm and Conflicts of Rights* (Princeton University Press, forthcoming 2000) and is currently writing a book on trauma and memory.

LORRAINE CODE is distinguished research professor of philosophy at York University in Toronto. She is the author of *Epistemic Responsibility* (University Press of New England, 1987), *What Can She Know? Feminist Theory and the Construction of Knowledge* (Cornell, 1991), and *Rhetorical Spaces: Essays on (Gendered) Locations*

(Routledge, 1995). She is currently developing an ecological model for naturalistic epistemology and editing a one-volume *Encyclopedia of Feminist Theories* (Routledge, 1999).

SUSAN DODDS is a senior lecturer in philosophy and the deputy director of the Institute of Social Change and Critical Inquiry at the University of Wollongong in Australia. She has published work in political philosophy, bioethics, philosophy of mind, and philosophy of feminism. With Rebecca Albury, she is currently working on a critical examination of the debate about policymaking in reproductive technology, analyzing the demand for regulation in terms of women's status as persons and as citizens.

ANNE DONCHIN is professor of philosophy at Indiana University, Indianapolis, and former director of their women's studies program. She teaches and writes principally in the areas of bioethics and feminist philosophy and has published numerous articles in leading bioethical and feminist journals. She is coeditor (with Laura Purdy) of *Embodying Bioethics: Recent Feminist Advances* (Rowman & Littlefield, 1999) and is currently completing *Procreation, Power, and Personal Autonomy: Feminist Reflections* (Temple University Press, forthcoming). She is also a founder and coordinator of the International Network on Feminist Approaches to Bioethics.

MARILYN FRIEDMAN is professor of philosophy at Washington University in St. Louis. Her special interests are in ethics, social philosophy, and feminist theory. She is the author of *What Are Friends For? Feminists Perspectives on Personal Relationships and Moral Theory* (Cornell, 1993), the coauthor of *Political Correctness: For and Against* (Rowman & Littlefield, 1995), and the coeditor of *Feminism and Community* (Temple, 1995) and *Mind and Morals: Essays on Ethics and Cognitive Science* (Bradford/MIT, 1996).

GENEVIEVE LLOYD is professor of philosophy at the University of New South Wales in Sydney. She is the author of *The Man of Reason: "Male" and "Female" in Western Philosophy*, 2nd ed. (Routledge, 1993), *Being in Time: Selves and Narrators in Philosophy and Literature* (Routledge, 1993), *Part of Nature: Self-Knowledge in Spinoza's Ethics* (Cornell, 1994), and *Spinoza and the Ethics* (Routledge, 1996).

CATRIONA MACKENZIE is a senior lecturer in philosophy at Macquarie University in Sydney. She works primarily in ethics, feminist theory, and moral psychology and has published articles in a variety of journals and edited collections. Her current research includes a book on the interconnections among emotion, imagination, embodiment, and autonomy.

CAROLYN MCLEOD is a PhD candidate in the philosophy department at Dalhousie University in Halifax, Canada. She has been awarded postdoctoral fellowships by the Center for Human Bioethics, University of Minnesota and the Social Sciences and Humanities Research Council of Canada. Her dissertation is on the nature of self-trust and its role in autonomous decision making.

DIANA TIETJENS MEYERS is professor of philosophy at the University of Connecticut, Storrs. She is the author of *Self, Society, and Personal Choice* (Columbia, 1989) and *Subjection and Subjectivity* (Routledge, 1994), and she has edited many collections, most recently *Feminists Rethink the Self* (Westview, 1997) and *Feminist Social Thought: A Reader* (Routledge, 1997). She is currently working on two books, one extending her procedural account of autonomy and the other examining how cultural figurations of gender confound agency.

SUSAN SHERWIN is professor of philosophy and women's studies at Dalhousie University in Halifax, Canada. She is the author of *No Longer Patient: Feminist Ethics and Health Care* (Temple, 1992) and is coordinator of the Feminist Health Care Ethics Research Network, which wrote *The Politics of Women's Health: Exploring Agency and Autonomy* (Temple, 1998). She is a founding member of Feminist Approaches to the Bioethics Network and is a member of the board of the International Association of Bioethics.

NATALIE STOLJAR received her PhD in philosophy from Princeton University in 1994. She is currently a senior lecturer in philosophy at Monash University, Melbourne. Her main research areas are moral and legal philosophy and feminist philosophy. She is currently working on a book on legal interpretation.

RELATIONAL AUTONOMY

INTRODUCTION

Autonomy Refigured

Catriona Mackenzie
Natalie Stoljar

Introduction

In the current climate of feminist theory, the notion of individual autonomy may seem an unlikely topic for a collection of feminist essays. Although the ideal of autonomy once seemed to hold out much promise, in providing both a liberatory goal and a moral standpoint from which to criticize sex-based oppression, autonomy is now generally regarded by feminist theorists with suspicion. Crudely stated, the charge is that the concept of autonomy is inherently masculinist, that it is inextricably bound up with masculine character ideals, with assumptions about selfhood and agency that are metaphysically, epistemologically, and ethically problematic from a feminist perspective, and with political traditions that historically have been hostile to women's interests and freedom. What lies at the heart of these charges is the conviction that the notion of individual autonomy is fundamentally individualistic and rationalistic.

The aim of this collection is to challenge this conviction. While it is true that feminist critiques of autonomy have identified serious theoretical and political problems with some historical and contemporary conceptions of autonomy, the notion of autonomy is vital to feminist attempts to understand oppression, subjection, and agency. Moreover, none of the major feminist critiques justifies repudiating the concept altogether. The challenge facing feminist theorists is rather to draw on aspects of the feminist critique of autonomy to reconceptualize and refigure the concept of individual autonomy from a feminist perspective. It is this refigured concept that we are calling "relational autonomy."[1]

The term "relational autonomy," as we understand it, does not refer to a single unified conception of autonomy but is rather an umbrella term, designating a range of related perspectives. These perspectives are premised on a shared conviction, the conviction that persons are socially embedded and that agents' identities are formed within the context of social relationships and shaped by a complex of intersecting social determinants, such as race, class, gender, and ethnicity. Thus the focus of relational approaches is to analyze the implications of the intersubjective and social dimensions of selfhood and identity for conceptions of individual autonomy and moral and political agency.

The purpose of this introduction is to situate relational approaches to autonomy in the context of both feminist critiques of autonomy and contemporary philosophical accounts of autonomy. We outline and assess five major feminist critiques of autonomy and then map out the conceptual terrain of contemporary philosophical accounts of autonomy, focusing in particular on the vexed relationship between autonomy and socialization. Finally, we draw on the conclusions of the previous two sections to provide a more detailed characterization of relational models of autonomy. Before proceeding to these more detailed discussions, however, it is worth providing a general overview of the notion of autonomy within contemporary moral and political philosophy.

The concept of individual autonomy has come to occupy a central, if contested, place in moral and political philosophy. For example, questions concerning the nature and value of individual autonomy and its compatibility with a recognition of the social embeddedness of persons are central to current debates in political philosophy among liberals, communitarians, and feminists.[2] Whereas the value of autonomy is contested in political philosophy, this is less the case in applied ethics and legal philosophy. In these areas, disputants on either side of a range of different debates often agree on the value, even the primacy, of autonomy but disagree about how it is best promoted. In bioethics, for example, appeals to patient autonomy figure prominently in debates about voluntary active euthanasia, in analyses of the physician-patient relationship, and in debates about the ethics of reproductive technologies and surrogate motherhood, with the different disputants in these debates each claiming to have autonomy on their side.[3] In legal philosophy, the appeal to individual autonomy has been used to defend an unrestricted right to freedom of speech in the context of debates concerning legal restrictions on hate speech and pornography. It has also been used to contest such a right.[4] Finally, recent debates about the nature of autonomy in moral philosophy and moral psychology intersect with, and have implications for, an increasingly broad range of philosophical debates. These include the free will–determinism debate; theories of personal identity; theories of practical reasoning and deliberation; conceptions of agency and selfhood; accounts of character and self-respect; and theories of oppression, embodiment, and subjectivity.

However, despite the importance of the notion of individual autonomy within contemporary moral and political theory, there is no consensus about what the concept means or when it can be legitimately employed. In bioethics, autonomy is often equated with informed consent. In rational choice theory, autonomy is equated with voluntary, rational choice. In other contexts, for example, within liberal political theory, autonomy is considered to be an individual right. For liberals of a libertarian persuasion, the right to autonomy is construed as negative liberty, a right of the individual to freedom from undue interference in the exercise of choice (moral, political, personal, and religious) and in the satisfaction of individual preferences. For Rawlsian liberals, autonomy is understood in Kantian terms as the capacity for rational self-legislation and is considered to be the defining feature of persons.

The conceptual thread that links these different uses of the notion of autonomy is the idea of self-determination or self-government, which is taken to be the defining characteristic of free moral agents. Notions of autonomy as individual choice or as a political right flow from, and are derivative of, this defining characteristic. Because of the core role of the idea of autonomy as self-determination, section 3 of this introduction focuses on the notion of autonomy as it is understood in moral psychology and on the debates within that literature concerning the conditions necessary for its development and exercise.

Despite the differences that we have identified among uses of the concept of individual autonomy, there are nevertheless important overlaps between the different senses of autonomy and between the different domains in which the concept is employed. There are clear historical and conceptual links among conceptions of choice, conceptions of political rights, and conceptions of individuality, autonomy and selfhood. These links explain why the concept of autonomy is so contested among liberals, communitarians, and feminists. And they also explain why debates about autonomy are often fraught with confusion—because the *concept* of autonomy is sometimes conflated with one particular *conception* of autonomy and its attendant conceptions of choice and rights. The most obvious example is the caricature of individual autonomy as exemplified by the self-sufficient, rugged male individualist, rational maximizing chooser of libertarian theory. It is this caricature that is often the target of feminist critiques of autonomy.[5] Given the widespread cultural association of individual autonomy with this caricature, it has been, and continues to be, important for feminists to contest this particular conception of autonomy. However, it is also imperative for feminists to reclaim and reconceptualize the concept of individual autonomy and to articulate conceptions of choice and of political rights that are more adequate from a feminist perspective. To do so, feminist theorists must draw on both mainstream philosophical theories of autonomy and on feminist critiques of culturally dominant conceptions of individuality, selfhood, and moral and political agency.

Five Feminist Critiques of Autonomy

This section briefly outlines five major feminist critiques of the notion of autonomy: *symbolic, metaphysical, care, postmodernist,* and *diversity.* In what follows, we outline the major components of each critique, arguing that none of them justifies rejecting the concept of autonomy altogether.[6]

Symbolic Critiques

The symbolic critique of autonomy has been articulated most clearly and force-fully by Lorraine Code.[7] Code's critique is not directed toward any particular the-ory of autonomy but rather toward the abstraction or character ideal of the "au-tonomous man." This character ideal, she claims, informs mainstream moral theory and epistemology, to their detriment, and is at the heart of what she regards as the "autonomy-obsession" of contemporary Western culture. Central to this character ideal is the notion of self-sufficient independence, which functions both descrip-tively and prescriptively to promote a particular conception of human nature and a particular conception of the telos of human life. The descriptive premise on which the character ideal is based is the notion that human beings are capable of leading self-sufficient, isolated, independent lives. From this premise is drawn the prescrip-tive conclusion that the goal of human life is the realization of self-sufficiency and individuality. Code explains:

> Autonomous man is—and should be—self-sufficient, independent, and self-reliant, a self-realizing individual who directs his efforts towards maximizing his personal gains. His independence is under constant threat from other (equally self-serving) individuals: hence he devises rules to protect himself from intrusion. Talk of rights, rational self-interest, expedience, and efficiency permeates his moral, social, and political discourse. In short, there has been a gradual alignment of *autonomy* with *individualism*.[8]

Although this character ideal is an abstraction that theorists recognize is un-likely ever to be attained, nevertheless, the ideal leads in practice to a number of problematic views. First, it supports valuing substantive independence over all other values, in particular over those arising from relations of interdependence, such as trust, loyalty, friendship, caring, and responsibility. Second, it promotes a very stripped-down conception of agents as atomistic bearers of rights, a conception in which the diversity and complexity of agents are pared away and agents are re-duced to an interchangeable sameness. Third, it suggests that values, social practices, relationships, and communities that are based on cooperation and interdependence threaten, or at least compromise, autonomy.

Code is right to be critical of the character ideal of the autonomous man, and she is correct in pointing out its influence in contemporary Western cultures. How-ever, the point of Code's critique is not to urge feminists to reject the concept of au-tonomy altogether. She acknowledges that critical reflection and assessment are of vital importance to individual women and to feminist political goals. Her point is rather that an adequate understanding of critical assessment must begin by reject-ing the conception of atomistic subjectivity characteristic of "hyperbolized auton-omy" and replacing it with a relational view of subjectivity, centered on the recogni-tion that persons are "second persons" who only become persons in relations with others.[9] Thus Code's critique is directed toward a cultural character ideal, rather than toward contemporary philosophical accounts of autonomy, and it does not provide reasons for rejecting the attempt to rehabilitate autonomy. The question that is raised, but not answered, by her critique is how to develop models of critical reflection that are consistent with a relational conception of subjectivity. Code's contribution to this collection takes up this question by examining the role that advocacy and testimony can play in furthering the autonomy of oppressed individuals and groups.

Metaphysical Critiques

The metaphysical critiques of the notion of autonomy are some of the most entrenched in the feminist literature. They claim that attributing autonomy to agents is tantamount to supposing that agents are atomistic, or separate, or radically individualistic. Since, as feminists and others have pointed out, agents are socially embedded and seem to be at least partially constituted by the social relations in which they stand, if attributing autonomy to agents is indeed to presuppose individualism or atomism, then it seems that the attempt to articulate autonomy rests on a mistake.[10] There are four possible positions within the metaphysical critiques that we wish to distinguish, which correspond to four different understandings of the term "individualism." Individualism can be understood as any of the following claims: first, that agents are causally isolated from other agents; second, that agents' sense of themselves is independent of the family and community relationships in which they participate; third, that agents' essential properties (that is, their natures, or metaphysical identities) are all intrinsic and are not comprised, even in part, by the social relations in which they stand; and fourth, that agents are metaphysically separate individuals. We consider each version of individualism in turn.

Annette Baier argues against individualism in the first sense by proposing that persons are what she calls "second-persons." This means that the development of persons requires relations of dependency on other persons: "Persons are essentially successors, heirs to other persons who formed and cared for them, and their personality is revealed both in their relations to others and in their response to their own recognized genesis."[11] Baier's claim is a causal one about the development of persons, their personalities and capacities. If she is right, individualism in the first sense is false. Persons are not causally isolated from other persons; indeed, the development of persons *requires* relations of dependency with others. We agree with Baier's version of anti-individualism. However, a commitment to this version of anti-individualism does not justify rejecting the concept of autonomy. Most theories of autonomy—especially those we discuss in the next section—are compatible with the notion that persons are relational in Baier's sense.[12] Baier's observations recommend that any reconceptualized notion should attend to the status of persons as second persons, not that autonomy should be ruled out altogether.

The second and third senses of individualism are often run together in a common feminist critique of autonomy. This critique alleges that theories of autonomy presuppose "abstract individualism," namely, the thesis that "logically if not empirically, human beings could exist outside a social context."[13] However, since persons, and hence their characteristics and capacities, are constituted, and not simply caused, by the relations to others in which they stand, theories of autonomy presuppose a flawed conception of selfhood and should be jettisoned. The claim that agents are constituted by the social context in which they participate is ambiguous between a psychological reading and a metaphysical one. Either it means that an agent's *sense* of herself is constituted by her social context, which denies individualism in the second sense, or it means that social relations are essential components of an agent's identity, which denies individualism in the third sense.

It is obviously correct to deny individualism in the second sense, yet to do so does not undermine the notion of autonomy. That is, we can accept that social relations influence and perhaps constitute agents' senses of themselves and their capacities, without concluding that capacities such as autonomy are nonexistent. As relational approaches to autonomy emphasize, reconceptualizations of autonomy must acknowledge the effect of social conditions on agents' senses of themselves, such as their senses of self-esteem and self-trust. Furthermore, denying individualism in the third sense, while more controversial,[14] does not undermine the notion of autonomy. Anti-individualism in the third sense entails that social relations are essential properties of persons. Yet, as far as we know, there are no theories of autonomy—with the possible exception of the hyperbolized notion described by Code—that take a stand on the question of the kinds of properties that are metaphysically essential to the existence and persistence of the autonomous agent. After all, the metaphysical question of the essential nature of persons is separate from and perhaps prior to the question of the nature of a person's characteristics and capacities, including her autonomy. Thus, even if both the second and third senses of anti-individualism are true, they provide no reason to reject autonomy.

Let us consider finally the fourth conception of individualism, which claims that agents are metaphysically separate individuals or entities. As Louise Antony points out, this sense of individualism is true even if we assume that social relations are essential properties of these individuals.[15] Moreover, the claim that the concept of individual autonomy presupposes individualism in the fourth sense is trivially true because the phrase "individual autonomy" implies that agents are separate entities with a capacity for autonomy. Thus, no theory of individual autonomy could presuppose anti-individualism in the fourth sense.

It follows that metaphysical critiques of autonomy are mistaken. If we understand "individualism" in any of the first three senses, most theories of autonomy do not presuppose individualism. If we understand "individualism" in the fourth sense, it is trivially true that theories of individual autonomy presuppose individualism. The moral of the discussion, therefore, is that the concept of individual autonomy should be distinguished from individualistic conceptions of individual autonomy. The task of this collection, namely, to rehabilitate individual autonomy, does not entail rehabilitating individualistic autonomy in any of the first three senses. Indeed taking the feminist critiques seriously is precisely to explore the possibilities for anti-individualistic conceptions of autonomy.

Care Critiques

According to care critiques, traditional ideals of autonomy give normative primacy to independence, self-sufficiency, and separation from others, at the expense of a recognition of the value of relations of dependency and interconnection. Since such relations have historically been central to women's lives and symbolically associated with femininity, it is argued that traditional conceptions of autonomy not only de-value women's experience and those values arising from it, such as love, loyalty, friend-ship, and care, but also are defined in opposition to femininity. Traditional concep-tions are thus masculinist conceptions.

Care critiques overlap with aspects of both symbolic critiques and metaphysi-cal critiques. They are to be distinguished from symbolic critiques because they do not characterize the concept of autonomy as inherently tainted by the connotations of masculinist conceptions of autonomy.[16] Rather the latter conceptions are criti-cized as normatively flawed. Similarly, care critiques differ from metaphysical cri-tiques because of their emphasis on the *value* of relations of nurturance and de-pendency for agents, rather than on the implications of these relations for the metaphysical nature of the self.

Care critiques appeal to Nancy Chodorow's psychoanalytic account of mascu-line and feminine psychic development.[17] On that account, in gender unequal soci-eties in which women are the primary caregivers, masculine psychic individuation and separation are conflated with separation from the mother. Masculine selfhood is thus defined as other than the feminine mother and psychic autonomy, or the de-velopment of a strong sense of self, is equated with self-sufficient independence. Feminine psychic development, by contrast, involves identification with the mother and so promotes capacities for connection and interdependence, often at the ex-pense of the development of a strong sense of self.

Virginia Held's account of the notion of the self that is at the heart of the care critiques, echoes this story:

> The self . . . is seen as having both a need for recognition and a need to under-stand the other, and these needs are seen as compatible. They are created in the context of mother-child interaction and are satisfied in a mutually empathetic relationship. . . . Both give and take in a way that not only contributes to the sat-isfaction of their needs as individuals but also affirms the 'larger relational unit' they compose. Maintaining this larger relational unit then becomes a goal, and maturity is seen not in terms of individual autonomy but in terms of competence in creating and sustaining relations of empathy and mutual intersubjectivity.[18]

The target of care critiques, and of Chodorow's critique of masculine selfhood, is autonomy understood as substantive independence. Although some care critiques unfortunately conflate autonomy with substantive independence, and therefore re-ject autonomy on the basis of this critique,[19] many are careful to distinguish them, as does Chodorow herself. Thus other theorists influenced by the care perspective, such as Jennifer Nedelsky, argue for a reconceptualization of autonomy modeled on the mother-child relationship.[20] Such reconceptualizations give normative primacy to the relations of care and connection identified by Chodorow and Gilligan and ar-ticulate autonomy within the context of these relations.

Similarly, Evelyn Fox Keller has developed a notion of dynamic autonomy, which she contrasts with static autonomy.[21] Keller sees autonomy as a kind of com-petence. The distinction between dynamic and static autonomy is a distinction be-tween, on the one hand, the kind of competence that promotes an enhanced sense of self and, on the other, the kind of competence and mastery that are pursued in the interests of domination, denied connectedness, and defensive separateness. Dynamic autonomy involves both relatedness to, and differentiation from, others. It promotes a sense of agency in a world of "interacting and interpersonal agents" and a sense of others "as subjects with whom one shares enough to allow for a recognition of their independent interests and feelings—in short for a recognition of them as other subjects."[22] Static autonomy, on the other hand arises from seeing others as a threat to the self, from insecurity about the self, and from fears of dependency and loss of self-control, leading to patterns of domination and control over others. In its extreme forms static autonomy gives rise to sadism.[23]

Care critiques, of the kind developed by Chodorow, Held, Nedelsky, and Keller thus do not repudiate the concept of autonomy altogether. Rather they recommend that autonomy be reconceptualized so that it is not defined in opposition both to femininity and to relations of dependence and connection. The issues raised by care critiques are therefore to some extent continuous with the project of articulating a relational conception of autonomy as we understand it. However, in focusing primarily on intimate dyadic relations, particularly between mother and child, care critiques provide a very circumscribed reconceptualization of autonomy. In particular, they fail to address the complex effects of oppression on agents' capacities for autonomy; and they provide a somewhat limited reconceptualization of the social dimensions of agency and selfhood. We discuss these issues further in the last section.

Postmodernist Critiques

What we are calling, rather loosely, postmodernist critiques of autonomy derive from a number of distinct theoretical perspectives: psychoanalytic theory, Foucauldian theories of power and agency, and feminist theories of sexual difference and otherness. As far as we are aware, there is no sustained and detailed critique of contemporary philosophical accounts of autonomy from any of these perspectives. Rather, critics draw on the so-called "critique of the subject" that emerges from one or more of these perspectives to criticize the assumptions that they allege to be implicit in the ideal of autonomy. In particular, it is claimed that the ideal assumes that agents are self-transparent, psychically unified, and able to achieve self-mastery. Critics who draw on psychoanalysis charge that since Freud, these assumptions have been shown to be illusory.[24] In contrast to the complete self-transparency, seamless psychic unity, and self-mastery supposedly required by autonomy, the picture of the psyche that emerges from psychoanalytic theory depicts agents as conflict-ridden, often self-deluded, fundamentally opaque to themselves, and driven by archaic drives and desires of which they may not even be aware, let alone able to master. Critics who draw on Foucauldian theories of power and agency suggest that theories of autonomy assume a pure Kantian free will, or a true self. This assumption naively ignores the fact that subjects are constituted within and by regimes, discourses, and micropractices of power. There is no pure, self-determining free will that somehow escapes the operations of power, nor is there a true self, there to be discovered through introspective reflection. Agency must be reconceptualized not as a matter of individual will but as an effect of the complex and shifting configurations of power.[25] Feminist theories of difference and otherness allege that the notion of autonomy is a historically, socially, and culturally specific ideal that parades as a universal norm. Not only does this norm suppress internal differentiation within the subject, but also in masking its specificity behind a veneer of universality, it functions coercively to suppress different others.[26]

Although they draw on rather divergent theoretical perspectives and criticize autonomy for rather divergent reasons, there is a unifying theme underlying the postmodernist critiques. The theme is that the notion of autonomy is a kind of conceit or illusion of the Enlightenment conception of the subject.[27] Thus it is charged that defenders of autonomy still cling to the Cartesian idea that consciousness can be transparently self-aware or to the Kantian view of persons as rational self-legislators, despite the fact that such views have been so decisively challenged since Nietzsche, Freud, and their heirs. Moreover, the persistence of such views is not just a harmless anachronistic hangover of the Enlightenment. It is complicit with structures of domination and subordination, in particular with the suppression of others—women, colonial subjects, blacks, minority groups—who are deemed incapable of achieving rational self-mastery.

We cannot do justice here to these different theoretical perspectives, nor have we space to discuss the complex, and conflicting, accounts of agency and subjectivity developed by each.[28] The question is whether the general critique presented by these perspectives justifies rejecting the notion of autonomy. Our view is that it does not. The general critique conflates the notion of autonomy with certain conceptions of autonomous *agents*. Conceptions of agents that require complete self-transparency and psychic unity are certainly vulnerable to the Freudian challenge. Kantian conceptions that conceive autonomous agents as free from empirical determination are vulnerable to Foucauldian critiques, among others. Likewise, some conceptions of autonomous agents have functioned historically to enforce exclusionary norms and ideals of the person. But for reasons that we discuss in the next two sections, the concept of autonomy need not be based on such assumptions about agents. It need not require agents to be completely self-transparent and psychically unified; assume that only a pure will, free from all empirical determination, can be self-determining; or enforce a hegemonic identity. Nevertheless, the postmodernist critiques are salutary, for they alert us to the need to develop notions of autonomy based on richer, more psychically complex, and more diverse conceptions of agents.

Diversity Critiques

Diversity critiques parallel postmodernist critiques in challenging the assumption that agents are cohesive and unified. Such critiques claim that each individual has a "multiple identity," which reflects the multiple groups to which the individual belongs. For example, Kimberlé Crenshaw argues that "the experiences of women of color are frequently the product of racism and sexism, and these experiences tend not to be represented within the discourses of either feminism or of antiracism."[29] Thus, the identities of individual women are "intersectional" in that they combine the group affiliations unique to that woman. A similar ambivalence inherent in the identities of women of marginalized groups has been described by María Lugones as the experience of living within and traveling between different "worlds."[30]

The idea of intersectionality may seem incompatible with the presuppositions of theories of autonomy. It implies that because different and sometimes conflicting group identities intersect in the formation of individual identity, many individuals do not have a unified or integrated sense of self. As with the postmodernist arguments we have already discussed, if theories of autonomy are thought to presuppose a transcendental self, the conception of the self offered by diversity theorists is incompatible with that offered by theories of autonomy. Even if theories of autonomy do not presuppose a transcendental self, as we show in the next section, notions of integration are central to many accounts of autonomy. Hence intersectionality does seem potentially to undermine conceptions of autonomy that require integration.

However, while intersectionality provides an important cautionary note for theories of autonomy, it need not undermine the claim that integration is a necessary condition of autonomy. It is plausible that certain radical kinds of disintegration of the self undermine the integration condition, for example, the disintegration as a result of trauma that is described by Susan Brison. But is the fragmentation of the self implied by intersectionality an analogous kind of disintegration?[31] If not, is the ambivalence implied by intersectionality, or indeed other kinds or degrees of ambivalence, perhaps *compatible* with the integration required for autonomy? Diana Meyers takes up these questions in her contribution to this volume.

In focusing on the particular features of individuals' identities, diversity theorists attempt to explain how and why individuals should not be absorbed into some group or other. Crenshaw claims that "in the area of rape, intersectionality provides a way of explaining why women of color must abandon the general argument that the interests of the community require the suppression of any confrontation around interracial rape."[32] The resistance to seeing individuals as replicating the interests and identities of the groups to which they belong is congenial to an emphasis on *individual* autonomy. Thus, despite the problems posed for certain theories of autonomy by the notion of intersectionality, we would argue that the insights of diversity critiques, especially that agents have *particular* identities and not group identities shared with other members of the group, enhance rather than reduce the need for feminist recharacterizations of individual autonomy.

Conceptions of Autonomy in Moral Psychology

We argued in the previous section that none of the five major feminist critiques justifies repudiating the notion of autonomy. The critiques, however, do require that attempts to refigure autonomy pay attention to the complex nature of the autonomous agent and to the differentiated social and historical contexts in which agents are embedded. Feminists have been particularly concerned, in this regard, with attending to and analyzing oppressive social contexts and their effects on agents. It is here that the concerns of feminist critiques of autonomy intersect with the concerns of mainstream theories of autonomy, to which we turn in this section.

From both a feminist perspective and that of many mainstream theories, oppressive socialization often seems inimical to agents' autonomy.

Contemporary accounts of individual autonomy hold that autonomy, or self-determination, involves, at the very least, the capacity for reflection on one's motivational structure and the capacity to change it in response to reflection. This view is underpinned by the intuition that there is an important difference between those aspects of an agent's motivational structure that she unreflectively finds herself with and those aspects that, as a result of autonomous reflection, she regards as "her own." Disagreements among different accounts of autonomy arise in explicating what is involved in the process of reflection, in explaining how reflection secures autonomy, and in making sense of the notion of "one's own."

The debates within the contemporary literature arise in response to two distinct sets of issues, which we refer to as the metaphysical problem and the socialization problem. The metaphysical problem focuses on the implications of determinism for autonomy and on whether a successful compatibilist response to the problem of determinism must rely on the notion of a "true" or "metaphysical" deep self. The socialization problem focuses on the implications of socialization for autonomy. Since our primary aim is to highlight issues within the mainstream literature on autonomy that intersect with feminist concerns and to explain the impetus toward the development of relational approaches to autonomy, our discussion in this section focuses mainly on the socialization problem.

We divide theories of autonomy into *procedural* and *substantive*. There are structural, historical, and competency versions of procedural theories and strong and weak versions of substantive theories. We argue that procedural theories encounter a series of difficulties in attempting to reconcile autonomous agency with socialization, especially oppressive socialization. In particular, since structural procedural theories analyze autonomy as a feature of an agent's occurrent mental states, they cannot do justice to the historical processes of socialization leading up to those states. Although historical theories address this problem, they nevertheless face trouble in explicating the difference between autonomous and nonautonomous processes of critical reflection. In addition, historical theories are to a large extent concerned with the negative effects of socialization on autonomy, rather than the global implications of socialization for autonomy. Meyers's competency account offers a fine-grained analysis of these global implications but falters when she attempts to preserve content neutrality for her theory. These problems with procedural accounts have led some theorists to the conclusion that only a substantive account of autonomy can explain how oppressive socialization impairs autonomy.

Procedural Theories of Autonomy

The vast majority of recent theories are variants of a basic procedural account. On procedural, or content-neutral, accounts, the *content* of a person's desires, values, beliefs, and emotional attitudes is irrelevant to the issue of whether the person is autonomous with respect to those aspects of her motivational structure and the actions that flow from them.[33] What matters for autonomy is whether the agent has subjected her motivations and actions to the appropriate kind of critical reflection. Where structural and historical versions of procedural theories differ from each other is in their different accounts of the processes of critical reflection necessary and sufficient to secure autonomy.[34]

Structural Theories.   Structural models of autonomy focus on the agent's occurrent motivational structure and on whether the present desires, beliefs, and values on which the agent acts have been subject to the appropriate kinds of critical reflection. Most structural theories are hierarchical. Hierarchical theories distinguish different, hierarchically ordered elements of the self and characterize autonomy as requiring a certain kind of structural organization of these different elements. Of the hierarchical accounts, the most influential is that of Harry Frankfurt, which characterizes autonomy as an accord between an agent's first-order desires and her second-order volitions.[35] Frankfurt identifies an agent's will with an effective first-order desire and claims that autonomy, or freedom of the will, requires both that the agent exercise control over her will and that she identify, at the level of her second-order volitions, with her will. Identification is the outcome of a process of reflection in which the agent distinguishes those desires that she endorses or regards as "her own" from those desires that she merely finds herself with and is either indifferent to or regards as external to herself.

Within the literature, a number of important objections have been raised against Frankfurt's hierarchical account. We discuss several objections that point to more general problems facing hierarchical theories. The first objection, articulated most forcefully by Gary Watson, is the regress objection. In a nutshell, Watson argues that Frankfurt's distinction between first-order desires and second-order volitions, and the notion of identification, do not provide sufficient conditions for autonomy. For what ensures that our higher-order identifications are themselves autonomous? Watson claims that since Frankfurt's account makes no qualitative distinctions among desires, the only resource available within his account to respond to this question is to introduce yet higher orders of desire. But then the same question can be asked about our identifications at each of these higher levels.[36]

The second objection, first articulated by Irving Thalberg, is that hierarchical theories give ontological priority to certain allegedly "higher" aspects of the self, which are regarded as the person's "true" or "real" self. But why should we equate a person's true self with her higher-order desires or her valuational system? Doesn't this view simply beg the question against, for example, a Freudian account of human psychology, which depicts us as "conflict-prone systems of libidinal, destructive, morbid, self-preserving, sociable, conscientious, guilt-ridden, and other 'forces,' 'principles' or 'mini-agencies'"?[37] Even if we might prize the rational aspects of ourselves or our capacities for judgment most highly, this does not provide a justification for giving those aspects of ourselves ontological priority.

Marilyn Friedman develops two further sets of objections to hierarchical theories. First, she claims that the distinction within hierarchical theories between higher- and lower-order aspects of the self entails a problematic ontological commitment, namely, to a "true self," which discloses the agent's real metaphysical identity. If autonomy involves discovering and acting in accordance with this true self, questions arise as to how the true self is formed and whether free agency requires the self to be undetermined. In other words, to be free, do we have to be metaphysically responsible for ourselves, or self-caused? If so, autonomy would be an impossibility.[38]

Friedman's second set of objections pinpoints the inadequacy of most hierarchical theories in dealing with, or even recognizing, the socialization problem. As Friedman points out, hierarchical theories either ignore the issue of socialization altogether or tend to assume that the higher-level self somehow transcends the influences of socialization to which the rest of the self is subject. But this assumption reintroduces a socialization version of the regress objection because the critically reflecting or higher-order self is just as subject to socialization as what we might call the "first-order" self. As a result, hierarchical theories cannot explain how agents can be autonomous with respect to their higher-level motivations, for the question can always be asked whether the higher-order aspects of the self have themselves been subject to critical reflection in the right ways. Furthermore, Friedman asks, why assume that a person's higher-level principles and values are indicative of what she really wants or values? In cases of oppressive socialization, an agent may reflectively endorse her thoroughly socialized higher-level principles and values, but it may be her apparently wayward first-order desires that are more indicative of what she really wants and values.

In response to these objections to hierarchical versions of the structural approach, Friedman proposes a nonhierarchical variant, which she calls an "integration" model. Instead of taking a "split-level" or "top-down" approach that favors higher-level assessment, in the integration model critical reflection is rather understood as a "two-way process of integration within a person's hierarchy of motivations, intermediate standards and values, and highest principles. Only if a person's highest principles have been subjected to assessment in accord with her intermediate standards and her motivations, would it be appropriate to consider them her 'own' principles."[39] Thus lower-level motivations provide the standpoint from which an agent can judge and critically evaluate her higher-order values and principles. According to Friedman, the autonomy-conferring status of critical reflection is secured because higher-level principles and values are assessed by reference to lower-level motivations and vice versa. Autonomy is achieved when the different levels of the self are integrated.

Friedman's integration model makes an important contribution toward understanding the effects of oppressive socialization on autonomy. In particular, it provides an explanation of the kind of self-alienation that characterizes failures of autonomy in oppressive social contexts. However, integration cannot provide a sufficient condition for autonomy. For, as Paul Benson points out, "An integration view detects threats to autonomy only when the total internalization of autonomy-inhibiting socialization fails to take hold or begins to break down."[40] Furthermore, Friedman's integration account, like other structural theories, takes a time-slice approach to autonomy and hence overlooks the historical processes of formation of the agent's beliefs, desires, values, and emotional attitudes.

Historical Models. In response to the problems arising from socialization that plague structural models, several philosophers, especially Gerald Dworkin and John

Christman, have introduced a historical dimension to analyses of autonomy. Dworkin argues that for critical reflection to be autonomy conferring, the processes of critical reflection must themselves be "procedurally independent."[41] Critical reflection must be understood as a capacity rather than as an occurrent state, a capacity that enables the agent to reflect on and critically assess the various processes (socialization, parental or peer influence, etc.) by means of which she came to acquire her desires, beliefs, values, and emotional attitudes. The agent is autonomous with respect to these processes if she endorses them.

John Christman argues that critical reflection yields autonomy when the processes of reflection have not been influenced by "illegitimate external influences."[42] Illegitimate external influences are those influences (for example, indoctrination, manipulation, brainwashing, and oppressive socialization) that interfere with agents' normal cognitive processes of reflection. Such influences are illegitimate if upon becoming aware of them as a result of critical reflection, the agent is led to revise her identifications. In a later article, Christman proposes a counterfactual analysis of autonomy in which a person is autonomous with respect to her values and higher-order identifications only if, upon becoming aware of the historical process through which she acquired them, she does not resist this process, or she *would* not resist it were she to become aware of it.[43] Both the illegitimate influences and the counterfactual conditions provide a compatibilist response to the problem of socialization. As long as our desires and preferences are not the products of illegitimate external influences, or that we do not or would not resist the way we came by these desires and preferences, they are autonomous.

However, there are at least two problems with Christman's analysis. First, it tends to equate autonomy with self-transparency. The more we are aware of the historical processes through which we acquired our desires, values, and so on, the more autonomous we will be. But if autonomy requires this kind of self-transparency, it is highly dubious that any of us are ever autonomous, for reasons that Thalberg points out. Second, although seeming too stringent from one perspective (requiring self-transparency), it is too weak from another because it allows agents whose processes of critical reflection are not autonomous to count as autonomous. Paul Benson points out that a person who has been thoroughly socialized to internalize certain norms, for example, the norms of feminine appearance, would be unlikely to revise her higher-order identifications as a result of critical reflection if she were to become aware that these identifications were the result of oppressive socialization.[44] It is not clear that such a person *would* modify either her identification with the desire to be attractive to men or her self-conception in which her sense of self-worth is tied to her physical appearance. Only an agent whose normal processes of reflection are *already* autonomous would be led to modify her identifications upon becoming aware that they are the result of socialization. The thoroughly socialized woman does not, or would not, resist these processes. Hence she counts as autonomous on Christman's view.

Whereas historical approaches thus draw attention to the importance of attending to the historical processes of belief-, desire-, and value-formation, they are nevertheless insufficient to grapple with the autonomy-impairing effects of oppressive socialization. Moreover, both the historical and structural versions of procedural theories that *are* attentive to the implications of socialization for autonomy nevertheless tend to represent socialization in largely negative terms, as an obstacle, or threat, to autonomy. So whereas it is admitted that our values, beliefs, and desires, as well as our characters and life plans, are inevitably shaped by socialization, autonomy tends to be represented as the quest to shape an identity for oneself in the face of, or against, this influence. As a result, both structural and historical theorists have failed to analyze the differences between the kinds of socialization, or aspects of socialization, that promote autonomy and those that impede or undermine it. They have also neglected the question of what skills and capacities are necessary for autonomy and what kinds of socialization are necessary to promote these skills and capacities. Competency theories have to a large extent addressed this problem.

Autonomy Competency. Diana Meyers's theory of autonomy competency[45] is motivated by a concern both to explain the autonomy-impairing effects of oppressive socialization and to develop a theory that is able to explain how agents who are subject to oppressive social circumstances may nevertheless be partially autonomous, or autonomous in certain domains of their lives but not in others. She argues that autonomy is a competency comprising a cluster of different skills and capacities, in particular skills of self-discovery, self-direction, and self-definition, all of which involve reflection. Autonomy involves the capacity to exercise these skills to achieve an integrated but dynamic self. Thus the notion of integration plays an important role in Meyers's theory, as it does in Friedman's structural account.[46]

Meyers's theory might best be classified as a self-realization approach to autonomy.[47] Unlike Aristotelian versions of self-realization, however, which are premised on a normative notion of flourishing, Meyers's approach is procedural. Since individuals differ so significantly in their talents, capacities, character traits, values, desires, beliefs, and emotional attitudes, she argues, there can be no blueprint for what constitutes an autonomous life. Rather autonomy can be secured only through the exercise of autonomy competency, or a coordinated repertoire of skills and capacities that enable each individual to fully realize himself or herself, whatever self-realization amounts to for each particular individual.

Meyers's account is explicitly relational in that she argues that autonomy competency can be developed only in the context of social relationships, practices, and institutions. The social context is important to the development of autonomy competency for at least three reasons. First, self-realization does not require an agent to be able to develop or realize all of her potentialities; rather it involves the capacity to develop those potentialities that are central to the agent's authentic self-conception, in the context of the agent's life plan. Since different social environments encourage or foster the development of different potentialities in any individual, the agent's social environment is crucial to the agent's ability to recognize and develop her important potentialities. Second, the connection between self-realization and the social environment explains how an agent's attempts to develop an authentic self may be thwarted or compromised by that environment. Since agents are more likely to develop or emphasize those aspects of themselves (character traits, potentialities, and talents) that are socially reinforced and to incorporate these aspects into their self-concepts, the quest for authenticity may be undermined by conventionality. Third, the social context may impair agents' capacities to achieve autonomy in a different way, namely, because certain kinds of socialization encourage the development of some of the skills that make up autonomy competency, at the expense of others. Patterns of gender socialization in contemporary Western cultures, for example, tend to encourage in women the skills involved in self-discovery because they encourage the development in women of emotional receptivity and perceptiveness. However, women are less likely to be encouraged to develop skills of self-direction and self-definition. It is precisely these skills that are more likely to be developed in men, at the expense of skills of self-discovery.

If autonomy competency comprises a range of skills that may be more or less developed, exercised, and coordinated, it makes sense to think of autonomy as a matter of degree. Hence Meyers distinguishes episodic autonomy from programmatic and narrowly programmatic autonomy. She argues that agents subject to oppressive socialization may exhibit high degrees of episodic autonomy, that is, the capacity to decide what one wants in weighing up one's desires or how to act in a particular situation. They may also exhibit narrowly programmatic autonomy, the capacity to make autonomous decisions in particular aspects of one's life, for example, choice of partner. Meyers's view is that women subject to traditional gender socialization are likely to exercise episodic or narrowly programmatic autonomy. However, their programmatic autonomy, their capacity to critically and reflectively decide major life issues such as whether or not to be a mother or whether to dedicate oneself to the pursuit of a career, is likely to be compromised. Like Rawls, Meyers sees self-realization as crucial to self-respect. If traditional gender socialization compromises women's capacities to achieve full autonomy and so damages their self-respect, this kind of socialization is oppressive.

Meyers's account aims to resolve a conundrum confronting feminist theorists, which she states in the preface to her book: "If women's professed desires are products of their inferior position, should we give credence to those desires? If so, we seem to be capitulating to institutionalized injustice by gratifying warped desires. If not, we seem to be perpetuating injustice by showing disrespect for those individuals."[48] Her answer to the conundrum is that not all desires should be afforded equal credence or weight. Autonomous desires, namely, those that express our "authentic selves," as developed through the exercise of skills of self-discovery, self-definition, and self-direction, are more worthy of satisfaction than desires that merely reflect uncritical acceptance of social norms or expectations. The suggestion, then, is that it is not the *content* of so-called warped desires that renders them less worthy of satisfaction but the fact that they have not been acquired or endorsed autonomously. The question we wish to raise concerning Meyers's theory is whether her content-neutral approach to self-realization really does provide a satisfactory solution, from a feminist perspective, to this conundrum. In particular, could warped desires, or desires that arise as a result of oppressive socialization, ever be autonomous? Or does the content of certain desires and choices show that the deliberative processes involved just could not meet the conditions necessary for autonomy?[49] In other words, does the notion of autonomy competency implicitly rely on a more normative and substantive view of what is required for women to flourish or achieve full autonomy? Furthermore, does a feminist perspective on oppressive feminine socialization require more stringent normative conditions on autonomy? It is this second concern that has led some feminists to argue that the problem of oppressive socialization suggests the need for a more substantive approach to autonomy.

Substantive Theories of Autonomy

Procedural accounts implicitly assume that the content-neutral procedural conditions they identify are both necessary and sufficient for autonomy. It is here that recent work focusing especially on the articulation of the possibility of autonomy in oppressive circumstances has revealed a flaw in procedural theories. Such work shows that whereas some set of procedural conditions may indeed be necessary for autonomy, it is not sufficient. We call those theories that maintain that procedural accounts must be supplemented by some nonneutral condition *substantive* theories.[50] There are two basic categories of substantive accounts: *strong substantive* and *weak substantive*. The former reject the content neutrality of procedural theories by requiring specific contents of the autonomous preferences of agents. The latter reject content neutrality by suggesting further necessary conditions on autonomy that operate as constraints on the contents of the desires or preferences capable of being held by autonomous agents. Both kinds of accounts, in different ways, are responding to objections to procedural accounts that derive from socialization.

Strong Substantive Theories. Susan Wolf and Paul Benson have both defended strong substantive accounts of autonomy. (We discuss Benson's more recent weak substantive theory below.) The central idea of these strong substantive accounts is that of normative competence: to be autonomous, agents must be competent, or have the capacity, to identify the difference between right and wrong. Since certain kinds of socialization, including socialization due to oppression, interfere with this capacity, agents subject to this kind of socialization are not autonomous. Consider Wolf's account of JoJo, the son of an evil and sadistic tyrant.[51] JoJo is raised to be evil and sadistic like his father; as an adult, he respects his father's values and emulates his desires. His father's evil and sadistic worldview is thoroughly internalized by JoJo. Wolf argues that since JoJo identifies in the appropriate ways with his first-order desires, on hierarchical accounts he would count as autonomous. Yet she argues that he is not autonomous nor morally responsible for the actions performed on the basis of his evil values, for "it is unclear whether anyone with a childhood such as his could have developed into anything but the twisted and perverse sort of person that he has become."[52] Wolf argues that to be free and responsible, one has to be "sane." Although JoJo acts according to his own values and desires in the way required by hierarchical theories, he is nevertheless "insane"—and hence neither free nor morally responsible—because his upbringing has blocked his capacity to distinguish right from wrong. In her book *Freedom within Reason*, Wolf articulates the failure of autonomy here as a failure of a capacity to track an aspect of the world, namely, the moral or the right. Since for Wolf the demands of morality are equivalent to the demands of "Reason," to be autonomous, agents must be capable of discerning the requirements of Reason. Wolf's theory, therefore, is a new version of the traditional Kantian account of autonomy, in which autonomy is understood as the capacity for rational self-legislation.[53]

In several papers, Paul Benson has advocated a similar strong substantive account of autonomy.[54] As we have seen, he points out that inadequate or inappropriate socialization (as in the case of children), as well as oppressive socialization, can undermine agents' normative competence. In particular, oppressive socialization can lead to the acceptance of norms, which once internalized, block agents' capacities for detecting whether the norms are correct. For example, when women internalize norms purveyed by the fashion industry, such as those that treat personal value as being dependent on stereotypical feminine appearance, the typical effect is to undermine their capacity to criticize the norms. Since the stereotype suggesting that personal appearance is a component of self-worth presupposes a *false* norm, when women lose the capacity to criticize the norm effectively, and thereby lose the capacity to detect that it is incorrect, they lose autonomy with respect to the area of their lives that they take to be governed by the norm. Because both Wolf and Benson are proposing that a necessary condition of autonomy is the capacity to formulate desires and preferences and endorse values, with specific contents, their theories are strongly substantive.

Weak Substantive Theories.   Benson has recently proposed a weaker normative competence theory. Consider the following passage from his article "Free Agency and Self-Worth":

> Imagine a feminist remake of *Gaslight* in which, as in the original, the female protagonist falls into a state of helplessness and disorientation as a result of a profound change in her view of herself. . . . [The husband] . . . is a physician . . . and regards women who are excitable, who have active imaginations and strong passions, and who are prone to emotional outbursts in public as suffering from a serious psychological illness. . . . The protagonist has the suspect traits, her husband makes the standard diagnosis, and the 'hysterical wife' ends up isolated, feeling rather crazy. . . . She arrives at her sense of incompetence and estrangement from her conduct on the basis of reasons that are accepted by a scientific establishment which is socially validated and which she trusts.[55]

Benson argues that neither structural nor historical procedural accounts explain the agent's apparent lack of autonomy in such a situation, for the agent satisfies the conditions offered by both accounts. What is lacking in such agents is a sense of worthiness to act, which "involves regarding oneself as being competent to answer for one's conduct in light of normative demands that, from one's point of view, others might appropriately apply to one's actions."[56] Lacking this sense of self-worth is quite compatible with agents retaining their "power to put [their] will into effect" and hence is quite compatible with agents retaining the capacities and undergoing the processes required by procedural theories. We are calling the type of condition offered by Benson *weakly substantive* because although it places constraints on the desires, preferences, and values that count as autonomous, it abandons the content specificity of strong substantive theories.[57] Similarly, Robin Dillon and Trudy Govier have implicitly endorsed weak substantive accounts in suggesting, respectively, that self-respect and self-trust are necessary conditions of autonomy.[58]

Both kinds of substantive accounts articulate convincing responses to apparent counterexamples to procedural accounts. They also provide a good starting point in explaining why agents who are operating within oppressive institutions and structures exhibit failures of autonomy. Broadly, two different kinds of explanation are being offered by the two kinds of substantive accounts. The first is that oppressive socialization impedes agents' abilities to discern the false norms accepted and perpetuated by the oppressive context in which they are operating. The objection that must be answered by this first kind of substantive account is that it is too stringently normative and conflates autonomy with moral responsibility.[59] The explanation offered by the second kind of substantive account sidesteps this objection by linking oppression to psychological impairment, for instance, impairment of one's sense of self-worth, self-trust, or self-respect, which impairment itself undermines autonomy. The question that must be answered by this kind of account is whether it sufficiently explains feminist intuitions regarding choices in oppressive social contexts. Natalie Stoljar's chapter in this volume takes up this question.

Both kinds of accounts treat autonomy as intrinsically relational and introduce necessary conditions of autonomy that derive from the social relations within which agents are embedded. Hence they implicitly presuppose a richer account of agency than do procedural accounts.

Relational Autonomy

The difficulties generated by providing an adequate explanation of impairment of autonomy in contexts of oppressive socialization, together with feminist critiques of traditional notions of autonomy, have provided the main impetus toward the development of a relational approach. Although the feminist critiques discussed earlier do not directly address the procedural and substantive theories of autonomy discussed in the previous section, their effect has been to focus attention on the need for a more fine-grained and richer account of the autonomous *agent*. The critiques emphasize that an analysis of the characteristics and capacities of the self cannot be adequately undertaken without attention to the rich and complex social and historical contexts in which agents are embedded; they point to the need to think of autonomy as a characteristic of agents who are emotional, embodied, desiring, creative, and feeling, as well as rational, creatures; and they highlight the ways in which agents are both psychically internally differentiated and socially differentiated from others.

One of the crucial concerns of relational approaches is to investigate the implications for our understanding of autonomy of this richer conception of agency. For example, conceptualizing agents as emotional, embodied, desiring, creative, and feeling, as well as rational, creatures highlights the importance to autonomy of features of agents that have received little discussion in the literature, such as memory, imagination, and emotional dispositions and attitudes. Recognizing that agents are both psychically internally differentiated and socially differentiated from others calls for a reconceptualization of certain notions that are central to the literature on autonomy, such as integration, identification, critical reflection, and self-realization.

Finally, analyzing the way in which socialization and social relationships impede or enhance an agent's capacities for autonomy has drawn attention to the connections among an agent's self-conception, her social context, and her capacities for autonomy. It is for this reason that many relational approaches investigate the relationship between autonomy and feelings of self-respect, self-worth, and self-trust.

A second concern of relational approaches is to analyze the specific ways in which oppressive socialization and oppressive social relationships can impede autonomous agency, at three interrelated levels. The first level is that of the processes of formation of an agent's desires, beliefs, and emotional attitudes, including beliefs and attitudes about herself. Relational approaches are particularly concerned with analyzing the role that social norms and institutions, cultural practices, and social relationships play in shaping the beliefs, desires, and attitudes of agents in oppressive social contexts. The second level is that of the development of the competencies and capacities necessary for autonomy, including capacities for self-reflection, self-direction, and self-knowledge. Diana Meyers's work has been particularly influential in analyzing the ways in which oppressive social environments can impair agents' autonomy at this level. The third level is that of an agent's ability to act on autonomous desires or to make autonomous choices. Autonomy can be impeded at this level not just by overt restrictions on agents' freedom but also by social norms, institutions, practices, and relationships that effectively limit the range of *significant* options available to them.[60]

These two concerns indicate that agents and their capacities should be conceived relationally. There are two ways of understanding this idea. One regards agents as intrinsically relational because their identities or self-conceptions are constituted by elements of the social context in which they are embedded. Another regards agents as causally relational because their natures are produced by certain historical and social conditions. The distinction between intrinsically and causally relational agency points to a corresponding distinction between relational conceptions of autonomy. Broadly, relational conceptions can be divided into *constitutively* (or intrinsically) relational conceptions and *causally* relational conceptions.[61] Those approaches focusing on the social constitution of the agent or the social nature of the capacity of autonomy itself, are constitutive conceptions, whereas those focusing on the ways in which socialization and social relationships impede or enhance autonomy are causal conceptions. The essays in this volume grapple with both kinds of relational autonomy. They also grapple with the connected question of whether procedural theories are sufficient to satisfy the demands of a relational approach to autonomy or whether a more normative account is necessary. However, there is no convergence among the contributors toward a single conception of relational autonomy, nor does there need to be. These questions are still open as far as relational approaches are concerned.

The articles are grouped under two main sections: "Autonomy and the Social" and "Relational Autonomy in Context." The articles in the first group explore a range of theoretical issues for conceptions of autonomy, agency, and moral responsibility that arise from the social dimensions of selfhood, particularly in oppressive social contexts. The articles in the second group examine the ways in which a relational approach to autonomy can contribute to a better understanding of autonomy and impaired autonomy in a variety of concrete contexts, for example, in health-care practice and decision making or in legal debates over freedom of expression.

Marilyn Friedman's and Linda Barclay's articles, which open the first group, examine the implications of feminist discussions of the social self for procedural accounts of autonomy. If the agent is socially constituted, as many feminists believe, capacities of the agent like autonomy are also constitutively social and relational. Whereas Friedman and Barclay are broadly sympathetic to the notion of the social self, they take issue with some accounts of it and with the conclusions about autonomy that some feminists have drawn from these accounts. Friedman's article, "Autonomy, Social Disruption, and Women," addresses the question of whether autonomy is antithetical to women's interests because it has the potential to disrupt social relationships, in particular those that historically have been central to women's lives and identities. Friedman argues that although popular conceptions of autonomy may seem to support this view, procedural autonomy is not intrinsically disruptive of social relationships, nor need it be inconsistent with values that arise from social relationships, such as love, loyalty, or trust. Although an exercise of procedural autonomy *may* sometimes disrupt social relationships, this need not always be problematic because in oppressive social circumstances, achieving autonomy may require the rejection of oppressive social relationships.

Barclay's article, "Autonomy and the Social Self," asks whether autonomy is compatible with the social self. Barclay distinguishes three different versions of the social self thesis: the socially determined self, the motivationally social self, and the constitutively social self. She argues that whereas a suitably nuanced conception of procedural autonomy is compatible with plausible versions of the socially determined and the motivationally social self, it is incompatible with strong versions of the socially determined and the constitutively social self. However, this incompatibility does not undermine the value of autonomy since these strong versions of the social self are implausible. Moreover, feminists should be wary of an alliance with communitarianism since the communitarian view that we are so constituted by social relations and shared values that we are unable to reconsider our attachment to them is incompatible with a feminist commitment to communities of choice.

The articles by Paul Benson and Natalie Stoljar both investigate the adequacy of procedural views to explain the impairment of agents' capacities for autonomy and moral responsibility in oppressive social contexts. In his article, "Feeling Crazy: Self-Worth and the Social Character of Responsibility," Benson argues that a sense of self-worth is an additional necessary condition of moral responsibility. The sense of self-worth is a sense of one's worthiness to account for one's actions to others, and hence moral responsibility depends conceptually on relations with others. Moreover, responsibility is relational in two further respects: publicly shareable norms regulate both the moral appraisal of an agent's actions and the account of her actions that she provides to others; and an agent's conception of herself as competent to account for her actions is dependent on her having the status of an eligible participant in the moral community. Thus Benson's account of moral responsibility, like his account of autonomy in "Free Agency and Self-Worth," offers a constitutively relational analysis of the relevant capacity of agents.

Natalie Stoljar's article, "Autonomy and the Feminist Intuition," argues that there is a tension between feminist intuitions regarding choices in oppressive contexts and a commitment to procedural autonomy. She extracts five conditions from procedural accounts of autonomy and argues that none fully explains the widely held feminist intuition that preferences and decisions motivated by oppressive norms are not autonomous. She argues that only a version of a strong substantive account of autonomy will do the job of explaining the intuition. Like Benson's, Stoljar's article explores the nature of the capacity for autonomy rather than the nature of the agent who exercises the capacity.

The articles by Genevieve Lloyd, Catriona Mackenzie, and Diana Meyers return to the issue of the social dimensions of selfhood. Genevieve Lloyd's article, "Individuals, Responsibility, and the Philosophical Imagination," explores the phenomenon of individuals taking responsibility for actions or events that lie beyond the scope of their agency, and suggests that understanding this phenomenon requires a reconceptualization of notions of individual identity and moral responsibility. Lloyd considers three different examples of such taking of responsibility: in friendship, in solidarity, and in historical responsibility for the actions of one's forebears. She argues that all three examples challenge the grip of standard philosophical conceptions of the individual, in particular conceptions of selves as sharply bordered units and of relations between individuals as contractual and voluntary. Lloyd argues that we forge our identities through relations of sympathetic identification with others. Moreover, the narratives of our individual lives, as they unfold in time, are not discrete but overlap with the narratives of others, including the narratives of the collective existence and its memories into which we are born. Thus Lloyd draws attention to an important connection between the social and temporal dimensions of selfhood.

The following three articles, by Catriona Mackenzie, Diana Meyers, and Lorraine Code, take up some of the issues raised by Lloyd. The temporal and social dimensions of selfhood that concern Lloyd are central to an analysis of self-definition developed by Mackenzie in "Imagining Oneself Otherwise." Mackenzie's main concern, however, is to explore the connections among autonomy, selfhood, and imagination. She proposes that agents' abilities to imagine themselves otherwise play an important but overlooked role in practical deliberation and self-definition. Understanding this role can provide an explanation of one way in which oppressive social environments can impair the autonomy of oppressed agents, namely through a restricted cultural imaginary that curtails agents' abilities to imagine alternate social and individual possibilities.

Diana Meyers's article, "Intersectional Identity and the Authentic Self: Opposites Attract?" takes up Lloyd's concern with understanding the implications of collective and social group identities for individual identity. Meyers's main concern is whether an integration account of the authentic self, of the kind she developed in her earlier work on autonomy, can accommodate selves whose identities are intersectional. She argues that although standard accounts of integration, of the kind proposed by Frankfurt, are inconsistent with intersectional conceptions of the self, her own model of dynamic integration is compatible with these conceptions. Indeed, she argues, acknowledging the intersectionality of one's identity is crucial for achieving the self-knowledge that is necessary for authenticity. Meyers's article directly tackles the postmodernist and diversity critiques of autonomy. In doing so, it explores how recognition of the internally and socially differentiated identities of agents calls for a reconceptualization of notions like integration, critical reflection, and self-realization.

The concern of many of the contributors to this volume is to provide an analysis of the effects of oppressive social contexts on individuals' capacities for autonomy and moral responsibility. In "The Perversion of Autonomy and the Subjection of Women: Discourses of Social Advocacy at Century's End," Lorraine Code turns away from this concern to provide a detailed analysis of the broader social and epistemic contexts within which autonomy is an issue for oppressed agents. In her analysis of these contexts she points to a tension or paradox concerning autonomy. On the one hand, the social imaginary of Western societies is dominated by a hyperbolized ideal of autonomy as self-sufficient individualism. This ideal is complicit with and underpins social structures of oppression and subjection in which those who do not attain self-sufficient autonomy are marginalized. On the other hand, in the struggle of the oppressed against their oppression, autonomy is a legitimate aspiration. The issue that concerns Code is how to develop a model of autonomy that answers to this aspiration. She sees the problem as a moral and epistemological one: those who are subject to oppression are less likely to achieve autonomy, partly because they are marginalized and delegitimized as knowers, even with regard to their own experiences. Code suggests that a cluster of moral and epistemic practices of what she calls "advocacy" on behalf of the oppressed may provide a response to this problem.

The issues raised by Code about the epistemic, social, and political conditions necessary for autonomy are taken up in very concrete ways by the four articles in the second section of the book, "Relational Autonomy in Context." Those by Susan Dodds, Anne Donchin, and Susan Sherwin and Carolyn McLeod are primarily concerned with health-care ethics. In "Choice and Control in Bioethics," Dodds takes issue with the way in which autonomy is narrowly conceptualized in much bioethical literature as equivalent to informed consent. She argues that one effect of this conception is to restrict the exercise of autonomy in health-care contexts to making choices among a limited set of options. Dodds argues that criticisms of this model by liberal, radical, and cultural feminists have been important in highlighting some of its shortcomings. However, she believes that a relational model of autonomy that draws on and develops some of these feminist criticisms provides the best basis for an appropriate conception of autonomy in health-care contexts.

Anne Donchin's article, "Autonomy and Interdependence: Quandaries in Genetic Decision Making," uses the example of genetic decision making to bring out the tensions between interpersonal dependencies and prevailing accounts of autonomy in bioethics. These tensions point to the need for a relational approach to autonomy in bioethics more broadly. Donchin makes an important distinction between weak and strong relational approaches to autonomy. The former acknowledge that selfhood and capacities for autonomy are developed in the context of social relationships. But they see social ties as only contingently related to agents' self-understandings and tend to regard social relationships as entirely voluntary. Focusing on a selection of case studies of individuals and families involved in genetic de-

cision making, Donchin shows that the complex interplay between individual autonomy and biological and social relationships, particularly nonvoluntary ones, requires the development of a strong relational model. This model recognizes that autonomy is not solely an individual enterprise and that respect for the autonomy of
others requires collaboration, long-term reciprocity, and equitable balancing of
power relationships.

The article by Susan Sherwin and Carolyn McLeod, "Relational Autonomy,
Self-Trust, and Health Care for Patients Who Are Oppressed," analyzes one dimension of the autonomy-undermining effects of oppression, namely, its effects on
agents' self-trust. Sherwin and McLeod distinguish three different kinds of self-
trust: trust in one's capacity to choose and decide effectively, trust in one's ability to
act on the decisions one makes, and trust in one's own judgment. All three kinds,
they maintain, are necessary for the exercise of autonomy competency. Furthermore, because self-trust in all three senses is relational, both causally and constitutively, it can be eroded to varying degrees by oppressive social situations. Sherwin
and McLeod illustrate the connections among impaired autonomy, oppression, and
self-distrust by considering a range of different cases in which patients' self-distrust,
arising from oppressive social situations, impairs their abilities to make autonomous
health-care choices.

One of the recurring themes in the articles by Dodds, Donchin, and Sherwin
and McLeod is the importance of a range of *significant* options to agents' abilities
to exercise autonomous choice. Susan Brison's article, "Relational Autonomy and
Freedom of Expression," is also concerned with the connections among autonomous
choice, agents' relations with others, and the range of options that are socially and
culturally available to agents. In explaining this connection, Brison draws on and develops Amartya Sen's capability account of human flourishing. She then considers
the implications of the capability account of autonomy for debates about hate
speech. A prominent defense of the right to free speech is that it is grounded in a
right to autonomy. Such a right, it has been argued, precludes restrictions on hate
speech. Brison argues that the capability account of autonomy does not support this
conclusion. Speech does not always enhance autonomy, but it can in some circumstances undermine autonomy by reducing the significant options available to agents,
affecting agents' beliefs about themselves, their preferences and options, and affecting others' beliefs about and attitudes toward agents.

In articulating relational approaches to autonomy, the articles collected in this
volume challenge and enrich contemporary philosophical debates about autonomy, while showing why autonomy is an important value for feminists to retain
and defend.

Notes

1. As far as we know, Jennifer Nedelsky was the first to articulate a conception of relational autonomy from an explicitly feminist perspective. See Nedelsky, "Reconceiving Autonomy: Sources, Thoughts and Possibilities," *Yale Journal of Law and Feminism* 1 (1989):
7–36; "Law, Boundaries and the Bounded Self," *Representations* 30 (1990): 162–189; "Recon-

ceiving Rights as Relationship," *Review of Constitutional Studies* 1 (1993): 1–26; and "Meditations on Embodied Autonomy," *Graven Images* 2 (1995): 159–170. For a recent exposition of the varieties of possible conceptions of relational autonomy, see Marilyn Friedman, "Autonomy and Social Relationships: Rethinking the Feminist Critique," in *Feminists Rethink the Self*, ed. Diana Tietjens Meyers (Boulder, Colo.: Westview, 1997), pp. 55–58.

2. For example, Seyla Benhabib, *Situating the Self: Gender, Community and Postmodernism in Contemporary Ethics* (New York: Routledge, 1992); Michael Sandel, *Liberalism and the Limits of Justice* (Cambridge: Cambridge University Press, 1982); Will Kymlicka, *Contemporary Political Philosophy* (Oxford: Oxford University Press, 1990).

3. For example, for autonomy-based defences of euthanasia, see Ronald Dworkin, *Life's Dominion: An Argument about Abortion and Euthanasia* (New York: Vintage, 1994), and Joel Feinberg, "Voluntary Euthanasia and the Inalienable Right to Life," *Philosophy and Public Affairs* 7 (1978). For autonomy-based discussions of surrogacy, see Susan Dodds and Karen Jones, "Surrogacy and Autonomy," *Bioethics* 3 (1989): 1–17, and Laura Purdy, "A Response to Dodds and Jones," *Bioethics* 3 (1989): 40–44.

4. Susan J. Brison, "The Autonomy Defense of Free Speech," *Ethics* 108 (1998): 312–339.

5. Marilyn Friedman, "Autonomy and Social Relationships."

6. For other discussions of feminist critiques of autonomy, see John Christman, "Feminism and Autonomy," in *Nagging Questions: Feminist Ethics in Everyday Life*, ed. Dana Bushnell (Lanham, Md: Rowman & Littlefield, 1995), and Friedman, "Autonomy and Social Relationships."

7. Lorraine Code, "Second Persons," in *What Can She Know? Feminist Theory and the Construction of Knowledge* (Ithaca, N.Y.: Cornell University Press, 1991).

8. Ibid., p. 78.

9. Annette Baier introduces the notion of second persons in "Cartesian Persons," in *Postures of the Mind: Essays on Mind and Morals* (Minneapolis: University of Minnesota Press, 1985).

10. This critique parallels certain well-known communitarian critiques of liberalism. Communitarians have argued that liberalism presupposes a flawed account of human nature, namely, that agents are (metaphysically) atomistic or unencumbered by the social contexts in which they are embedded. See note 2 above.

11. Baier, "Cartesian Persons," p. 85.

12. For more discussion, see Friedman, "Autonomy and Social Relationships."

13. Alison Jaggar, *Feminist Politics and Human Nature* (Totowa, N.J.: Rowman & Allanheld 1983), p. 29.

14. See Natalie Stoljar, "Essence, Identity and the Concept of Woman," *Philosophical Topics* 23 (1995): 261–294, and Charlotte Witt, "Anti-Essentialism in Feminist Theory," *Philosophical Topics* 23 (1995): 321–344, for discussions of the possibility of relations being essential to individual identity in a metaphysical sense.

15. Louise Antony, "Is Psychological Individualism a Piece of Ideology?" *Hypatia* 10 (1995): 157–174, 167. Also see Antony, "Sisters, Please, I'd Rather Do It Myself: A Defense of Individualism in Feminist Epistemology," *Philosophical Topics* 23 (1995): 59–94.

16. Although, as Marilyn Friedman points out in her discussion of what we are calling care critiques, these critiques do often slide between rejecting autonomy and rejecting masculinist conceptions of autonomy. Friedman, "Autonomy and Social Relationships."

17. Nancy Chodorow, *The Reproduction of Mothering* (Berkeley: University of California Press, 1978) and "Gender, Relation and Difference in Psychoanalytic Perspective" in *The Future of Difference*, ed. Hester Eisenstein and Alice Jardine (New Brunswick, N.J.: Rutgers University Press, 1985). See also Carol Gilligan, *In a Different Voice: Psychological Theory and Women's Development* (Cambridge, Mass.: Harvard University Press, 1982).

18. Virginia Held, *Feminist Morality* (Chicago: University of Chicago Press, 1993), p. 60.

19. Sarah Lucia Hoagland, *Lesbian Ethics: Toward New Value* (California: Institute of Lesbian Studies, 1988), pp. 143ff.

20. Nedelsky, "Reconceiving Autonomy," p. 12; Held, *Feminist Morality*, pp. 61–62.

21. Evelyn Fox Keller, *Reflections on Gender and Science* (New Haven, Conn.: Yale University Press, 1985), chap. 5.

22. Ibid., p. 99.

23. Keller's discussion refers to Jessica Benjamin's psychoanalytic work on erotic domination. See especially "The Bonds of Love: Rational Violence and Erotic Domination," in Eisenstein and Jardine, *The Future of Difference.*

24. Jean Grimshaw, "Autonomy and Identity in Feminist Thinking," in *Feminist Perspectives in Philosophy*, ed. Morwenna Griffiths and Margaret Whitford (Bloomington: Indiana University Press, 1988).

25. Judith Butler, *Gender Trouble: Feminism and the Subversion of Identity* (New York: Routledge, 1990); Drucilla Cornell, *Transformations: Recollective Imagination and Sexual Difference* (New York: Routledge, 1993), chap. 2; Jane Flax, "Postmodernism and Gender Relations in Feminist Theory," *Signs* 12 (1987): 621–643; Susan Hekman, "Subjects and Agents: The Question for Feminism," in *Provoking Agents: Gender and Agency in Theory and Practice*, ed. J. K. Gardiner (Champagne-Urbana: University of Illinois Press, 1995); "Reconstructing the Subject: Feminism, Modernism and Postmodernism," *Hypatia* 6 (1991): 44–63; and "Review of *Self, Society and Personal Choice*," *Hypatia* 6 (1991): 222–225; Diana T. Meyers, "Personal Autonomy or the Deconstructed Subject? A Reply to Hekman," *Hypatia* 7 (1992): 124–132.

26. Benhabib, *Situating the Self*, chap. 5; Butler, *Gender Trouble*; Cornell, *Transformations*; Code, "Second Persons"; Flax, "Postmodernism and Gender Relations"; Hekman, "Reconstructing the Subject."

27. Hekman, "Reconstructing the Subject."

28. The question of whether postmodernism is able to provide an adequate account of agency is the subject of an important debate in contemporary feminist theory. We are unable to address this debate here. However, we are broadly sympathetic with Seyla Benhabib's discussion of this issue in *Situating the Self*, chap. 7. Benhabib criticizes feminist appropriations of the rhetoric of the "death of the subject," such as those of Flax ("Postmodernism and Gender Relations") and Butler (*Gender Trouble*), on the grounds that they are ultimately incoherent and that feminism cannot afford to reject notions such as agency, autonomy, and selfhood.

29. Kimberlé Williams Crenshaw, "Mapping the Margins: Intersectionality, Identity Politics, and Violence Against Women of Color," in *Critical Race Theory: The Key Writings*, ed. Crenshaw et al. (New York: New Press, 1995), p. 358.

30. María Lugones, "Playfulness, 'World'-Travelling, and Loving Perception," *Hypatia* 2 (1987): 3–19.

31. Susan J. Brison, "Outliving Oneself: Trauma, Memory and Personal Identity," in *Feminists Rethink the Self*, ed. Diana Tietjens Meyers (Boulder, Colo.: Westview, 1997), 12–39.

32. Crenshaw, "Mapping the Margins," p. 377.

33. For discussions of the notion of content neutrality, see John Christman, "Autonomy and Personal History," *Canadian Journal of Philosophy* 21 (1991): 1–24, and Paul Benson, "Free Agency and Self-Worth," *Journal of Philosophy* 91(1994): 650–668.

34. We take the distinction between structural and historical theories from Paul Benson, "Free Agency and Self-Worth," pp. 653–654.

35. Harry Frankfurt, "Freedom of the Will and the Concept of a Person," *Journal of Philosophy* 68 (1971): 5–20. See also S. I. Benn, "Individuality, Autonomy and Community," in *Community as a Social Ideal*, ed. Eugene Kamenka (New York: St Martin's Press, 1982), and "Freedom, Autonomy and the Concept of a Person," *Proceedings of the Aristotelian Society* 76 (1976): 109–130; Gerald Dworkin, "Acting Freely," *Nous* 3 (1970): 367–383, and *The Theory and Practice of Autonomy* (New York: Cambridge University Press, 1988); Joel Feinberg, "Autonomy," in *The Inner Citadel: Essays on Individual Autonomy*, ed. John Christman (New York: Oxford University Press, 1989); Robert Young, "Autonomy and Socialisation," *Mind* 84 (1980): 565–576, and *Personal Autonomy: Beyond Negative and Positive Liberty* (London: Croom Helm, 1986).

36. Gary Watson, "Free Agency," *Journal of Philosophy* 72 (1975): 205–220. In response to this objection, Watson develops his own variant of the hierarchical approach by distinguishing between a person's motivational system and her valuational system. Although these systems must overlap, the problem of free agency arises because they can sometimes come apart. Watson identifies the agent's point of view, or the aspects of the self that are truly "one's own," with the agent's valuational system. An agent acts freely when her motivational and valuational system are integrated; she acts nonautonomously or unfreely when her actions conflict with her valuational system. However, this account faces problems of its own in explaining the special autonomy-conferring authority accorded to a person's values. Watson does make a distinction between values that are the product of acculturation (acculturated attitudes) and values that are judgments, that is, values that have been subjected to processes of rational critical assessment, claiming that only the latter are autonomy conferring. But he does not provide an account of the processes of assessment that distinguish values that are judgments from mere acculturated attitudes, nor does he explain how these processes of assessment confer autonomy on those values that have been scrutinized in this way. For further discussion, see Harry Frankfurt, "Identification and Wholeheartedness," in *Responsibility, Character and the Emotions*, ed. Ferdinand Schoeman (New York: Cambridge University Press, 1987).

37. Irving Thalberg, "Hierarchical Analyses of Unfree Action," *Canadian Journal of Philosophy* 8 (1978): 211–225.

38. See Diana T. Meyers, *Self, Society, and Personal Choice* (New York: Columbia University Press, 1989), for a similar objection. We would argue that this metaphysical objection, as discussed by Friedman, Meyers, and within the literature more generally, arises from certain misunderstandings of hierarchical models. First, the idea that hierarchical views involve an ontological commitment to a metaphysically distinct "true self" there to be discovered misrepresents the process of critical reflection. On our reading of hierarchical theories, critical reflection should be understood as a process of self-constitution. As Frankfurt makes clear (especially in "Identification and Wholeheartedness"), the self is not a static, deep metaphysical entity but is constantly being reconstituted through the processes of reflection, deliberation, and decision, by means of which we define our cares, commitments, and values. Second, as Susan Wolf has argued convincingly, the metaphysical problem conflates moral responsibility for the self with metaphysical responsibility for the self: Wolf, "Sanity and the Metaphysics of Responsibility," in *Responsibility, Character and the Emotions*, ed. Ferdinand Schoeman (New York: Cambridge University Press, 1987), and *Freedom within Reason* (New York: Oxford University Press, 1990). Autonomy requires only that we are morally responsible, or capable of self-revision. It does not matter that our desires may arise from sources within or external to ourselves that we do not control, nor does it matter that we did not invent the values that guide our lives. What matters is that we are capable of revising ourselves in the light of critical reflection. Thus, as far as the metaphysical problem is concerned, there

is no significant difference between Friedman's integration model and hierarchical models. Both are attempting to provide accounts of self-revision and both see some kind of integration among the elements of the self as central to autonomy. Where they differ is in their accounts of critical reflection.

39. Marilyn Friedman, "Autonomy and the Split-Level Self," *Southern Journal of Philosophy* 24 (1986): 19–35, 32.

40. Paul Benson, "Autonomy and Oppressive Socialization," *Social Theory and Practice* 17 (1991): 385–408, 395.

41. Dworkin, *Theory and Practice of Autonomy*, chap. 1.

42. John Christman, "Autonomy: A Defense of the Split-level Self," *Southern Journal of Philosophy* 25 (1987): 281–293.

43. Chistman, "Autonomy and Personal History"; see also "Feminism and Autonomy."

44. Benson, "Autonomy and Oppressive Socialization."

45. Meyers, *Self, Society, and Personal Choice,* and "Personal Autonomy and the Paradox of Feminine Socialization" *Journal of Philosophy* 84 (1987): 619–628.

46. See Meyers's article in this volume for a development of this account of integration in the context of an intersectional approach to identity.

47. For a liberal approach to self-realization, see, for example, John Rawls, *A Theory of Justice* (Cambridge, Mass.: Harvard University Press, 1971). For an Aristotelian approach, see, for example, Martha C. Nussbaum, "Human Capabilities, Female Human Beings," in *Women, Culture and Development: A Study of Human Capabilities,* ed. Martha C. Nussbaum and Jonathan Glover (Oxford: Clarendon Press, 1995), and Amartya Sen, *Inequality Reexamined* (Cambridge, Mass.: Harvard University Press, 1992).

48. Meyers, *Self, Society, and Personal Choice,* p. xi.

49. These questions arise repeatedly in debates in the feminist literature about cosmetic surgery, surrogacy, and reproductive technologies. On cosmetic surgery, see Kathryn Morgan, "Women and the Knife: Cosmetic Surgery and the Colonization of Women's Bodies," *Hypatia* 6 (1991): 25–53. On surrogacy, see Dodds and Jones, "Surrogacy and Autonomy," and Purdy, "A Response to Dodds and Jones." On reproductive technologies, see Margaret Radin, "Market Inalienability," *Harvard Law Review* 100 (1987): 1849–1937; Marjorie Schultz, "Reproductive Technology and Intent-based Parenthood: An Opportunity for Gender Neutrality," *Wisconsin Law Review* 2 (1990): 287–398; Suzanne Uniacke, "*In Vitro* Fertilization and the Right to Reproduce," *Bioethics* 1 (1987): 241–254; Mary Anne Warren, "IVF and Women's Interests: An Analysis of Feminist Concerns," *Bioethics* 2 (1988): 37–57.

50. We borrow this terminology from Benson, "Free Agency and Self-Worth."

51. Wolf, "Sanity and the Metaphysics of Responsibility."

52. Ibid., p. 54.

53. Thomas E. Hill, Jr., "The Kantian Conception of Autonomy," in Christman, *Inner Citadel.* Philip Pettit and Michael Smith offer a different set of arguments for a version of a Kantian theory of autonomy in "Backgrounding Desire," *Philosophical Review* 94 (1990): 565–592; "Practical Unreason," *Mind* 102 (1993): 53–79; and "Freedom in Belief and Desire," *Journal of Philosophy*: 93 (1996): 429–449.

54. Paul Benson, "Freedom and Value," *Journal of Philosophy* 84 (1987): 465–486; "Feminist Second Thoughts About Free Agency," *Hypatia* 3 (1990): 47–64; and "Autonomy and Oppressive Socialization."

55. Benson, "Free Agency and Self-Worth," p. 656.

56. Ibid., p. 660.

57. See Benson's discussion of content neutrality and content specificity in "Free Agency and Self-Worth," pp. 663–665.

58. Robin Dillon, "Toward a Feminist Conception of Self-Respect," *Hypatia* 7 (1992): 52–69, and Trudy Govier "Self-trust, Autonomy and Self-Esteem," *Hypatia* 8 (1993): 99–120.

59. See Benson's discussion of this issue in "Free Agency and Self-Worth," p. 665.

60. The importance of options to autonomy is emphasized by Joseph Raz, *The Morality of Freedom* (Oxford: Clarendon Press, 1986), pp. 205, 373ff.

61. Friedman, "Autonomy and Social Relationships," pp. 57–58.

I

AUTONOMY AND THE SOCIAL

1

AUTONOMY, SOCIAL DISRUPTION, AND WOMEN[1]

Marilyn Friedman

Of Autonomy and Men

Are women in Western societies alienated by the ideal of autonomy? Many feminist philosophers have recently suggested that women find autonomy to be a notion inhospitable to women, one that represents a masculine-style preoccupation with self-sufficiency and self-realization at the expense of human connection.

Paul Gauguin's life epitomizes what many feminists take to be the masculine ideal of autonomy. Gauguin abandoned his family and middle-class life as a banker in Denmark to travel to Mediterranean France, Tahiti, and Martinique in search of artistic subjects and inspiration. He deserted his wife and five children, one might say, to paint pictures in sunny locales. Biographies of Gauguin's life reveal that he agonized for some time over the decision to leave his family. He once wrote: "One man's faculties can't cope with two things at once, and I for one can do *one thing only*: paint. Everything else leaves me stupefied."[2] Gauguin's self-reflective agonies, I believe, would qualify as autonomous, according to many contemporary definitions.

How has Western culture assessed Gauguin's life and work? Gauguin was *canonized* by Western art history. Of course, he had the moral good luck to have painted important pictures, something that Bernard Williams might call a "good for the world."[3] Whereas his fame is certainly based on his paintings and not on his familial desertion, nevertheless, the fact of his having left behind a wife and five children for sunnier prospects has done nothing to tarnish his stature. If anything, it has added a romantic allure to his biography.

Narratives of this sort suggest that autonomy in practice is antithetical to women's interests because it prompts men to desert the social relationships on which many women depend for the survival and well-being of themselves and their children. In the past, because of women's restricted opportunities, the loss of support suffered by abandoned women has often been worse than the heterosexual relationships on which they depended.

Men are supposed to "stand up like a man" for what they believe or value, including the simple assertion of their self-interests. Women are instead supposed to "*stand by* your man." The maxim "stand up like a *woman!*" has no serious meaning. It conjures up imagery that is, at best, merely humorous. There is no doubt which model of behavior as exhibited by which gender receives the highest honors in Western public culture.

Still today, women in general define themselves more readily than men in terms of personal relationships. In addition, women's moral concerns tend to focus more intensely than those of men on sustaining and enhancing personal ties.[4] Also, popular culture still presumes that women are more concerned than men to create and preserve just the sorts of relationships, such as marriage, that autonomy-seeking men sometimes want to abandon.[5] Feminist analysis has uncovered ways in which close personal involvement and identification with others have been culturally devalued, in tandem with the devaluation of women, by comparison with the public world of impersonal relationships that men have traditionally monopolized.[6] Focusing on the importance of the social is one feminist strategy for combating these traditions of thought and for elevating social esteem for women. Many feminist philosophers have thus emerged as champions of social relationships and of relational approaches to diverse philosophical concepts.[7]

The cultural understanding of autonomy needs to change if the concept is to be relevant for women. I discuss three such changes: new paradigms of autonomy that involve female protagonists, redefinitions of autonomy that avoid stereotypically masculine traits, and redefinitions of autonomy that somehow involve social relationships or are at least not antithetical to them. Indeed such an account has been under development for some time in philosophical literature, and my suggestions on these points are not new. Of course, nothing guarantees a priori that we will find an account of autonomy that synthesizes these elements consistently with the core notion of self-determination that sets limits to our understanding of autonomy. I am optimistic, however, that a female-friendly account of autonomy can be, and has in part already been, developed.

At any rate, I mention these points merely to set the stage for my fourth, and primary, thesis: at the same time that we embrace relational accounts of autonomy, we should also be cautious about them. Autonomy increases the risk of disruption in interpersonal relationships. Although this is an empirical and not a conceptual claim about autonomy, nevertheless, the risk is significant. It makes a difference in whether the ideal of autonomy is genuinely hospitable to women.

After providing a capsule characterization of autonomy that is typical of accounts in the contemporary philosophical literature, I address each of the preceding points in turn.

Personal Autonomy: A Capsule Account

Autonomy involves choosing and living according to standards or values that are, in some plausible sense, one's "own." A plausible sense of "ownness" involves at least two dimensions. First, someone must reflect in an autonomy-conferring manner on the particular choices she makes and the standards or values by which she will be guided. Autonomy-conferring reflection, in my view, is not confined to rational reflection. Such terms as "critical," "reflection," "consideration," "evaluation," "scrutiny," and "choice," as I use them, encompass emotional as well as strictly rational or narrowly cognitive dimensions of personal processes.[8]

Second, the reflection itself must be relatively free of those varieties of interference that impede the achievement of autonomy. What varieties these are I do not specify except to say that socialization does not as such impede autonomy, whereas coercion as such does do so.[9] These circular terms ("autonomy-conferring reflection" and "autonomy-impeding interference") are not meant to articulate the notions in question but merely to serve as placeholders for a fully fleshed account of the nature of autonomy, which is not my present concern.

For the most part, my discussion focuses on personal autonomy, something best defined by reference to moral autonomy. Moral autonomy has to do with what one regards either as morally required or as morally permissible. It involves choosing and living according to rules that one considers to be morally binding. Personal autonomy involves acting and living according to one's own choices, values, and identity within the constraints of what one regards as morally permissible.[10]

Of Autonomy and Women

First, I consider the historic association of autonomy with men. Autonomy, its constituent traits, and the actions and lives that seem to manifest it are publicly esteemed much more often in men than in women. As noted earlier, the preponderance of men in narratives of autonomy could easily cast a masculine shadow over the concept.

Does a concept become irrevocably shaped by the paradigms that initially configure its usage? I believe that it does not and that autonomy can accordingly be freed of its historically near exclusive association with male biographies and male-identified traits. Doing so will require systematic rethinking. In part, we need new paradigms of autonomy that feature female protagonists.[11]

A particularly *feminist* appropriation of the concept of autonomy requires narratives of women who strive in paradigmatically or distinctively female situations against patriarchal constraints to express and refashion their deepest commitments and senses of self. Such narratives are already widely available. Susan Brison, for example, writes of regaining autonomous control over her life after she was tragically raped and almost murdered.[12] Patricia Hill Collins explains the power and importance of self-definition to African-American women, who are fighting the dominating cultural images of themselves as mammies, matriarchs, and welfare mothers.[13] Minnie Bruce Pratt tells of how she struggled to live as a lesbian while at the same time renouncing the racism and antisemitism that she had derived from her family and community of origin.[14]

In addition, there are women's autonomy narratives that are not particularly about overcoming patriarchal constraints. Sara Ruddick's account of maternal thinking, for example, draws heavily on stories of women who reflected deeply on how to care well for their children, an otherwise conventional female task.[15] In short, there is already available a large variety of narratives that exemplify women's autonomous struggles, both feminist and nonfeminist.

It is, in addition, helpful to remember that autonomy is not always valued in men. Whole groups of minority men have had their autonomous aspirations crushed by white Western societies. Moreover, white men do not always tolerate autonomy from one another. In traditional, patriarchal hierarchies, such as military or corporate structures, even many *white* men are routinely punished for being autonomous, for challenging accepted norms and authoritative dictates, for not being a "team player."[16]

Some male philosophers, in addition, criticize the ideal of autonomy in at least some of its versions. Male communitarians challenge what they take to be the overly individualistic and ungrounded autonomy of the liberal tradition.[17] Sounding a different note, Loren Lomasky regards autonomy as a source of "massive dislocation" and "widespread human misery." He criticizes autonomy as a rallying cry of the "Red Guards" and of proponents of the welfare state who reject the "traditional ways" of family life.[18]

Thus, the historical link between autonomy and men is not uniform. It is being further challenged today by the growing diversity of women's lives. Autonomy is now available to, and sometimes celebrated in, women, and it is not always celebrated in men. The gender paradigms of autonomy are shifting. On the basis of paradigms alone, autonomy is no longer straightforwardly male-oriented or alien to women.

Autonomy and Gender Stereotypes

My second point is that we should seek redefinitions of autonomy that avoid stereotypically masculine traits. Autonomy has often been conceptualized in terms of traits that suggest an antifemale bias. Traditional ideals of autonomy, for example, have been grounded in reason. Genevieve Lloyd and others have argued that traditional conceptions of reason have excluded anything deemed "feminine," such as emotion.[19] The exclusion of emotion from the concept of reason, however, is less prominent a view today than it once was. Some recent accounts of rationality by both feminists and mainstream philosophers blur the boundary between reason and emotion and thus promise to undermine this traditional dichotomy.[20] In case those accounts prove to be well grounded, this particular philosophical basis for thinking that autonomy is an antifemale ideal would have been eliminated.[21]

Besides connecting autonomy to reason, popular Western culture has also associated autonomy with other masculine-defined traits, for example, independence and outspokenness.[22] Traits popularly regarded as feminine, by contrast, have no distinctive connection to autonomy—social interactiveness, for example.[23] Thus popular gender stereotypes have associated autonomy with men but not with women; these stereotypes might invidiously infect philosophical thinking about autonomy.

To be sure, because of gender differences in socialization, autonomy might actually occur less often in women than in men. As Diana Meyers has documented, male socialization still promotes autonomy competency more effectively than does female socialization.[24] Overall, men have had far greater opportunities than women to act and live autonomously.[25] Such modes of action and living have in the past been closed to most women because they required unavailable (to women) resources such as political power, financial independence, or the freedom to travel unmolested in public space—to jog safely, for example, through New York City's Central Park.

The more frequent appearance of autonomy in men than in women, combined with the association of stereotypically masculine but not feminine traits with autonomy, might unwittingly bias philosophical investigations of autonomy. Together with their nonphilosophical peers, philosophers might fail to recognize manifestations of autonomy by women. Philosophers who try to conceptualize autonomy might do so with autonomous males in mind as paradigm cases. They might go on to mistake what are merely masculine traits for the traits that make up autonomy competency as such. Thus contemporary philosophical accounts of autonomy should be scrutinized particularly with a view to eliminating any covert masculine paradigms that might lie behind them.

In addition to creating a male bias that might influence philosophical reflections on autonomy, male stereotypes are also easy to exaggerate in ways that could further distort the conception of autonomy. The male-stereotyped traits of independence and self-sufficiency have often been interpreted, both in general culture and in philosophical traditions, in asocial, atomistic terms that seem to sanction detachment from close personal relationships with others.[26] Many feminists have argued that this illusory goal of atomistic self-sufficiency has indeed structured male development and male perspectives in those cultures that require men to repudiate the feminine to consolidate their own masculine gender identity.[27] Some feminists worry that the very concept of autonomy has been irremediably contaminated by this atomistic approach, which neglects the social relationships that are vital for developing the character traits required for mature autonomy competency.[28] Much of that socialization consists of women's traditional child-care labor.

Philosophical accounts might err in this regard more by omission than by commission. Some contemporary accounts, for example, fail to mention how the human capacity for autonomy develops in the course of socialization.[29] By neglecting to mention the role of socialization in the development of mature autonomy competency, traditional accounts of autonomy ignore one crucial way in which autonomous persons are ultimately dependent persons after all, and in particular, dependent on women's nurturing. This philosophical omission does nothing to undermine the conceited cultural illusion of the "self-made man" as a paradigm of autonomy.

To be sure, no respectable philosopher today would *explicitly* deny that a social upbringing and ongoing personal interaction are necessary to become autonomous. These conditions impart the self-concept and resources for critical reflection that autonomy requires. Also, no respectable philosopher would deny that women's labors still make up the lion's share of child care, especially in the crucial years of early formative socialization. Careful philosophical thought on these issues should correct the pop-cultural view of some men as impossibly "self-made," a view that denies women their proper share of credit for nurturing or supporting the autonomy competency found in those men. The point is that philosophers must actively take pains to weed out inappropriate male paradigms that might contaminate their own or a wider cultural understanding of key philosophical notions.

In virtue of disregarding the fundamentally social nature of autonomy and autonomous persons, the myth of the self-made man rests on a mistake. The fact that mistaken conceptions of autonomy are male-biased, however, does not show that autonomy *properly understood* is male-biased or antifemale.

Social Reconceptualizations of Autonomy

My third point is that we need an account of autonomy that brings out its relational character. Fortunately, a relational approach to autonomy has been emerging for some time. Two developments are relevant to this issue: a procedural conception of autonomy and a relational or intersubjective conception of autonomy.[30]

According to a procedural account, personal autonomy is realized by the right sort of reflective self-understanding or internal coherence along with an absence of undue coercion or manipulation by others. Autonomy, in this sort of view, is not a matter of living substantively in any particular way.[31] My own capsule account of autonomy in the previous section is a procedural account. Although this sort of account can be debated,[32] it is nevertheless common in philosophy today. In a procedural conception, avoiding or abandoning close personal relationships is in no sense required by autonomy. Nor is it for any reason inherently a better way for any individual to strive for autonomy.

Although the language of autonomy in popular culture might still suggest asocial atomistic images of the self-made man, academic philosophers now seldom share this view. The atomistic "self-made" conception of autonomy is a substantive conception of a particular sort of life or mode of behaving that someone must choose in order to realize autonomy. Such an ideal falls outside the bounds of procedural accounts of autonomy. It is not a proper part of them.

In addition to focusing mainly on procedural matters, many contemporary philosophers of autonomy have also tended to gravitate toward relational or intersubjective accounts of autonomy. This is true of both feminist and mainstream philosophers. At present, both construe autonomy in social, relational, interpersonal, or intersubjective terms.[33]

According to the relational approach, persons are fundamentally social beings who develop the competency for autonomy through social interaction with other persons. These developments take place in a context of values, meanings, and modes of self-reflection that cannot exist except as constituted by social practices. Also, according to some theorists, autonomy is itself the capacity for a distinctive form of social and, in particular, dialogical engagement.[34]

Autonomy is no longer thought to require someone to be a social atom, that is, radically socially unencumbered, defined merely by the capacity to choose, or to be able to exercise reason prior to any of her contingent ends or social engagements.[35] It is now well recognized that our reflective capacities and our very identities are always partly constituted by communal traditions and norms that we cannot put entirely into question without at the same time voiding our very capacities to reflect.

We are each reared in a social context of some sort, typically although not always that of a family, itself located in wider social networks such as community and nation. Nearly all of us remain, throughout our lives, involved in social relationships and communities, at least some of which partly define our identities and ground our highest values. These relationships and communities are fostered and sustained by varied sorts of ties that we share with others, such as languages, activities, practices, projects, traditions, histories, goals, views, values, and mutual attractions—not to mention common enemies and shared injustices and disasters.

Someone who becomes more autonomous concerning some tradition, authority, view, or value in her life does not stop depending on other persons or relationships, nor does she evade her own necessarily social history of personal development. Her initial detached questioning does not arise in a social vacuum but is likely to be prompted by commitments reflecting still other relationships that for the present time remain unquestioned and perhaps heteronomous. A shift in social relationships or commitments is not equivalent to, nor need it betoken, wholesale social detachment.

Autonomy does not require self-creation or the creation of law ex nihilo, a limitation that we need not join Richard Rorty in lamenting.[36] Becoming more procedurally autonomous concerning particular standards, norms, or dictates involves reflecting on them in a language that one did not create—according to further norms and standards that one has almost surely taken over from others—in light of what is most central to that product of social development that is oneself.[37] Also, autonomy is always a matter of degree, of more or less. Reflective consideration still counts as a gain in autonomy even if done in the light of other standards and relationships not simultaneously subjected to the same scrutiny.

How Autonomy Disrupts Personal Relationships

Feminists have sought a relational account of autonomy to render it relevant to women. Philosophers in general have sought such an account to make good on a widely shared intuition that autonomy is not antithetical to other social values and virtues that concern us all, such as love, friendship, care, loyalty, and devotion.[38] Many philosophers seem to expect that most of what we want or value in interpersonal relationships will prove to be consistent with the ideal of autonomy, once we develop an appropriately social conception of it.

That conviction, however, may be unfounded. It underestimates, I believe, the disruption that autonomy can promote in close personal relationships and in communities. Although autonomy is not inherently antithetical to social relationships, nevertheless, in practice autonomy often contingently disrupts particular social bonds. How it sometimes interferes with social relationships and what this implies about its value for women make up the fourth and primary theme of this article.

Human relationships and communities, as noted, are held together by a variety of ties that persons share, including languages, practices, traditions, histories, goals, views, and values. Any of these elements in someone's life can become the focus of her critical scrutiny. Whenever someone questions or evaluates any tie or commitment that binds her to others, the possibility arises that she may find that bond unwarranted and begin to reject it. Rejecting values that tie someone to others may lead her to try to change the relationships in question or simply to detach herself from them. Someone might also reflect on the very nature of her relationships to particular others and come to believe that those ties are neglecting or smothering important dimensions of herself. To liberate those aspects of herself, she might have to distance herself from the problematic relationships.

Most personal and communal relationships are multifaceted and based on more than one sort of tie. Kinship, for example, keeps many people in contact with relatives whose values would otherwise repel them. Childhood friends who travel disparate paths in life may retain shared memories that keep them ever fondly in touch with each other. A shared ethnic identity may link economically diverse people in the pursuit of collective political ends or cultural self-affirmation. Thus, friends, relatives, or other associates who diverge over important values may still remain related to each other in virtue of other shared ties.

The resilience of social relationships is, of course, not always a blessing. Relationships in which one partner exploits or abuses the other can also, and regrettably, last for years.[39] Sometimes, however, a person becomes so disenchanted with her relationships or their underlying values that they become, to her, unbearable. At that level of discontent, and assuming viable alternatives, she may begin to withdraw from the relationships. In so doing, she displays just the sort of relational disconnection that can stem from a person's autonomous reflections on (and growing dissatisfaction with) her prior commitments.

Alternatively, someone's increasing autonomy might result in the breakup of a relationship not because she rejects it but rather because other parties to the relationship reject her. They might despise the changes in her behavior that they are witnessing. Some parents, for example, disown children who rebel too strongly against deeply held parental values. Peer groups often ostracize their members for disregarding important norms that prevail in their own subcultures.

Strictly speaking, to say that autonomy unqualified (sometimes) disrupts social relationships is misleading. The mere capacity for autonomy is not intrinsically socially disruptive. What disrupts a social relationship in a particular case is the actual exercise of the capacity. More strictly still, the differences that arise between people as a result of one party's autonomous rejection of values or commitments that the other party still holds may lead one party to draw away from or reject the other. Thus, to borrow a rhetorical turn of phrase from the U.S. lobbying group the National Rifle Association (!), it is not *autonomy* (as a dispositional capacity) that disrupts social relationships; it is *people* who disrupt social relationships.

The exercise of autonomy, it should be emphasized, is not sufficient as such to disrupt particular relationships. The connection between autonomy and social disruption is merely contingent. Someone's autonomous reflections increase the chances of disruption in her social relationships but do not make it a necessary consequence. In certain sorts of circumstances, autonomy may not even make social disruption more likely than it already is. Someone's reflective consideration might lead her to appreciate in a new light the worth of her relationships or the people to whom she is socially attached and to enrich her commitment to them. In such cases, autonomy would strengthen rather than weaken relational ties. Even if someone began to disagree with significant others about important matters, their relationship might still not suffer. People use many interpersonal strategies to keep differing commitments from disrupting social harmony—"never discuss religion or politics," for example.[40]

Thus, someone's autonomy is not a *sufficient* condition for the disruption of her social relationships. Nor is it a *necessary* condition. A person might end a relationship because of new commitments that she has reached heteronomously. Peer pressure, for example, can promote knee-jerk rebelliousness that disrupts personal relationships as much as the greatest soul searching and critical self-reflection. Someone's attitudes can also change as the result of traumatic experiences over which she had no control. These changes may occasion deep rifts in her relationships with close others.[41] Someone's increasing autonomy is thus neither a sufficient nor a necessary cause of disruption in social relationships.

Nevertheless, the contingently possible connection between autonomy and social disruption is of noteworthy importance. When a culture places great value on autonomy, members of that culture are thereby encouraged to question their prior allegiances and the standards that impinge on them. Autonomy as a cultural ideal creates a supportive climate for personal scrutiny of traditions, standards, and authoritative commands.[42] Public discourse in such a culture will tend to promote open dialogue and debate over values and traditions. Autonomy-idealizing societies may protect such discourse, and the normative critiques it can foster, with a legal right to a substantial degree of freedom of expression.

Thus, other things being equal, in a culture that prizes autonomy, all traditions, authorities, norms, views, and values become more vulnerable to rejection by at least some members of the society than they would be in a society that devalued autonomy. No commitment in such a culture remains entirely immune to critical scrutiny, whether the commitment concerns religion, sex, family, government, economy, art, education, race, ethnicity, gender, or anything else.

Once such scrutiny takes place, the likelihood increases that people who are socially linked to each other will begin to diverge over views or values they previously shared, including the value of their social ties. Once people begin to diverge over important matters, they are more likely than they were before to disagree and quarrel with each other or to lose mutual interest and drift apart. In this way (other things being equal), an autonomy-idealizing culture increases the risk of (though it certainly does not guarantee) ruptures in social relationships.

To be sure, cultures that idealize autonomy do not always extend this ideal to all social groups. Sometimes certain sorts of people, white men, for example, receive the lion's share of the social protections and rewards for being autonomous. Also, even an autonomy-idealizing culture may shield certain norms or values from criti-

cal scrutiny. In such a society, values that protect dominant social groups, those privileged to enjoy the value of autonomy, might not get as much critical attention as
they deserve. Whereas limitations on rampant autonomy might be necessary to prevent wholesale social breakdown, they can also create bastions of unquestioned autonomous privilege. In such a culture, autonomy might well be a restricted, domes-
ticated, socially nonthreatening luxury.

Nevertheless, as long as autonomy is culturally valued even for only some
groups and for only certain issues, its very cultural availability opens up the possibility for wide social transformation. Even if idealized for only a privileged few, it
can always fall into the "wrong" hands. New groups might coincidentally acquire
autonomy competency in virtue of social changes, such as the spread of literacy and
formal education. They might then go on to contest norms and values previously
left unscrutinized. This possibility has been historically crucial for women and other
subordinated groups. The ideal of autonomy is thus always a potential catalyst for
social disruption in interpersonal relationships.

Notice also that the rupture that autonomy can promote in any one particular
social relationship does not necessarily amount to an overall decline in the societal quantity of relationality, to put the point inelegantly. Typically, when someone
questions some prior commitment, such as a religious commitment, which ce-
mented certain relationships in her life, she is probably doing so in company with
other skeptics whose reflections prompt and reinforce her own rising doubts.
When she turns away from her prior religious community, she is likely to be turn-
ing toward a different community, perhaps a religiously neutral secular community or a new religious group. Those with whom someone shares her new commitments may have given her a vocabulary or perspective for reflecting on her
central concerns. Without any empirical backing for this claim, I nevertheless es-
timate that in most cases in which autonomous reflection does lead people to reject the commitments that bound them to particular others, they are at the same
time taking up new commitments that link them through newly shared conviction to *different* particular others. This is one important reason for thinking of autonomy as social in character.

Although people in an autonomy-valuing society might have as many interpersonal relationships as those in a society that devalued autonomy, it is reasonable to speculate that the nature of people's relationships would differ in the two
cases. Where people are permitted with relative ease to leave relationships that
have become dissatisfying to them, we should expect attachments to be less stable,
to shift and change with greater frequency, than in societies in which personal autonomy (or relational mobility) is discouraged. The types and qualities of relationships in an autonomy-promoting culture would also probably differ from
those of an autonomy-discouraging culture. Relationships into which people are
born and in which they are first socialized—those of family, church, neighbor-
hood, friendship, and local communities—would probably be disrupted first, if
any, by widespread individually autonomous reflections on basic values and commitments. In a culture that values autonomy, it is likely that more people than
otherwise would gravitate toward voluntary relationships formed in adult life
around shared values and attitudes.[43]

Women and the Social Disruptions of Autonomy

What difference should it make to our theory of autonomy that autonomy, however social its nature or origin, might promote the disruption of social relationships? More precisely in the present context, what difference does this possibility make to *women*? If autonomy is sometimes socially disruptive, does that make it inimical to the relational orientation that many feminists celebrate in women and display in their own moral concerns?

Some people exhibit what I call autonomophobia, or fear of autonomy. What they usually fear is not their own autonomy; it is the autonomy of *others* that scares them. Their concern is that autonomous people will disrupt or desert valuable, *shared* relationships. Which relationships are thought to be valuable will be specified differently from distinct critical perspectives. Feminists, and many women in general, often worry about the relationships on which many women depend for material and emotional sustenance.

Whether or not any particular woman benefits or suffers in virtue of the exercise of autonomy depends on how she is positioned in relation to it. When a woman is connected to someone else whose autonomous pursuits disrupt their relationship, the immediate effect on her is likely to be simply a loss—of whatever benefits she derived from their relationship. Autonomophobia is thus a legitimate concern. It arises from the ways in which our lives are intertwined with those of other persons. When others who are close to us reflect on their own deepest commitments, they might well find grounds for challenging or abandoning the relationships and communities that we share with them. We might find ourselves helpless as a result. Social relationships and communities are collective projects. They function best when sustained jointly by people with important values or norms in common. In a culture that idealizes autonomy, each individual faces the insecurity of investing herself in relationships and communities that the other participants might, on critical reflection, come to reject.

Historically, the disruption of personal relationships has had a different impact on men than on women. Because women were usually limited to dependence on men for financial support, whereas men had no comparable limitation, women doubtless suffered more than they benefited from the cultural idealization of autonomy. Men have been historically better situated than women to forsake personal relationships that came to seem dissatisfying to them. Unlike most women, many men have had the material and cultural resources with which to support themselves, as well as greater opportunities to seek more satisfying relationships elsewhere. Men were able to abandon their responsibilities to women and children to pursue forms of personal fulfillment unavailable to women.

Men who, like Gauguin, produced good enough subsequent works have been celebrated for autonomous pursuits that involved neglecting or abandoning relationships that supported women and children. Dependent women and children have suffered greatly from these male desertions. Women's own autonomous living, by contrast, brought them much more censure and hardship than praise.[44] Since women tend to be more financially dependent on men than men are on women even today, autonomophobia is understandably still more often a female than a male concern. Thus, men's autonomy would have done women little direct good and could have imposed serious harm.

On the other hand, many social relationships constrain and oppress women, indeed the very women who work to sustain them. Apart from whether or not women *want* to devote their lives to maintaining close personal ties, gender norms have required it of them. Women have been expected to make the preservation of certain interpersonal relationships such as those of family their highest concern regardless of the costs to themselves. Women who have had important commitments other than those of taking care of family members were nevertheless supposed to subordinate such commitments to the task of caring for loved ones. Many men, by contrast, have been free to choose or affirm their highest commitments from among a wide panorama of alternatives. Indeed, men are sometimes lauded for just the sort of single-minded pursuit of an ideal that imposes sacrifices on all the people close to them.

Traditionally, the majority of women derived their primary adult identities from their marriages and families. For at least some groups of women, however, social and economic opportunities have broadened in the late twentieth century. Because of expanding financial opportunities in the West, many women no longer need to accommodate themselves *uncritically* to traditional marriages or other relational ties to sustain themselves. As many feminists have well recognized, there is no reason to defend social relationships without qualification. There is nothing intrinsic to each and every social relationship that merits female or feminist allegiance.[45] The traditional relational work of women has included sublime joy and fulfillment but also abuse, exploitation, and subordination. There are some, perhaps many, relationships that women, too, should want to end.

Thus, the disruption of social relationships that can follow someone's growing autonomy is not itself inherently alien to women, nor is it a dimension of the ideal of autonomy that women today should automatically reject. What should matter to any particular woman in any given case is the worth of the relationship in question and how its disruption would bear on herself and on innocent others. The old question, "can this marriage be saved?" should be revised to, "can this marriage be saved from *oppressiveness*?" Some relationships should be preserved and others should be abolished. Even relationships that should be preserved can always be improved. Sometimes what disrupts social relationships is good for particular women. Since the socially disruptive potential of autonomy can at least sometimes be good for women, it does not constitute a reason for women to repudiate the ideal of autonomy.

Indeed, reflecting on one's relationships or the norms or values that underlie them might be the *only* way someone can determine for herself the moral quality of those relationships. A woman who does not reflect on her relationships, communities, norms, or values is incapable of recognizing for herself where they go wrong or of aiming on her own to improve them. Her well-being depends on those who control her life and on their wisdom and benevolence—regrettably, not the most reliable of human traits. Autonomy is thus crucial for women in patriarchal conditions, in part *because* of its potential to disrupt social bonds. That autonomy is sometimes antithetical to social relationships is oftimes a good for women. With all due respect to Audrey Lorde, the "master's tools" *can* "dismantle the master's house."[46]

Thus, although women still have occasion to fear *men's* autonomy, it seems that many women have good reason to welcome our *own*. When a woman is the one who is exercising autonomy, even if its exercise disrupts relationships in her life the value of her gain in autonomous living might well make the costs to her worth her while. She may plausibly fear what increasingly autonomous others might do to the relationships between herself and them, but it would not make sense for her to reject autonomy for herself. A woman might choose not to *exercise* autonomy under certain conditions. She might, for example, devote herself loyally to an ideal that she can only serve by working with a group of persons who sometimes take specific actions she does not understand or endorse. She can hardly want to give up, however, the very option of so devoting herself. To reflect on the standards or values according to which one will behave or live one's life, as one does when resolving to dedicate oneself to a particular ideal, is already to exercise a degree of autonomy. It would be self-defeating, at the same time, to reject autonomy altogether as a value for oneself.

Once women admit that autonomy might be a value for us, it would be difficult to deny its value for persons in general. The capacity for autonomy seems instrumentally valuable as a means for resisting oppression and intrinsically valuable as part of the fullest humanly possible development of moral personality. In these respects it seems valuable for anyone. The problem arises with the need for reciprocity. We cannot esteem autonomy in women while deprecating it in men. Yet men's autonomy and the social disruption it can promote does sometimes threaten women's well-being. I have argued that when women have access to means for their own material support, this risk is lessened.[47] Women can then gain at least as much from a generalized cultural idealization of autonomy as they risk by it.

There are, as well, certain mitigating possibilities that reduce, even though they do not eliminate, the likelihood that autonomy might cause social disruption. Autonomy does not necessarily lead someone to reject her prior commitments. Someone else's increasing autonomy might instead enhance her appreciation of her close relationships. Even if she comes to regard a relationship as seriously flawed, she might work to improve it rather than abandoning it.

These possibilities suggest that alongside autonomy as a cultural ideal, we should also idealize the values and responsibilities that make relationships and communities worthwhile.[48] We can emphasize, for example, the ways in which close relationships are vital sources of care for the most vulnerable members of our society.[49] We should articulate these values in public dialogues in which all can participate, including those who might become autonomously skeptical about those social ties.

This balanced pursuit of the values of community along with the ideal of autonomy is a partial response to the concern that the empirical social disruptiveness of autonomy lessens the value of autonomy for women. There is no way, however, to alleviate this concern fully. The possibility of social disruptiveness is one risk that must be faced by persons and cultures who would idealize personal autonomy.[50] I have argued that social disruptiveness is, at least, a mixed curse, one that harbors the potential for good, as well as bad, consequences.

In addition, the mantra of "family values" that is invoked uncritically in so much public debate in the United States should remind us as feminists of the hazards of allowing any relationships, including those we most cherish, to be entirely insulated from the critical reflection of all their participants. Even care for the most vulnerable can usually be improved. It is a form of respect toward those with whom we most want affiliation to want *them* to find forms of commitment to us that reflect *their* most cherished values.

Notes

1. I am grateful to Natalie Stoljar and Catriona Mackenzie for helpful editorial suggestions on an earlier draft of this article.

2. Yann le Pichon, *Gauguin: Life, Art, Inspiration* (New York: Abrams, 1987), p. 26.

3. Bernard Williams's discussion of moral luck deploys the hypothetical biography of an artist whose life resembles that of the historic Gauguin; see Williams, "Moral Luck," in *Moral Luck* (Cambridge: Cambridge University Press, 1981), p. 37. See my discussion of Williams on the Gauguin-like example in my *What Are Friends For?: Feminist Perspectives on Personal Relationships and Moral Theory* (Ithaca, N.Y.: Cornell University Press, 1993), pp. 163–170.

4. See the germinal work on this topic by Carol Gilligan, *In a Different Voice* (Cambridge, Mass.: Harvard University Press, 1982), and Nel Noddings, *Caring: A Feminine Approach to Ethics and Moral Education* (Berkeley: University of California Press, 1984).

5. See Susan Faludi's discussion of the popularization of research results alleging that women's chances of marrying fall precipitously after age forty, in *Backlash: The Undeclared War against American Women* (New York: Crown Publishers, 1991), chap. 1. Faludi argues persuasively that the conclusions were misrepresented in the mass media. My point is a different one: these research results would not have received popular attention if it hadn't been for the presumption that people, including women, would want to know about them.

6. See Gilligan, *In a Different Voice*, chap. 1.

7. See, for example, Helen Longino, *Science as Social Knowledge* (Princeton, N.J.: Princeton University Press, 1990).

8. For an account of emotion as a source of autonomy, see Bennett W. Helm, "Freedom of the Heart," *Pacific Philosophical Quarterly* 77 (1996): 71–87. Harry Frankfurt discusses caring and love as sources of autonomy but uses those terms to refer to states of will rather than of emotion; see, for example, *The Importance of What We Care About* (Cambridge: Cambridge University Press, 1988), and "Autonomy, Necessity, and Love," in *Vernunftbegriffe in der Moderne: Stuttgarter Hegel-Kongress 1993*, ed. Hans Friedrich Fulda and Rolf-Peter Horstmann (Stuttgart: Klett-Cotta, 1994), pp. 433–447.

9. Of course, socialization might itself be coercive. See John Christman's approach to this problem in "Autonomy and Personal History," *Canadian Journal of Philosophy* 20 (1991): 1–24.

10. Diana T. Meyers, *Self, Society, and Personal Choice* (New York: Columbia University Press, 1989), pp. 13–17.

11. Morwenna Griffiths explores the importance of narratives in the cultural understanding of autonomy in *Feminisms and the Self: The Web of Identity* (London: Routledge, 1995).

12. Susan Brison, "Surviving Sexual Violence," *Journal of Social Philosophy* 24, no. 1 (Spring 1993): 5–22.

13. Patricia Hill Collins, *Black Feminist Thought: Knowledge, Consciousness, and the Politics of Empowerment* (New York: Routledge, 1991), especially chaps. 4 and 5.

14. Minnie Bruce Pratt, "Identity: Skin Blood Heart," in *Yours in Struggle: Three Feminist Perspectives on Anti-Semitism and Racism*, ed. Elly Bulkin, Minnie Bruce Pratt, and Barbara Smith (Brooklyn, N.Y.: Long Haul Press, 1984), pp. 9–63.

15. Sara Ruddick, *Maternal Thinking: Toward a Politics of Peace* (New York: Ballantine, 1989).

16. The chancellor at a university near my own, for example, was recently fired by his university's governing board. The faculty members who supported him thought the problem was, as one of them put it, that the chancellor was "too autonomous, too independent." Faculty supporters described the governing board as wanting a "team player" instead. See Susan C. Thomson and Kim Bell, "Mizzou Chancellor Wants Buyout," *St. Louis Post-Dispatch*, June 14, 1996, C7. Note that the figure of a "team player" is a historically masculine metaphor for a cooperative social agent. The differences between women's and men's paradigm images of social cooperation deserve some study.

17. Michael J. Sandel, *Liberalism and the Limits of Justice* (Cambridge: Cambridge University Press, 1982), and Alasdair MacIntyre, *After Virtue*, 2nd ed. (Notre Dame, Ind.: University of Notre Dame Press, 1984).

18. Loren E. Lomasky, *Persons, Rights, and the Moral Community* (New York: Oxford University Press, 1987), p. 249. In the now common procedural account of autonomy, a view that I share (see the section on social reconcepualizations), no particular choices are intrinsic to autonomy. An autonomous person might embrace traditional relationships, reject traditional relationships, welcome the Red Guards, or abhor the Red Guards. What matters is how she arrived at her political views and whether those views reflect her own considered convictions. Lomasky construes autonomy as a failing only of those who make political choices he rejects, but this is just as mistaken as assuming that autonomy is a virtue only of those who make what one considers to be the right political choices.

19. Genevieve Lloyd, *The Man of Reason: "Male" and "Female" in Western Philosophy* (Minneapolis: University of Minnesota Press, 1984). See also Lorraine Code, *Rhetorical Spaces: Essays on Gendered Locations* (New York: Routledge, 1995), especially chap. 10, "Critiques of Pure Reason."

20. Feminist sources include Code, *Rhetorical Spaces*, and Alison M. Jaggar, "Love and Knowledge: Emotion in Feminist Epistemology," in *Gender/Body/Knowledge*, ed. Alison M. Jaggar and Susan R. Bordo (New Brunswick, N.J.: Rutgers University Press, 1989), pp. 145–171. Nonfeminist sources include Allan Gibbard, *Wise Choices, Apt Feelings: A Theory of Normative Judgment* (Cambridge, Mass.: Harvard University Press, 1990).

21. A different approach would be to argue that the stereotypic association of women with emotion was always groundless and that women are as able as men to exercise a narrowly cognitive mode of reason. See Louise M. Antony and Charlotte Witt, eds., *A Mind of One's Own: Feminist Essays on Reason and Objectivity* (Boulder, Colo.: Westview Press, 1993), especially the essays by Margaret Atherton and Louise Antony. See the discussion of these essays by Code, *Rhetorical Spaces*, pp. 217–223.

22. See Susan Golombok and Robyn Fivush, *Gender Development* (Cambridge: Cambridge University Press, 1994), pp. 7–8.

23. Ibid., p. 18. A social or relational account of autonomy, such as that presented here, is one that construes social relationships as necessary for autonomy but not sufficient for it. There is nothing about social interconnection as such that entails, causes, or suggests autonomy.

24. Meyers, *Self, Society and Personal Choice*, especially part 3.

25. This point is, of course, not universal throughout Western cultures. Men of op-

pressed groups, such as racial minorities, may not have had significantly greater opportunities than the women of their own groups to act and live autonomously.

26. Many feminists have charged the traditional philosophical ideal of autonomy with excessive individualism; see, for example, Lorraine Code, "Second Persons," in *What Can She Know?: Feminist Theory and the Construction of Knowledge* (Ithaca, N.Y.: Cornell University Press, 1991), pp. 76–79.

27. See, for example, Evelyn Fox Keller, *Reflections on Gender and Science* (New Haven, Conn.: Yale University Press, 1985); Nancy Chodorow, *The Reproduction of Mothering: Psychoanalysis and the Sociology of Gender* (Berkeley: University of California Press, 1978); and Jessica Benjamin, *The Bonds of Love: Psychoanalysis, Feminism, and the Problem of Domination* (New York: Pantheon, 1988).

28. Annette Baier, "Cartesian Persons," in *Postures of the Mind: Essays on Mind and Morals* (Minneapolis: University of Minnesota Press, 1985). See also the discussion of this notion in Code, "Second Persons."

29. One prominent philosopher who neglects socialization, and, indeed, social relationships generally, in his account of autonomy is Frankfurt, *Importance of What We Care About*.

30. See the discussion of both of these points by John Christman, "Feminism and Autonomy," in *"Nagging" Questions: Feminist Ethics in Everyday Life*, ed. Dana E. Bushnell (Lanham, Md.: Rowman & Littlefield, 1995), pp. 17–39.

31. Gerald Dworkin provides one example of a procedural account of autonomy; see his *The Theory and Practice of Autonomy* (Cambridge: Cambridge University Press, 1988), pp. 18, 21–33.

32. See Marina Oshana, "Personal Autonomy and Society," *Journal of Social Philosophy* 29, no. 1 (Spring 1998): 81–102.

33. Feminist theorists who have developed this view include Keller, *Reflections on Gender and Science*; Jennifer Nedelsky, "Reconceiving Autonomy: Sources, Thoughts, and Possibilities," *Yale Journal of Law and Feminism* 1, no. 1 (Spring 1989): 7–36; Meyers, *Self, Society, and Personal Choice*; and Code, "Second Persons." Mainstream theorists who have developed this view include Joseph Raz, *The Morality of Freedom* (Oxford: Clarendon Press, 1986); Dworkin, *Theory and Practice of Autonomy*; and Joel Feinberg, "Autonomy," in *The Inner Citadel*, ed. John Christman (New York: Oxford University Press, 1989), pp. 27–53. For a discussion of the convergence of these two groups around a social conception of autonomy, see Christman, "Feminism and Autonomy," and my "Autonomy and Social Relationships: Rethinking the Feminist Critique," in *Feminists Rethink the Self*, ed. Diana T. Meyers (Boulder, Colo.: Westview Press, 1997), pp. 40–61. Some mainstream philosophers deny that the traditional notion of autonomy, even in its rigorous Kantian formulation, ever really excluded or ignored the importance of interpersonal relationships; see J. B. Schneewind, "The Use of Autonomy in Ethical Theory," in *Reconstructing Individualism: Autonomy, Individuality, and the Self in Western Theory*, ed. Thomas C. Heller, Morton Sosna, and David E. Wellbery (Stanford, Cal.: Stanford University Press, 1986), and Thomas E. Hill, Jr., "The Importance of Autonomy," in *Autonomy and Self-Respect* (Cambridge: Cambridge University Press, 1991).

34. See, for example, Jurgen Habermas, *Moral Consciousness and Communicative Action*, trans. Christian Lenhardt and Shierry Weber Nicholsen (Cambridge, Mass.: MIT Press, 1990), and Joel Anderson, "A Social Conception of Personal Autonomy: Volitional Identity, Strong Evaluation, and Intersubjective Accountability," Ph.D. dissertation, Northwestern University, Evanston, Ill., 1996.

35. See, for example, Sandel, *Liberalism and the Limits of Justice*, p. 19.

36. Richard Rorty, *Contingency, Irony, and Solidarity* (Cambridge: Cambridge University Press, 1989).

37. Gerald Dworkin notes the impossibility of creating our own moral principles. Such a requirement "denies our history. . . . We . . . are deeply influenced by parents, siblings, peers, culture, class, climate, schools, accident, genes, and the accumulated history of the species. It makes no more sense to suppose we invent the moral law for ourselves than to suppose that we invent the language we speak for ourselves" (*The Theory and Practice of Autonomy*, p. 36).

38. Ibid., p. 21.

39. If abusive relationships persist for long periods of time, it is usually because the abused partner has, or thinks she has, no other viable options or because she sacrifices her own well-being to that of her abuser. For a survey of why long-time battered women finally seek court orders of protection against abusive male partners, see Karla Fischer and Mary Rose, "When 'Enough is Enough': Battered Women's Decision Making around Court Orders of Protection," *Crime and Delinquency* 41, no. 4 (October 1995): 414–429.

40. I do not endorse this maxim; I merely cite it as an example of the strategies that people use to keep disagreements from disrupting social relationships.

41. See Brison's discussion in "Surviving Sexual Violence," of the difficulties that arose in her relationships with family, friends, and others after she was violently raped.

42. As Dworkin notes, "Those who practice in their daily life a critical reflection on their own value structure will tend to be suspicious of modes of thought that rely on the uncritical acceptance of authority, tradition, and custom" (*The Theory and Practice of Autonomy*, p. 29).

43. For further discussion of this theme, see my *What Are Friends For?* chap. 9.

44. See Alison MacKinnon, *Love and Freedom: Professional Women and the Reshaping of Personal Life* (Cambridge: Cambridge University Press, 1997), on the hurdles faced by women in Australia at the end of the nineteenth and beginning of the twentieth century who sought higher education and careers outside the home.

45. There are many feminist discussions of problems that women face in social relationships; see, for example, Susan Moller Okin, *Justice, Gender, and the Family* (New York: Basic Books, 1989).

46. See Audrey Lorde, "The Master's Tools Will Never Dismantle the Master's House," *Sister Outsider* (Freedom, Cal.: Crossing Press, 1984), pp. 110–113.

47. On this topic, see the essays in Martha Nussbaum and Jonathan Glover, eds., *Women, Culture and Development: A Study of Human Capabilities* (Oxford: Clarendon Press, 1995).

48. See the essays in *Feminism and Community*, eds. Penny Weiss and Marilyn Friedman (Philadelphia: Temple University Press, 1995).

49. See, for example, Robert E. Goodin, *Protecting the Vulnerable: A Reanalysis of Our Social Responsibilities* (Chicago: University of Chicago Press, 1985); Neera Kapur Badhwar, ed., *Friendship: A Philosophical Reader* (Ithaca, N.Y.: Cornell University Press, 1993); Joan C. Tronto, *Moral Boundaries: A Political Argument for an Ethic of Care* (New York: Routledge, 1994).

50. Should we devalue autonomy for individuals, perhaps recasting it as an ideal for groups only? The notion of group autonomy is extremely important, especially for oppressed groups; see, for example, Laurence Mordekhai Thomas, *Vessels of Evil: American Slavery and the Holocaust* (Philadelphia: Temple University Press, 1993), pp. 182–189. Group autonomy, however, does not necessarily help individuals when they face oppressive conditions in isolation. It complements but does not replace individual autonomy. In addition, group autonomy promotes its own risk of social disruption in the relationships between groups. The possible advantages, as well as the possible costs, of autonomy's socially disruptive potential simply reappear at a more encompassing level of social integration.

2

AUTONOMY AND THE SOCIAL SELF[1]

Linda Barclay

Widespread dissatisfaction with the ideal of individual autonomy is a prominent feature of feminist and communitarian perspectives on moral and political theory. Whether attention is focused on moral impartialism, Kantian ethics, modern political theory, or in particular, contemporary liberalism, a frequently voiced concern is that individual autonomy is overemphasized and that an "atomistic" or "abstract individualistic" conception of the self is presupposed. Both feminists and communitarians have claimed that numerous moral and political theories promote a vision of the autonomous self as essentially independent and self-sufficient, a vision that denies the inescapable connectedness of selves and the fact that their immersion in networks of relationships forms their desires, aspirations, indeed their very identities. In other words, what is denied is that the self is essentially social.

Lorraine Code, for example, claims that the prevailing notion of autonomy posits human beings as "self-sufficient, independent, and self-reliant," a partial and ultimately distorted view that blithely ignores the fact that we are also interdependent and cooperating.[2] For similar reasons Jennifer Nedelsky argues that "feminism requires a new conception of autonomy," one that is able to "recognize the inherently social nature of human beings."[3] Sarah Lucia Hoagland, somewhat more pessimistically, claims that "autonomy . . . is a thoroughly noxious concept" that "encourages us to believe that connecting and engaging with others limits us . . . and undermines our sense of self."[4]

Similar objections can be traced through communitarian critiques of liberalism. Alasdair MacIntyre repudiates the liberal assumption that "individuals . . . are primary and society secondary" and that individual interests are assumed to be "prior to, and independent of, the construction of any social bonds between them." Such a picture ignores the fact that "individuals inherit a particular space within an interlocking set of social relationships."[5] Similarly, Michael Sandel argues that liberals assume we each choose our ends, an assumption belied by the fact that the self does not so much choose its ends as "discover" them as constituents of its identity, ends that are derived from the communities of which it is a part.[6]

In short, both communitarians and feminists have championed social conceptions of the self, which they argue are denied, or at least underplayed, by the prominence afforded to individual autonomy in a range of theories. Their apparently shared concerns seem in fact to be "strikingly similar,"[7] leading a number of feminists to question whether there is scope for an explicit alliance between feminism and communitarianism.[8]

In fact, a number of quite distinct issues is often concealed by the very general suggestion that the concept of autonomy presupposes an asocial conception of the self. In what follows I set out three distinct senses in which feminists and communitarians have defined the social self and assess the accusation that the notion of autonomy is incompatible with each. The three senses in which the self is said to be social are deterministic, motivational, and constitutive.[9]

I develop these three distinct accounts of the social self in the next three sections. I attempt to demonstrate that a suitably nuanced conception of autonomy is compatible with plausible versions of the socially determined and motivationally social self, but it is incompatible with particularly strong versions of the socially determined and the constitutively social self. However, I also argue that these strong versions of the social self are not in fact plausible and thus should not threaten our commitment to a suitable conception of autonomy. In the final section I consider whether there are grounds for a communitarian-feminist alliance against the ideal of autonomy. I argue that despite very superficial similarities, feminist and communitarian claims about autonomy and the social self are quite distinct and, in the main, incompatible. It is therefore doubtful that feminists can wholeheartedly embrace communitarianism as an ally.

The Socially Determined Self

Among the numerous philosophers writing on autonomy, broad consensus on some kind of procedural notion has been emerging.[10] Generally, autonomy is said to consist of a capacity, or the exercise of certain competencies,[11] that enables one to reflect on one's aims, aspirations, and motivations and choose one's ends and purposes through such a reflective process. One of the most frequently voiced criticisms of autonomy is that it is in tension with the fact that the self's very identity is determined by the communities of which one is a part, that is, by the pervasive influence of parents, peers, and culture. A procedural notion of autonomy—which envisions a person critically reflecting on her desires and aspirations—could be thought to presuppose that the self can somehow simply transcend the influence of all of these

factors and make oneself anew, to become a fully "self-made (wo)man." But this denies the obvious reality that none of us is self-made in this fashion for we are all, inescapably, "a product of our environment." This is the claim that the self is socially
determined. The claim is broad and can incorporate four quite distinct concerns.

The Global Influence of Social Determinism

The first and strongest way of expressing concern about the relation between autonomy and the fact that the identity of the self is socially determined is to deny
that individual autonomy is possible. For every value, plan, or project endorsed by
the self, there is a set of social influences that can account for why one makes the
"choices" one does. Autonomy is an illusion. Even if we go through the motions of
reflecting on our motivational structure to critically reconsider our ends and purposes, the "choices" we make are themselves just as much a product of the social environment as our prereflective ends and purposes are.

This claim about the impossibility of autonomy bears a strong resemblance to
the familiar free will versus determinism debate. From this perspective, the problem is to explain how autonomy is possible, given the truism that for any action
we perform or any intention that we form there is a set of antecedent causes that
explains why we do what we do or why we think what we think. In other words,
there are social (and biological) facts that explain why we do what we do or why
we think as we do; the *sources* of the self's ends and purposes are sources external
to oneself. How is autonomy possible, given the indisputable facts of determinism? It seems ineluctably in conflict with the fact that the self is determined, all
the way down.

I would argue that the claim that social determinism undercuts the possibility
of autonomy—whether that claim is expressed in terms of the metaphysical threat
of determinism, or of the pervasiveness of socialization—is based on a misunder-
standing of the notion of autonomy. Determinism is only a global threat to the possibility of autonomy on the assumption that agency is only genuinely autonomous if
it is uncaused, or determined by no reasons whatsoever. However, that one is autonomous does *not* mean that one's choices are uninfluenced or uncaused, for it is
doubtful that such a notion is even coherent. Autonomous agency does not imply
that one mysteriously escapes altogether from social influence but rather that one is
able to fashion a certain response to it.

Such responses to the problem of social determinism are now widely known.
For example, Harry Frankfurt argues that persons are unique in having the ability
to critically reflect on and choose which of their desires they identify with and which
they reject. [12] Diana Meyers's detailed descriptions of autonomous agents abound
with examples of people whose preferences, ends, and projects can be thought to be
authentically their own.[13] Authenticity does not refer to the hidden inner self, which
is finally revealed after the effects of socialization have been stripped away. Rather,
autonomous people exercise a complex array of what she calls autonomy competencies, which include diverse self-reading and self-actualizing skills. The authentic self
continually emerges throughout this ongoing process of exercising autonomy com-

petency. It is not hidden and then found: it is *constructed* throughout the process of exercising one's autonomy. Numerous other theorists of autonomy have developed accounts of how autonomous people can negotiate the effects of socialization. Robert Young, like Meyers, emphasizes the importance of self-knowledge and gaining understanding of how the influence of one's culture, family, and so on has shaped one's aims, aspirations, and values.[14] Stanley Benn emphasizes the importance of resolving conflicts within the self to achieve a degree of coherence, something also stressed by Marilyn Friedman.[15]

On these various accounts, the difference between an autonomous person and a person who fails to be autonomous is not the difference between a person who mysteriously escapes the forces of socialization and one who does not. Both the autonomous and the nonautonomous are conditioned by the forces of society. The difference is that the autonomous person is not a passive receptacle of these forces but reflectively engages with them to participate in shaping a life for herself. Thus the strong sense in which autonomy is said to be incompatible with the socially determined self—the claim that because we are socially determined, autonomy is an illusion—is to be rejected because it is committed to an unrealistic conception of autonomy. Once we understand that autonomy does not imply the simple shedding of social influence but the ability to fashion a certain response to it, then social determinism does not entail that autonomy is an illusion.

Degrees of Social Determinism

A second, weaker concern raised about the relationship between autonomy and social determinism relates to the *extent* that a person must critically reflect on her ends to achieve autonomy. Although we may fashion more or less autonomous responses to social influence, our aspirations and aims will always bear the markings of those social relationships most pervasive in our lives—to family, culture, and so on. Nobody ever wholly manages to critically reconsider all of the socially determined values, aims, and aspirations that indelibly shape her identity, no matter how often she exercises her autonomy competency. Ultimately, to what extent one believes this undermines autonomy will depend on the degree to which one believes autonomy competency should be exercised before a threshold has been attained.

Attempts to specify this degree run the risk of either exaggerating or underplaying the extent to which such critical reflection is both possible and desirable. Will Kymlicka, for example, quite rightly criticizes some communitarians for their presumption that the liberal notion of self-determination presupposes a pure rational will, devoid of any social traits.[16] As Kymlicka argues, the claim that an autonomous or self-determining person can question her social roles and values does not mean she questions them all at once, that she rejects them all and then starts afresh on the basis of nothing but the will. Someone who is nothing but a free, rational will would have no reason to choose one way of life over another. Rather, in exercising our autonomy we hold many of our ends and purposes in place while critically reflecting on some other particular commitment. Yet, Kymlicka is himself guilty of excess in this enthusiastic claim:

No particular task is set for us by society, no particular practice has authority that is beyond individual judgment and possible rejection. We can and should acquire our tasks through freely made personal judgments about the cultural structure, the matrix of understandings and alternatives passed down to us by previous generations, which offers us possibilities we can either affirm or reject. Nothing is "set for us"; nothing is authoritative before our judgment of its value.[17]

If this is meant to be a claim about the psychological capacity of each and every individual, it disregards the force and pervasiveness of social determinism and is clearly false. To be fair to Kymlicka, his view that every possible end is capable of evaluation and possible rejection may not be a psychological claim about each individual self. The claim may be a normative one, which I discuss in more detail in the third section, "The Constitutively Social Self."

Negative Forms of Social Determinism

In addition to the global concern about social determinism and the weaker question about the exact degree of social determinism that is compatible with autonomy, there is a third concern, which focuses on the incompatibility between autonomy and certain *forms* of social determinism. In particular, the emphasis shifts somewhat from the impact of social determinism on the content of our ends, from the question of whether our ends are really anything more than socially determined, to the slightly different issue of the impact of social determinism on the *capacities* we need to be able to exercise autonomous agency. There are certain forms of socialization that uncontroversially militate against the development of the kinds of competencies that are required of a person exercising procedural autonomy.

Feminists have been particularly concerned with the question of socialization and the pervasive reality of gender subordination. Diana Meyers documents the way in which gender socialization renders women less likely to develop autonomy competency at the level that men often achieve.[18] Despite the pervasive and often detrimental influence of gender socialization, feminists have argued that it is frequently ignored by theorists purportedly concerned with individual autonomy. For example, one of the central feminist criticisms of contemporary liberalism is that its exclusive emphasis on formal equality and individual rights as a means to protect individual autonomy consistently fails to deliver substantial equality and individual freedom, precisely because of its failure to address those social forces, such as gender socialization, that radically delimit the actual choices available to some individuals.[19]

We cannot presuppose that we each acquire autonomy competency as a natural consequence of maturation. For even if social determinism per se does not threaten autonomy, certain forms certainly do, either in virtue of what skills they fail to encourage or in virtue of what is actively discouraged and penalized. It follows that a commitment to protect the autonomous individual in social and political life requires scrutiny of the various social forces that affect the development of autonomy competency and a preparedness to alter them.

The Positive Influence of Social Determinism

While it may well be true that certain forms of social determinism militate against the development of autonomy competency, it is equally true that the very precondition of our being able to develop and sustain our capacity for autonomy is attributable to our developing and remaining embedded within a network of social relationships. The capacity and aspiration for autonomy is not something we are born with but something we develop only in society. The fact that any of us has the capacity for autonomous agency is a debt that we each owe to others.

Although this point seems almost truistic, it is a truism often ignored. Feminists argue that numerous theorists ignore that fact that we each inescapably experience long periods of total dependency through which we develop capacities like autonomy. For example, the often invoked metaphor of the "state of nature" presupposes that in the beginning man is essentially alone, as though, says Hobbes, we each spring out of the earth and are suddenly fully mature, "like mushrooms." Seyla Benhabib argues that "this vision of men as mushrooms is an ultimate picture of autonomy."[20] What is denied in the mushroom metaphor is that it is primarily women's labors, especially in the early years, that contribute most significantly to the development of the skills required for autonomous agency.[21] Similarly, Susan Moller Okin demonstrates how more contemporary champions of individual autonomy, such as John Rawls and Robert Nozick, presuppose women's labor and care for the family and at the same time deny, even if implicitly, that they are politically relevant.[22]

It is not only in virtue of our dependency on others in the family that we acquire a capacity for autonomy. In an interesting contrast with feminist critiques, Charles Taylor denies that the acquisition of an autonomous identity is acquired only, or even primarily, in the family.[23] He argues that it is only in the context of a whole civilization, where the value of autonomy is implicit within a whole range of common practices—the arts, the legal system, intellectual debates, and politics—that we can each acquire the aspiration and the ability to be autonomous. Of course most feminists would not deny the broader relevance of the whole society, yet it is true that their emphasis is often on the family, in particular, women's labor, whereas communitarians have tended more to emphasize traditions, nations, and society. The important point, however, is that both feminists and communitarians argue that our capacity for autonomy is acquired in contexts where we are dependent on others.

As well as dependency, the importance of *interdependency* should not be overlooked. Even after a capacity for autonomy is acquired through a long period of dependency, our ongoing success as an autonomous agent is affected by our ability to share our ideas, our aspirations, and our beliefs in conversation with others. It is unlikely that any vision or aspiration is sustained in isolation from others. As Taylor argues, "A human being can always be original, can step beyond the limits of the thought and vision of contemporaries, can even be quite misunderstood by them. But the drive to original vision will be hampered, will ultimately be lost in inner confusion, unless it can be placed in some way in relation to the language and vision of others."[24] Our ongoing public debates about moral and political issues, our more personal conversations with particular others, and even our ability at times to imagine conversations with fictional or historic interlocutors enable us to effectively exercise and maintain autonomous agency. The crucial point is that in many respects our dependency is *ongoing*. We do not merely acquire autonomy competency in childhood and then become fully independent. Although the degree and nature of a person's dependency certainly shift, that dependency never vanishes.

What emerges from this discussion is the need to acknowledge that our autonomy competency is a debt we owe to others. As Annette Baier argues, we are each "second persons." A person—a being capable of language, of mathematics and cultural skills, and, we might add, autonomy—

> is best seen as one who was long enough dependent upon other persons to acquire
> the essential arts of personhood. Persons essentially are *second* persons, who grow
> up with other persons. . . . The fact that a person has a life history, and that a
> people collectively have a history, depends upon the humbler fact that each person has a childhood in which a cultural heritage is transmitted, ready for adolescent rejection and adult discriminating selection and contribution. Persons come
> after and before other persons.[25]

I would only add that autonomous persons not only come after and before other persons, but to flourish they must live concurrently with other persons as well.

In this section I have addressed the multifaceted claim that the self's ends, aspirations, and capacities are socially determined. I began by considering whether this fact renders autonomy nothing more than an illusion. I argued that once we rid the concept of autonomy of any association with the incoherent idea that there is a core "inner self" untainted by social influence, there is no conceptual incompatibility between autonomy and the socially determined self. This implausible global claim in fact diverts our attention from more interesting and complex concerns about what forms of social influence are detrimental to autonomy and what forms contribute to its development. I acknowledged that *certain* types of social determinism may well be at odds with the development and flourishing of autonomy, as feminists in particular have emphasized. But finally, I emphasized that it is only in virtue of the fact that we are exposed to social influence in multifarious ways that we are ever capable of being autonomous at all, a point that further exposes the incoherence of the idea that truly autonomous people must escape the forces of social determinism.

The Motivationally Social Self

Most of the issues raised in discussions of the socially determined self are concerned with a set of descriptive facts and whether those descriptive facts about the self are compatible with autonomy. In this section and the next I consider conceptions of the social self that incorporate descriptive claims but also question whether the autonomous self is to be *valued* and promoted. Proponents of these conceptions claim that a social account of the self provides a more valuable conception of agency and selfhood.

Some feminists have suggested that the concept of individual autonomy presupposes that the self is disconnected from enduring attachments to others, avoids intimacy, and is essentially an egoistic or self-interested maximizer. Such a self is motivated above all by its own narrowly conceived self-interest and eschews the interests and comfort of others. For example, Lorraine Code argues, "A cluster of derivative assumptions now attaches to ideals of autonomy. Autonomous man is—and should be—self-sufficient, independent, and self-reliant, a self-realizing individual who directs his efforts toward maximizing his personal gains."[26] The concern here is not with the fact that the self is socially determined but with the idea that human beings are presumed to have a certain individualistic nature, a nature presupposed, either implicitly or explicitly, by the notion of autonomy. This individualistic notion of the self incorporates both a descriptive and a normative claim. Descriptively it asserts that we are by nature self-interested. Normatively, it argues that these are valuable character traits. Feminists deny both the descriptive and the normative claim and defend instead the view that the self is motivationally social.

Numerous philosophers have presupposed that selves are primarily self-interested and that *the* moral or political problem is to secure the legitimate means for social cooperation, a cooperation that more efficaciously enables each individual to pursue her legitimate self-interest without interfering with the similarly self-interested pursuits of others. A number of feminists have claimed that such a picture of the self is implicitly presupposed in a range of contractarian approaches to moral and political philosophy, which begin with the ideal of self-interested individuals reaching mutually advantageous agreement with one another.[27] Some take John Rawls to be a contemporary paradigm of this approach, graphically illustrated by the device of the original position, in which "mutually disinterested" individuals seek to secure as many primary goods for themselves as possible. Similarly, approaches that emphasize individual rights at the core of moral and political life presuppose that the isolated individual needs above all to be protected from encroachment by others.[28]

It is hardly surprising that feminists have focused on the individualistic conception of the self, as it is starkly at odds with many women's experience, as well as the norms of femininity. Traditionally, women's lives have been devoted to the care of others, and if anything the problem has been to find a space for the expression and pursuit of one's own interests. The relationship of parent to child, the traditional conception of what it is to be a wife, or caring for a frail and aging parent can hardly be characterized as a form of cooperation for the efficacious pursuit of self-interest. Feminist theory has contributed to the development of alternative theory, which focuses moral concern more on the qualities and activities appropriate to care of others than on legitimizing individual rights as the means for protecting individuals from one another. They have argued that as we are in fact selves characterized as much by our capacity for care and concern for others as by our self-interest, we need moral and political theories that are shaped according to this fact.[29]

Although it is undoubtedly the case that certain moral and political theories presuppose an individualistic conception of the self, it is not plausible to suggest that the concept of autonomy itself presupposes such a conception of the self. As Marilyn Friedman has argued, this position conflates the concept of autonomy with that of substantive independence.[30] According to most procedural accounts of autonomy, a person's choices must be procedurally independent, rather than substantively independent. There is no requirement that one make any particular substantive choices—such as to live as independently of others as possible or to eschew commitments. It is consistent with a procedural account that an autonomous person may be motivated above all by a sense of solidarity or attachment to various people, causes, or communities.

On this account, a person's individual autonomy is not threatened by a deep attachment to other people and thus there is no reason to suspect that there is any incompatibility between autonomy and the motivationally social self. The only reason for questioning the autonomy of someone deeply committed to social and altruistic ends would be if we believed that she had never questioned or thought about her attachment to those ends, that is, if she had somehow failed to exhibit procedural autonomy with respect to them. But as Friedman points out, doubts about someone's autonomy in this respect could equally apply to a man who unthinkingly accepts the masculine stereotype of the cold, distant figure. A man who truly exhibits procedural independence in reflecting on his motivational structure is after all just as likely to "be the one at home changing his baby's diapers [as] the one riding off into the sunset on his Harley."[31] None of this is to deny that the abstract individualism feminists have rejected does not in fact pervade a great deal of moral and political theory. My argument is that this kind of individualism is not a part of the core ideal of autonomy.

Nevertheless, although autonomy is not threatened by enduring attachments and the motivation to further the interests of others, the converse does not necessarily hold: the exercise of individual autonomy may threaten certain relationships to particular others. In fact, given the recent feminist emphasis on the importance of relationships of attachment, particularly those between mothers and their children, and the insistence of some feminists that the value of those relationships is not derived from their being objects of choice,[32] it might be that feminists should be suspicious of even a procedural account of autonomy on *evaluative* grounds. It could be thought that a procedural notion of autonomy valorizes critical reflection and choice over and above the integrity and longevity of relationships of attachment and the accompanying motivation to further the interests of others.

There are two distinct although related concerns here. First, it might be argued that it is regrettable that a person may exercise her autonomy and choose to sever some particular attachments and thus to cease being motivated to further another's interests. A person may autonomously decide to end a relationship to a particular other or to a commitment, cause, or community. Although this is true, I would suggest that the flip side of this particular concern is the possibility of autonomously deciding to sever an oppressive, exploitative, or unsatisfactory relationship. As Friedman suggests, we cannot defend the value of relationships of attachment without qualification, and although the endurance of some relationships is jeopardized by the exercise of autonomy, sometimes this is a good thing.[33] Even when it is not a good thing that a particular relationship is ended by an autonomous person, we should not disparage the worth of a certain capacity because it is sometimes exercised in a bad way.[34]

A second concern is that a procedural account of autonomy seems to encourage constant ratiocination and critical reflection on one's attachments to others in the light of the acquisition of new ends, desires, or values. It is quite reasonable to suppose that the integrity and quality of our most valuable attachments and loyalties will not survive constant scrutiny and assessment. This concern falsely presupposes that an autonomous agent must *constantly* reassess her various attachments and commitments each time she acquires new ends or aspirations. I see no reason to burden the idea of individual autonomy with this implausible account of how often and to what degree it must be exercised. It may be ideal that people critically reflect on their decision to become parents or to marry a particular person, but it should not necessarily be a requirement of autonomy that one be able or prepared to critically reflect on these ends after they have been chosen. A person who is at every moment reassessing her attachment to the care and concern of particular others seems more anomic than autonomous. Part of making an autonomous decision to commit oneself to a particular person or project precisely involves a decision to close off certain possibilities in the future, to make a decision or choice to no longer consider other options as ongoing possibilities. Perhaps at moments of crisis or when explicit tensions and incompatibilities arise, one may have to reconsider a relationship that one had chosen in the past, but I see no reason to believe that this would, or should, inevitably collapse into constant ratiocination.

In this section I have considered the relationship between autonomy and the view that people are motivationally social, that is, motivated by care and concern for others. I have argued that a procedural notion of autonomy is compatible with the view that the self is motivationally social and does not presuppose that we are by nature essentially self-interested. In addition, I have argued that the exercise of a person's autonomy may nonetheless lead her to sever some particular relationships and thus no longer have as one of her ends a commitment to the needs and interests of a particular other. Provided that we do not suppose that an autonomous person must constantly assess her commitments to others, the fact that autonomous agency may sometimes lead to the rejection of certain commitments cannot always be classified as a regrettable outcome. Thus our commitment to the value of the motivationally social self is not incompatible with a commitment to the ideal of autonomy.

The Constitutively Social Self

The idea of the constitutively social self, which has been developed by a number of communitarian critics of liberalism, stresses that the *identity of the self* is constituted by various social attachments. The claim that the self is constitutively social incorporates the claim that the self is socially determined, for it certainly suggests that the self's aims and aspirations are determined by the communities of which one is a part. However, the constitutively social self is also meant to capture the idea that the *content* of the self's ends are social, in the sense that they represent not just my ends but also our shared ends. Compare the following two examples, only the second of which captures the idea of the constitutively social self. A person's aspiration to be a doctor may be determined by the strong influence of his father's preferences, in which case the person's aspiration is socially determined. Another person's deep commitment to the value of Catholicism is also socially determined for he was raised within a Catholic community, where he acquired his unwavering faith. But the commitment is one he shares with the community of Catholics and is not, therefore, just his own end but a socially shared end. The idea of the constitutively social self stresses that many of our ends are not only socially determined or derived but socially shared in this way as well.

As with feminist arguments about the motivationally social self, communitarian concerns about the constitutively social self go beyond descriptive claims and incorporate various normative arguments as well, particularly about the value of autonomous agency and the purpose of politics. In this section I consider the communitarian claim that the ideal of autonomy denies that we are constitutively social and presents a less valuable conception of agency and selfhood than a normative commitment to the constitutively social self allows.

Probably the most sustained critique of autonomy on the grounds of incompatibility with the constitutively social self is Michael Sandel's Hegelian-inspired critique of Rawls's theory of justice.[35] Sandel acknowledges the point made in the second section that the concept of individual autonomy is fully compatible with the notion that the self's ends may include a concern for others and an abiding interest in promoting their welfare. In other words, he acknowledges that the autonomous self can be motivationally social. Sandel argues, however, that there is a further sense in which the self is bound to community that *is* incompatible with some of the more exalted claims made in the name of individual autonomy. According to this further sense,

> to say that the members of a society are bound by a sense of community is not simply to say that a great many of them profess communitarian sentiments and pursue communitarian aims, but rather that they conceive their identity—the subject and not just the object of their feelings and aspirations—as defined to some extent by the community of which they are a part. For them, community describes not just what they have as fellow citizens but also what they are, not a relationship they choose . . . but an attachment they discover, not merely an attribute but a constituent of their identity.[36]

On this view, to speak of the social self is not merely to suggest we experience a spirit of benevolence or cooperation with others or that we choose attachments of solidarity, love, or commitment. Rather the claim is that certain ends and values *constitute* our identity and that these ends and values are fundamentally social in nature. Sandel argues that it is by reference to these shared ends that we each determine our good. When the self engages in the sort of self-reflection that theorists of autonomy describe, when one reflects on what one wants or what one should do, what one *discovers* are "shared values partly constitutive of a common identity or form of life."[37] It is these shared values, partly constitutive of a common form of life—"whether a family or tribe or city or class or nation of people"—that constitute the self's identity. Famously, Sandel argues that the fundamental question for the constitutively social self is not "What ends shall I choose?" but "Who am I?" and the latter question is answered by looking inward and discovering one's shared constitutive ends. Sandel argues that because a conception of autonomous agency presupposes that the self chooses rather than discovers one's ends, it is incompatible with a conception of the self as constitutively social. Thus, at this descriptive level Sandel suggests an incompatibility between the concept of autonomous agency and the constitutively social self.

But there is normative incompatibility as well. Sandel claims that agency which proceeds via the discovery of constitutive ends is more valuable, deeper, than autonomous agency. Sandel finds a shallow notion of autonomous agency in Rawls's account of how we each come by our ends and purposes. According to Rawls, a person comes by her life plan by exercising deliberative rationality, a process that involves working out what one wants and how much these things are wanted and then choosing the plan that satisfies as many of these wants as possible. What Sandel deplores about this conception of agency are the conceptions of choice and reflection that underpin it. Within deliberative rationality there is no reflection on the worth or *value* of desires, only reflection on their relative intensities. For agency to be worth our respect, it proceeds not simply by closer inner inspection of one's desires and inclinations but also on the basis of the values that constitute one's identity. But, Sandel claims, it is only inasmuch as we have constitutive social traits, shared values constitutive of a shared way of life, that we have languages of worth and qualitative hierarchies with which to evaluate our desires and preferences. If our agency is to consist of more than merely sorting out which of our desires is strongest, "we must be capable of a deeper introspection than a 'direct self-knowledge' of our immediate wants and desires allows."[38] Such deep introspection reveals values that express a common identity or way of life.

I will discuss Sandel's descriptive and normative claims in turn. In considering his descriptive claim that autonomy is incompatible with the constitutively social self, let us concede from the beginning that critical reflection on one's ends often does proceed with explicit reference to one's values, and thus autonomous agency is not (always) just a matter of working out which of one's desires is most intense. But why must we assume that insofar as our values are relied on to structure our critical reflection, they themselves are not subject to such critical reflection? Why must we assume that they are simply the "discovered" values of tribe, nation, and family? To be sure, not everything—values, desires, aspiration, aims—can be up for critical assessment at the same time. Something (most things) are usually held in place. Thus our values, insofar as they are relied on in reflection, are not themselves at that time subject to critical questioning. But it does not follow that at other times these values themselves are not subject to autonomous consideration. We can agree that values are socially influenced and often socially shared by parents, peers, and culture. We can follow Gerald Dworkin, who suggests, "It makes no more sense to suppose we invent the moral law for ourselves than to suppose that we invent the language we speak for ourselves."[39] But it doesn't follow that such values are necessarily constitutive of our identity in the sense of not themselves being subject to revision and rejection.

Sandel's critique of autonomous agency ultimately hinges on an ambiguity regarding what is meant by the descriptive claim that one is constituted by shared ends. There are two possible interpretations of this claim. The strong version says that the self is so constituted by her social ends that she is unable to reconsider or reject them. This is very implausible. Most theorists of autonomy believe that the exercise of individual autonomy may well be directed at such socially derived and shared values, which are then vulnerable to reshaping or even rejection. It is worth reiterating here that this is not an implausible psychological claim that any individual can, at any time, reflect on and reject such attachments. Perhaps many of us, with respect to certain ends, cannot. But conversely, it is equally implausible to imply that we can conceptually hive off that part of individual identity defined by socially derived and shared values as necessarily invulnerable to critical scrutiny and possible rejection. In certain circumstances and through the deployment of certain competencies, some individuals can and do reshape their attachment to particular values, including those that define a common way of life. As Marilyn Friedman insists, we know "that attitudes and behavior sometimes *are* independent. We know that there are social critics and social deviants."[40]

There is a second, weaker interpretation of the claim that we are constituted by our shared ends that simply claims that even the most autonomous person's identity is always mediated to some extent by community. Our starting point will always affect where we end up, so that even if some particular shared values are rejected by the individual, she will continue nonetheless to bear as part of her identity some markings of her original communities of family, nation, and tribe. Sandel himself sometimes offers a version of this claim: "As a self-interpreting being, I am able to reflect on my history and in this sense to distance myself from it, but the distance is always precarious and provisional, the point of reflection never finally secured outside the history itself."[41] But this claim is compatible with a suitable account of autonomous agency, as I argued in the first section. Nobody makes radical choices from an empty starting point. The key question remains: are socially shared values sometimes rejected by individuals, even if, of course, no individual can reshape herself de novo? The only plausible answer is yes, which immediately undercuts the strong version of the claim that the self is constitutively social. It turns out that many of us are not, after all, doomed to live out the roles and embrace the particular ends that are given to us by family or nation. This is fully compatible with most procedural accounts of autonomy.

The difficulties for Sandel's view do not end here, for his normative claims are also vulnerable to objection. Sandel claims that agency which proceeds via the discovery of constitutive ends is more valuable, deeper, than agency that proceeds on the basis of working out which of one's desires is stronger or more intense, that is, agency that he caricatures as autonomous. Let us suppose for a moment that reflection on the intensity of one's desires really is all that autonomous agency amounts to. It is still not obvious that such agency would be less worthwhile than agency in which we discover those shared values that define us each in the constitutive sense. Why exactly does this second kind of agency exhibit greater *depth* than the kind of agency that Sandel so deplores in Rawls's account? It is unclear how this could be so if the qualitative or evaluative distinctions the self draws on are *nothing* more than the discovered ends of tribe, family, and nation.

Consider the following example.[42] A particular woman has as one of her most abiding values the belief that a woman's place is in the home, particularly if one is a mother. This woman's constitutive ends are shared ends in just the sense that Sandel champions, for she lives in a close-knit community defined by its deep commitment to gender roles and the centrality of motherhood in women's lives. These values represent their shared way of life. In reality, this particular woman is persistently dissatisfied with her life in the home and fantasizes often about a different life, one centered around projects other than full-time parenting. Despite this, she never questions her values, for they are constitutive of her identity and it is by reference to them that she is able to critically assess her desires and preferences. Thus, she is inclined to feel disgusted with herself for her selfish desires.

Similarly, a single man quite consistently finds his sexual desires oriented toward other men and often indulges in a fantasy in which he develops an ongoing relationship with another man. He reflects on these desires and decides that they are wrong, indeed absolutely disgusting. The values that he employs to reflect critically on his desires are values both derived from and shared with his community, a community that staunchly embraces the heterosexual family unit as constitutive of its shared way of life. He persistently represses his mere desires and ends up, unsurprisingly, a miserable person.

In each of these cases, although a person acts on the basis of her or his constitutive values as opposed to mere desires, it is far from clear that either exhibits the kind of agency that deserves respect. Each case represents an example of the kind of agency that follows from being constitutively social and deploying these discovered, shared values in reflection. Yet it is difficult to appreciate why the kind of agency represented in each case is "deeper" or deserves greater respect than that which is primarily devoted to a closer inspection of one's desires and inclinations. Values may well play a significant role in autonomous agency, but to play an important role, they have to be more than purely discovered, constitutive social traits. Values themselves must to some extent be subject to the self's autonomous scrutiny. This suggestion is supported by the fact that what seems wrong in both of our not-so-imaginary examples is that they portray stark examples of a person laboring under socially imposed and uncritically accepted values in a way that thwarts individual autonomy. Each has been unduly influenced by the values of others.

I have argued that neither Sandel's descriptive nor his normative criticisms of autonomous agency based on the ideal of the constitutively social self are plausible. The only plausible descriptive account of the constitutively social self is a weaker version fully compatible with the idea of autonomy. The normative value attributed to agency based on the discovery of shared ends and values is also highly debatable. Thus, whereas it may well be true that particular versions of the constitutively social self are incompatible with the idea of autonomy, it is these versions of the constitutively social self that we should repudiate, not the idea of autonomy.

The Value of Autonomy: Rejecting a Communitarian and Feminist Alliance

So far I have distinguished three different senses in which the self is social in order to consider more specifically the claim that autonomy is incompatible with social conceptions of the self. Although social conceptions of the self have been promoted by both feminists and communitarians, I have attempted to highlight the differences between them. I now want to argue more explicitly that the concerns that feminists and communitarians have voiced about autonomy are only superficially similar and conceal a deep division over the value of autonomy. Some communitarians believe we should repudiate the value of autonomy, whereas, I argue, feminists should not reject its value. To see how feminism and communitarianism pull in different directions over the value of autonomy, it is important to understand the very different *motivations* each has for focusing on the fact that selves are social and the distinct conclusions each draws from such views.

One of Sandel's more explicit normative aims, an aim shared by many communitarians, is to see our shared, constitutive values embodied within political institutions. Communitarians reject liberal neutrality, the principle that the state itself is to play no role in deciding which ways of life are better than others. Many liberals argue that state neutrality protects individual autonomy and enables individuals to decide for themselves which values and ways of life they will endorse and which they will reject.[43] Communitarians criticize the liberal assumption that the state's highest duty must always be to protect individual autonomy. A good state also acts to protect shared values and a shared way of life. Indeed, Sandel explicitly suggests that when political institutions embody shared values, we can "know a good in common that we cannot know alone."[44] In other words, embodying our common, constitutive values within our shared institutions represents a more powerful vision of what politics can be than the favored liberal alternative, which begins with the assumption that individuals must be protected in seeking their own individual conceptions of the good.

Where individual autonomy thrives within a political community, very few shared values remain invulnerable to critical rejection. Underpinning some communitarian objections to the valorization of autonomy is precisely the fact that individual autonomy renders shared values vulnerable to rejection. Individual autonomy, therefore, should be subordinated to the alternative task of enabling shared values to flourish. Politics, on this view, goes better when individual autonomy is subordinated to the aim of building a flourishing political community based on shared values. On this view, the incompatibility between autonomy and the social self is a normative incompatibility, one whose resolution calls for a repudiation of the value of autonomy.

Should feminists join communitarians in repudiating the value of autonomy in favor of the common good? Of course, balancing the value of autonomy with the value of a community of shared ends is difficult, and I cannot attempt an exhaustive discussion of this issue here. My rejection of Sandel's normative defense of agency based solely on the discovery of shared ends in the previous section indicates that feminists should certainly be cautious about repudiating the value of autonomous agency. I want to conclude this chapter by building on this concern in order to suggest that feminists should respond with a cautious "no" to a proposed feminist-communitarian alliance.

It is clear from the first and third sections that communitarians and feminists share some version of the descriptive claim that selves are socially determined. But for feminists, the importance of this insight is that it opens up the possibility of changing our identities and challenging existing social structures. Precisely because our identities—our aims, aspirations, and capacities—are *socially* determined, we can repudiate the historically entrenched view that women (and others) have a certain fixed and immutable nature, a nature that suits them for specific roles and disqualifies them for others. Similarly, if women have lacked the skills and capacities, as well as the opportunity, to do certain things, such as exercise autonomy, this is not a natural fact about women but a consequence of social determination. The truth that selves are socially determined carries with it a certain *liberating* potential, a denial that social roles *need* be fixed and a repudiation of the claim that selves have an immutable nature that determines their roles. As Benhabib and Cornell argue, feminists begin "with the situated self but view the *renegotiation* of our psychosexual identities, and their *autonomous reconstitution* by individuals as essential to women's and human liberation."[45]

In a striking contrast, some communitarians seem to draw precisely the opposite conclusion. The fact that we are each born into certain social relations within which our identities are shaped is a feature of ourselves not to be questioned but embraced. The fact that our identity is socially determined does not expose the contingency of that identity for the communitarian but entrenches the view that it is normatively vacuous to attempt to challenge or reshape the boundaries of our social roles and values. Of course, communitarians do not think that these roles and identities are given by nature, but they do seem to believe that they are, or should be, more immutable than any feminist could be satisfied with. Alasdair MacIntyre writes:

> It is through his or her membership in a variety of social groups that the individual identifies himself or herself and is identified by others. I am brother, cousin and grandson, member of this household, that village, this tribe. These are not characteristics that belong to human beings accidentally, to be stripped away to discover "the real me." They are part of my substance, defining partially at least and sometimes wholly my obligations and my duties. Individuals inherit a particular space within an interlocking set of social relationships; lacking that space, they are nobody, or at best a stranger or an outcast.[46]

There are versions of MacIntyre's claim that we could agree with, one example being that we cannot be autonomous in the absence of social relationships. But MacIntyre explicitly insists on the necessity of *inherited* relationships, which he believes we cannot do without. Feminists have argued that not only can we do without the particular roles and identities we inherit but also that sometimes, at least, we are better off without them. As Penny Weiss argues, "Communitarians are concerned with the *loss* of 'traditional boundaries,' while feminists are concerned with the *costs* of those boundaries, especially for women."[47]

For feminists, the liberating potential opened up by a recognition that our identities are socially determined is particularly crucial, given that those identities are often indisputably *oppressive*. It has been noted by a number of feminists that communitarian valorization of "traditions," "community," "tribe" and "nation" frequently ignore their sexist and racist practices and the multifarious ways in which they contribute to gender oppression, the subjugation of certain ethnic groups, the exclusion of gays, and so on.[48] It is precisely the kinds of communities celebrated by communitarians that women have often rejected because of their exploitative or oppressive nature. Feminism as a shared movement has been largely defined by the various ways it has resisted and challenged traditional communities.

These considerations enable us to express caution toward the normative attachment to a community of shared ends that communitarians have championed. Communitarians like Sandel argue that our common good, our shared values, should be embodied in the social and institutional arrangements of society and that the value of a common good of this nature takes precedence over the value of individual autonomy. But we cannot both be alert to the potentially oppressive features of social relationships and assign unconditional worth to them. Indeed, as I argued in the second section, this same problem arises in the context of the motivationally social self. Similarly, in the previous section, I rejected Sandel's normative defense of agency that is based solely on the discovery of shared values precisely because such agency consigns many individuals to oppressive social roles. We need to consider *which* particular attachments to nourish, *which* particular shared values should be part of our common good. The answer to these questions cannot fail to be enormously complex once we squarely face up to the fact that the flourishing of autonomy means the loss of traditional, hermetically sealed communities characterized by shared values and the lack of dissent. There are losses here undoubtedly; but for women and many others, there have also been incomparable gains.

Some feminists, like Friedman, have wondered why communitarians valorize unchosen communities like family, tribe, and nation and ignore "communities of choice" like friendships.[49] The answer is that to acknowledge that some of our enduring and most valuable social relationships are communities of choice, as feminists have done, and that some of our most cherished values grow out of a rejection of other inherited ones is to concede implicitly both the possibility and the value of autonomous agency. To value communities of choice is to reject the strong descriptive claim that we are so constituted by social relations and shared values that we are unable to reconsider our attachment to them. But it is also to reject the value of agency that is based solely on the discovery of shared ends and the value of thwarting the individual's ability to decide for herself which communities she will belong to in the name of the common good. Precisely because feminists are committed to communities of choice, I think it is doubtful that we could transform "the communitarian vision of self and community into a more congenial ally for feminist theory."[50]

To consider which particular attachments we should reshape, which to reject, which to choose, and which to promote, we need autonomy. We do not simply want to endorse what we inherit and later discover. This is neither a descriptively accurate assessment of what our agency is capable of nor a liberating vision of what kind of agency deserves our evaluative endorsement. Nor is it a liberating vision of political community. We need and should cherish the capacity to decide and choose. This will always be a shared task, one that we do in concert and conversation with others. It is also something that any of us can do in virtue of the fact that we experience long periods of dependency and interdependency. It will be a task motivated by deep, sometimes irreconcilable differences but also by equally unshakeable shared commitments and concern for others. The truth of these claims shows that we are quite compatibly both autonomous agents and deeply social selves. It also shows that some versions of communitarianism are perilous allies for feminists.

Notes

1. I would like to thank Catriona Mackenzie and Natalie Stoljar for their helpful and thorough feedback on an earlier draft of this article.

2. Lorraine Code, *What Can She Know? Feminist Theory and the Construction of Knowledge* (Ithaca, N.Y.: Cornell University Press, 1991), p. 77.

3. Jennifer Nedelsky, "Reconceiving Autonomy: Sources, Thoughts and Possibilities," *Yale Journal of Law and Feminism* 1 (1989): 7–36.

4. Sarah Lucia Hoagland, *Lesbian Ethics. Toward New Value* (Palo Alto, Cal.: Institute of Lesbian Studies, 1988), pp. 144–145.

5. Alasdair MacIntyre, *After Virtue. A Study in Moral Theory* (Notre Dame, Ind.: University of Notre Dame Press, 1981), 32, pp. 232–233.

6. Michael Sandel, *Liberalism and the Limits of Justice* (Cambridge: Cambridge University Press, 1982).

7. Marilyn Friedman, "Feminism and Modern Friendship: Dislocating the Community," in *What Are Friends For? Feminist Perspectives on Personal Relationships and Moral Theory* (Ithaca, N.Y.: Cornell University Press, 1993), p. 232.

8. See for example, ibid.; Penny A. Weiss, "Feminism and Communitarianism: Comparing Critiques of Liberalism," in *Feminism and Community*, ed. Penny A. Weiss and Marilyn Friedman (Philadelphia: Temple University Press, 1995); Elizabeth Frazer and Nicola Lacey, *The Politics of Community. A Feminist Critique of the Liberal-Communitarian Debate* (London: Harvester Wheatsheaf, 1993). The attempt to assess whether or not there are grounds for a feminist-communitarian alliance has been a decidedly one-sided affair, with communitarians overwhelmingly displaying no interest in feminist theory.

9. Of course these three senses of the social self overlap, so I am not therefore suggesting that the deterministic, motivational, and constitutive senses of the social self are entirely unconnected. Nonetheless they are distinct claims, which for purposes of clarity and effective critique I have disentangled.

10. See, for example, Gerald Dworkin, *The Theory and Practice of Autonomy* (Cambridge: Cambridge University Press, 1988); Diana Tietjens Meyers, *Self, Society, and Personal Choice* (New York: Columbia University Press, 1989); Robert Young, *Personal Autonomy: Beyond Negative and Positive Liberty* (London: Croom Helm, 1986).

11. Meyers, in *Self, Society, and Personal Choice*, refers to autonomy as a set of key competencies—the skills of self-reading, self-definition, and self-direction.

12. Harry Frankfurt, "The Freedom of the Will and the Concept of a Person," *Journal of Philosophy* 68 (1971): 5–20.

13. Meyers, *Self, Society, and Personal Choice*.

14. Young, *Personal Autonomy*.

15. S. I. Benn, "Freedom, Autonomy, and the Concept of a Person," *Proceedings of the Aristotelian Society* 76 (1975/1976): 109–130; Friedman, "The Social Self and Partiality Debates," in *What Are Friends For?*

16. Will Kymlicka, *Contemporary Political Philosophy. An Introduction* (Oxford: Oxford University Press, 1990), pp. 207–216.

17. Ibid., pp. 210–211.

18. Meyers, *Self, Society, and Personal Choice*, part 3.

19. See, for example, Frazer and Lacey, *Politics of Community*; Seyla Benhabib and Drucilla Cornell, eds., *Feminism as Critique: Essays on the Politics of Gender in Late-Capitalist Societies* (Cambridge: Polity Press, 1987), introduction.

20. Seyla Benhabib, "The Generalized and the Concrete Other," in *Situating the Self: Gender, Community and Postmodernism in Contemporary Ethics* (New York: Routledge, 1992), p. 156.

21. See Marilyn Friedman, "Autonomy, Social Disruption, and Women," in this volume.

22. Susan Moller Okin, *Justice, Gender, and the Family* (New York: Basic Books, 1989), chap. 4; Robert Nozick, *Anarchy, State and Utopia* (New York: Basic Books, 1974).

23. Charles Taylor, "Atomism," in *Philosophy and the Human Sciences: Philosophical Papers,* vol. 2 (Cambridge: Cambridge University Press, 1985).

24. Charles Taylor, *Sources of the Self: The Making of Modern Identity* (Cambridge: Cambridge University Press, 1989), p. 37. See also Friedman, "Friendship, Choice and Change," in *What Are Friends For?* for a discussion of the importance of friendships in sustaining the possibility of individual autonomy.

25. Annette Baier, "Cartesian Persons," in *Postures of the Mind: Essays on Mind and Morals* (Minneapolis: University of Minnesota Press, 1985), pp. 84–85.

26. Code, *What Can She Know?* p. 77.

27. Thomas Hobbes is, of course, one of the better-known theorists who presupposes such a picture of persons, but there are contemporary exponents as well, such as David Gauthier, *Morals by Agreement* (Oxford: Oxford University Press, 1986).

28. See, for example, Nedelsky, "Reconceiving Autonomy," p. 12; Virginia Held, "Non-Contractual Society: A Feminist View," *Canadian Journal of Philosophy*, Supplementary 13 (1987): 111–137; Code, *What Can She Know?* p. 77. I should note here that I actually think this is a mistaken way to understand the role played by the notion of mutual disinterest in Rawls's theory.

29. See in particular Carol Gilligan's *In A Different Voice: Psychological Theory and Women's Development* (Cambridge, Mass.: Harvard University Press, 1982). Some of the literature inspired by Gilligan includes Eva Feder Kittay and Diana Tietjens Meyers, eds., *Women and Moral Theory* (Totowa, N.J.: Rowman & Littlefield, 1987); Virginia Held, ed., *Justice and Care: Essential Readings in Feminist Ethics* (Boulder, CO: Westview Press, 1995).

30. Marilyn Friedman, "Autonomy and Social Relationships," in *Feminists Rethink the Self*, ed. Diana Tietjens Meyers (Boulder, Colo.: Westview Press, 1996).

31. Ibid., p. 53.

32. See Annette C. Baier, "The Need for More Than Justice," in Held, *Justice and Care*; Held, "Non-Contractual Society."

33. See Friedman, "Autonomy, Social Disruption and Women," for an extensive discussion of this point.

34. This seems quite obvious once we consider that an autonomous person can make evil or malicious choices.

35. Sandel, *Liberalism and the Limits of Justice*. My aim is not to assess Sandel's critique of Rawls but to consider his claims about autonomous agency more generally.

36. Ibid., p. 150.

37. Ibid., p. 167.

38. Ibid., p. 172.

39. Dworkin, *Theory and Practice of Autonomy*, p. 36.

40. Friedman, "Social Self and Partiality Debates," p. 76 (emphasis in the original).

41. Sandel, *Liberalism and the Limits of Justice*, p. 179.

42. I take the example from Marilyn Friedman, "Autonomy and the Split-Level Self," *The Southern Journal of Philosophy* 24, no. 1 (1986): 19–35.

43. See John Rawls, *A Theory of Justice* (Oxford: Oxford University Press, 1971), and Kymlicka, *Contemporary Political Philosophy*.

44. Sandel, *Liberalism and the Limits of Justice*, p. 183.

45. Benhabib and Cornell, *Feminism as Critique*, p. 13 (emphasis in the original).

46. MacIntyre, *After Virtue*, p. 32.

47. Weiss, "Feminism and Communitarianism," p. 167.

48. See ibid.; Friedman, "Feminism and Modern Friendship"; Frazer and Lacey, *Politics of Community*.

49. Friedman, "Feminism and Modern Friendship."

50. Ibid., p. 234.

3

FEELING CRAZY

Self-Worth and the Social Character of Responsibility[1]

Paul Benson

Crazy *a*. 1. Full of cracks or flaws; damaged, impaired, unsound; liable to break or fall to pieces.

(*Oxford English Dictionary*)

I can hear you say, "What a horrible, irresponsible bastard!" And you're right. I leap to agree with you. Irresponsibility is part of my invisibility; any way you face it, it is a denial. But to whom can I be responsible, and why should I be, when you refuse to see me? And wait until I reveal how truly irresponsible I am. Responsibility rests upon recognition, and recognition is a form of agreement.

(Ralph Ellison, *Invisible Man*)

Feminist Interests in Responsibility

The notion of responsibility has figured prominently in feminist theorizing. Feminists have explored ways in which received conditions of blameworthiness and excuse mask and thereby sustain social arrangements that oppress women. Men who reap advantages from such arrangements are commonly in a position to justify their conduct by appealing to gendered social norms that grant men special prerogatives ("Lighten up! Surely there is nothing wrong in my just looking, teasing . . .") or by professing their innocent motives ("I didn't mean any harm by it"). Alternatively, men may exempt themselves from responsibility by deflecting accountability away from individuals to larger social systems over which individuals seem powerless ("It's not my fault; that's just the way the system works"). In such ways, conditions of responsibility are interpreted so as to license male irresponsibility. Systematic distortion of responsibility is a feature of most resilient forms of social oppression, not only gender-based oppression.

Responsibility also has been at the heart of much feminist practice and activism. Feminists have sought to demystify responsibility by clearly naming male perpetrators of violence, abuse, exploitation, and harassment and by giving voice, as ones who have been wrongly blamed for the harms inflicted on them, to their own ethical identities and integrity. In the process of struggling with the paralyzing and polarizing effects of self-blame and the reproach of other women, feminists have also underscored the importance of women's *taking responsibility* for their feelings, perceptions, desires, beliefs, and actions as a prerequisite for reclaiming and expanding their personal and political agency. Part of the significance of consciousness raising for feminism has been that it offers women a way to take responsibility, collectively and individually, for their own interpretations of their experiences and activities.[2] In this vein, Virginia Held writes, "Feminist thought is committed to keeping experience in mind, and feminist experience must include personal test cases of a self, a female subject, taking responsibility for resisting the language and thought and practices that confront us and maintain our subordination."[3]

Perhaps since responsibility has served these conflicting roles—at once a tool for reinforcing oppressions leveled against women and also a valuable component of resistance—philosophical work in feminist ethics has displayed considerable ambivalence about responsibility. On the one hand, responsibility, conceived in terms of interpersonal responsiveness, attention, and care, has been favored in many formulations of an ethic of care.[4] On the other hand, many feminists have regarded responsibility with deep suspicion. The notion of personal moral responsibility in particular has been associated with abstract, individualistic, or atomistic moral psychologies that have their historical home in the liberal moral and political theories of the Enlightenment. So conceived, the responsible person is the self-governing, self-constituting, and self-sufficient agent whose natural freedom and moral identity do not essentially depend on socially elaborated powers, roles, and relationships. Many feminists have argued that such conceptions of agency obstruct forms of critical social and psychological analysis useful for advancing women's interests and frustrate the articulation of women's experiences of socially situated, interpersonally constituted motives, decisions, and actions.[5]

Seen in this light, it is unsurprising that women's purported responsibility and blameworthiness (for "choices" of body size and shape, of poverty, of unruly sexuality and emotion, and of violence-ridden lives) should be a common theme of moral discourse in male-dominated societies. Accordingly, many feminist ethicists have taken pains to highlight the dangers of responsibility attribution and blame in oppressive social contexts.[6] Sarah Hoagland contends:

> Once we begin considering questions of praise and blame among the oppressed, we find the extremes of blaming the victim or victimism. As it stands now, someone who is harmed under oppression is held responsible for everything that happens to her—not only for her choices, but for the situation itself (women invite rape, slaves never resisted slavery, jews [*sic*] were willing victims, and so on). Alternatively, she is perceived as a total victim, as if she were not making choices and trying to survive and go on. . . . Moral accountability as we understand it . . . does not present us with a viable concept of choice under oppression.[7]

The result is that extended treatment of conditions of personal moral responsibility has belonged largely to philosophical projects that are not motivated explicitly by feminist concerns. My project in this article will be to hold some main-stream accounts of moral responsibility more accountable by examining a theoret-ically neglected form of diminished responsibility that shows those accounts to be insufficient. This form of impaired responsibility comes to light by analyzing the profound self-doubt that rigid feminine norms can instil when internalized. I argue that standard conditions of responsibility oriented around agents' abilities of re-flective self-control or the reasons-responsiveness of their actions turn out to be in-sufficient for responsibility when studied in the light of persons' own standpoints toward their agency, especially their sense of worthiness to answer for their actions. In this way, I hope to respect Alison Jaggar's dictum that "from a feminist point of view, the call to reflect on women's moral experience is politically and method-ologically indispensable."[8]

Furthermore, the unorthodox condition of responsibility that I begin to de-velop promises to bear fruit for feminist ethics by clarifying the extent to which re-sponsibility is a social, or relational, matter. This condition highlights overlooked ways in which responsible agency is not only shaped causally and developmentally by social conditions but also intrinsically depends on various types of interpersonal, moral relations.

I begin by considering a historically located example of a horrifying—and philosophically illuminating—sort of self-doubt.

The Rest Cure and Self-Doubt

Let us imagine that Charlotte,[9] a white, middle-class American woman who is com-ing to adulthood in the 1880s, finds the rigid, conventional roles that women of her class are expected to take up—wife, mother, and housekeeper—to be nearly in-tolerable. She detests conventional feminine roles so thoroughly that she wants very much to leave her husband and young child to pursue an artistic career, writing, painting, and lecturing. But these interests are so alien from the standpoint of middle-class Victorian norms of womanliness that Charlotte's friends and family fear for her sanity. She is sent to a well respected physician, who diagnoses her as suffering from a serious nervous disorder. The physician prescribes the rest cure: Charlotte is to re-main in bed as much as possible, without visitors, and is not to read, write, or paint. Charlotte concurs with the doctor's judgment, feeling that she really must be emo-tionally ill if she cares about a potential artistic career more than her domestic responsibilities. However, she simply cannot endure the rest cure and the doctor's in-sistence on "moral medication."[10] She feels that she may not survive it. She also be-lieves that she has become an excessive burden to her husband and child. So she leaves them and sets out in hope of launching her career. All the while she contin-ues to feel that she must be quite emotionally deranged to be doing such a thing. In fact, she regards her leaving as good evidence of her mental infirmity.

I want to consider some of the effects that Charlotte's internalization of the restrictive norms of femininity of her day, and her resulting feelings of craziness, could have on her capacity for moral agency. For my present purposes, what is sig-nificant about Charlotte's predicament is not simply the fact that she experiences a practical conflict that arises from conflicting ethical responsibilities; nor does my concern lie merely with the fact that this conflict arises from social expectations that severely narrow the options Charlotte could pursue without facing condemnation from her peers. Rather, I want to explore the fact that having internalized oppressive social conventions, Charlotte decides to leave her family while doubting her very capacities to make such decisions in a morally competent way, and she regards that decision as a symptom of her craziness. Charlotte's sense of derangement takes the form of moral self-doubt. Furthermore, her sense of craziness may implicate an important element of her sense of moral worth, namely, her sense of her *worthiness to answer for her conduct.* Charlotte's inner conflict about her capability to care about both her domestic responsibilities and relationships and her artistic aspirations in ways that seem to her and her peers to be appropriate might displace her sense that she has the standing in the moral community that would allow her to give an account of herself as a moral agent in response to others' potential moral criticisms of her. The feature of Charlotte's case that I concentrate on, then, is that her sense of craziness comes about in such a way that she doubts her own moral capacities; and this doubt jeopardizes that portion of her moral self-respect that consists in her sense of her worthiness to answer for her actions.[11]

I examine some of the effects that Charlotte's attitudes about her craziness might have on her capacity for moral agency by focusing on her responsibility for leaving her family. In drawing attention to her moral responsibility, I am not supposing that her action was wrong. Nor am I supposing that we are in a good position to determine what it would have been right (much less best) for her to do. However, this does not mean that taking up the question of Charlotte's responsibility is artificial or inappropriate. Given the divisions in Charlotte's attitudes toward her moral competence and her worthiness to give an account of her conduct, and because most of her contemporaries (along with too many of ours, I fear) would be inclined to judge her behavior as a serious moral wrong, there is a live question about what Charlotte's action can reveal about her as a moral agent and about what range of responses to her would be appropriate. Moreover, it will be instructive to see how three recent, influential accounts of responsibility would treat Charlotte's conduct. As I argue in the next section, none of these accounts can fully explain the significance that Charlotte's diminished sense of worth has for her responsibility.

Consider Jay Wallace's view of responsibility.[12] A person is a morally accountable agent, Wallace maintains, just when she possesses "the powers of reflective self-control."[13] These powers are general psychological capacities that admit of degrees and are susceptible of influence by the agent's social and political circumstances. Reflective self-control consists in "the power to grasp and apply moral reasons" and "the power to control or regulate [one's] behavior by the light of such reasons."[14] The latter ability, in turn, requires a capacity for critical reflection, the power to make choices through deliberation, and the capacity to translate choices into behavior.[15] According to Wallace, a person who possesses these normative powers can reasonably be held to moral obligations, whether or not she actually exercises these powers when she acts, and so can fairly be held accountable for what she does.[16]

Full responsibility for a particular action, on Wallace's view, demands that the agent be accountable and also that she not have excuses (such as inadvertence, physical constraint, or coercion) for the action. Legitimate excuses exist only on those occasions when an agent has not intentionally done anything wrong, when her action does not display a culpable choice.

Applying Wallace's theory to Charlotte, we see that it is possible that Charlotte does not have any ordinary excuses for her action. Notwithstanding the conflict she felt toward her motives, she had her reasons for fleeing the rest cure—she believed she would not survive it and that she had become unjustifiably burdensome to her husband and child—and she acted for those reasons. She did not act inadvertently or as a result of physical force. Had she submitted to the rest cure, she probably would have had the excuse that she was coerced to do so, but that is precisely what she did not do.

More important, nothing in Charlotte's moral self-doubt dictates her lack of sufficient capacities of reflective self-control to be morally accountable by Wallace's lights. It is possible that moral self-doubt could diminish these capacities, to be sure. Her doubts about her competence could make her so confused that she could not recognize relevant moral considerations or apply them in her deliberations; or self-doubt could obstruct her control. In the most extreme case, her self-doubt might threaten to cloud Charlotte's consciousness with manifestly contradictory beliefs and aims, and thereby undo her fundamental ability to maintain a minimally coherent standpoint from which to deliberate, choose, and act.[17] But my description of Charlotte also leaves room for the possibility that despite her self-doubt, she retains a basic level of competence to recognize and apply moral reasons, along with the capacity to reflect critically on possible courses of action and to form intentions accordingly. The very fact that Charlotte feels tremendous conflict about the conventions of womanliness that she has internalized and intentionally defies the rest cure gives us good reason to think that Charlotte has far greater capability for reflective self-control than she or her peers give her credit for. Charlotte's attitude toward her emotional health may mean that she does not exercise her reflective capacities as she otherwise might, but this is compatible with her accountability, in Wallace's theory.

There is another possible way in which Charlotte's feelings of craziness and incompetence might impede her reflective self-control, although this is a possibility that Wallace apparently fails to recognize. Charlotte's self-doubt could alienate her from her power to grasp and apply moral reasons. She might feel dissociated from any exercise of that power, so that the results of any critical reflection she might carry out would seem to her to be no more her own than decisions arrived at by someone else. Divorced from her judgments of what morality counsels, those judgments would not serve as grounds on which she could form, authorize, and take responsibility for her choices. This is an important possibility to note since contemporary discussions of responsibility normally presume that persons are necessarily engaged in or identified with their power of critical reflection in such a way that the actual or potential operation of that power *just is* the full presence of the person in her motivation and behavior.[18] Thus, Charlotte's form of self-doubt may, but need not, interfere with the satisfaction of Wallace's conditions for responsibility.

Consideration of John Martin Fischer's and Mark Ravizza's theory of responsibility likewise confirms that Charlotte may meet standard conditions of responsibility. Fischer and Ravizza argue that agents are morally responsible for their actions just when they have actual causal control, or "guidance control," over them.[19] The most important element of such control is that agents' actions must issue from weakly reasons-responsive mechanisms. These are mechanisms that are counterfactually responsive to some sufficient reasons to do otherwise. In other words, the mechanism that produces a bodily movement is weakly reasons-responsive when there exists some possible world, governed by the same natural laws as the actual world, in which the agent has a sufficient reason to do otherwise, and the same type of mechanism operates, leading the agent to do otherwise for that reason.[20] As long as the agent meets standard epistemic requirements, such as that she knows what she is doing and knows enough about the likely consequences,[21] the reasons-responsiveness of the process that actually produces her action suffices for her responsibility for the action.

Since, as noted, Charlotte's feelings of craziness and incompetence might not actually disrupt her capacities for reflective self-control, the process that leads Charlotte to decide to leave her family, however serpentine it may be, could be counterfactually responsive to some reasons for her to do otherwise. Imagine, for instance, the world in which Charlotte not only feels that she is a burden to her family but also believes that her child would never adjust to her leaving and would suffer permanently impaired emotional growth as a result. Holding fixed the process that leads to Charlotte's decision to leave in the actual world, this additional belief may have been sufficient for Charlotte to decide to stay home. Similarly, were Charlotte to believe that she lacks enough talent for an artistic career, it is plausible to think that she would not leave her family. Surely the mechanism that actually yields her decision to leave can be weakly responsive to possible reasons for her to do otherwise despite her fear that there really is something crazy about her defiant attitudes toward her proper place in respectable society.

Whereas Charlotte's self-doubt could be compatible with being fully responsible in both Wallace's view and Fischer and Ravizza's theory, a third influential account would disagree. According to this third view, persons are morally responsible for their actions just when those actions are *capable of disclosing* what morally matters to them. This claim makes up the core of what Susan Wolf terms the "Real Self View" of responsibility.[22] In this view, persons are responsible when their actions are properly attributable to their "real selves," this being the case when persons are able to govern their wills on the basis of their valuational systems and to govern their actions on the basis of their wills.[23] Gary Watson has endorsed such a position,[24] holding that

> we are responsible for our conduct not because of its causal complexity but because and when it is self-disclosing; because, as John Dewey put it, "that conduct is ourselves objectified in actions." On this view excusing, mitigating and exempting conditions indicate circumstances that prevent or qualify self-disclosure.[25]

Thus far, our discussion of Charlotte's responsibility might be taken to indicate that her decision to leave her family can disclose her values and commitments since she may continue to have the power to control her conduct reflectively despite her distrust of her own competence. Charlotte leaves her family intentionally. She is aware of her reasons for leaving (her horror of the rest cure, her belief that she is useless to her child and husband, and her devotion to art), and these reasons seem genuinely to be *her own* reasons. So it seems that her leaving can disclose what really matters to her, and, therefore, we can morally evaluate *her* in light of her conduct, not merely appraise her behavior.[26] At first glance, Charlotte seems to satisfy the self-disclosure account of responsibility.

Charlotte appears otherwise, however, when we recall that her self-doubt can lead her to feel that she is *unworthy* of answering for her action. Although Charlotte's doubts about her moral competence will not directly interfere with the self-disclosive potential of her conduct,[27] if they undermine her sense of worthiness to give an account of herself, this will impede normative self-disclosure. If Charlotte feels that it is no longer her place to answer for her actions, she will also feel implicitly that it is not her place to express through her actions what really matters to her. The social status of one who is worthy to give a moral account of her conduct (by seeking to justify it, excuse it, admit fault, or the like) is also that of one worthy to disclose her valuational system through her actions. So Charlotte's sense that she has lost full standing in the moral community will bring with it a change in her attitude toward her worthiness to disclose her values and commitments to others through her actions. In turn, Charlotte will not regard leaving her family, or any other actions of hers that would be assessed in relation to the norms of conventional femininity of her day, as actions that could disclose her values and commitments to others. But if she does not regard this portion of her conduct as potentially self-disclosing, then, setting aside the possibility of unconsciously adopted aims or values (for that is not at issue in Charlotte's case), neither can we legitimately draw inferences about what really matters to her on the basis of her conduct. Charlotte's conduct cannot be self-disclosing when she cannot regard it as being so because of her sense of unworthiness to express and answer for her values. Thus, Charlotte's sense of unworthiness can diminish her responsibility according to the self-disclosure account.

This review of three current theories of responsibility and their handling of Charlotte's form of self-doubt is instructive for three reasons. First, none of these theories has been designed to treat agents' attitudes toward their own moral status in a straightforward way. They attend to agents' powers and capabilities, or to the character of the processes by which their decisions emerge, but not directly to the persons' sense of what they are worthy of as moral agents. Second, although all three accounts will grant that there are ways in which moral self-doubt conceivably could impair responsibility, Wallace's theory and Fischer and Ravizza's account will be more inclined to count Charlotte as responsible for her action than will the self-disclosure account. The latter theory will be more sensitive to agents' sense of worth, although this is a feature of the theory that its proponents have not noted. Accordingly, this reason for a possible divergence between the self-disclosure view and the other theories has not been appreciated. Third, as I hope to demonstrate in the subsequent section, there is a very different way in which a diminished sense of self-worth can bear on responsibility, independently of the considerations reviewed in this section. If I am correct about this, none of the theories reviewed here supply conditions of responsibility that are both sufficient and theoretically adequate.

A Self-Worth Condition of Responsibility

The argument that having a certain sense of one's worth is necessary for one's being fully responsible for one's actions begins by underscoring the connection between being responsible and being *held* responsible. Persons who are morally responsible for their actions are properly liable to be held responsible for them. This means, in part, that responsible agents can appropriately be objects of reactive attitudes such as blame, indignation, or resentment when their actions run afoul of reasonable expectations.[28] Furthermore, holding a person responsible enacts a moral relationship with her in which one characteristically expects that she should respond to appropriate criticisms of her. This expectation is not primarily descriptive, a belief about the likelihood that the person will respond. It is a normative expectation concerning standards of response for one who is fairly held responsible. Thus, being morally responsible involves being worthy of a certain social standing, that of an eligible participant in various kinds of moral exchange, such as offering reasons, seeking excuse, begging forgiveness, and so forth.[29] As Gary Watson has suggested, we might understand the conditions of moral responsibility as conditions of intelligible moral address.[30]

This normative dimension of holding someone responsible is revealed, for example, when we openly express blame (or some other central reactive attitude such as indignation or resentment).[31] When we openly blame someone, we characteristically expect that the person blamed should respond in certain ways, by admitting fault and attempting to set it right, say, or by attempting to show that her actions were justified, despite appearances. We need not expect the person blamed to respond right then and there. Sometimes the response is called for at another time (after thoughtful consideration, for example) or in another setting (when the persons to whom harm was done can be present, for instance). There may also be cases in which the magnitude or depth of the wrong is so great that no standard response is called for because none of the usual options—justification, excuse, admission of fault, or apology—will do. The gravity of the wrong done in such cases seems to outstrip the normal human repertoire for moral response—which is not to say that failure to respond is acceptable but rather that no response can ever be enough. Nevertheless, openly blaming someone standardly calls for her to respond because blaming or, more generally, holding persons responsible is not merely a matter of appraising the quality of their actions, motives, or traits. It is also a matter of calling forth a moral relationship with the person in which appropriate blame demands a response, and the person blamed is expected to recognize the legitimacy of that demand.[32]

The appropriateness of holding someone responsible, therefore, will depend on the appropriateness of holding the person to this characteristic normative demand for a suitable response. This is one reason that, as Wallace recognizes, having capacities for moral competence and control is necessary for being properly held responsible. Persons who lack those powers (through no fault of their own) cannot reasonably be expected to give a suitable moral response to moral criticism; they are not suitable candidates for the type of interpersonal exchange that responsible agency warrants. Likewise, the appropriateness of the normal expectation of moral response also requires that those at whom it is directed not regard themselves as unworthy of engaging in just that sort of relationship. If Charlotte regards herself as unworthy of giving an account of her action (and is not to blame for having this attitude),[33] she will not be an entirely appropriate object of the characteristic demand that she respond properly if blamed for leaving her family. This is not a point about Charlotte's general moral capabilities. She may, as I have noted, have the capabilities necessary to give suitable moral responses to potential criticisms. The point is, rather, that it is not reasonable to demand that someone participate in a certain type of relationship when she has been made to feel so deeply that she is not worthy to engage in that relationship.

To confirm the plausibility of this argument, it is helpful to remind ourselves of how an agent's internalization of oppressive social norms can impede the development of or undermine her sense of worthiness to answer for her actions. Let us imagine a society with a rigid, hierarchical caste system that places members of the lowest caste beneath consideration as moral equals. Persons of this caste are not immune to evaluative appraisal, but it is not considered to be their place to attempt to justify, seek excuse for, or admit fault for their purported failings. It is not only that these persons' efforts to answer for themselves would make no difference to how others treat them; I am supposing that any efforts they might make to speak for their own actions would be perceived as transgressing established demarcations of social status, and so would simply not count morally. Persons in the lowest caste are neither to accept nor refuse responsibility for their acts. They are simply to undergo the judgments of their "betters" and submit to the consequences that attach to those judgments.

Persons who have internalized the prevailing norms of this society and who are unfortunate enough to be assigned to the lowest social stratum will feel, and will be given much reason to feel, that it is not their place to answer for their conduct. This attitude will be one element of the broader lack of moral self-respect, the failure to recognize their fundamentally equal moral worth as persons, which they are likely to suffer. This attitude will probably be secured by an ideological framework that instructs that members of this caste are infantile or bestial or impure, incapable of the kinds of moral sensitivity, reasoning, and self-control that would warrant their recognition as fully accountable agents. Like Charlotte, members of this class typically will harbor grave doubts about their own competence as moral agents. This might obstruct whatever moral competence they actually have (and the competence of many in this caste will probably be severely underdeveloped, given their social location), or it might dissociate them from their powers of moral reflection. But self-doubt may also affect these individuals in a further way, as it does Charlotte: it may engender the attitude that they are not worthy of being moral interlocutors, of answering for their own actions in response to their betters' appraisals of them. This is an attitude about one's position or status as a moral agent in relationship to others, not merely about one's abilities as an individual to discern various reasons and modify one's choices accordingly.

This example supports the plausibility of my claim that persons who, through no failing of their own, feel that it is not their place to give accounts of their actions are also not appropriately held fully responsible for what they do. Charlotte's case obviously differs from the caste example in notable ways. Charlotte has much greater moral competence than members of the lowest caste are likely to have. She feels conflicted about the conventions of femininity that she has been brought up to embrace, and her conflict leads her intentionally to defy those conventions. Perhaps most significantly, Charlotte probably has been treated in the past as being worthy of answering for herself, particularly with regard to matters less fully regulated by specific gender norms. So Charlotte may retain a sense of self-worth in relation to other spheres of her life, as persons trapped in the lowest caste may not.[34] But these distinctive features of Charlotte's situation can only affect her responsibility if they modify the appropriateness of holding her responsible. And the caste example reinforces the idea that an agent's socially instilled and legitimized attitude toward her own self-worth can alter the appropriateness of holding the agent responsible. Thus, even though Charlotte's responsibility and the responsibility of a person in the subjugated caste will be assessed differently, the agent's sense of worthiness to answer for her actions will directly affect her responsibility in each case.

Another, more familiar example suggests that common views about the effects of trauma on responsibility reflect the belief that socially sensitive attitudes of self-worth are necessary for full accountability. Consider a young adolescent who has suffered through an unusually deprived and traumatic childhood. Depending on the particular characteristics of her trauma, this young person may be incapable of appreciating certain types of moral consideration, or she may be unable to control her actions adequately on the basis of her reflective judgments. These deficiencies in her competence would justify lessening the extent to which she is held responsible for some of her actions.[35] But childhood trauma is widely thought to affect its victims in other ways as well, for example, by profoundly disrupting the development or sustenance of their sense of personal worth. Among the components of self-worth that can be obstructed by childhood deprivation is the sense of one's worthiness to answer for one's actions, a normally important part of one's sense of equal moral standing as a person and thus of one's relation to the rest of the moral community. In this respect, the victim of a severely deprived upbringing may be similar to the person confined to the invidious social hierarchy in the previous example; both may have good reason to feel that it is not their place to take responsibility for their actions by answering for themselves. The common (albeit not uncontroversial) view that the adolescent's traumatic childhood would lessen her responsibility for some of her actions, even if she possesses basic moral competence, can be upheld if she has a seriously impaired sense of her worth and if possessing a more robust sense of worth is necessary for being fully responsible.[36]

My argument for admitting a self-worth condition of responsibility respects more fully the relational character of holding persons responsible than do the three accounts of responsibility discussed in the previous section. We can better understand this feature of my position and clarify its value for feminist projects in ethics, as well as mark the comparative shortcomings of the other three accounts, by noting three overlapping social dimensions of responsibility that the self-worth condition brings clearly to view. First, since the sense of worth required for full responsibility concerns one's worthiness to give account of one's actions *to others*, this condition serves to remind us that responsibility depends conceptually on there being others who could morally criticize us and expect us to answer for our actions. Thus it makes sense, as Wallace realizes, to approach responsibility by analyzing being *held responsible by others*.[37] This does not mean that we are responsible only in the actual presence of others who might respond to our actions and to whom we could give an account of ourselves. The point is just that the conceptual possibility of relating to others in certain ways is necessary for responsibility, even in the remote instance when such relations are not physically possible.

This first relational aspect of responsibility points beyond the purely conceptual, for it is also a developmental fact about us that only through being expected by others to speak for our actions do we become responsible agents and acquire the requisite sense of our worth. I also suspect that it is only through being held responsible by others that we can come to hold *ourselves* responsible and learn how to answer to ourselves since being held responsible by others seems to be a necessary step in learning how to hold anyone responsible and becoming susceptible in appropriate ways to the range of reactive emotions.[38]

The conceptual and developmental primacy of being expected to account for one's actions to others affords a theoretical framework that complements feminist theories of the narrative construction—and reconstruction—of personal identity. For example, as Susan Brison explains in her compelling discussion of the remaking of selfhood in the wake of trauma, "In order to construct self-narratives, then, we need not only the words with which to tell our stories but also an audience able and willing to hear us and to understand our words as we intend them."[39] Of course, in the case of trauma survivors, this dependence on an audience is bound to be actual and concrete, not merely conceptual.[40] Nonetheless, recognizing in a theory of responsibility the need for at least a potential audience to whom agents are expected to give an account of themselves reveals a natural point of commonality between narrative theories of selfhood and my view of responsibility.

This first relational feature of responsibility also helps to explain the evident empirical fact that the relevant sense of worth typically is highly sensitive to the attitudes that others display toward the agent.[41] If responsible agents' sense of self-worth depends on (potentially) being expected to make sense of their actions to others, it is understandable that this sense of worth would normally be sensitive to others' expressed attitudes toward the agent's worth. This point coheres with feminist insistence that an adequate view of moral agency must attend to the interpersonal context within which the agent is situated. Such attention is necessary not just to characterize the choices the agent faces but also to reveal the role that others' attitudes may have in shaping the person's own sense of her status as an accountable agent.

A second relational aspect of responsibility manifested in the self-worth condition is that *publicly shareable norms* must regulate both moral appraisal of an agent's actions and the account of her conduct that she might give in response. Agents can be in a position to respond to others' moral criticisms of them only if all parties to this possible dialogue can share an understanding of the norms reflected in these criticisms and the norms according to which responses can properly be made. The social intelligibility of norms of moral appraisal and response does not require that all parties must actually understand these norms equally well. Nor does it require that any responsible agent must accept these norms or accept them for the same reasons that others do.

Although it seems obvious that moral responsibility is possible only if everyone to whom moral norms of criticism, justification, and excuse apply can understand them, the significance of this second social feature of responsibility has not been well appreciated. For instance, it highlights another respect in which justified attributions of responsibility depend on the context of the social relationships within which they are made. If someone is an intimate friend of mine, as opposed to being just a familiar face in the grocery store or a total stranger at the bus station, what she can understand me to hold her accountable for and what kinds of justification or excuse she can expect me to accept may differ considerably from these other cases. Social relationships modify the kinds of moral dialogue that are possible among people and, in doing so, influence the terms of moral responsibility that are possible between them.[42] When persons are subjected to relations of subordination and domination, the public intelligibility of norms of criticism and response is likely to be undermined, yielding contested attributions of responsibility. This is especially the case when subordination is effected precisely by holding persons to conflicting expectations, ensnaring them in moral double binds that make it impossible for them to reach a coherent understanding of how they could ever adequately defend or excuse their own conduct.[43]

A third relational aspect of responsibility illuminated by the self-worth condition is that being responsible is itself a matter of occupying a certain social position, having *the status of an eligible participant in a community of moral dialogue*. Someone who regards herself as being in a position to speak for her own agency, should others criticize it, and who also has the competence necessary for answering for her actions (powers that include reflective self-control) is, then, in just such a position. Whether others recognize it or not, she is in a position to take full part in a moral dialogue with others who can properly hold her responsible and whom she can hold responsible. This point is particularly relevant to feminist ethics in two respects. It shows why feminists, who are necessarily concerned about ways in which women are denied the status of full social actors, also have reason to care deeply about whether or not women are held fully responsible for their actions. Exempting women from responsibility can in some cases serve sexist purposes by not respecting their status as moral interlocutors.[44] This third feature also brings to view a route by which feminist accounts of the mechanisms used to deny or obscure women's rightful social status can be extended to instruct us about the nature of responsibility. I have begun to explore one branch of that route in the case of Charlotte's socially manufactured craziness.

Fischer and Ravizza's reasons-responsiveness account will allow social aspects of a person's deliberations or circumstances to affect responsibility only to the extent that those aspects influence her actual causal control over her behavior. This account seems, at first, quite alien to many feminist interests in the relational dimensions of women's moral selfhood. For instance, since it focuses on the counterfactual responsiveness of action-*mechanisms* rather than on the capabilities of *agents* (as Wallace's view does), it can appear to neglect the integrity of individual agents considered as wholes, not to mention the character of relationships among persons. However, a reasons-responsiveness condition can apprehend some social features of responsibility that would be important for feminist ethics. Such a condition remains neutral about the source and nature of reasons to act, thereby allowing action generated through mechanisms that are responsive to emotional considerations or considerations grounded in physical need to count as responsible. By refusing to accord privilege to modes of rational consideration that are emotionally cold, abstract, or impersonal, the account makes room for rational responsiveness to the sorts of affectively colored states that figure prominently in interpersonal attachments.

More important, Fischer and Ravizza's view is essentially historical. It ties responsibility to features of the *process* by which an action is generated, not simply to features realized in the time slice during which the action is performed.[45] Taking seriously the history of actions permits the theory to be sensitive to elements of context and narrative development, thus making the account conducive to feminist elaboration.

Nevertheless, the fact that the reasons-responsiveness condition is rooted in features of action-mechanisms that need not reflect the perspectives of agents themselves sharply limits the theory's serviceability for feminist ethics. As we saw in Charlotte's case, the way an agent regards herself as a moral agent can jeopardize her responsibility even when the mechanism through which she acts remains counterfactually sensitive to possible reasons to act otherwise. Moreover, Fischer and Ravizza examine the nature of an agent's control in conceptual isolation from the nexus of relationships within which personal control becomes relevant to moral responsibility. Control matters for responsibility because various degrees of control are required within the complex form of moral dialogue that defines what it is to be responsible. The reasons-responsiveness condition cannot fully reflect the normative demands of such dialogue, as I have argued. Attending to agents' sense of worth, by contrast, helps to advance feminist commitments to take women's experiences and perspectives seriously. Of course, it does not follow that agents' feelings or beliefs about their own responsibility are incorrigible.[46]

Wallace's account of the conditions of responsibility does much better than Fischer and Ravizza's in recognizing the level at which social considerations contribute to responsibility. For Wallace, having the powers of reflective self-control makes one accountable because one is appropriately held responsible when one possesses those powers (so long as one has no excuses in cases of wrongful behavior). Wallace contends, as I do, that holding someone responsible is a matter of opening the possibility for a certain form of moral relationship with her. This means that relational considerations operate not merely as incidental causal influences on responsibility; social relationships also shape responsibility more profoundly.

> The main hazards to accountability may be posed not by our physical and biological nature but by the social and political circumstances in which we develop and live. The conditions of responsibility I have identified . . . describe an ideal that is regulative of our social interactions, the ideal of a community of people capable of participating constructively with each other in the exchange of moral criticism and justification. No doubt many of the people we interact with conform to this ideal sufficiently to make it fair to hold them fully accountable. . . . But approximation to the ideal is a matter of degree, and it is liable to be affected by such common phenomena as childhood abuse, psychological trauma, and the persistence of extreme poverty and violence in the midst of general affluence.[47]

Yet, like Fischer and Ravizza, Wallace ignores considerations having to do with persons' experience of their own agency.[48] He approaches responsibility primarily from the standpoint of evaluation, the standpoint of holding persons responsible (including oneself). He considers aspects of the agent's perspective on her own conduct only to the extent that they pertain to conditions framed from the evaluator's standpoint. However, as I have contended throughout this discussion, failure to respect the agent's perspective fully, particularly with regard to her sense of worthiness to speak for her own conduct, occasions failure to understand the full effects of oppressive social conditions on responsibility and, accordingly, occasions failure to grasp how deeply the relational aspects of responsibility run. The social relations that affect responsibility are not only those that modify *what we are capable of doing* but also those that mold *who we regard ourselves as being.*

Thus, the two criticisms I set before Fischer and Ravizza's reasons-responsiveness approach—that it focuses on control, to the neglect of persons' perspectives on their own agency, and that it attempts to detach a conception of control from the context of interpersonal moral relations that determines what responsibility is—are not entirely independent of each other. Examining the relational context that defines responsibility leads us to take seriously the agent's perspective on the exchange of moral criticism and response. Conversely, taking seriously the agent's perspective enables us to understand more fully the social character of responsibility.

Of the three accounts that I have considered in addition to my own proposal, the self-disclosure view comes the closest to reflecting the three intrinsically relational aspects of responsibility that I have noted. This is not surprising since the notion of self-disclosure naturally points toward the context of relationships within which what an agent really cares about can be disclosed to others through her conduct.[49] And, as we saw in the second section, a self-disclosure view of responsibility could recognize the effect that diminished self-worth has on an agent's responsibility by arguing that adequate self-disclosure is possible only when an agent regards herself as worthy of expressing through her actions what she values. Hence, if I am correct that a theory's sensitivity to the relational dimensions of responsibility makes it particularly valuable for feminist purposes, a self-disclosure account of responsibility warrants much more feminist interest than it has received.

Nevertheless, it remains the case that a self-disclosure approach has not in fact been developed in ways that explicitly draw out its relational implications. My discussion of the approach is (to my knowledge) the first to point out these implications and to consider the possible role of a socially articulated sense of self-worth in self-disclosure. I suspect that this type of account has been insufficiently developed along these lines because it was initially formulated by thinking about the internal psychological conditions under which an agent's motives constitute her *real* wants (as in Wolf's formulation of the Real Self View), instead of by conceiving self-disclosure as a matter of entering into certain forms of moral relationship with others who can appropriately expect the agent to answer for the features of her moral self that her conduct may disclose.

Some Worries

I have mainly been concerned in this article to show three things. First, I have argued that three influential accounts of responsibility have failed to appreciate adequately the role of persons' own perspectives on their agency. Taking those perspectives seriously gives rise, I have proposed, to an unorthodox self-worth condition of full responsibility.[50] Second, I have used the self-worth condition of responsibility to show that responsibility is sensitive to social relations in ways that other theories have obscured. Finally, I have suggested that considering the intrinsically relational aspects of responsibility that I have identified will help to advance feminist reflection about the significance of responsibility for liberatory approaches to ethics.

In closing, I want to discuss briefly some likely worries about the proposed condition of self-worth. First, some may worry that because it can be difficult to gather adequate evidence about whether persons have the requisite sense of worth, the proposed view would make it very difficult to assess persons' responsibility. I admit this but deny that it is a good reason to reject the self-worth condition. It is a feature of many ordinary conditions of responsibility that their application can be extremely difficult to verify, which is one reason why ascriptions of responsibility are so commonly contested. It would be unreasonable to demand that an adequate account of responsibility make it easier than it actually is to determine whether, or to what degree, a person is responsible for some action.

A second, related worry is that requiring a sense of self-worth for unqualified responsibility would make it too easy to evade responsibility. Persons could plead reduced accountability simply by denying that they felt worthy of answering for their acts or, more extremely, by intentionally trying to sabotage their sense of worth. I do not see why my proposal would have this consequence. For one thing, whereas it is a simple matter to *say* that one does not have the requisite sense of worthiness, what one says by no means settles the question of whether one actually has it or not. Compare this with the ordinary condition of control. It is difficult to verify the extent of an agent's control over her actions, and it is easy to deny that one has much control. But this does not threaten the plausibility of requiring some sort of control as a condition of responsibility. Furthermore, it would be very difficult to destroy deliberately one's sense of worthiness to account for one's conduct without damaging many other valuable aspects of one's moral agency, too. Even if one could do so, it would be an irrational strategy for evading responsibility. An agent who deliberately destroyed her sense of self-worth would normally be responsible for that very act.

The proposed self-worth condition could also seem to permit unwarranted evasions of responsibility because many agents who suffer serious blows to their self-worth, through no fault of their own, do not appear to be less responsible as a result. For instance, persons who were victims of abuse as children may become abusers as adults, in part because of the dramatic loss of self-worth brought on by their early experiences of abuse. Yet the fact that these abusers often feel relatively worthless as persons does not seem automatically to lessen their responsibility for inflicting abuse on others.[51]

Such cases do not pose a genuine difficulty for my position, however. I have made a claim only about the role that one particular component of our sense of moral self-worth, namely, worthiness to give account of our actions, plays in our responsibility. There are many elements of our general sense of personal worth or esteem that are independent of this specific component of our self-regard.[52] The example of abuse victims who become abusers illustrates this. The self-contempt these abusers are likely to suffer does not normally entail reluctance to give an account of their actions. Abusers are, if anything, all too ready to advance justifications for their violence (justifications that in fact often reflect indirectly their damaged self-esteem and repressed rage). This is entirely different from persons like Charlotte, whose socially inflicted self-doubt leads them to feel unworthy of speaking for themselves as morally answerable agents. Of course, there are other live questions about the responsibility of victims of abuse (especially concerning the level of self-control that it is fair to expect of them), but there is no general problem here for my proposed condition of responsibility.

Third, one might object that my analysis of Charlotte's predicament complicates matters unnecessarily. Would it not be simpler to argue that Charlotte's responsibility is diminished only to the extent that she has been subjected to coercive or manipulative social influences? If this were the case, impairment of her responsibility could be explained entirely in terms of disruptions of her ability to act freely, without reference to her attitudes toward her worth. This might be adequate when external threats or deceits force persons to conform to oppressive social practices. But Charlotte does not act in conformity with social expectations, and in any case, she has internalized many of the prevailing expectations that regulate women's judgments and behavior (in her day). She views many of the social influences that operate on her as providing good evidence about how she should feel about herself. This is precisely why she is so profoundly conflicted. Analyzing her responsibility solely in terms of socially instituted threats and deception would radically oversimplify her predicament. It is precisely because she does act through reasons-responsive processes and can act on her own judgments despite her "craziness" that her situation calls for more subtle analysis.

One might worry, alternatively, that diminished self-worth does compromise moral agency, but not by reducing responsibility. Perhaps diminished self-worth just makes it more difficult to discern what is morally acceptable and translate it into action, so that we should not hold persons afflicted by this sense of unworthiness to the same standards that we would expect others to meet. But this would not involve reduced responsibility. We should still hold such persons accountable in relation to the revised expectations.

There is much to agree with in this objection. It develops the point (noted in the second section) that an agent's sense of worth could interfere with her capacities of reflective self-control. However, this does not deflect my arguments that self-worth may influence responsibility through other routes, too. It also underestimates the seriousness of a plight like Charlotte's to think only that it is just a bit more difficult for her to know what to do than it would be for her doctor or husband. This fails to appreciate how her self-doubt can change her relationship to the entire process of deciding what to do in the face of others' expectations.

Finally, I should note the more sweeping concern that making self-worth a necessary condition of full responsibility seems to be at odds with the political purposes of feminism. The worry is that many women may feel unworthy of giving accounts of their actions on equal terms with men, and so the proposed condition would, in effect, condemn them to the position of pure victims, rendering them demoralized and frustrating the possibility that they could take responsibility for developing resistance to the oppressions leveled against them. In other words, if my proposal makes full responsibility too difficult to attain under oppressive social conditions, widespread acceptance of the view could disempower many women and make the project of building women's collective and individual resistance just that much more difficult.

I can only give a partial response here to a concern that really calls for a systematic account of how moral agency can be reconstructed from within oppressive contexts. Many others have offered significant proposals about whether attributions of responsibility should be given an important role in fighting women's demoralization.[53] I restrict my comments to three points, which indicate that women who feel unworthy to answer for their actions need not be pure victims.

First, as I noted in the previous section, the sense of self-worth that pertains to responsibility is sensitive to social context. One's sense of worthiness to account for one's actions can reasonably vary from one domain of normative expectations to another, and so can vary from one network of relationships to another. Persons' sense of their moral standing can vary as the context for action shifts from family relationships to the social demands of citizenship, and so forth. Thus, diminished responsibility that results from a depressed sense of worth in one domain of relationships, relative to one cluster of ethical expectations, does not necessarily entail diminished responsibility in every area of activity, for all moral choices. Since oppressions typically burden some areas of activity more than others, their effects on persons' responsibility are far from uniform. Persons who feel hopelessly victimized in some respects can often find resources for reaffirming their self-worth in other contexts, where their status as accountable agents receives greater social recognition. A powerful illustration is the way in which patriarchal expectations that assigned black women slaves in the United States virtually total responsibility for managing slaves' domestic needs thereby provided a meaningful context of accountability, self-worth, and power from which slave women could criticize and resist institutionalized slavery.[54]

Furthermore, as Charlotte's case shows, if self-worth can modify responsibility while the agent's powers of reflection and self-control remain intact (though underused), it is hardly the case that diminished self-worth renders such a person a completely disempowered victim. On the contrary, if the agent retains her powers to recognize, apply, and act on moral considerations, she has tools that are essential for analyzing and, ultimately, dismantling social systems that subordinate her. True, these tools will be of little use to her until she can gain adequate trust in herself to employ them. But it is hardly the case that a person in Charlotte's predicament has to rebuild her capacities for moral agency from scratch.

Also, the task of reclaiming and sustaining the relevant sense of worthiness from within oppressive conditions is far from impossible, however difficult it may be. As I have noted, our sense of our fitness to give accounts for what we do is highly sensitive to social recognition. Just as venomous, degrading, inferiorizing social relations can break down our sense of our fitness to speak for ourselves as moral agents, so also caring, dignifying, democratizing social relations can repair damaged self-worth. Taken together with the preceding points about the context-dependence of self-worth and the compatibility of normative competence with loss of self-worth, this suggests that means for recovering a sense of accountability are normally available even for those who appear hopelessly victimized.

Notes

1. I am grateful to the editors of this volume for making numerous helpful comments on an earlier draft of this article. Whereas the content of the position I have defended is my responsibility alone, whatever clarity I have managed to achieve in explaining it owes a good deal to the editors' assistance.

2. This is compatible with Catharine MacKinnon's view that consciousness raising has not only been a useful resource for feminists but also the distinctive methodology of feminism. According to MacKinnon, "The key to feminist theory consists in its *way* of knowing. Consciousness raising is that way." Catharine A. MacKinnon, *Toward a Feminist Theory of the State* (Cambridge, Mass.: Harvard University Press, 1989), p. 84 (emphasis in original).

3. Virginia Held, *Feminist Morality* (Chicago: University of Chicago Press, 1993), pp. 14–15.

4. Margaret Urban Walker maintains, however, that a feminist ethic of responsibility is more properly understood as a broad family of views, including but not restricted to an ethic of care. See Walker's "Picking Up Pieces: Lives, Stories, and Integrity," in *Feminists Rethink the Self*, ed. Diana Tietjens Meyers (Boulder, Colo.: Westview Press, 1997), pp. 64–65.

5. For representative feminist criticisms of the abstract individualism that has been associated with personal responsibility, see Alison M. Jaggar, *Feminist Politics and Human Nature* (Totowa, N.J.: Rowman & Allanheld, 1983), especially pp. 39–47, and Lorraine Code, *What Can She Know?: Feminist Theory and the Construction of Knowledge* (Ithaca, N.Y.: Cornell University Press, 1991), pp. 71–79.

6. See, for instance, María C. Lugones, "Playfulness, 'World'-traveling, and Loving Perception," *Hypatia* 2 (1987): 3–19; Lugones, "On the Logic of Pluralist Feminism," in *Feminist Ethics*, ed. Claudia Card (Lawrence: University Press of Kansas, 1991); Cheshire Calhoun, "Responsibility and Reproach," *Ethics* 99 (1989): 389–406; Sandra Lee Bartky, "Shame and Gender," in *Femininity and Domination* (New York: Routledge, 1990); Susan Wendell, "Oppression and Victimization: Choice and Responsibility," *Hypatia* 5 (1990): 15–46; Elizabeth V. Spelman, "The Virtue of Feeling and the Feeling of Virtue," in Card, *Feminist Ethics*; and Anita M. Superson, "Right-Wing Women: Causes, Choices, and Blaming the Victim," in *"Nagging" Questions: Feminist Ethics in Everyday Life*, ed. Dana E. Bushnell (Lanham, Md.: Rowman & Littlefield, 1995). For a thoroughgoing critique of blame as demoralizing in the context of lesbian community, see Sarah Lucia Hoagland, *Lesbian Ethics: Toward New Value* (Palo Alto, Cal.: Institute of Lesbian Studies, 1988), pp. 215–221. Barbara Houston, "In Praise of Blame," *Hypatia* 7 (1992): 128–147, offers an opposing view. While urging "a feminist transformation of blame" (p. 142), Houston nevertheless affirms blame as necessary for developing women's moral agency, integrity, and sense of self in community (pp. 140–142).

7. Hoagland, *Lesbian Ethics*, p. 215.

8. Alison M. Jaggar, "Feminist Ethics: Projects, Problems, Prospects" in Card, *Feminist Ethics*, p. 90.

9. I name her for feminist author Charlotte Perkins Gilman, whose life is reflected in

many (though not all) features of this case. I thank John Christman for reminding me about Gilman's short story "The Yellow Wallpaper" in conjunction with my work on free agency.

10. Gilman's neurologist, S. Weir Mitchell, used this term to describe the process by which his female patients would gradually turn to him for moral guidance. Mitchell wrote, "If you tell the patient she is basely selfish she is probably amazed and wonders at your cruelty. To cure the case you must morally alter as well as physically amend, and nothing else will answer." See Ann J. Lane, *To "Herland" and Beyond: The Life and Work of Charlotte Perkins Gilman* (New York: Pantheon Books, 1990), p. 117.

11. I regard the sense of one's worthiness to answer for one's conduct as one component of one's respect for one's own personhood, one's "recognition self-respect," as Stephen Darwall terms it in "Two Kinds of Respect," *Ethics* 88 (1977): 36–49. Lacking recognition of self-respect does not entail that one fails to grasp one's worthiness to answer for one's conduct, however. And whereas failing to appreciate one's worthiness to give a moral account of oneself will stand in the way of fully recognizing one's moral worth, it would be possible for one to retain some appreciation of one's worth as a person nevertheless. For some helpful distinctions among different types and elements of self-respect and a survey of numerous ways in which self-respect can be degraded, see Robin Dillon, "How to Lose Your Self-respect," *American Philosophical Quarterly* 29 (1992): 125–139.

12. R. Jay Wallace, *Responsibility and the Moral Sentiments* (Cambridge, Mass.: Harvard University Press, 1994). I will not discuss theories that place incompatibilist requirements on responsibility since I do not think that debates about the metaphysical compatibility of responsibility and deterministic explanations of human action have much to contribute to feminist ethics.

13. Ibid., p. 157.

14. Ibid.

15. Ibid., p. 158.

16. Compare ibid., pp. 161, 183–186.

17. Compare John Christman's discussion of the ways in which obstacles to self-awareness and inconsistent beliefs and desires may block an agent's autonomy. See "Autonomy and Personal History," *Canadian Journal of Philosophy* 21 (1991): 1–24, especially 13–18.

18. I have discussed this mode of alienation from reflective powers in "Free Agency and Self-Worth," *Journal of Philosophy* 91 (1994): 650–668, especially 657–659.

19. John Martin Fischer, "Responsiveness and Moral Responsibility," in *Responsibility, Character, and the Emotions*, ed. Ferdinand Schoeman (Cambridge: Cambridge University Press, 1987); John Martin Fischer and Mark Ravizza, "Responsibility and Inevitability," *Ethics* 101 (1991): 258–278; John Martin Fischer and Mark Ravizza, "Responsibility for Consequences," in *Perspectives on Moral Responsibility*, ed. Fischer and Ravizza (Ithaca, N.Y.: Cornell University Press, 1993); John Martin Fischer, *The Metaphysics of Free Will* (Cambridge: Blackwell, 1994). (Fischer and Ravizza's most recent work, *Responsibility and Control: A Theory of Moral Responsibility* [Cambridge: Cambridge University Press, 1998], appeared after this article was written.)

20. Fischer and Ravizza distinguish weak from strong reasons-responsiveness, where the latter requires responsiveness of the act-mechanism to *any* possible sufficient reason to act otherwise. See Fischer, "Responsiveness and Moral Responsibility," pp. 86–90; Fischer and Ravizza, "Responsibility and Inevitability," pp. 269–270; and Fischer, *The Metaphysics of Free Will*, pp. 166–168.

21. Fischer and Ravizza are primarily interested in the "freedom-relevant" component of responsibility, that is, in the sort of control that responsibility requires. They discuss the epistemic requirements of responsibility only briefly. See Fischer, "Responsiveness and Moral

Responsibility," p. 267, n.10; Fischer and Ravizza, "Responsibility for Consequences," p. 338, n. 22; and Fischer, *Metaphysics of Free Will*, p. 238, n. 4.

22. Susan Wolf, *Freedom within Reason* (New York: Oxford University Press, 1990), chap. 2. Wolf does not endorse the Real Self View. She argues that it provides only a necessary condition of responsibility, not a sufficient condition, since it does not entail the ability to recognize and appreciate the right reasons for action.

23. Ibid., p. 33.

24. However, Watson has backed away from his early account of the role of valuational systems in free and responsible agency. For that account, see "Free Agency," *Journal of Philosophy* 72 (1975): 205–220. He has argued more recently that actions for which a person is responsible can disclose her values without necessarily reflecting her judgments about what is valuable or worthwhile and without endorsing those values from some general evaluational standpoint. See "Free Action and Free Will," *Mind* 96 (1987): 145–172, especially 149–150.

25. Gary Watson, "Responsibility and Normative Competence," unpublished paper, delivered at the Pacific Division Meetings, American Philosophical Association, March 1992, p. 11. John Dewey's statement is from his *Outlines of a Critical Theory of Ethics* (New York: Hillary House, 1957), p. 161. A revised version of Watson's paper appeared as "Two Faces of Responsibility," *Philosophical Topics* 24 (1996): 227–248.

26. The self-disclosure account will grant, of course, that features of Charlotte's circumstances, such as the extreme psychological and social pressures enacted in the rest cure, are relevant to a sound interpretation of what her actions reveal about what matters to her. This view does not take the simplistic position that what persons care about can be directly read from the actions for which they are responsible, independently of the circumstances and history of those actions.

27. This assumes that self-doubt does not alienate Charlotte from her reflective capacities, a possibility I considered when discussing Wallace's account. If such alienation were to occur, the value judgments that Charlotte would arrive at through reflection would not necessarily express what really matters to her. In that case, it is hard to see how Charlotte could be capable of governing her actions through her valuational system and thereby disclosing what she really cares about through her actions.

28. For an extended treatment of the conceptual relationship between the appropriateness of holding persons morally responsible and their actually being responsible, see Wallace, *Responsibility and the Moral Sentiments*, chap. 4. Wallace argues that a person is morally responsible for an action just in case it would be appropriate to hold her morally responsible for it, where the relevant standards of appropriateness are moral norms of fairness.

29. I am indebted here to T. M. Scanlon, Jr., "The Significance of Choice," in *The Tanner Lectures on Human Values,* vol. 8, ed. Sterling M. McMurrin (Salt Lake City: University of Utah Press, 1988), especially pp. 166–176. Scanlon emphasizes connections between holding a person morally responsible and the person's inter- and intrapersonal responsiveness. However, I do not endorse Scanlon's thesis that the forms of responsiveness necessary for responsibility are dictated by the content of moral judgments alone. For a valuable discussion of Scanlon's account, see Wallace, *Responsibility and the Moral Sentiments*, pp. 74–81.

30. See Gary Watson, "Responsibility and the Limits of Evil," in Schoeman, *Responsibility, Character, and the Emotions*. As Jay Wallace reminds us, however, this does not mean that holding someone accountable involves moral communication in each instance or always requires an interest in having a moral exchange with the person (see *Responsibility and the Moral Sentiments*, pp. 164–165).

31. I am not suggesting that blame, whether expressed or unexpressed, is strictly necessary for holding someone responsible. I focus on cases of holding persons responsible for per-

ceived wrongs, hence on negative reactions such as blame or indignation, because these cases best display the relational aspects of responsibility in which I am interested here. However, I readily admit that philosophers would do well to spend more time reflecting on the role of positive reactive attitudes, such as admiration, pride, or praise.

32. See Watson, "Responsibility and the Limits of Evil," pp. 264–265; Scanlon, "The Significance of Choice," pp. 171–172; and Wallace, *Responsibility and the Moral Sentiments*, pp. 164–165.

33. I assume that Charlotte is not to blame for feeling unworthy of giving an account of her actions because of the oppressive circumstances she faces. In such circumstances, a person could not reasonably be expected to feel any differently about herself. A person whose sense of self-worth erodes because of some character flaw under more favorable conditions would be in a very different position, however.

34. I explore the importance of this point more fully in the last section.

35. In *Freedom within Reason*, chap. 4, Susan Wolf suggests that traumatic childhoods may reduce responsibility primarily by impeding the development of adequate abilities to recognize certain kinds of good reasons for acting. Wallace proposes instead that many kinds of childhood deprivation reduce accountability by affecting the capacity to control behavior (see *Responsibility and the Moral Sentiments*, pp. 231–233).

36. However, as I underscore in the last section, not just any sort of diminished self-worth that is associated with traumatic upbringings will reduce responsibility, in my view. The childhood trauma must specifically modify the sense of worthiness to give an account of one's actions in order to engage the proposed condition of responsibility.

37. I argue shortly, however, that Wallace goes too far in the direction of analyzing responsibility from the third-person perspective of appropriately holding others responsible. He omits due consideration of the agent's own perspective on her agency.

38. As Galen Strawson notes, admitting these developmental facts is consistent with holding that "the true centre of one's commitment to the notion of human freedom [and responsibility] lies in one's attitude to and experience of oneself." See *Freedom and Belief* (New York: Oxford University Press, 1986), p. 110.

39. Susan J. Brison, "Outliving Oneself: Trauma, Memory, and Personal Identity," in Meyers, *Feminists Rethink the Self*, p. 21.

40. Ibid., p. 27.

41. This point is also important for understanding the political possibilities for restoring accountability in oppressive contexts (see the final section).

42. Christine Korsgaard's work on a Kantian account of responsibility suggests a different route by which to arrive at the idea that responsibility is properly relative to interpersonal relationships. See Christine M. Korsgaard, "Creating the Kingdom of Ends," in *Creating the Kingdom of Ends* (Cambridge: Cambridge University Press, 1996). Korsgaard maintains that responsibility should be conceived practically, as a matter to be decided, not a fact about persons to be discovered. To hold someone responsible, in this view, is to decide to place oneself in a relationship of reciprocity with the person (or to affirm the reciprocal relations one already has with her). Hence, Korsgaard reasons, "It may be perfectly reasonable for me to hold someone responsible for an attitude or an action, while at the same time acknowledging that it is just as reasonable for someone else not to hold the same person responsible for the very same attitude or action" (ibid., p. 199). Whereas Korsgaard sees responsibility as relative to relationships because of the decision to enter or continue relations of the sort in which responsibility attributions make sense, my claim is that relationships can modify facts about responsibility in virtue of affecting the shareability of particular norms of criticism and response.

43. See Kathryn Pauly Morgan, "Women and Moral Madness," in *Feminist Perspectives*,

ed. Lorraine Code et al. (Toronto: University of Toronto Press, 1988), for a classic discussion of how patriarchy traps women in unavoidable moral paradoxes and thereby deepens their demoralization through feelings of "moral madness."

44. Cf. Houston, "In Praise of Blame."

45. Fischer and Ravizza argue that this dependence on historical features is not only epistemic but also metaphysical. Their condition of responsibility is, therefore, genuinely historical, not just apparently so. See John Martin Fischer and Mark Ravizza, "Responsibility and History," in *Midwest Studies in Philosophy: Philosophical Naturalism*, ed. Peter A. French (Notre Dame, Ind.: University of Notre Dame Press, 1994).

46. Here I disagree with a related claim that Jennifer Nedelsky makes about autonomy in "Reconceiving Autonomy: Sources, Thoughts and Possibilities," *Yale Journal of Law and Feminism* 1 (1989): 7–36. Nedelsky correctly notes that theories of autonomy typically have ignored persons' feelings of autonomy. But she maintains, further, that the feeling of autonomy is "an inseparable component" of the capacity of autonomy (p. 25) and that someone who feels autonomous (when autonomy is properly reconceived) must actually be autonomous (p. 24). For reasons implied in my discussion of Charlotte's capabilities (second section), feelings of autonomy are neither necessary nor sufficient for the possession of capacities of autonomy. The important goal of granting greater authority to such feelings can be met without making them immune to possible error.

47. Wallace, *Responsibility and the Moral Sentiments*, p. 234.

48. This is clear from Wallace's discussion of childhood deprivation. Ibid., pp. 231–233.

49. The fact that Watson is interested in both a self-disclosure analysis of responsibility (in "Responsibility and Normative Competence" and "Two Faces of Responsibility") and a Strawsonian view that concentrates on the conditions of intelligible moral address (in "Responsibility and the Limits of Evil") is a further indication that the former type of account may be capable of recognizing the importance of relational considerations.

50. Of course, giving due attention to persons' sense of who they are as moral agents will be likely to do more than simply reveal the place of their sense of worthiness to answer for their actions in their responsibility. I have focused on this particular element of agents' standpoints because it is especially useful for bringing to view relational aspects of responsibility that are significant for many feminist purposes.

51. I thank Catriona Mackenzie and Natalie Stoljar for urging me to address this problem.

52. Compare note 11 on the relation of this specific component of self-worth to recognition self-respect.

53. See the references in note 6.

54. See Angela Davis, "Reflections on the Black Woman's Role in the Community of Slaves," *The Black Scholar* 3 (1971): 3–15.

4

AUTONOMY AND THE FEMINIST INTUITION[1]

Natalie Stoljar

Introduction

Feminist philosophers rightly have been suspicious of old-fashioned theories of autonomy, in which it was equated with the masculinist ideals of substantive independence and self-sufficiency. Lately, however, a different set of theories of autonomy has become dominant, namely, procedural theories. Many such theories argue that it is the capacity for *procedural independence* or *independence of mind,* rather than the capacity for substantive independence, that is necessary and sufficient for autonomy.[2] In such accounts, an agent's preference or decision is autonomous if and only if the process of formation of the preference or decision has satisfied certain standards of critical reflection. Once a preference or decision has passed such formal or procedural tests, it is autonomous, no matter what its content. Hence, procedural theories are "content-neutral."[3]

The implication of content neutrality, namely, that there is no restriction on the content of preferences that may be chosen by autonomous agents, is an advantage from some feminist perspectives, especially when contrasted with the idea that autonomy presupposes preferences for substantive independence or self-sufficiency. For instance, for feminists inspired by the care perspective of Carol Gilligan, it is important that autonomy be compatible with maintaining the relations of care and dependence that are characterized as valuable components of female agency. Jennifer Nedelsky writes that "the most promising model, symbol or metaphor for autonomy is child rearing. There we have encapsulated the emergence of autonomy through relationship with others."[4] Unlike self-sufficiency accounts of autonomy, procedural theories allow that preferences for dependence and connection can be autonomous. Moreover, as Marilyn Friedman points out, procedural theories are compatible with another characteristic of autonomy noticed by Nedelsky, who says, "If we ask ourselves what actually enables people to be autonomous, the answer is not isolation, but relationships—with parents, teachers, friends, loved ones—that provide the support and guidance necessary for the development and experience of autonomy."[5] Finally, content neutrality allows different agents autonomously to opt for a range of different life plans and conceptions of the good, thus respecting recent feminist concerns to preserve the diversity among and the multiplicity of agents. Procedural theories, therefore, are congenial to a feminist emphasis on the relational features of persons in three senses: first, they are compatible with agents' desires to establish and maintain valuable relationships of care and dependency; second, they allow for the insight that capacities for autonomy and critical reflection are the *product* of family influences, socialization, and so on; and third, they respect differences among agents, especially with respect to life plans and conceptions of the good, which are produced by the different social contexts in which agents are embedded.

Despite the apparent advantages, however, feminists should be cautious about adopting a purely procedural account of autonomy. In certain cases, even preferences satisfying the standards of critical reflection that are required by procedural accounts would still be regarded as nonautonomous by many feminists. This is because such preferences are influenced by pernicious aspects of the oppressive context. They therefore attract what I call *the feminist intuition*, which claims that preferences influenced by oppressive norms of femininity cannot be autonomous.

In the first section, I illustrate the feminist intuition by using examples from Kristin Luker's study of women who take contraceptive risks.[6] I suggest that the response that such women are not autonomous is a manifestation of the feminist intuition. In the second section, I argue that the feminist intuition cannot be explained by any of the conditions suggested as necessary for autonomy by procedural theories. If I am right, we have to either reject the feminist intuition or reject purely procedural theories of autonomy. In the final section, I propose that to explain the feminist intuition, we need to endorse a substantive rather than a procedural account of autonomy.[7] Substantive theories claim that there are further necessary conditions of agents' autonomy in addition to the formal conditions derived from procedural theories. For example, some theorists argue that agents must have a sense of self-trust or self-worth, in addition to relevant capacities for critical reflection; others argue that agents' preferences must have certain specified contents. I argue that only a strong substantive theory, namely, one that places restrictions on the contents of agents' preferences, explains the feminist intuition. Although I cannot provide any detailed development of such a theory here, I hope at least to show that feminists committed to the feminist intuition must take on the task of articulating a strong substantive theory of this sort.

Autonomy, Rationality, and the Feminist Intuition

In her book, *Taking Chances*, Luker describes a study of a group of about five hundred women who attended an abortion clinic in California in the early 1970s. Detailed interviews were done with fifty women, who were selected on the basis of medical records. Luker's aim was to investigate the relationship between abortion and contraception, in particular to answer this question: "Why do women who can presumably use freely available methods of contraception end up having unwanted pregnancies which result in induced abortions?"[8] Among the women studied, the unwanted pregnancies were not due to ignorance or lack of skills or access to contraception. Luker's study showed that over half had used a prescription method of birth control, and 86% had used some method of birth control in the past. Yet 40% used no contraception in the month prior to becoming pregnant, and 26% used contraception inconsistently, including such methods as rhythm.[9]

A typical response to the decision making of Luker's subjects is to label it irrational or perhaps even crazy. Luker's aim in the book is to challenge this intuition, to argue that the decision making leading up to the decision not to use contraception or effective contraception is, although risky, nevertheless rational. According to Luker, these "contraceptive risk-takers" engaged in a process of tacit bargaining with themselves over the costs and benefits of using contraception and in the end chose to take a risk. If she is right, her subjects' decision not to use contraception is not prima facie irrational or crazy. There is no more significant occurrence of irrationality among these women than there is in the population at large in situations of decision making "under risk conditions" such as smoking or failing to wear a safety belt in a car.[10] More strongly, she argues that "their behaviour leading up to the unwanted pregnancy is both reasonable and logical given their *own* definition of the situation."[11]

Luker provides a strong defense of her subjects' rationality. In so doing, she challenges the stereotypical antifeminist idea that women's decision making, when it is difficult to explain or does not conform to expectations, is likely to be irrational. I argue here that the example of Luker's subjects also triggers the intuition that they are not autonomous. However, the cases of rationality and autonomy are not symmetrical because it is precisely the intuition that the subjects are *not* autonomous that is the feminist intuition. In the next sections, I sketch some connections between rationality and autonomy, and then I outline the reasons adopted by Luker's subjects in the bargaining process and explain why it attracts the feminist intuition.

Rationality and Autonomy

Luker's study raises the issue of the relationship between rationality and autonomy. Many theories of autonomy propose that rationality is a necessary condition of autonomy or, more strongly and in the Kantian spirit, reduce autonomy to a capacity for rational decision making. For instance, procedural theories of autonomy often impose a rationality condition on autonomous preference formation, typically a "minimal rationality" condition.[12] As one would expect of a condition of a purely procedural theory of autonomy, the minimal rationality condition is itself purely procedural, requiring agents to manifest formal consistency among the relevant beliefs and desires. On the other hand, substantive theories of autonomy tend to reduce it to substantive rationality. In Susan Wolf's theory, for example, autonomy is a capacity to form preferences that track objective standards of "Reason."[13]

More significant in this context, there are structural parallels between theories of rationality and theories of autonomy. Both divide into the procedural and the substantive. For example, in a recent response to Luker's argument, Elizabeth Anderson in "Should Feminists Reject Rational Choice Theory?" identifies various theories of rational choice. The *formal theory* describes rationality as the disposition to maximize utility, namely, to weigh up preferences in the light of subjective assessments of their costs and benefits and choose the option that maximizes the utility of the overall scheme. Since the content of preferences is irrelevant to maximizing the overall scheme, the formal theory is purely procedural.[14] On the other hand, in the *rhetorical theory of rational choice*, an agent is rational when she has certain substantive characteristics, for instance, those of self-reliance, autonomy, and self-confidence.[15] Thus, the rhetorical theory is substantive.

Anderson draws out the relationship between autonomy and rationality. She interprets Luker as adhering to the formal theory of rational choice. Luker's subjects are not irrational in this theory because rationality requires only that they order their preferences to maximize utility. It does not matter that weighing up the costs and benefits of contraception leads to taking a contraceptive risk or that the contents of the preferences adopted by Luker's subjects may be criticized from a feminist point of view. Anderson herself adopts the rhetorical theory, which she argues has greater explanatory power because it offers a richer account of agency. In the rhetorical theory, autonomy is one of the characteristics that a rational agent must display. Since Anderson thinks that Luker's subjects are not autonomous, they cannot be rational either.

The conception of autonomy that Anderson takes to be implicit in the rhetorical theory of rational choice is as follows. She suggests, first, that autonomous agents must regard themselves as authorized to act on their own interests and ordering of preferences, that they not "bow down to social convention, tradition, or even morality," or "take other people's reasons for how they should act as their reasons for action." Second, autonomous agents must "regard themselves as self-originating sources of claims."[16] The first condition has a stronger and a weaker formulation. The stronger is that autonomous agents must not take others' reasons for action as their own, and the weaker is that autonomous agents must *regard themselves* as authorized to act on their own interests. The stronger formulation is false, however, because procedural theories (rightly) treat autonomy as compatible with socialization, and acting on reasons generated through socialization is inevitably a case of taking others' reasons as one's own. The question for all theories of autonomy is what kinds of socialization are incompatible with autonomy. The weaker formulation, while plausible, is not a purely procedural condition, and neither is the second condition that Anderson describes, that is, that autonomous agents must regard themselves as self-originating sources of claims. Procedural accounts would not typically conceive failures *to regard* one's interests or claims as self-authorizing or self-originating as sufficient to undermine autonomy. Such failures are closer to failures of confidence or trust in one's ability to make claims than to flaws in the capacity for critical reflection. For example, Luker's subjects lack confidence in asserting their sexual agency and, as a result, do not have a robust sense of their own authority in asserting their claims. (I return to this issue in the final section.) Thus, the two conditions Anderson identifies seem to go beyond the conditions for autonomy required by recent procedural accounts. The conception of autonomy implicit in the rhetorical theory of rationality is a substantive conception.

The Feminist Intuition

I suggest that Anderson's reaction to the question of the autonomy of Luker's subjects is an example of the feminist intuition. They are judged to be nonautonomous because they are overly influenced in their decisions about contraception by stereotypical and incorrect norms of femininity and sexual agency. Unlike risk-takers in other domains, such as those who smoke or fail to wear safety belts in a car, Luker's subjects are motivated by oppressive and misguided norms that are internalized as a result of feminine socialization. Because of the role of such norms in the decision to take a contraceptive risk, Luker's subjects attract the feminist intuition.

Let us consider in more detail the kinds of reasons weighed up by Luker's subjects in the tacit bargaining process at the time of the decision to take a contraceptive risk. She lists both the costs of contraception and the anticipated benefits of pregnancy in the "bargaining set." For example, among the costs of contraception are the social and cultural costs, the costs of obtaining and maintaining contraception, and the medical and biological costs. The social and cultural costs and benefits described by Luker provide the best evidence of the kinds of social norms that are motivating her subjects. Among the costs, there are the social costs of acknowledging intercourse by planning and using contraception. For example, there is the cost of public censure for engaging in premarital sex. Consider the following excerpt from an interview:

> I: Why didn't you use more effective contraception?
>
> R: I always thought about it, but never did anything about it. I used to think about the pill, but my sister used it, she's married now and stuff, and my mother used to tell me she'd die. She's really Catholic. But it seems as if most of my friends are on it.[17]

A second kind of social cost is that of flouting internalized religious or other norms. This cost is to some extent removed by avoiding deliberate planning for sex by not using adequate contraception:

> I: Did you think you might get pregnant not using contraception?
>
> R: I thought so, I mean, I knew it was a possibility. But there was this problem of my religious background. If you are familiar with the Catholic Church it is against the Church to use contraception or to have pre-marital sex. . . . Just using a contraceptive seems like you're planning.[18]

A third cost identified by Luker is that of appearing to be a sexually active agent.[19] A pattern identified by Luker is ceasing to use contraception after the breakdown of a relationship with a husband or boyfriend. She observes that "continuing contraception implies that one expects intercourse with a new partner, and this flies in the face of a strong taboo."[20]

Luker argues that in many cases her subjects tacitly weighed up the costs of obtaining and using contraception against what they anticipated would be benefits of pregnancy. (The perceived benefits of pregnancy usually vanished once the pregnancy became a reality.) Luker's subjects anticipated that pregnancy would benefit them by proving fertility, establishing true womanness and increasing self-worth, forcing the sexual partner to define his relationship to the woman, and forcing significant others such as parents to pay attention to the pregnant woman. For example:

> I: You said you had a strong maternal urge. So you think that could have been a factor in getting pregnant?
>
> R: I think so, yeah. I don't know exactly, but taking a wild stab, I think that getting pregnant means having someone who will take my love and care, 'cause lots of times I think noone else wants it.[21]

The overall picture derived from these interviews is one of women motivated in large part by the following norms: it is inappropriate for women to have active sex lives; it is unseemly for women to plan for and initiate sex; it is wrong to engage in or be seen to engage in premarital sex; pregnancy and childbearing promote one's worthiness by proving one is a "real woman"; it is normal for women to bargain for marriage by, for instance, proving their fertility to their partners or their partners' families; and women are worthwhile marriage partners only if they are capable of childbearing.

Contrast this picture with a hypothetical picture of risk taking by smokers. Assume that, like Luker's subjects, their risk taking is not explained by a lack of skills or access to professional help. Imagine that many cases involve tacit bargaining, paralleling the tacit bargaining of Luker's subjects. For example, suppose that the financial and health costs of continuing to smoke are weighed against its benefits, such as that smoking is pleasurable, that it is relaxing or therapeutic, or that it would be financially onerous or otherwise too much trouble to seek professional help to overcome the habit. For smokers who engage in a tacit bargaining process of this sort, although we may judge them weak-willed or wrong in giving too little weight to the medical costs, we are unlikely to judge that their decisions are not autonomous because smokers are not typically opting to smoke on the basis of false and oppressive norms. Notice, however, that when smokers (especially children) do opt to smoke on the basis of false and oppressive norms, for example, in response to images of smoking as glamorous and promoting one's desirability, the intuition that they are not autonomous is triggered. Unlike risk taking among smokers, the contraceptive risk taking of Luker's subjects attracts the feminist intuition because the internalized norms motivating the decision to take a contraceptive risk have criticizable contents. They are norms of religion, femininity, and sexuality that are oppressive to women.

Procedural Theories

We saw in the preceding section that Luker's argument that her subjects are not irrational succeeds if we take her to be endorsing a purely procedural theory of rational choice, namely, the formal theory described by Anderson. Because of the parallels between theories of rational choice and theories of autonomy, this suggests that in procedural theories of autonomy, Luker's subjects should count as autonomous, or at least should not be ruled nonautonomous. In this section, I examine in detail whether Luker's subjects would count as nonautonomous in procedural theories. In general terms, procedural theories claim that for a desire or preference to be autonomous, it must satisfy certain standards of critical reflection. That is, critical reflection must be autonomy conferring in the relevant way. I extract five necessary conditions of autonomy from different procedural accounts: *counterfactual, internal coherence, endorsement, self-knowledge,* and *inhibiting factors.* I argue in each case that many of Luker's subjects satisfy the condition and hence cannot be ruled nonautonomous on that basis. Thus procedural theories are at best equivocal on the question of whether Luker's subjects are autonomous. They do not vindicate the feminist intuition.

The Counterfactual Condition

In providing an analysis of autonomous preference formation, Christman introduces a counterfactual condition, as follows: an agent is autonomous with respect to a certain preference or desire only if she did not resist its development when attending to the process of its development or would not have resisted had she attended to the process.[22] So, for example, suppose out of habit an agent chooses to go on vacation every year to the same location. The fact that the agent fails to attend critically each time to the processes of formation of the preference does not rule out its being autonomous unless, counterfactually, had the agent reflected on the process of development of the preference, she would have resisted the development of the preference. Since in most cases of this sort agents would not have resisted the preference had they attended to it, such preferences are not ruled nonautonomous on the counterfactual condition.

Does the preference of Luker's subjects to take a contraceptive risk fail the counterfactual condition? One approach is to take Luker's description of her subjects as bargainers at face value. If her description is right, it is not plausible to claim that they failed to attend to the process of formation of the preference. On the contrary, they weighed up the costs and benefits of using contraception and decided to take a risk. Since they attended to the process, there is no need to invoke the counterfactual condition. On the other hand, since the bargaining described by Luker was mostly tacit, it is likely that Luker's subjects did not sufficiently attend to their motivational structure, in particular to the influence of the norms of femininity and sexual agency on the bargaining process; hence that they did not sufficiently attend to the process of formation of the preference. If they had attended, would they have resisted?

To answer this question, it is useful to consider cases in which desires are formed on the basis of external standards or internalized norms and as a result appear to be nonautonomous. For example, Feinberg distinguishes two paradigm patterns of nonautonomous, or inauthentic, desires.[23] The first is that of a "habitual and uncritical conformist who receives his signals from some group whose good opinion he needs, or from unknown tastemakers in the advertizing agencies and public relations firms"; the second is that of an agent who is subject to "standards [that] are implanted in the child by his parents, their authoritative source internalized, so that they become his forever more."[24] Suppose that both types of agents do not sufficiently attend to the formation of their preferences when the preferences are based on either the external standards to which they habitually defer or the internalized standards that have been operating since childhood. Would they have resisted the formation of these preferences had they attended to the influence of the standards or norms on their desires? It is unlikely that they would have, precisely because the habits of deference and the internalized norms, that is, the values that govern the agent's motivational structure, would themselves justify holding the relevant desire. In other words, agents who attend to the influence of the values on their preferences would be more likely to endorse the preferences than to resist them.

Paul Benson makes the same point, using a different example:

> Consider the eighteen year-old college student who excels in her studies, is
> well-liked by her many friends and acquaintances, leads an active, challenging life,
> yet who regularly feels bad about herself because she does not have "the right
> look." . . . So, on top of everything else she does, she expends a great deal of time
> and money trying to straighten or curl her hair, to refine her cosmetic technique,
> to harden or soften her body, and so on.[25]

In claiming that the student is not autonomous, Benson expresses the feminist intuition. He argues that the counterfactual condition cannot explain why the student is not autonomous because even had she reflected on the fashion norms she has internalized, as well as the process of development of her preferences and its relationship to the norms, she would not have resisted the process. As Benson explains, the fact that the norms are internalized blocks the capacity of the agent to resist the development of preferences based on the norms. If we consider only this procedural condition, therefore, the student's decision to devote so much time and energy to her appearance is procedurally competent and autonomous.

Many of Luker's subjects are influenced by internalized norms of feminine sexual agency. Consider, for example, subjects who judge that one of the anticipated benefits of pregnancy is to allow them to "bargain for marriage":

> I: How did you feel about getting pregnant?
>
> R: I thought I would probably get married, that he would want to. I never, ever thought
> I'd go through an abortion. That never entered my mind at all.[26]

Although the case is somewhat underdescribed here, one way of interpreting this woman's beliefs is that she is in the grip of feminine norms about the dependency of women on men in sex, pregnancy, and marriage. Luker's phrase, "bargaining for marriage," suggests that many of her subjects conceived of themselves as being unable to offer themselves as equal partners in marriage unless they brought some stereotypical female value to the arrangement, especially the promise of children. Moreover, they considered that once a man had "got them pregnant," he had some obligation to fulfil his end of the bargain by providing her with institutional status through marriage. Like Benson's student, these women are acting on internalized norms, which they accept. Even if they had not sufficiently attended to the process of formation of their preference to take a contraceptive risk, it is unlikely that they would have resisted that process, and hence the counterfactual condition does not rule out their autonomy with respect to the preference.

The Self-Knowledge Condition

A second condition of autonomous critical reflection that has been offered is that the agent not be self-deceived in the formation of her desires and preferences. For example, Diana Meyers claims that acting on one's authentic self, and hence being autonomous, is the result of successfully exercising a number of skills, one of which is the skill of self-discovery. She says that a typical autonomous person displays "active involvement in shaping herself and intimate knowledge of her evolving self."[27] For Meyers, the authentic self is not something hidden and static, which autonomous people successfully reveal to themselves; rather it is generated through the exercise of the further skills of self-direction and self-definition. Christman also includes a self-knowledge condition, which he describes as the requirement that agents not tell themselves a "cover story" about the process of development of their preferences.[28]

Recall that one of the costs of contraception described by Luker is the cost of acknowledging oneself as an active sexual agent. If Luker's subjects are radically self-deceived (as Anderson suggests[29]) because they do not acknowledge themselves as active sexual agents, it is hard to see how they could satisfy the self-knowledge condition. On the other hand, the motivations of Luker's subjects are diverse and complex, and there is no uniform lack of acknowledgment *to oneself* of one's sexual agency among them. Consider the following two contrasting cases:

I: Did you ever think about getting pregnant?

R: Sometimes I thought about it, but I didn't really pay too much attention, because we weren't really into . . . we were goofing around . . . in an intimate . . .

I: Could you clarify that?

R: We started in on one thing and then we would go on to another thing and finally we would have intercourse. We never said, "Well, we're going to do it today." It just happened.

(It "just happened" almost every night for over a year.)[30]

I: You said that you had used the pill previously but had run out. Where did you get the pills the first time?

R: A family-planning clinic in Southwest City.

I: Why didn't you get the prescription filled?

R: Because of my father. . . . We live in a small town, and the medical and dental people are very close, and I couldn't go to another doctor without his finding out and I think that would hurt him.[31]

A lack of acknowledgment *to oneself,* which amounts to self-deception, as in the first case, should be distinguished from a lack of acknowledgment *to others,* as in the second. In the second case, although the agent is influenced by norms of sexual agency to the extent that she wishes to be seen to be observing them, she is not deceiving herself about either the norms she subscribes to or the influence of the norms on her preference formation. Her case is not one of *self*-deception.

Nor are different kinds of cases described by Luker obvious cases of self-deception. One set of examples is of women who wish to engage in an active sex life while at the same time being committed to religious or feminine norms that restrict women's sexual agency. The motivations of such women are conflicting, and their decisions not to plan for sex, and hence not to use adequate contraception, are attempts to reconcile their conflicting desires. These women face an unfortunate dilemma, and it may be weak-willed not to either wholeheartedly reject the norms and plan for contraception or wholeheartedly accept the norms and forego an active sex life. However, weakness of will does not amount to self-deception. Another set of examples is that in which women hope for pregnancy in the misguided belief that it will promote their self-worth or increase their value as potential marriage partners. Although these women are in the grip of false norms of femininity and sexual agency, it does not follow that they are self-deceived about the influence of the norms on their decision to take a contraceptive risk. Thus, although it is plausible that the autonomy of the agent for whom sex "'just happened' every night for almost a year" is extinguished as a result of her lack of self-knowledge, this is not the case for most of Luker's subjects. In most cases, the decision to take a contraceptive risk is the product of a complex array of factors, including a wish, based on pragmatic reasons, not to be *seen to be* violating norms of female sexual agency.

The Internal Coherence Condition

It has been proposed that the desires and preferences of autonomous people must be *integrated* in some sense. I examine two ways of spelling out the notion of integration in this and the following sections: integration as internal coherence and integration as endorsement. Christman's "minimal rationality" offers one kind of internal coherence condition. His requirement demands that there be no *manifest* inconsistencies among the beliefs and desires in the set of beliefs and desires that contribute to the processes of reflection.[32] Since minimal rationality is understood as internal consistency among agents' beliefs and desires, not as consistency between beliefs and the world, it is an internalist requirement of rationality. Marilyn

Friedman suggests another kind of internal coherence condition. She argues that higher- and lower-order desires must be integrated in the sense that higher-order desires are subject to revision in light of lower-order desires, and vice versa. In her account, autonomy requires a reflective equilibrium among higher- and lower-order desires.[33]

To judge whether Luker's subjects violate an internal coherence condition, we need a fine-grained account of the kinds of inconsistencies among desires that can plausibly be said to be autonomy undermining. Many inconsistencies, especially conflicts among first-order desires, are innocuous and should not count as autonomy undermining, even if contained within the desire set leading to the formation of the relevant preference. Moreover, some types of incoherence seem to be *required* by proper processes of rational reflection. Indeed, this situation is typical of members of oppressed groups who are attempting to integrate the norms that govern themselves with those that govern a nonoppressed outside world.[34]

Consider again the difference between the woman whose "decision" to risk sexual intercourse without contraception is the product of paralyzing ambivalence and the woman whose decision not to use contraception is the result of a conflict between the desire to have sex and the desire not to reveal her sex life to her father. The former is plausibly an example of a manifest breakdown of internal coherence, whereas the latter is closer to a conflict among first-order desires, which should not be characterized as autonomy undermining. This is so in particular if the motivation for her behavior is to be seen by her father as acting on the basis of acceptable norms, rather than the norms of femininity or religion per se. The decision not to use contraception in these particular circumstances is an imaginative way of bringing the values of respect for one's parents into reflective equilibrium with first-order desires.

Only a minority of Luker's subjects display a level of ambivalence that is sufficiently extreme to count as a *manifest* violation of the internal coherence condition. Yet many are torn between the norms of sexual agency that apply to women as an oppressed group and the norms of sexual agency that *should* apply to them, that is, the norms that apply to the relatively nonoppressed group of men. On the one hand, the decisions of Luker's subjects are influenced by stereotypical ideas, such as that sexual intercourse is appropriate for women only within marriage or a similarly committed relationship; on the other hand, their decisions reflect the influence of more "liberated" notions of sexual agency. Does this constitute autonomy-undermining internal incoherence?

Luker's subjects are often attempting to reconcile the norms of the two groups to which they belong: the preliberated group, to whom the stereotypes of female sexual agency are applicable, and the postliberated group of active sexual agents in whom the difference between the sexes is not salient. This kind of situation is typical of members of oppressed groups. For example, Cheshire Calhoun argues that it is precisely this kind of ambivalence that is experienced by women who are both Latina and lesbian.[35] The sexual norms imposed by Hispanic communities are often irreconcilable with those of the gay and lesbian communities. Hence, for someone in such a situation, experiencing ambivalence about both their sexual and their Hispanic identities is an inevitable consequence of reflecting on the situation in which they find themselves. Although Calhoun's argument is a discussion of internal co-herence as a necessary condition of integrity, not of autonomy, her conclusions par-allel those appropriate for the latter. She argues that the ambivalence or internal in-coherence of such agents does not undermine their integrity because integrity in fact *requires* that agents who are members of different groups simultaneously face up to the ambivalence inherent in their experience. Similarly, the ambivalence experienced by Luker's subjects is often a product of an attempt to liberate themselves from the oppressive norms of sexual agency that are applied to the group of women. It does not constitute a manifest breakdown in the capacity for critical reflection, which would be incompatible with autonomy. Rather, a proper exercise of critical reflec-tion requires acknowledgment of the incoherence inherent in one's circumstances.

Procedural theories rely on characterizing autonomous preference formation as the result of processes of critical reflection. For internal incoherence to count as being incompatible with autonomy, therefore, it must be sufficiently problematic to count as a breakdown of the processes of critical reflection required by procedural accounts. I suggest that only extreme breakdowns of coherence are problematic enough to count.

The Endorsement Condition

An alternative way of understanding the integration condition is as that of iden-tification or endorsement rather than simply consistency or internal coherence. In Frankfurt's account, for example, first-order desires are autonomous just in case they are endorsed by second-order desires. More precisely, a first-order desire is autonomous only if an agent has a second-order desire (a second-order "volition") that the first-order desire be effective.[36] A good example of a failure of endorsement being autonomy undermining is Frankfurt's example of the unwilling addict. The unwilling addict has a desire to take drugs but a desire to desire not to take drugs. He does not therefore desire that the first-order desire be effective; it is not endorsed by a second-order volition. This suggests that his first-order desire is not under his control and that it is not autonomous.[37]

Failure to satisfy an endorsement condition is a possible way of explaining the prima facie nonautonomy of some of Luker's subjects. For example, many desire premarital sex yet do not seem to endorse this desire at the second-order level. In Frankfurt's terms, they do not "have the will they want" because at a second-order level, they want their behavior to be governed by norms of femininity or religion that are incompatible with having premarital sex. Thus, since a decision to take a contraceptive risk is a product of an unendorsed first-order desire, it is not au-tonomous.

For most of the subjects, however, the motivational structure is not as simple as this. First, in many cases of the tacit bargaining that Luker describes, there is no fail-ure to endorse the first-order preference to take a contraceptive risk. Consider a woman who thinks that deliberate planning for sex is distasteful and also that get-ting pregnant will have the benefit of testing her partner's commitment to her. The cost of using contraception together with the benefit of not using it lead her to de-cide to take a contraceptive risk. In this kind of case the preference seems to be endorsed by a set of norms, all of which lead in the same direction, that is, *against* using contraception. Second, several of Luker's cases are ones in which the second-order desires conflict, not those in which there is a failure to endorse a first-order desire. Anderson observes that Luker's subjects are often "caught between contradictory norms of femininity," for example, that it is not nice to have premarital sex and that in situations of sexual intimacy, women should subordinate their desires to those of their male partners.[38] In cases in which a woman's partner wishes to have premarital sex, the norms come into conflict. If any of Luker's subjects, or women like them, are in the grip of conflicting or contradictory norms such as these, a conflict of desire at the first-order level can be traced back to one at the second-order level. It is not a case, as in the unwilling addict, of a conflict between an unendorsed first-order desire and a second-order volition because here *both* first-order desires are endorsed at a second-order level.[39] If I am right, the endorsement condition will not explain the nonautonomy of many of Luker's subjects.

The Inhibiting Factors Condition

The final condition I wish to address is articulated by Christman. He claims that the lack of resistance to the development of a preference or desire must not have taken place (or would not have taken place) under the influence of factors that inhibit self-reflection (unless exposure to such factors was autonomously chosen, in which case that choice had to be made without such factors).[40] There are at least two kinds of factors that might inhibit self-reflection, external factors and internal factors. An example of the former is offered by Christman's own "happy slave" case. Suppose a "'happy slave' has expunged her desires for freedom only as a result of the oppressive presence of the restraints she faces."[41] In other words, the slave has adapted to the oppressive circumstances imposed on her and no longer desires to be free of them. Her desires are nevertheless not autonomous, even if she has not resisted their process of formation, because the desires to adapt and remain unfree were formed only as a result of the presence of oppressive external factors that she could not avoid. External factors that operate to inhibit self-reflection are not present in the case of Luker's subjects. Unlike happy slaves, Luker's subjects are not subject to external constraints that make it impossible to extract themselves from an oppressive situation. Their lack of resistance to the formation of the preference to take a contraceptive risk is not the product of adapting to circumstances that they cannot avoid.

There are several kinds of internal factors that might inhibit self-reflection. The classic examples are those of obsession, addiction, and compulsion. A different kind of internal factor that inhibits self-reflection is one that derives from certain norms of femininity themselves. For example, historically women have been characterized as emotional rather than rational, as agents whose motivations are influenced more by intuition than by careful critical scrutiny. If childhood socialization has encouraged the internalization of such norms, an agent may simply fail to develop the capacity to critically examine her own motivations in the way required for autonomy. Thus, even if she does not resist the process of development of her desires, the lack of a sufficient capacity to reflect on her motivational structure may be an inhibiting factor, undermining the autonomy of those desires.

The question of whether internal factors are present to inhibit Luker's subjects' capacity for self-reflection is difficult to answer. As Meyers has pointed out, feminine socialization typically hampers the development of the skills of critical reflection that are essential for an agent to have a high degree of autonomy.[42] Since there are degrees of capacities for autonomy, however, feminine socialization will not extinguish female agents' autonomy altogether. Even women socialized through stereotypical feminine socialization will often have developed good capacities for critical reflection and hence for autonomy. Thus it would be rash to conclude that Luker's subjects have severely hampered critical capacities, to the extent that their preferences to take contraceptive risks, and indeed most of their other preferences, are automatically nonautonomous. Moreover, such a conclusion would fly in the face of Luker's own description of her subjects as bargainers.

Normative Competence Theories

None of the five conditions that I have extracted from procedural theories of autonomy vindicates the feminist intuition. If I am right, feminists who endorse both the intuition and a procedural theory of autonomy are faced with a dilemma: either they reject the intuition, or they reject the position that procedural conditions are sufficient for autonomy. In this section, I look at two different *substantive* theories of autonomy. Both are normative competence theories and both have been defended (at different times) by Paul Benson. I suggest that only the stronger of the two theories fully explains the feminist intuition, and hence unless feminists reject the intuition, they must take on the task of defending this stronger theory.

The weaker normative competence theory offers the following necessary condition of autonomy: agents must have a "sense of worthiness to act [which involves] regarding oneself as being competent to answer for one's conduct in light of normative demands that, from one's point of view, others might appropriately apply to one's actions."[43] One element of the conception of autonomy endorsed by Anderson—that agents fail to be autonomous when they fail to regard themselves as "self-originating sources of claims"—could be explicated by using a normative competence theory of this kind. To say that agents must regard themselves as the self-originating sources of claims suggests that agents must have a subjective sense of their authority to answer for their own preferences and actions. Agents who lack this subjective sense, through lack of self-confidence, self-trust, or self-esteem, will fail to be autonomous.[44] An example of an agent who lacks normative competence is Benson's "gaslighted" woman. This woman has characteristics—she is passionate, excitable, and "prone to emotional outbursts in public"—as a result of which her husband and the scientific establishment believe that she is significantly unstable. Since she trusts these external judgments of her character and behavior, her sense of her own competence as an agent capable of answering normative demands placed on her is seriously eroded. Her disorientation and self-conception as crazy undermine her capacity for autonomy without undermining the capacities for critical reflection required for autonomy by procedural theories.[45]

The stronger normative competence theory claims that what is required for autonomy is "an ability to criticize courses of action competently by relevant normative standards."[46] Benson argues that the effective internalization of false or irrelevant norms together with the fact that such norms *are* false or irrelevant diminish or extinguish agents' capacities for autonomy with respect to decisions governed by the norms. As Christman puts it, in this theory, normative competence, and hence autonomy, is impaired because agents do not "have an understanding of the correct norms applying to their actions."[47] An example of an agent who lacks autonomy on the stronger but not the weaker normative competence theory is that of Benson's eighteen-year-old student who has internalized the norm purveyed by the fashion industry that most women's natural physical appearance is deficient. The very internalization of the norm blocks her capacity to effectively criticize this "false construal of [her] personal value," and hence she fails to be autonomous with respect to the domain of her decision making that is governed by the norm.[48]

The weaker normative competence theory might be thought, prima facie, to explain failures of autonomy in Luker's subjects. First, certain subjects believe that pregnancy and motherhood will raise their self-esteem and their standing as women in the eyes of family members or society at large. This suggests that they have a low sense of self-worth, which may hamper their normative competence. Second, Anderson observes that Luker's subjects sometimes frame their actions as excuses, especially as excuses for not having sex with their partners. She argues that to do so "is to concede his presumptive authority over one's actions" and hence to fail to regard one's claims as self-authorizing or originating.[49] If she is right, perhaps this indicates that Luker's subjects do not regard *themselves*—but rather their partners or society—as normatively competent. Third, certain of Luker's subjects are ashamed of their sexual agency, and as Benson points out, shame is sometimes sufficient to erode the sense of self-worth necessary for normative competence.[50]

Let us consider each reason in turn. Certain subjects do judge (at the time of deciding whether to use contraception) that the benefits of pregnancy outweigh the disadvantages precisely because they accept the norm that pregnancy and motherhood increase women's worthiness. If their low self-esteem involves a failure to regard themselves as competent to answer others' expectations and demands, a decision to take contraceptive risks may fail to be autonomous. On the other hand, accepting and acting on the norm that pregnancy increases self-worth suggests that the women concerned take themselves as competent to answer the normative demands that they regard as applicable to them. The wish to become pregnant is precisely a wish to increase their self-esteem by increasing their standing in the normative community to which they belong. The sense of self-worth that is lacking in Luker's subjects is not tied in the appropriate way to a lack of a sense of normative competence. Neither does framing a reason as an excuse convincingly show that the agent lacks the relevant kind of self-worth. Framing a reason as an excuse could indicate weakness of will or a desire to resolve conflict in a nonconfrontational way, rather than a failure to regard oneself as normatively competent. Even if it does indicate a failure of a sense of self-worth sufficient to undermine normative competence, only a small minority of Luker's subjects use the decision not to use contraception as an excuse. Yet, by hypothesis, *most* of Luker's subjects' decision making, even when not characterized as an excuse, is informed by oppressive and misguided norms and hence is not autonomous. Finally, whether or not shame is sufficient to undermine one's sense of normative competence is a matter of degree. Whereas many of Luker's subjects are ashamed to some degree of their desire for sexual agency, most do not exemplify a level of breakdown of the sense of self-worth sufficient to undermine their capacity to regard themselves as members of the normative community. In the case of Benson's gaslighted woman, the sense of self-worth that is eroded is precisely the sense of worthiness to participate as a full member of the normative community. However, the shame experienced by Luker's subjects is typically a *result* of failing to desire to live up to norms—those of religion or femininity— that the subjects take as applicable to them. This suggests that whereas they are often wrong in their judgment that those particular norms apply to them, they are not failing to take themselves as normatively competent to answer the demands that from their point of view others appropriately apply to them.

The intuition that Luker's subjects are not autonomous is underpinned not by the lack of normative competence in the weaker sense but rather by the lack of normative competence in the stronger sense. Women who accept the norm that pregnancy and motherhood increase their worthiness accept something *false*. And because of the internalization of the norm, they do not have the capacity to perceive it as false. Most of Luker's examples can be explained in these terms. The reason that Luker's subjects are judged not to be autonomous is that the reasons weighed up in the bargaining process—the costs of active sexual agency, as well as the benefits of pregnancy—are often derived from false norms that have been internalized, such as that women should not actively desire sex or prepare for sex in advance, that pregnancy is an expression of "real" womanhood, or that pregnancy is likely to lead to a marriage commitment from one's partner and that this is a good thing. It is the content of these norms that can be criticized from a feminist point of view, not the way in which Luker's subjects engage in the bargaining process. To vindicate the feminist intuition that the subjects are not autonomous, therefore, feminists need to develop a strong substantive theory of autonomy.[51]

Notes

1. I am grateful to Linda Barclay, Ian Gold, Catriona Mackenzie, and an audience at the Department of Philosophy, Wollongong University, for helpful comments on earlier drafts of this article.

2. Gerald Dworkin, *The Theory and Practice of Autonomy* (New York: Cambridge University Press, 1988), especially chap. 1; John Christman, "Autonomy: A Defense of the Split-Level Self," *Southern Journal of Philosophy* 25 (1987): 395–420; "Autonomy and Personal History," *Canadian Journal of Philosophy* 20 (1990): 1–24; and "Liberalism and Individual Positive Freedom," *Ethics* 101 (1991): 343–359.

3. For discussions of the notion of content-neutrality, see Christman, "Autonomy and Personal History" and Paul Benson, "Free Agency and Self-Worth," *Journal of Philosophy* 91(1994): 650–668.

4. Jennifer Nedelsky, "Reconceiving Autonomy: Sources, Thoughts and Possibilities," *Yale Journal of Law and Feminism* 1 (1989): 7–36, 12.

5. Marilyn Friedman, "Autonomy and Social Relationships: Rethinking the Feminist Critique," in *Feminists Rethink the Self*, ed. Diana Tietjens Meyers (Boulder, CO: Westview, 1997). Quote from Nedelsky, "Reconceiving Autonomy," p. 12. See Diana T. Meyers, *Self, So-*

ciety, and Personal Choice (New York: Columbia University Press, 1989), for an extensive discussion of the ways in which socialization affects the development of capacities for autonomy.

6. Kristin Luker, *Taking Chances: Abortion and the Decision Not to Contracept* (Berkeley: University of California Press, 1975). I am indebted to a paper by Elizabeth Anderson, "Should Feminists Reject Rational Choice Theory?" presented to the APA Eastern Division Meetings, 30 December 1996, which suggested the idea of using Luker's examples to discuss autonomy. I have benefited greatly from Anderson's discussion. All references to Anderson's as yet unpublished paper are with permission.

7. Paul Benson defends substantive theories of autonomy in "Freedom and Value," *Journal of Philosophy* 84 (1987): 465–486; "Feminist Second Thoughts about Free Agency," *Hypatia* 3 (1990): 47–64; "Autonomy and Oppressive Socialization," *Social Theory and Practice* 17 (1991): 385–408; and "Free Agency and Self-Worth." My approach in this article owes a great deal to Benson's work. Sarah Buss defends a different kind of substantive theory in "Autonomy Reconsidered," in vol. 19 of *Midwest Studies in Philosophy*, ed. P. A. French, T. A. Uehling and H. K. Wettstein (Minneapolis: University of Minnesota Press, 1994): 95–121. Substantive theories are discussed in greater length in Catriona Mackenzie and Natalie Stoljar, "Autonomy Refigured," in this volume.

8. Luker, *Taking Chances*, p. 13.

9. Ibid., pp. 20, 23–24.

10. Ibid., pp. 17, 34–35.

11. Ibid., p. 17.

12. For example, Christman, "Liberalism and Individual Positive Freedom," pp. 349–351.

13. For a discussion of autonomy as rationality, see Richard Lindley, *Autonomy* (London: Macmillan, 1986), chap. 2. For Susan Wolf's theory of autonomy, see *Freedom within Reason* (New York: Oxford University Press, 1990). In *A Theory of Justice*, Rawls defines persons as autonomous when they act from principles that express their nature as free and rational beings: *A Theory of Justice* (Oxford: Oxford University Press, 1971), p. 515.

14. Anderson, "Should Feminists Reject Rational Choice Theory?" pp. 8–9.

15. Ibid., p. 10.

16. Ibid., pp. 10, 25. The latter formulation corresponds to Rawls's formulation of autonomy in "Kantian Constructivism in Moral Theory: The Dewey Lectures," *Journal of Philosophy* 77 (1980), 515–572, 543.

17. Luker, *Taking Chances*, p. 46; for a full description of the bargaining process, see chaps. 4 and 5.

18. Ibid., p. 45.

19. Ibid., pp. 47–48.

20. Ibid., p. 48.

21. Ibid., p. 68.

22. Christman, "Autonomy and Personal History" and "Liberalism and Individual Positive Freedom," p. 347.

23. Joel Feinberg, "Autonomy," in *The Inner Citadel: Essays on Individual Autonomy*, ed. John Christman (New York: Oxford University Press, 1989), p. 42.

24. Ibid.

25. Benson, "Autonomy and Oppressive Socialization," p. 389.

26. Luker, *Taking Chances*, p. 70

27. Meyers, *Self, Society, and Personal Choice*, p. 47.

28. Christman, "Autonomy and Personal History," p. 17.

29. Anderson, "Should Feminists Reject Rational Choice Theory?" p. 25.

30. Luker, *Taking Chances*, p. 4.

31. Ibid., p. 44.

32. Christman, "Liberalism and Individual Positive Freedom," pp. 349–351.

33. Marilyn Friedman, "Autonomy and the Split-Level Self," *Southern Journal of Philosophy* 24 (1986): 19–35.

34. For a detailed discussion, see Diana Tietjens Meyers, "Intersectional Identity and the Authentic Self? Opposites Attract," in this volume.

35. Cheshire Calhoun, "Standing for Something," *Journal of Philosophy* 92 (1995): 235–260, 236–241.

36. Harry Frankfurt, "Freedom of the Will and the Concept of a Person," *Journal of Philosophy* 68 (1971): 5–20.

37. Notice that an alternative explanation for the lack of control here is that the desire is the product of addiction.

38. Anderson, "Should Feminists Reject Rational Choice Theory?" p. 26.

39. The situation attracts one of the common objections to Frankfurt's theory, namely, that the endorsement condition introduces a regress. When agents experience conflicts among second-order desires, Frankfurt's theory must introduce a third-order level at which one of the second-order desires must be endorsed for it, rather than the others, to count as autonomous. See Gary Watson, "Free Agency," *Journal of Philosophy* 72 (1975): 205–220.

40. Christman, "Liberalism and Individual Positive Freedom," p. 347.

41. Ibid., p. 354.

42. Meyers, *Self, Society, and Personal Choice.*

43. Benson, "Free Agency and Self-Worth," p. 660.

44. For a development of the idea that a sense of self-trust is necessary for autonomy, see Carolyn McLeod and Susan Sherwin, "Relational Autonomy, Self-Trust, and Health Care for Patients Who Are Oppressed," in this volume.

45. Benson, "Free Agency and Self-Worth," pp. 655–657.

46. Benson, "Freedom and Value," p. 469.

47. Christman, "Liberalism and Individual Positive Freedom," p. 357.

48. Ibid., p. 389.

49. Anderson, "Should Feminists Reject Rational Choice Theory?" p. 26.

50. Benson, "Free Agency and Self-Worth," pp. 657–659.

51. As Benson has noted, there are prima facie objections to a strong normative competence theory. He accepts the objection that a strong normative competence theory like his or Susan Wolf's conflates autonomy with responsibility (ibid., p. 660). This is one reason he now rejects the strong theory. However, Philip Pettit and Michael Smith offer a set of arguments for a version of a normative competence theory in which autonomy is conceptually linked to responsibility. Hence they implicitly respond to the charge that strong normative competence accounts of autonomy conflate autonomy and responsibility. See "Backgrounding Desire," *Philosophical Review* 94 (1990): 565–592; "Practical Unreason," *Mind* 102 (1993): 53–79; and "Freedom in Belief and Desire," *Journal of Philosophy* 93 (1996): 429–449. Moreover, there may be other ways of spelling out the strong substantive component of autonomy than by using a notion of normative competence.

5

INDIVIDUALS, RESPONSIBILITY, AND THE PHILOSOPHICAL IMAGINATION[1]

Genevieve Lloyd

The "Situated" Self: Feminist Critique of Individualism

Themes of connection and interdependence have been strong in feminist ethics, political theory, and epistemology. Many feminist philosophers have emphasized the need for a relational approach to selfhood—the need to highlight the connections between persons rather than what separates them, community rather than individuality, sociability rather than the solitary self. The nature of the desired conceptual shift is illustrated in, for example, Virginia Held's *Feminist Morality*. Held describes feminist reconceptualization of the concept of the self as a challenge to "standard moral theory." "To be adequate," she says, "moral theories must pay attention to the neglected realm of particular others in the actual relationships and actual contexts of women's experience."[2] Social relationships, especially that between "mothering person" and child, move to the center of Held's refocused approach to ethical theory. Feminist philosophers are urged to recognize the centrality of human projects of nurturance and growth to our understanding of moral subjects. Although some feminists have suggested that friendship should be the central category to be contrasted with the "rational contracting" of standard moral theory, mothering relations have for Held the advantage of being more distant from, and hence more challenging to, common preoccupation with contractual relations.[3]

I do not wish to deny that it can be an enlightening thought experiment to attempt

112

to think through what is lacking—what is distorted or remains unrepresented— when we think about relations of nurturance or friendship through the idea of the "contracting individual." That construct undoubtedly fits some forms of social interaction better than others. In seeing where it does not fit, we become more reflectively aware of areas of human life that have been neglected in ethical, political, and epistemological theory. There is, nonetheless, something perplexing about the relations between such feminist attempts at reconceptualization and the theories they try to challenge. There are unresolved methodological issues here. Can we really replace at will in our theorizing the model of contracting individual with that of mothering person or friend and have the alternatives serve the same function as those they replace? If not, what light does that throw on the point and scope of moral theory and on how it might change under the impact of feminist critique?

The exercise of imagination is often central to feminist challenges to moral theory. Often their implicit strategy is to take a theoretical model that has become so familiar as to be invisible and confront it with undertheorized areas of experience. In trying to think of friendship or nurturance in terms of contracting individuals, we become aware of a misfit or distortion. In moving between concrete experience and theoretical constructs of selves in relation, we are aware of a greater dissonance in the area of human nurturance or friendship than in more commercial interactions, which may indeed have provided the original context of the model. The dissonance confronts us with the lack of appropriate theoretical models for neglected areas of human interaction; it also makes visible things we might otherwise miss about common theoretical models of selfhood. The methodological point is spelled out by Seyla Benhabib, in the introduction to *Situating the Self,* where she argues that the Enlightenment conception of a "disembedded and disembodied" subject can be seen to be an illusion when we confront it with the realities of human development, which force us to recognize that "subjects of reason" can be "finite, embodied and fragile creatures" such as human infants.[4]

In challenging received models of selfhood, feminist critics do not thereby offer new conceptual models or alternative, competing theories of what is involved in selfhood. Feminist philosophy does not change moral or political theory simply by slotting mothering person, friend, or infant into the places traditionally occupied by contracting individual. The confrontation of abstract models with concrete realities is just the beginning of the exercise of reconceptualization. What must come next is the challenge of thinking through what is involved in relations of interdependence to give content to the desired reconceptualization of the self.

In this article I want to open up some of these issues in the reconceptualizing of selfhood by exploring a social phenomenon whose reality challenges, from a different direction, some of the same assumptions addressed in feminist discussion of the "situated" self: the fact that individuals can take responsibility for things that lie beyond the scope of their individual agency. The collective dimensions of responsibility intersect with the collective dimensions of selfhood. By looking more closely at the processes through which we make ourselves responsible for what we have not ourselves done—the processes through which human beings enter relations of solidarity that challenge oppositions between self and other—we can gain insight into how our models of selfhood might change to accommodate the realities of interdependence. The crucial shifts, I argue, involve a new emphasis on the temporal dimensions of selfhood.

Imagining Responsibility

Although collective responsibility has received considerable philosophical attention in recent years, there is a striking rigidity in the conceptualization of what is involved in being a bearer of responsibility. Acceptance of the claim that responsibility can be a collective matter seems to have had little impact on how we think of selfhood and agency. Even when responsibility is attributed explicitly to collectivities, the idea of the individual seems to have a grip on the philosophical imagination, which resists conceptual change. In trying to make sense of collective responsibility, we may think of the collectivity as an overarching super individual, whose responsibilities are not reducible to those of the individuals that compose it; alternatively, we may think of the collectivity as a fiction, whose responsibilities can ultimately be cashed out in terms of the familiar old individuals who have traditionally borne them. We see these alternatives, for example, in how we think of corporations when attributing praise or blame to them, holding them accountable for policies that produce unjust or inequitable outcomes. In some circumstances the responsibilities of the corporation are regarded as distributing to the individuals that compose them; in others the collectivity itself is treated as having responsibilities that do not thus distribute. Either way, our conceptualization of responsibility remains centered on the idea of the individual.

Paradoxically, in its very insistence on claims of collective responsibility, philosophical discussion seems to have entrenched the grip of the individual as a theoretical construct. With regard to responsibility, collectivities seem to function as metaphorical extensions of individual persons. As bearers of responsibility they are centers of agency and hence appropriate objects of praise and blame. There is nothing amiss in this. Collectivities are appropriately held responsible for what they do; and the possibility of moving between their responsibilities and the allocation of responsibilities to individuals is crucial to many important issues of accountability. My concern here is with the idea of the individual through which we think these collective responsibilities. How might we think of selfhood if we let our imagination run from the collectivity to the individual rather than in the other direction? Imaginatively accommodating the realities of collective responsibility might change how we think of both selfhood and responsibility. It would allow, I hope to show, some shift of emphasis away from preoccupation with issues of praise and blame, as well as some insight into less individualistic ways of thinking of selfhood.

By thinking through what is involved in the relations of sympathetic identification and solidarity involved in friendship we can gain insight into the nexus between individual and collective identity—between a self and its "other selves." Understanding the kinds of connection between selves that undermine easy oppositions between individual and group—between self-interest and concern for the good of others—can clarify the limitations of prevailing notions of selfhood and open up space in which we can begin to transform them. To bring the issues into focus, I want now to look at two illustrations of the interactions between relations of sympathetic identification and responsibility. The first example comes from the reflections on friendship and responsibility offered by Jacques Derrida in *Memoires for Paul de Man*, the second from the depiction of solidarity and self-sacrifice in Pat Barker's novel *Regeneration*.

Friendship and Solidarity

In "Like the Sound of the Sea Deep Within a Shell: Paul de Man's War," published as an addition to the revised edition of *Memoires for Paul de Man*, Derrida addresses the scandal of allegedly anti-Semitic journalism published by the young de Man in occupied Belgium, between 1940 and 1942.[5] Derrida's essay is a richly layered set of reflections on interwoven aspects of responsibility, especially its connections with friendship and with time. It is written out of the distress of bereaved friendship, in response to the discovery of allegedly anti-Semitic remarks in articles written by de Man in journals associated with Nazi collaborators. As well as being a *response* to the scandal, the essay is also a highly self-conscious reflective act of *taking* responsibility out of friendship with the dead. Themes of time, memory, and mourning run through the essay. The connections between memory and responsibility had been already addressed in the earlier lectures in the volume, where Derrida's reflections on bereaved friendship are woven into his rereading of de Man's own writings on memory, mourning, and autobiography. Memory and responsibility, Derrida suggests in the preface to the French edition, cannot here be thought without one another: "What is recalled to memory calls one to responsibility."[6]

Those themes from the earlier essays in the volume take on added poignancy with the subsequent eruption of the scandal. Derrida's reflections on the impact of later events on how the earlier ones are construed present the future rather than the past as the primary perspective for the consciousness of temporality. The future makes determinate what occurs in the present. The "absolutely unforeseeable," he says, is always the condition of any event. "Even when it seems to go back to a buried past, what comes about always comes from the future."[7] The point here is not the relatively straightforward one that from the perspective of the present what has not yet happened will come from the future. The point is rather that the determination of what is happening now—the determinate content of what it is—depends on what is now still future. What happens now is determinate only from a perspective not yet available. Yet it is in this indeterminate present that we have to answer, to respond to what is happening. So we *take* responsibility, in situations we neither choose nor control, by responding to unforeseeable appeals, that is, to appeals from the other that are addressed to us "even before we decide on them." Derrida's response, his "answering for" de Man is already implicit in their preexisting friendship, when the appeal is still unforeseeable.[8]

Derrida responds to the scandal out of the promise implicit in a bereaved friendship, which could not anticipate the ordeal the future held in store for that friendship. He responds for de Man, as he says, not "judging or approving" of what he did but speaking once again "of-him-for-him," at a moment when de Man is no longer there to speak in his own name.[9] Since this was a friendship imbued with intellectual life, the response involves assuming an intellectual responsibility to meticulously read the whole body of journalistic writings that form the context of the offensive remarks: "Through the indelible wound, one must still analyze and seek to understand."[10] De Man's legacy becomes "the gift of an ordeal, the summons to a work of reading, historical interpretation, ethicopolitical reflection, an interminable analysis."[11] Derrida responds, then, with resolutely attentive reading and with an attempt to make possible close readings by as many others as choose to read: "As quickly and as radically as possible, it was necessary to make these texts accessible to everyone. The necessary conditions had to be created so that everyone could read them and interpret them in total freedom. No limit should be set on the discussion. Everyone should be in a position to take his or her responsibilities."[12]

The taking of responsibility here is, in Derrida's analysis, not just a standing in for—a speaking in the place of—the friend who, being absent, as it happens, through death, cannot speak for himself. The responsibility enacts the structure of bereaved friendship; it is an answering *to* as much as *for* the friend: "Before answering, responding for oneself and *for* that purpose, in order to do so, one must respond, answer to the other, about the other, *for* the other, not in his place as in the place of another 'proper self' but *for* him."[13] There is, for Derrida, an "impossibility" about this responsibility—an impossibility that arises from its undecidability and reflects the rich concept of "impossible mourning," which he has developed in the earlier essays. In the death of the other we recognize the possibility of the impossible—the interiorization of the other in memory—which in turn encounters the resistance of the other to the closure of that interiorizing memory.[14]

The shifts that occur on the uncertain borders of self and other—of interiorization and recognition of the other—are for Derrida central to the understanding of friendship, of mourning, and of selfhood. Grief brings the attempt to incorporate the lost other into the self—an attempt that is thwarted by the reality of friendship, with its demands for recognition of the other: "An aborted interiorization is at the same time a respect for the other as other, a sort of tender rejection, a movement of renunciation which leaves the other alone, outside, over there, in his death, outside of us."[15] The distinctions between self and other here take on an uncertainty that is unresolvable, for it is an uncertainty that is the very core of friendship, of mourning, and of selfhood itself. The distress the living friend feels is also the distress of the dead. It is in this area of uncertain boundaries—somewhere between the self and the ambiguously other self of the friend—that the realities and the "impossibilities" of both friendship and selfhood are enacted. The ambiguities of self and other here are expressed in our being called to *take* responsibility in circumstances in which we can not be appropriately *held* responsible for what has been done. Contributory guilt is in no way involved in our example; what is at stake is not the issue of blame. Derrida's task in taking responsibility is not that of clearing his dead friend of blame; he cannot know in advance that this is how it will go. The task is to answer for and to his dead friend—to assimilate whatever is found to be true into the ongoing, open-ended, and incompletable task of friendship beyond death.

The complexities of solidarity with the dead and their bearing on issues of responsibility are at stake also in my second illustration from the first volume, *Regeneration*, of Pat Barker's trilogy on the experience and aftermath of shell shock in

World War I. Barker's central character, modeled on the war poet Siegfried Sassoon, is a pacifist, committed to a mental hospital because no one knows quite what else to do with him. Sassoon is readily able—on plausible, even if untrue, medical grounds —to avoid, if he so chooses, being returned to the trenches. (The issue of whether it is Sassoon that is irrational or the principles and practices of wartime Britain is another central theme in the books.) His decision to return is against all self-interest, nor is it motivated by any patriotic altruism. It is also at odds with the pacifist principles Sassoon has embraced.

Barker provides hints to the explanation of her character's apparently strange behavior in fragments of the war poems of the historic Sassoon: a solidarity with the dead and with those awaiting death, which fills his imagination to the point where it excludes all other motivation. Solidarity with the dead sustains the character's sense of self, and with it a sense of responsibility to those no longer able to escape—"the homeless ones, the noiseless dead"—and to those still living, but doomed to death —the "Battalion in the mud:

> Out of the gloom they gather about my bed
> They whisper to my heart, their thoughts are mine.
>
> "Why are you here with all your watches ended?
> 'From Ypres to Frise we sought you in the line."
> In bitter safety I awake, unfriended.[16]

The sense of responsibility here seems irrational. It has nothing to do with the patriotic ideology of self-transcendence or self-sacrifice, which is supposed to sustain the soldiers' lives and give meaning to their impending deaths. Those sentiments are meaningless to Barker's character. He feels lost and angry among his compatriots who are living in England, distanced from the reality of war deaths while they mouth patriotic platitudes. All that engages him are the ties of companionship and loyalty that bind him to the dead and to the about-to-die. Imagination cannot bridge the gap between the vacuously alive and the pointlessly dead. He takes on responsibility out of solidarity with others, with whom he shares the strange middle ground between self and other—the uncertain borders of self articulated in Derrida's talk of the "impossibility" of mourning and of responsibility. For Sassoon it is impossible to continue safely alive while those with whom he shares this shifting selfhood are dead or facing death. Let us now see how all this bears on the broader issues of collective responsibility and selfhood.

Neither of these examples of taking responsibility out of friendship or solidarity can be readily accommodated into our familiar ways of thinking of selves as sharply bordered units. In both examples we see that individuals act out of a sense of themselves as bound up with others, in ways that resist clear-cut divisions between self and other. Their taking of responsibility is explicable only through relations that forge identities, in situations in which there can be no clear-cut distinction between self and other, between egoism and altruism. What emerges is a picture of the construction and constant transformation of identities through relations of sympathetic identification that underlie, but are also themselves made possible by, the taking of responsibility. Responsibilities taken on in this way make visible relations of sympathetic identification through which are constituted the identities of individuals as parts of wider wholes. The examples suggest that the explanation of the fact that responsibility can be a collective matter lies in the fact that the formation of selfhood is also a collective matter. Processes of formation and transformation of selves interact with the assuming of responsibilities, in contexts of interdependence and friendship; and this in turn creates further possibilities of subjectivity and agency.

The illustrations I have chosen are examples of friendship, solidarity, and loyalty. Responsibilities that arise in a context of close friendship operate in some respects, of course, very differently from responsibilities in the context of larger and more impersonal collectivities. But we can gain insight from Derrida's analysis of the responsibilities that are integral to bereaved friendship into something more general: how it is that we can appropriately take responsibility for what we have not ourselves done. The operations of emotion and imagination involved in the formation of social wholes can perhaps be seen more clearly here than in either the formation of more impersonal ties in wider collectivities or in the more intense interweavings of self and other in sexual love or parent-child relations. But wherever processes of sympathetic identification operate, we can see similar enabling shifts between ideas of self and other and similar implications for the temporal dimensions of selfhood.

Derrida's essay shows us that responsibility does not always rest on preexistent identities. The retrospective responsibility for the dead that Derrida describes resists understanding through ideas of free contracts. Responsibilities can be projected back into a past, which precedes the friendships that make them possible; and they can depend on future perspectives, which are in principle unavailable at the time of action. These aspects of responsibility demand models of selfhood that take seriously the temporal dimensions of human consciousness—its complex shifts between past and future. These temporal dimensions of responsibility are interconnected with temporal dimensions of selfhood.

The inherent temporality of selfhood—the multiple forming and re-forming of identities over time and within the deliverances of memory—is an important strand in the political dimensions of collective responsibility. Often those political aspects of responsibility involve our taking responsibility for a past in which we did not ourselves act, perhaps did not even exist. What our forebears did "comes from the future," in Derrida's phrase—the future that is now our present. The retrospective determination of what they did—a perspective not necessarily available to them—is an important part of what we now are; and it is our being what we now are that grounds our taking responsibility in the present, even where there is nothing in the past for which we can be blamed.

The point of bringing consideration of relations of friendship and sympathetic identification to bear on the understanding of collective responsibility is not that preexisting sympathetic identifications constitute a criterion for the attribution of collective responsibility. The point is rather that through understanding those processes in which the taking of responsibility is intertwined with the formation of identities, we can understand how it is that responsibilities can be a collective matter. Emotion plays an important part in the interconnection between responsibility and the formation of identities. But the claim is not that the presence of emotional ties justifies holding people responsible for what they have not themselves done.

Emotion figures rather in the understanding of how individuals come to appropriately *take* responsibility for what they have not themselves done. Having understood that process, we can also see that in some circumstances it may be appropriate to *hold* people responsible for not having thus *taken* responsibility for the past. To clarify what is at stake here, both for responsibility and for selfhood, it is helpful to revisit an old debate in which Joel Feinberg and Hannah Arendt address the question of how emotion—especially sympathetic identification—bears on collective responsibility.

Emotion, Individuals, and Community

In her response to Feinberg's treatment of collective responsibility, Arendt strongly attacks the tendency to conceptualize collective responsibility in terms of shared emotion.[17] Her concern is to establish a firm distinction between guilt and responsibility. Collective responsibility should be understood as a special case of vicarious responsibility; talk of such "misplaced feelings" as vicarious guilt, in contrast, confuses the issues. In postwar Germany, she says the cry, "We are all guilty," which at first sounded so noble, actually served to exculpate to a considerable degree those who actually were guilty. Guilt, unlike responsibility, is "strictly personal"; it always singles out: "Where all are guilty, no-body is."[18]

What is relevant for my purposes in Arendt's criticism of Feinberg is her rejection of the notion of "sympathetic identification," which he invokes to explain the formation of bonds of solidarity that make individuals identify themselves as part of a group. Arendt argues that Feinberg's use of this notion blurs the crucial distinction between guilt and responsibility. But despite Arendt's dismissal of the relevance of sympathetic identification to collective responsibility, we can, in the light of Derrida's reflections, see a place for it in understanding the expansion of subjectivity and agency that makes it possible for individual selves to take responsibility for what they have not done. Such understanding, in turn, can help us to understand an important strand in the notion of collective responsibility.

Arendt's central idea is to insist on the political dimensions of collective responsibility. The term "collective responsibility" and the problems it implies, she suggests, owe their relevance and general interest to political predicaments, as distinct from legal or moral ones, which always relate to persons and what persons have done. These political issues, she argues, should not be allowed to disappear into just a special case of matters subject to "normal legal proceedings" or "normal moral judgments."[19] What is at stake in such discussions of collective responsibility is whether the individual is responsible because of his or her participation in a group undertaking. In her own approach, which stresses in contrast the political dimensions of collective responsibility, the whole point is that the individual is responsible just because of his or her membership in the group. The responsibility belongs to us as members of a community, and we can escape it only by leaving the community—that is, since we cannot live without being in some community or another, by exchanging one community for another. So the only really nonresponsible people, she concludes, are the outcasts—refugees, the stateless.

It is a striking feature of Arendt's analysis of the political form of collective responsibility that it shifts the focus away from issues of blame and guilt to the need for remedy. The concept of collective responsibility, she observes, belongs primarily in situations in which Socrates's question of whether it is worse to do or to suffer evil ceases to be important—where what matters is not who should be blamed but what should be done about it. But what is at stake here is not a generalized response to the presence of injustice or oppression but the assumption of a responsibility that is specifically "ours," despite our not being to blame for the injustice.[20]

Arendt's political form of collective responsibility highlights for us the distance of this concept from the model of the self as "contracting individual." We do not acquire these responsibilities through any decisions we make as individuals, nor do we acquire them by contracting into a group whose actions or policies we thereby accept. We acquire them by being born into a community. These are responsibilities we have just by virtue of being who we are. But if we think of what it is to be a self in terms of a model of self-contained individuals—capable of freely opting in and out of collectivities and contracts—it is difficult to understand how we come to have such responsibilities. In *The Human Condition*, Arendt introduces a concept of "natality" as a kind of second birth, an initiation of words and deeds—a principle of beginning through which we become members of a community. To make sense of the claim that we can be born into responsibilities, she suggests, we must think of the beginning of a self in terms of entry into a community rather than the physical facts of birth.

Such an entry cannot be captured through the idea of a contracting individual, which assumes a preexisting self. Arendt's account of these collective responsibilities seems to demand a complementary account of selfhood. What must a self be if it is possible for it to have such responsibilities? What model of selfhood can accommodate this political form of collective responsibility? How can it be that simply by being born into a community we can be regarded as taking on its burdens of responsibility for past injustices—injustices in the production of which we played no role? Here we see a convergence between the demands that arise from feminist critiques of individualism and the need for a theoretical construction of selfhood and agency that can accommodate the political dimensions of collective responsibility articulated by Arendt. By bringing the two sets of concerns together, we can perhaps make some progress toward a reconceptualization of selfhood and agency that can accommodate both. The consideration of the operations of solidarity and sympathetic identification that Arendt dismisses as irrelevant to the political dimensions of collective responsibility can, at another level, contribute to our understanding of the kind of theoretical construction of selfhood that is needed.

I have argued that we can give content to Arendt's version of collective responsibility by supplementing it with an understanding of the processes of sympathetic identification that allow individuals to take on responsibilities for what they have not themselves done—including actions whose agency lies not only with others but also with the irrevocable absence of the dead. Being attuned to the operations of sympathetic identification can help us see the nexus between self and other that undermines easy oppositions between the individual and the group. It can help us see the join between individual and group identity, as well as the points where the opposition between self-interest and concern for the good of others breaks down. Let us now see what emerges for the reconceptualization of selfhood.

Temporality and the Self

Talk of blurring of the boundaries between self and other quickly becomes vacuous when we think in terms of a spatial imagining of the self; and spatial metaphors are powerful in our prevailing political ideals of selfhood, helping to reinforce the grip on the philosophical imagination of the idea of the sharply bordered individual. Jean Bethke Elshtain has remarked on the interconnections between ideals of individual and political sovereignty in "The Risks and Responsibilities of Affirming Ordinary Life." "What rights have become to individuals in the modern West," she suggests—namely, "marks of a sovereign self"—sovereignty is to states: "the sovereign state is immanentised, thereby constituting a view of citizens, or political subjects, as sovereign selves."[21] Spatial metaphors are caught up in this movement of thought. The sovereignty of the self takes in aspects of the sovereignty of the state, which reinforce our thinking of selves as sharply bordered unities modeled on spatial territories; and the projection operates also in the opposite direction—from the idea of a discrete, self-contained individual to the idea of a sovereign state.

What might it be to think otherwise of the relations between individuals and the collectivities to which they belong, and how might it affect the ways we think of ourselves and of our responsibilities? If we think of agency, letting our imaginations run from the collectivity to the individual rather than in the other direction, the self takes on something of the complexity and multiplicity of a collectivity. But to avoid this collapsing into unhelpful metaphors of blurred spatial borders, we need to make a shift that Derrida's reflections have already prepared us for—a shift from space to time in our imagining of the self. Stressing these temporal dimensions of selfhood can help clarify what is involved in taking responsibility for a past for which we cannot be blamed. Blame for the unjust treatment of Australian indigenous people might belong entirely in the past, but that does not remove present collective responsibility, of the kind Arendt is articulating. Nor is our collective responsibility in the present removed if it can be shown that past policies were blameless by the standards and beliefs that prevailed at the time. We are still responsible in the present, from the perspective of which the determinate content of the evil done by the group with which we are identified is now accessible.

The sovereign, bounded self described by Elshtain is a construct modeled on space—on parts, wholes, and borders. We are responsible, in this way of thinking of selfhood, for what lies on our side of the borders and for the changes that come about beyond those borders as a result of what we do on our side. But we have seen that there are complexities of selfhood and related complexities of responsibility that are not captured by this spatial model—complexities that arise from the temporal aspects of being a self. These complexities spring not from the self's relations with an external world but from its own inner relations with time—from its not being confined to the here and now or even to what has ever been present to it.

Selves struggle for coherence, for unity—struggle to make themselves well-functioning temporal, no less than spatial, wholes, brought together out of the rich but confusing deliverance of memory and imagination. In their relations to time, the limits of selves are less stable than in their spatial dealings with the world. The capacities for memory and imagination, although they may be preconditions for rational agency, are also sources of instability, of a lack of fixity. The capacity to have a past and to reflect on it is crucial to selfhood; and having, in the relevant sense, a past is not something that admits of tidy borders between the individual existence that is mine and the collective existence that precedes me, into which I am born. The fact that a self is intrinsically something that has a past means that there is an internal multiplicity of selfhood, an open-ended source of possibilities for what a self can appropriate and enact. For each self there is a multiplicity of narratives into which it can insert itself and from which it can rupture.

A self is born into a future in which it will make individual decisions, for which it will be held responsible, praised or blamed. But it is also born into the past of its communal life—a past that both precedes it and awaits it; a past of collective memory and imagination—which must be reckoned with in the present. The endless multiplication of possibilities for what a self can be and do is kept under restraint by the limitations of, and on, the here-and-now self that interacts spatially with the world.

Both spatial and temporal dimensions of selfhood are essential. They do not compete for exclusive rights to represent the truth of selfhood, and there is room for disagreement about which of them best helps the theorization of different facets of human action and interaction. They are more like two registers between which we move in attempting to understand selfhood. Neither can be reduced to the other; any more than our responsibilities can always be reduced to those that rest on happenings for which there is some kind of individual to blame.

Notes

1. For helpful comments on earlier versions, I am grateful to Peta Bowden, Lorraine Code, Penelope Deutscher, Moira Gatens, Catriona Mackenzie, Ross Poole, Amélie Rorty, Robert Sparrow, and Natalie Stoljar.

2. Virginia Held, *Feminist Morality: Transforming Culture, Society, and Politics* (Chicago: University of Chicago Press, 1993), p. 59.

3. Ibid., p. 72.

4. Seyla Benhabib, *Situating the Self: Gender, Community and Postmodernism in Contemporary Ethics* (New York: Routledge, 1992), pp. 4–5.

5. Jacques Derrida, *Memoires for Paul de Man*, rev. ed., trans. Cecile Lindsay, Jonathan Culler, Eduardo Cadava, and Peggy Kamuf (New York: Columbia University Press, 1989), pp. 155–263.

6. Ibid., p. xi.

7. Ibid., p. 160.

8. Ibid., p. 164.

9. Ibid., p. 166.

10. Ibid., p. 216.

11. Ibid., p. 229.

12. Ibid., p. 219.

13. Ibid., p. 30.

14. Ibid., pp. 149–150.

15. Ibid., p. 35.

16. Pat Barker, *Regeneration* (London: Penguin, 1992), p. 189.

17. See Joel Feinberg, "Collective Responsibility," *Journal of Philosophy* 65, no. 14 (July 1968): 674–688, and Hannah Arendt, "Collective Responsibility," in *Amor Mundi: Explorations in the Faith and Thought of Hannah Arendt*, ed. James W. Bernauer (Dordrecht: Martinus Nijhoff, 1987), pp. 43–50.

18. Ibid., p. 43.

19. Ibid., p. 44.

20. Here, as elsewhere throughout her work, Arendt makes a sharp distinction between the political and the ethical. For a helpful discussion of the rationale for the sharpness of Arendt's version of this distinction and of the problems it raises, see Seyla Benhabib, "Judgment and the Moral Foundations of Politics in Hannah Arendt's Thought," in *Situating the Self*, pp. 121–147.

21. Jean B. Elshtain, "The Risks and Responsibilities of Affirming Ordinary Life," in *Philosophy in an Age of Pluralism: The Philosophy of Charles Taylor in Question*, ed. James Tully (Cambridge: Cambridge University Press, 1994), p. 76.

6

IMAGINING ONESELF OTHERWISE[1]

Catriona Mackenzie

In the literature on autonomy, a few theorists have suggested in passing that imagination might play a role in autonomous reflection, deliberation, and action. In her account of autonomy competency, for example, Diana Meyers mentions imagination as one of the capacities involved in its exercise and suggests that one way in which autonomous agents can test and refine their self-portraits is through imaginative enactment.[2] It has also been suggested that one way in which oppressive social relationships and institutions may impair autonomy is by restricting agents' imaginative repertoires. Thus, Paul Benson writes that oppressive socialization "can erode competence at rational consideration by restricting persons' capacities for imagining with sufficient sensitivity and seriousness major alterations in the prevalent gender system."[3] Aside from these few remarks, however, the possible relationship between the various activities of the imagination and the capacity for autonomy has not been the subject of serious investigation in the literature. When one reflects on the extent to which our waking mental life is taken up with different kinds of imaginative thought, this neglect is striking and rather puzzling. My conjecture is that this neglect is due to a tendency to think of critical reflection in overly rationalistic terms, at the expense of a recognition of the extent to which critical reflection can be prompted by the imagination and by emotion, desire, and bodily feelings.

This article is largely exploratory, but the exploration is guided by two central aims. First, I want to lay the groundwork for an investigation of the connection between autonomy and the imagination by investigating the role played by imaginative thought in self-understanding, self-reflection, and practical deliberation about the self. To focus my analysis, I concentrate on one kind of imaginative activity only, namely, imagistic or representational thinking. However, the analysis could be extended to other kinds of imaginative mental activity, for example, mental conversations between an agent and an imaginatory interlocutor. My argument is that a variety of different kinds of representational and imagistic thinking play a central but often overlooked role in the processes of self-reflection and deliberation. This role is an ambivalent one. The various activities of the imagination do not always promote adequate self-reflection or ideal deliberation. The imagination can be, and often is, delusional. But because of its affective force and cognitive power, imaginative mental activity is crucial to the various processes by means of which we try to sort out what we want; what matters to us; and what ideals, goals, and commitments shape our lives.

My account of the connections among imagination, self-definition, and deliberation is developed in the first two sections of this article. In the first, I outline Richard Wollheim's analysis of a person's point of view and explain the role played by this notion in Wollheim's accounts of the mental activities of visually remembering, imagining, and previsaging.[4] In the second, I use Wollheim's analysis of a person's point of view to provide an integration account of the process of self-definition. I then argue that imaginative mental activity is central to this process.

The second aim of this article is to suggest that an understanding of the role played by imaginative mental activity in self-reflection and in deliberation about the self can provide some clues about the connection between failures of autonomy and dominant cultural metaphors, symbols, images, and representations or, in short, the cultural imaginary. Feminist philosophers, literary critics, anthropologists, and film theorists, among others, have drawn attention to the way in which normative stereotypes of gender relations and cultural fantasies of sexual difference are enforced and perpetuated through metaphors, symbols, and visual representations.[5] They have also stressed the need for alternative representations by means of which women can structure and understand sexual relationships and their own experience. Even in a context of formal legal equality of opportunity, social reform has limited power to reshape people's lives and opportunities if the cultural imaginary is predominantly phallocentric.

One question that is raised by these analyses, however, is *how* cultural metaphors, symbols, images, and representations can structure the experiences, self-concepts, and gender identities of individuals. Psychoanalysis provides one kind of explanation. In the third section, I sketch out an alternative explanation, one that is not hostile to psychoanalysis but, rather than focusing on the formation of the unconscious, focuses on the self-formative activities of self-reflection and deliberation. Drawing on and extending the account of self-definition developed in the second section, I argue that self-definition is not purely an introspective activity but also depends on social recognition. Understanding the social dimensions of self-definition helps explain the connection, particularly in oppressive social contexts, between the imaginative projects of individuals and the cultural imaginary. The suggestion I develop is that in self-reflection and deliberation, our own imaginative activities, our abilities to imagine ourselves otherwise, draw on a cultural repertoire of images and representations. When this cultural repertoire is predominantly phallocentric, the culturally available images on which women can draw seriously constrain their imaginative possibilities and hence their self-conceptions.

Imagistic Thinking and Point of View

A great deal of our waking mental life consists of imagistic or representational thinking of a variety of kinds. In event or experiential memory, for example, we visualize the event or experience we remember, sometimes as a series of unfolding scenes, sometimes as a succession of disjointed snapshot images. Sometimes one particular image can come to stand for, or be emblematic of, a whole phase of our lives. In future-directed anticipations, or previsaging, we represent our future selves to ourselves, doing, thinking, and feeling what we believe we will be doing, thinking, and feeling at that point in the future. And in imaginative visualizing, or what Richard Wollheim calls iconic imagination, we imagine ourselves, either as ourselves or as someone else, doing what we want or hope to be doing or being the kind of person we might want to be.

Often we simply find ourselves engaged in a sequence of imagistic remembering or imagining or anticipating, and because imagistic thinking has this involutary and associational character we can be quite surprised by what we find ourselves thinking. However, we can also engage voluntarily in these different kinds of representational mental activities, for a range of purposes. We visually rehearse events in the past to convince ourselves that they really happened or to try to understand their significance; we try to visualize the face of a friend who has died or from whom we are separated to remind ourselves of that person; we recall encounters with others to interpret the meaning of their gestures. In previsagement or future-directed anticipation, we represent our future selves and activities to ourselves, perhaps because we dread a possible future situation or something we will have to do. By actively prefiguring the future in this way, we try to prepare ourselves emotionally for what we dread or to think out different ways in which we might be able to handle the situation. Or in other cases, we previsage the future because we might want to experience a foretaste of anticipated future pleasures.

These examples bring out two important features of mental imaging of this kind. First, whether it is voluntarily elicited or whether it surfaces involuntarily, mental imaging has affective force. In visualizing the past, the activity of visualizing very often reactivates at least some of the emotions that we originally experienced and the bodily sensations kindled by them. For example, visualizing a past experience that was embarassing not only rearouses the embarassment but also our cheeks may start to burn. We can find ourselves smiling with joy in anticipation of a future encounter or close to tears as a result of some imaginative sequence, like imagining the death of a child. It is this capacity to arouse and rekindle emotions and bodily sensations that contributes to the psychic force of mental imagery. The second feature of mental imaging of this kind is that partly because of its affective force, it has cognitive power. We use mental imaging not only as a mnemonic device or to provide us with pleasurable relief from the humdrum of our daily lives but also as an aid in understanding ourselves and others.

In *The Thread of Life*, Richard Wollheim develops a detailed analysis of imagistic thinking to explain its affective force and cognitive power within our mental and bodily lives. In this section I outline this analysis, focusing in particular on Wollheim's notion of a person's point of view and on his account of the connections and differences among iconic imagination, event memory, and previsaging. In the next section I then draw on and develop aspects of this analysis to explain the role played by imaginative mental activity in self-definition and self-understanding.

Centrally Imagining

In his discussion of iconic imagination Wollheim draws a distinction between acentered and centered visualizing or imagining.[6] When I am visualizing or imagining acentrally, no point of view is represented in what I imagine. When I am imagining or visualizing centrally, I am imagining from the point of view of someone who is represented in the scene imagined. For example, I can acentrally imagine a scene in which someone is receiving an Oscar. I might be able to imagine the scene in a great deal of detail: I can visualize the audience, the auditorium, the face of the actor receiving the award, and the dignitary presenting it, as well as what they are both wearing. But this visual sequence unfolds in my mind as though I am watching the scene from a distance, uninvolved. By contrast, in centrally imagining, I represent to myself the same scene but this time from the point of view of one of the characters in it, the protagonist. For instance, I imagine that I am the famous actor who is receiving the award.

I want to highlight four features of Wollheim's account of centrally imagining that will be vital to my discussion later. First, although in centrally imagining I represent the imagined scene from the point of view of the protagonist, the protagonist that I imagine need not be the real, empirical me. In some cases the protagonist will be me, and I will imagine the scene from my point of view. In these cases, the act of imagining will not require me to leave behind my character, dispositions, ideals, or my specific body. Indeed, these may inform the nature of the scene visualized, although the act of imagining may involve foregrounding, perhaps exaggerating, certain of my dispositions, characteristics, or capacities and deemphasizing or overlooking others. However, I can also centrally imagine a scene from the point of view of a protagonist who is not me. In these cases I am imagining being someone else, for instance, I can imagine *being* Emma Thompson receiving an Oscar.

In imagining being someone else I suspend my point of view. I don't believe that I am the person I imagine; I just suppose it.[7] Wollheim explains how this is possible by likening centrally imagining to a kind of internal theater, in which the imaginer is simultaneously internal dramatist, internal actor or protagonist, and internal audience. In the imaginative project, these roles are of course not distinguished: "we represent the internal narrative to ourselves even as we concoct it . . . and even as we respond to it."[8] As internal dramatist, the imaginer assigns to herself, as protagonist, lines and actions but also thoughts, feelings, and experiences. These thoughts, feelings, and experiences not only provide the background that makes sense of what she says and does but also provide the perspective through which the other characters appear in the narrative. The other characters appear from her point of view. As internal actor, the imaginer represents to herself the actions, lines, thoughts, feelings, and experiences of the protagonist *as though* they were her own. The qualification "as though" is the important distinguishing mark between centrally imagining being someone else, where the point of view I represent is someone else's, and centrally imagining myself, where I am the protagonist and where the point of view I represent is my own.

In characterizing the internal audience, Wollheim argues that in the activity of centrally imagining, the internal audience is akin to an empathic audience in a theater rather than to either a detached or a sympathetic audience. On the one hand, a detached audience is emotionally uninvolved with the characters, as in Brechtian drama. Thus although it makes favorable or unfavorable judgments about the characters, these judgments do not give rise to any affective response on its part. In contrast, a sympathetic audience *is* emotionally involved with the characters, and its favorable or unfavorable judgments do give rise to the appropriate affective responses. But these responses arise from judgments about the worth or otherwise of the various characters and their actions. On the other hand, the response of an empathic audience is based on affect, rather than judgment, and in particular on an affective response toward a particular character, whom it selects as protagonist and with whom it emotionally identifies. This kind of emotional accord or resonance on the part of the audience need not be accompanied by a favorable judgment of the protagonist's actions or character. One can emotionally identify with a protagonist whom one may nevertheless judge to be despicable. In centrally imagining, the imaginer is like an empathic audience toward her own imagining, and it is her emotional identification with the protagonist she invents or imagines that plays the decisive role in selecting that character as the protagonist of the imagining. Centrally imagining being someone else is adopting another's point of view and emotionally identifying with it.

The second important feature of Wollheim's account of centrally imagining is his insight that this kind of imaginative project has cogency. The mental activity of representing to oneself the thoughts, feelings, and experiences of the protagonist, as though they were one's own, will leave one in the condition—cognitive, conative, affective—that one would be in were one actually to have the mental states one imagines. It is its cogency that gives centrally imagining its psychic force. The degree of cogency of an imagining will, of course, vary according to the extent of the repertoire assigned to the protagonist. In centrally imagining myself, my repertoire will be extensive, and hence the imagining is likely to have a greater degree of cogency. In centrally imagining someone else, my repertoire is likely to be more impoverished and the imagining less psychically cogent. Representing to oneself someone else's point of view, then, involves assuming or adopting that person's repertoire, to the extent that one can.

The third noteworthy feature of centrally imagining is Wollheim's distinction between internal audience and internal observer. As internal audience, the imaginer is part of the imaginative project and is moved cognitively, conatively, and affectively by the imagining in the same way as she would have been moved by the event that the imagining simulates. The internal observer, however, is outside the imaginative project and reflects on and reacts to it with emotions and judgments that may be quite different than those aroused by the imagining. Wollheim gives as an example an erotic daydream in which the imaginer may come to feel sexually aroused by an imagining, but in reflecting on the daydream and the desire it has aroused may react in a whole range of different ways—surprise, embarassment, disgust, or increased arousal. Thus even when I am the protagonist of an imagining, and hence even when the point of view represented in the imagining is my point of view, that point of view need not coincide with my self-conception. I return later to the issues of cogency and to the role played in self-understanding by the possible noncoincidence between the point of view of an imagining and a person's self-conception.

Fourth, and finally, Wollheim makes the important point that we initiate central imagining in the service of two distinct intentions—either to gain knowledge or to experience pleasure or satisfy desire. The imagining will bear different relations to our total body of beliefs, desires, and emotions, depending on which of these intentions it serves. When iconic imagining expresses desire, the repertoire that is invoked in the imagining is intentionally restricted, and beliefs, desires, and emotions that may conflict with the desires that are seeking satisfaction in the imagining are filtered out "so that nothing in my psychology that could disrupt the pleasing effect of imagining desire satisfied is afforded recognition."[9] In other words, the information we supply to ourselves about the background of the desire is minimized to ensure pleasure. By contrast, when we initiate imagining to gain knowledge about ourselves or about our relations with the world, the repertoire on which we draw in the imagining must be as rich and complex as possible if the imagining is going to yield for us the kind of understanding we are seeking. Wollheim does not pay close attention to the issue of how imagining can work in the service of self-understanding, but I attempt an explanation in my account of the relationship between self-definition and imagining oneself otherwise.

Point of View: Past, Present and Future

So far I have mentioned the role played by adopting a point of view in centrally imagining, but I have not explicated what constitutes a person's point of view. This is in fact the central concern of Wollheim's book. His analysis of a person's perspective or point of view is phenomenological in character; it involves understanding what he calls the process of life, or what it is to live the life of a person.[10] On his analysis, understanding this process hinges on understanding the relationships among a person's present mental states and dispositions, the events that constitute her past, and the future toward which she projects herself. These relationships are not a matter of contingent connection or association. The past and the future inhere in our present and they do so in two interrelated ways.[11] First, because our present perspectives or points of view trace out a particular temporal trajectory, they are characterized by a present awareness of the influence of our past and a present concern for our own future. To live the life of a person, as Wollheim puts it, is to live at a crossroads between the present, into which we enter; our past, which influences us; and our self-concern for our own futures.[12] It is the internal relations among past, present, and future mental and bodily states, in particular an agent's awareness of these relations, that account for the qualitative distinctness of her perspective or point of view.

The second way in which past and future inhere in the present is in the content of our present mental states, which include memories of past states and previsagements of future states. Wollheim argues that iconic representations, in the form of experiential memory and previsagement, and in particular the psychic force of these representations, play a pivotal role in giving rise to our sense of ourselves as creatures persisting through time and to the sense that the various events that occur in our lives are connected to ourselves in a noncontingent way. My later account of self-definition draws on Wollheim's temporal account of a person's point of view and on his explanation, outlined below, of the role played by experiential memory and previsagement in constituting that point of view.

The crucial similarity between iconic imagination and experiential memory is that because of their iconicity, they both have cogency and, in particular, affective force. The activity of remembering an event in my life by representing it to myself not only preserves my knowledge of the event but also rekindles the emotions associated with that event, leaving me to some extent in a similar condition as the one I was in when I experienced the event. Thus experiential memories preserve and transmit the psychic force of the original events that they represent and in so doing bring us under the influence of the past. Wollheim's explanation for this phenomenon turns on a dispositional account of experiential memory. One of the ways in which experiential memory differs from imagining is that a memory state stands in a dependence relation to an earlier event. This dependence relation is a causal relation in two ways. First, the memory state is causally related to an earlier event via a disposition. The disposition is an effect of the original event, and the disposition in turn manifests itself in the memory state. Second, the role of the disposition is to keep the event causally alive, to preserve and transmit its causal effect, and this role is furthered by the manifestation of the disposition in the memory state. Thus "dependence is at once an instance of causality and an agent of causality: it exemplifies and diffuses one and the same causal influence."[13] However, because the causal relation between earlier event and memory state is mediated by a disposition—which has a history in the history of the person and stands in changing relations to other dispositions, as well as to beliefs, emotions, and desires—the causal influence of the earlier event is not always preserved in its original form; it changes over time. Furthermore, the causal relation between disposition and occurrent memory state is not just a one-way relation. The manifestation of the disposition in an occurrent memory state can modify or reshape the disposition, altering its strength, for example, or its content. Wollheim observes that "the feedback from mental state to disposition is an essential element in the way in which we try to control the lives that we lead."[14] One way in which this might occur is through the agency of the internal observer, who may respond to the emotions elicited by the memory with quite different emotions. I return to this point later.

Another important way in which experiential memory differs from iconic imagination has to do with point of view. Experiential memories, Wollheim argues, are paradigmatically centered. However, unlike iconic imaginings, which can represent from a point of view other than that of the imaginer, the only point of view from which an experiential memory can represent is the point of view of the rememberer. This follows from the dependence relation between the earlier event and the memory state: an experiential memory is a memory of an event that the person remembering has lived through; it is a memory of her experience, and in remembering it, the person remembers it as she experienced it, that is, from her point of view. Wollheim's arguments against the possibility or intelligibility of quasi memories, that is, memories in which a person allegedly centrally remembers an event that another person lived through, are important in illuminating what it is to have a point of view.[15] His arguments bring to the fore the way in which memories are not just backward looking but also forward looking; that is, they exert the influence of the past on the present and the future, and in so doing help constitute our points of view.[16] The central argument is that quasi memories are not consistent with the dispositional character of memories. Because dispositions stand in complex networks of relations with other dispositions and with beliefs, desires, and emotions, for the idea of quasi memories to be intelligible the following would need to be explained: how to make sense of the idea that parts of this complex network could be transferred intact from one person to another; how to determine how much of this complex network would have to be transferred from one person to another for a particular memory to be transferred; how to account for those of my current dispositions that conflict with the network of dispositions within which the quasi memory is embedded. Against the suggestion that we should think of quasi memories as akin to centrally imagining being someone else, Wollheim points to a salient difference between imagining being someone else and imagining oneself. To imagine being someone else, I must select and adopt that person's repertoire—at least to the extent of my knowledge. In imagining being myself, there are no such epistemic limits and no assumption of repertoire is involved; I simply draw on my own repertoire. I want to describe what Wollheim calls drawing on my own repertoire as "unselfconscious identification" and to say that what distinguishes my point of view from another point of view I might assume is that I identify with my point of view in an unselfconscious way. In the case of memory, unselfconscious identification is explained by two features of representational memory that are inconsistent with the assumption of a repertoire: first, the causal link between disposition and mental state; second, the involuntary character of much remembering.

Whereas experiential memory reveals the extent to which our present is shaped by the influence of the past, previsagement is a manifestation of self-concern, that is, of our concern for our own futures. As with experiential memory, in centered previsagement I identify unselfconsciously with the protagonist or subject of the representation; I can only centrally previsage my future from my own point of view. However, previsagement differs from experiential memory in two significant ways, which reflect the asymmetry of past and future. First, previsagement involves no dependence relation: the future has no causal hold over the present, and there is no direct causal relation between the present representation and the future that it represents. Second, and following from the first, whereas in experiential memory I represent to myself a past that I have experienced, in previsagement I can and very often do represent to myself a future that does not take place. In this respect, previsagement is more akin to iconic imagination than to experiential memory. A further feature that previsagement shares with both experiential memory and iconic imagination is its affective force. Because previsagement is a manifestation or mode of self-concern and because of its iconicity, the activity of previsaging our own futures has the power to arouse in us the kinds of emotions we would feel were we to experience the events we previsage. I return to these issues later.

In addition to Wollheim's three modes of imagining from one's own point of view—centrally imagining, experiential memory, and previsagement—I want to suggest two others that are closely akin; in fact, they are species of iconic imagining. The first, which I call counterfactual speculation, stands somewhere between experiential memory and iconic imagination. In counterfactual speculation, we speculate about the course our lives might have taken had certain features of those lives been different. In these kinds of speculation, we imagine that at some point in the past, for example, at the juncture at which an important decision was made, the course of our lives diverged from the course that our lives have actually taken. From that point on, we imagine a different past for ourselves and hence a different present and future. What characterizes this mode of imagining is that although we imagine ourselves living a different life, we nevertheless identify unselfconsciously with the protagonist of the imagining; the life we imagine is still recognizably our own.

The second mode of imagining, which I call future-directed fantasy, stands somewhere between previsagement and iconic imagination. In this mode of imagining, I represent to myself a future I might have or might have had. So, once again, I imagine from my point of view a life that is still recognizably mine but one that diverges at some point in the future from the life I am likely to lead or believe I will lead. Thus an adolescent fantasizes that her talent for acting will be spotted; whether or not she has such a talent is irrelevant to the fantasy, and she imagines a future life of fame and pleasure, without really believing that such a future is a genuine possibility for her. The difference between counterfactual speculation and future-directed fantasy, on the one hand, and experiential memory and previsagement, on the other, is therefore that they manifest different dispositions. In the latter case, the representation of my past or my future is accompanied by a belief that what I represent did happen to me or is likely to happen to me. In the former case, I just suppose that this might have been my past or that this might be my future, without believing that what I represent was or will be a genuine possibility.

I have discussed the role played by different kinds of mental imaging in the phenomenology of a person's perspective or point of view. Following Wollheim, I have characterized the point of view of a person as a network of interrelated emotions, beliefs, desires, and mental and bodily states and dispositions, shaped by the influence of the past and directed by self-concern for the future. I have characterized the phenomenological distinctiveness of that point of view as unselfconscious identification with that network. In the following section I provide an account of self-definition that centers on the triadic relationships among a person's point of view; her self-conception; and her ideals, values, commitments, and cares. I then explain the role played by the different modes of imagining in the process of self-formation or self-definition.

Self-Definition, Deliberation, and Imagination

Diana Meyers has argued that self-definition is one of the capacities necessary for autonomy.[17] I develop, concurrently, three interrelated suggestions concerning self-definition. The first is that the process of self-definition should be thought of as a process of negotiation among three related but distinguishable elements of the person: her point of view; her self-conception; and her values, ideals, commitments, and cares, in short, what matters to her. The aim of this process of negotiation is to achieve a kind of reflective equilibrium among these different elements of the self.[18] A reflective equilibrium is achieved when these elements are integrated in a relatively stable way, that is, when there are not serious and persistent conflicts among them. Thus, I am proposing an integration account of self-definition. I regard the kind of integration I describe as a necessary, if not a sufficient, condition for autonomy.[19] Second, I characterize the process of formation of a person's *self-conception* as a process whereby, through reflection guided by her values, ideals, commitments, and cares, a person constitutes certain elements of herself, or certain features of her point of view, as external to herself while appropriating others. Third, I argue that the various modes of imagining already described play an important but overlooked role in the formation of a person's self-conception and in the process of achieving an integration among the different elements of the self.

Integration and Self-Definition

Following Wollheim, I have characterized a person's *point of view* as a network of interrelated emotions, beliefs, desires, and mental and bodily traits and dispositions, shaped by the influence of the past and directed by self-concern for the future. A person's *self-conception* delimits that part of the network that the person regards as defining herself or with which she identifies. Wollheim's metaphors of the empathic internal audience and the reflective internal observer help clarify the relationship between a person's point of view and her self-conception. Recall that the difference between internal audience and internal observer is that whereas both are internal, they stand in different relations to the imaginative project. The internal audience is caught up within the imaginative project and emotionally identifies with it. The internal observer, on the other hand, stands outside the imaginative project; may react to it emotionally in a range of different ways; and reflects on and evaluates the desires, emotions, and beliefs represented or manifested in the imagining.[20]

Elaborating from these metaphors, we can identify two salient features of the relationship between a person's point of view and her self-conception. First, like internal audience and internal observer, both my point of view and my self-conception are internal to me in the sense that both are constitutive aspects of my identity. To characterize a person's identity solely in terms of one of these aspects rather than both would be mistaken because both motivate our actions and our responses. Thus, on the one hand, our actions are often motivated, in ways that we either may not be aware of or cannot change, by mental or bodily dispositions and habits, desires, character traits, and so on that do not accord with our self-conceptions.[21] On the other hand, part of what it is to be an agent is to be able, at least within certain limits, to modify oneself in line with one's self-conception.

Second, although both our points of view and our self-conceptions are constitutive of our identities, like the internal observer we shape our self-conceptions by reflecting on different aspects of our points of view. This reflective activity can be thought of as a process of externalizing, distancing, or dissociating ourselves from certain aspects of ourselves and appropriating others.[22] The activity of externalizing an element of oneself, for example, a desire, involves reconfiguring the network or structure of beliefs, emotions, dispositions, desires, and so on that constitute one's point of view in order to lessen, perhaps eventually eliminate, the motivational pull of this desire. So to externalize an element of oneself is to reject it as a motivating factor in one's actions. To appropriate an element of onself is to acknowledge and accept it as one of the aspects of one's identity that guides one's actions. It is in this sense that we identify ourselves, or our self-conceptions, with those aspects of ourselves that we appropriate. In some cases, appropriation may involve endorsement. But appropriation may also be consistent with equivocal endorsement or in some cases just with acceptance.

The metaphor of the internal observer brings into focus two central features of externalizing and appropriating, namely, that they involve both emotional response and evaluation. In reflecting on and reacting to our own desires, habits, character traits, and so on, we respond to these affectively—with pride, shame, or embarassment, for example. These emotional responses are both guided by and shape our self-conceptions. So, for example, we might feel shame when we find ourselves acting on a desire that conflicts with our self-conception. But our emotional responses and our self-conceptions are in turn guided by our valuations and our judgments about what matters. Several philosophers have argued that our identities or self-conceptions are shaped by what matters to us. Thus Williams talks of a person's identity as being bound up with her "ground projects" and commitments;[23] Ronald Dworkin aligns the person with her critical, as opposed to experiential, interests, that is, with those interests that incorporate a person's critical or reflective judgments about what constitutes a good life, what is important, what is worth doing and valuing, what ideals she should live her life by, and so on;[24] and Frankfurt suggests that the boundaries of a person's will are defined by what she cares about.[25] For the purposes of this discussion, I ignore some of the philosophical differences among these accounts and draw on some of the intuitions that unite them in order to clarify the evaluative dimension of externalizing and appropriating.

Two central intuitions are shared by these views. The first is that our projects, cares, values, or critical interests guide the process of distinguishing our self-conceptions from our points of view. The judgment of whether we wish to appropriate or dissociate ourselves from a desire, disposition, or characteristic is related to our assessment of whether this element of our psychology strengthens or undermines our commitment to these cares, values, or critical interests.[26] So the formation of a person's self-conception could be understood as the attempt to bring the different aspects of the self into line with what matters to her. At the same time, making judgments about whether we wish to appropriate or dissociate ourselves from certain aspects of ourselves is a process that also involves engaging in a reflective assessment of our values, ideals, cares, or in short what matters to us. In reflecting on whether a certain desire or set of desires, for example, undermines our commitment to what we care about, we are also reflecting on whether what we care about is worth caring about or worth caring about in the way or to the extent that we do.[27]

The second intuition is that what we are and what matters to us are not simple matters of choice. To say that what we are is not a simple matter of choice is to say that the network or configuration of emotions, beliefs, dispositions, and desires that constitute our points of view is, to some degree, not voluntary. Our identities are shaped in fairly determinate ways by our various characteristics, by the relations between these characteristics and our social context, and by what matters to us. To say that what matters to us is not a simple matter of choice is that say that to a certain degree, we just find certain things mattering to us. This may be because we are disposed in certain ways by the manner in which different aspects of our identities, for example, our temperament and talents, reinforce one another; what matters to us may be connected with commitments to others, for example, parents, that are not entirely of our choosing;[28] or, what matters may be the result of significant events in our particular histories or of decisions we made in the past that are now no longer a matter of choice. Thus, we cannot simply choose to abandon our cares or to give up what matters to us. Or rather, we cannot do so without forfeit or loss. Certainly what matters to a person may change, perhaps because of a decision she has made or because of an event or action that has intervened to disrupt the reflective equilibrium she had established among different aspects of herself.[29] But something that has mattered usually cannot simply cease to matter. It can only do so, or come to matter in a different way, as a result of a process of readjustment of the elements of the self.

However, although what we are and what matters to us are not under our immediate voluntary control, this should not be taken to imply that we are passive with respect to ourselves. Self-definition or self-formation is a matter of actively negotiating the relationships among one's point of view, one's self-conception, and one's values. A reflective equilibrium among the different aspects of one's self is achieved when these elements are integrated in a relatively stable way, that is, when there are not serious and persistent conflicts among them. The notion of stability does not imply that there cannot be tension or inconsistency within or among the different elements of the self, that the self is seamless. Nor does it imply that an integrated self is static. In fact the process of self-integration is an ongoing and dynamic process precisely because of inevitable tensions and inconsistencies within the self and because the different elements of the self are constantly undergoing transformation.[30] The notion of stability does imply, however, that an agent who is persistently internally divided or whose sense of self is seriously fragmented cannot achieve the kind of reflective equilibrium necessary for unified agency.[31] By unified agency I mean the kind of practical unity necessary to deliberate, make decisions and choices, and act.[32]

Imagination, Deliberation and Self-Definition

For the remainder of this section I want to develop the idea that imaginative mental activity plays a crucial role in self-definition, as I have characterized it, and in the deliberative processes that precede self-formative decisions. To explain this role, I want to recall two points that were made earlier in the discussion. The first is that mental imagery, because of its iconicity, has psychic force or cogency; it is able to rearouse emotions or simulate the effect of emotions. The second is that in discussing the relationship between a person's point of view and her self-conception, I likened this relationship to that between Wollheim's internal audience and internal observer. This comparison brought to the fore two central features of the kind of reflection that is involved in negotiating the relationships among our points of view, our self-conceptions, and what matters to us, namely, that reflection involves both an affective and an evaluative response.

Putting these two points together, we can begin to see the role played by the various modes of imagining in the process of self-definition. By virtue of its power to rearouse or simulate emotions, imaginative mental activity initiates self-reflection by prompting an emotional response and, through that, an evaluative judgment. The cognitive power of this process is reasonably evident in the case of experiential memory. Because experiential memories are representations of experiences we have lived through, such memories can enable us to understand and reshape ourselves by enabling us to understand the ways in which our present points of view, self-conceptions, values, ideals, and commitments have been influenced by our past. The memories rearouse the emotions associated with the original experience. But the interval between the past and the present and the way in which the web of dispositions within which the memory is embedded has been modified by the history of the person during that interval, enable the person to respond to the original emotions with a further set of emotional reactions, which I call reactive emotions. These reactive emotions then prompt evaluative judgments, which enable the person to gain some understanding of the significance of past experiences and to gain some measure of control over the psychic force of those experiences. For example, the process of sifting through and evaluating memories, externalizing some and appropriating others, is one way in which a person can come to terms with a traumatic event in her past and reestablish some kind of equilibrium among the different elements of herself.[33]

However, it might be thought that if there is some truth to the claim that iconic mental representations have cognitive power and motivational force, if it is true that they are indeed able not only to yield self-understanding but also to inaugurate a reconfiguration of the various elements of the self, that this will be true mainly of those cases of imagining that are accompanied by belief, namely, experiential memory and previsagement. On the other hand, it might seem that because they typically manifest desire, iconic imagining, future-directed fantasy, and counterfactual speculation are modes of imagining that are more likely to be invoked in the service of self-deception than as an aid to self-understanding. Although I try to show that imagining of these varieties can contribute in a positive way to practical deliberation about the self, this objection certainly has force. The imagination can be delusional, and its role in self-understanding is ambivalent. There are a number of ways in which imagining can block, rather than aid, self-understanding and practical deliberation about the self. The first, discussed previously, is when the imaginer intentionally restricts the repertoire invoked in the imagining, so that no beliefs, desires, or emotions that might threaten the pleasure she seeks gain admittance to the imaginative project. This kind of restriction of the imaginative project can, of course, also occur when experiential memory and previsagement are invoked in the service of desire. The second way is when a person's imaginings and the repertoire she invokes in her imaginative projects are limited by the culturally available images and representations that provide the raw material on which we draw in our own imaginative activities. I turn to this issue later.

To understand the role that the species of imagining that includes counterfactual speculation, future-directed fantasy, and iconic imagination can play in self-definition, I want to focus a bit more closely on the emotional response prompted by an imagining. My emotional response to an imagining involves a number of interwoven components, including my response to the content of the representation, my response to the emotions that I perceive to have been aroused or simulated in me by the representation, and my response to what I perceive the representation and the emotions it generates in me disclose about me. For example, let us say that I imagine myself being told of the death of someone I believe I love. This imagining might arise involuntarily or it might be invoked deliberately to represent to myself my own feelings for this person. But let us say that as the imagining unfolds, I unexpectedly find myself representing myself, as the protagonist, as experiencing somewhat mixed emotions to this event: dread, grief and sorrow, to be sure, but also relief. As internal audience, the imagining simulates in me the effect of these different emotions. As internal observer, I respond to these different emotions with reactive emotions. My reactive emotions include those that are in accord with the emotions simulated by the imagining, for example, a heightening of sorrow and dread. These reactive emotions are direct responses to the content of the representation, that is, to the representation of the loss of the loved person, and they are also responses to the emotions simulated by the imagining. Furthermore, since I believe I love this person, these emotions concur with and confirm my self-conception. However, in this case my reactive emotions will also include a response to the apparently anomalous emotion simulated by the imagining, the emotion of relief, which takes me by surprise as the imagining unfolds. My reactive emotions to this emotion may include bewilderment, shame, and anxiety. These reactive emotions will in turn prompt self-reflection and evaluative judgment—of the imagining and the anomalous emotion of relief represented in it, of the various reactive emotions that arose in me in response to this simulated emotion, and of my self-conception and my sense of what matters. The judgment I arrive at may be that this simulated emotion is indeed anomalous and external to me, and so the judgment confirms my self-conception. However, it may be that this imagining sets in train, or at least forms part of, a process of coming to realize that I do not love this person any more, and so of reconfiguring my self-conception and my sense of what matters.

This example shows that in imagining, we present aspects of ourselves to ourselves for reflection and evaluation, not only directly or indirectly in the content of the representation, but also because their cogency enables such representations to provide a window into our own emotional states, our points of view, and our self-conceptions. In those cases in which imagining is invoked in the service of self-knowledge, we allow as much knowledge of ourselves as we can into the representation in order to make this window as wide as possible. In those cases in which imagining is invoked in the service of desire, we narrow this window, sometimes to guarantee that the imagining will afford maximum pleasure, sometimes to ensure that we see of ourselves only what we want to see. Thus we manipulate our imaginings so that they conform to, or at least do not conflict with, our self-conceptions. However, even in these cases, we very often find ourselves unable to control the imagining to the extent that we want—beliefs, desires, and emotions that conflict with the intention of the imagining can creep in as the imagining unfolds and can provide a sometimes unwanted window into those aspects of ourselves that we would rather not see.

The example also shows that representational imagining can provide this kind of window into the self because it can abstract us from our habitual modes of understanding ourselves and our relations with others. By putting ourselves at a remove from these habitual modes of understanding, we are able to reflect on and evaluate them, and so to test our satisfaction with them. But this is not the only way in which representational imagining can aid self-understanding and self-definition. By removing us from the habitual, imagining also opens up a space within which we can try out different possibilities for ourselves—different possibilities of action, desire, emotion, and belief. This trying out of different possibilities or postures of the self is a central feature of counterfactual speculation and future-directed fantasy. In assuming different postures, say in imagining a different past for ourselves or fantasizing about the future, we hold certain elements of ourselves stable and play around with others. Thus we place in the foreground certain aspects of our identities, for example, certain ideals, characteristics, or talents, and downplay others. As internal observer, we then respond, emotionally and evaluatively, to these alternative representations of ourselves. Through this process we start distinguishing those possibilities that may be genuine possibilities for us from those possibilities that are not really thinkable for us at all. An obvious example is the kind of previsaging of different possibilities that we engage in when we are trying to make a decision between alternative courses of action—for example, choosing between two jobs in two different cities. In making decisions of this kind, much of our deliberative activity involves imaginative projection. We represent to ourselves the different kinds of life we believe we would live, given the different options, and by evaluating our responses to these representations we gradually get ourselves into a position to make a decision.

For reasons that I have already indicated, this imaginative playing around with our identities, or imagining ourselves otherwise, does not always promote adequate self-reflection or ideal deliberation. In the case of previsagement, counterfactual speculation, and future-directed fantasy, an additional problem is that these kinds of imagining can be more or less impoverished. Our ability to imagine a different past for ourselves, for example, peters out fairly quickly because we simply do not know enough about what our lives would have been like had they taken a course such as the one we imagine. Similarly, although in the kind of deliberative previsagement that precedes decisions, we build in as much knowledge of ourselves and of the different possibilities as we can to make the imagining as rich and informative as possible, in retrospect these imaginings often strike us as impoverished. Thus, after the event, we can find ourselves thinking that we might have made a different, and better, decision if only we had known ourselves better or taken into account a consideration that in retrospect seems so obvious or predicted an unforeseen outcome of our actions.

Nevertheless, bearing in mind these reservations, I contend that our ability to imagine ourselves otherwise—that is, our ability to imaginatively distance ourselves from our habitual modes of self-understanding and to envisage, in imaginative representations, alternate possibilities for ourselves—plays an important role in practical reflection and deliberation about the self, and hence in self-definition.

Imagination, Social Recognition, and the Cultural Imaginary

From the way I have been describing imaginative projection so far it may seem as though our individual lives are completely discrete and self-contained; as though our mental and bodily lives, our memories, our self-concern for our own futures, and the repertoires on which we draw in our imaginings refer only to our own experiences and points of view; and as though these exist in some kind of vacuum. But, of course, this is not so. We are social creatures who are formed and transform ourselves in our intimate and nonintimate relationships with other people.[34] We become persons and live our lives in particular social, cultural, and historical communities. Our sense of our lives as temporal, our points of view, our self-conceptions, and our values, are therefore shaped by these relationships and these communities. So, too, are our imaginative mental activities. So how can the relationship between our individual imaginative projects and the social world in which we live our lives be characterized? Or, since this is a rather large question, let me narrow it by asking how we can understand the relationship between our own imaginative representations of ourselves and cultural images and representations. In particular, how can a person's imaginative projects, and hence her capacity for self-transformation and autonomy, be stymied by the dominant cultural imaginary? These are also very large questions that cannot be explored here adequately, but I want to sketch out one possible answer. The first part of my answer involves an analysis of the role played by social recognition in self-definition and autonomous agency. The second part draws some connections between social recognition and the social imaginary.

Social Recognition and Intrapsychic Integration

Previously, I suggested that self-definition should be understood as a process of attempting to achieve a dynamic integration of the different elements of the self. Here I want to argue that social relationships more generally, and social recognition in particular, play a crucial role in achieving this kind of integration, and hence in achieving autonomy. There are two crucial ways in which social recognition is necessary for self-definition. First, it is necessary because self-knowledge is crucial to self-definition and because we achieve self-knowledge in social relationships. Self-knowledge involves knowing which aspects of one's point of view—which desires, characteristics, traits, and so on—one identifies with; knowing what one values and cares about; and knowing how one feels and what one wants. It is precisely this kind of self-knowledge that is lacking in the case of agents whose self-conceptions are fragmented or who experience persistent conflict between different aspects of themselves. Most of the time this kind of self-knowledge is tacit and taken for granted. However, in crises or when we face difficult decisions, not only does it need to become more explicit but also our knowledge of ourselves and our self-conceptions are often seriously challenged.[35] Thus an enlarged or altered self-understanding may emerge during the process of deliberating and deciding—if all goes well. If all does not go well and self-knowledge only emerges after a decision has been made and actions undertaken, the result is often serious regret. Regret reveals the importance of self-knowledge to self-definition. An agent who persistently regrets her decisions is an agent whose capacity for autonomy is significantly compromised.[36] However, the affective, evaluative, and imaginative processes of reflection—by means of which we clarify what we value, distinguish our self-conceptions from our points of view, and so achieve self-knowledge—cannot be purely introspective. Our emotional responses to aspects of our identities such as our temperamental characteristics—responses, for example, of shame or pride—are shaped by and responsive to the estimations and responses of others. And these responses, at least in part, form the basis for our judgments about ourselves. Thus we come both to know and to define ourselves in our interactions with others.[37]

Second, social recognition is necessary for self-definition because a sense of self-worth is necessary to the achievement of a reflective equilibrium among the different aspects of the self and because self-worth is bound up with social recognition. In what follows I want to elaborate this second point by explaining the connections among integration, self-worth, and social recognition.[38] Having a sense of self-worth is necessary for integrated and self-defining agency for at least two reasons. One reason is that agents are motivated to act only if they have a conception of their actions as effective, as making a difference. This in turn requires that agents have a conception of themselves as capable of effective action—as having the necessary capacities, talents, and attributes. Without a sense of her own worthiness as an agent and of the worthiness of her capacities, her desires, and her beliefs, an agent will not be able to conceive of herself as capable of effective action.[39] Another reason is that an agent's capacity to resolve internal conflicts is tied to whether or not she thinks that what she does or thinks or feels makes a difference. It is also tied to her sense of whether or not she thinks that it is important for her to be able to define and express herself, in other words, with whether or not she thinks that who she is matters. If an agent has little or no sense of self-worth, she will think that who she is or what she does makes no difference, and hence she will have no motivation for resolving internal conflicts, for trying to establish a reflective equilibrium among the different elements of her self.

However, having a sense of self-worth is not an all-or-nothing matter. Since our identities are complex, an agent may have a reasonably strong sense of self-worth with respect to certain aspects of herself, for example, certain talents or capacities, but a rather fragile sense of self-worth with respect to other aspects of herself, for example, her physical appearance or her ability to form intimate relationships.[40] More important, self-worth is not an all-or-nothing matter because self-worth is fundamentally social. Agents live their lives in a number of overlapping but distinct social spheres, including the spheres of intimate interpersonal relationships—such as familial relationships, love relationships, and close friendships—as well as those of nonintimate social contacts and acquaintances; the sphere of work; the spheres of sport, social clubs, and artistic pursuits; the spheres of group-based ethnic or community identities and social life; the spheres of political activity and participation; and so on. These different spheres bring out different, sometimes conflicting, aspects of agents' identities and reinforce or undermine these aspects. An agent's sense of the worthiness of different aspects of her identity is bound up with the extent to which the social sphere in which those aspects are salient reinforces or undermines the relevant aspect of her sense of self-worth.

Another way of putting this point is to say that an agent's sense of self-worth is bound up with social recognition. I would suggest that there are three interconnected but distinct types of social recognition. The first, most fundamental type, which is obviously Kantian in flavor, involves recognition of the agent as a human being worthy of respect. It involves recognition of the agent as a person whose life matters to her and to others and as a being capable of feeling, thought, and self-defining agency. It is this kind of recognition that is violated by extreme forms of oppression, such as slavery or genocide, and by acts of violence committed by others, whether in their impersonal forms in warfare or in their more direct, personal forms in rape, assault, abuse, and murder. The power of this kind of violation is attested to by Susan Brison's remark that "one assailant can undo a lifetime of self-esteem."[41] The second type of social recognition involves recognition of the worth of the social group to which the agent belongs—where social groups may be defined in terms of class, racial, ethnic, gender, cultural, or religious identity or intersections of these.[42] This second dimension is clearly much more tied to sociopolitical structures and to social norms and expectations than the first. Systematic denial of social recognition of this kind tends to characterize oppressive social relations. The third type of social recognition operates at a more directly personal level and involves recognition of the worth of different aspects of an agent's identity, including her talents and capacities, mental and bodily traits and dispositions, emotions and desires, temperamental characteristics, and so on; recognition of the worth of her self-conception; recognition of her values, commitments, and ideals; and recognition of the worth of her social relationships. One of the consequences of a lack of social recognition of this kind is that it undermines an agent's sense of her own worthiness at a personal, social, and political level. I suggest below that in oppressive social contexts, this third kind of social recognition is systematically withheld from individual members of oppressed groups or is available to them only in very truncated and restricted forms.

I have argued that a sense of self-worth is necessary for integrated agency, and hence for autonomy, and that self-worth is tied to social recognition of all three kinds. However, the relationship between social recognition of the third kind and self-worth is ambivalent as far as autonomy is concerned. On the one hand, because self-worth is tied to social recognition, we emotionally invest ourselves in those aspects of our identities and self-conceptions and those social spheres that provide social recognition and that reinforce our sense of self-worth. This investment provides the kind of direction needed for autonomy. On the other hand, this kind of investment of our self-worth can be perilous and undermining of autonomy because it leaves us highly vulnerable to changes in our personal and social circumstances; witness the profound disorientation experienced by many men upon retirement, if their sense of self-worth has been overly invested in work, or by many women when their children grow up and leave home.

It is perhaps because of this ambivalence that philosophers have traditionally thought of autonomy as requiring independence from social norms, expectations, and recognition. I think this is a mistaken inference. Rather, the ambivalent relationship between self-worth and the third kind of social recognition illuminates the importance for autonomy of a robust sense of self-worth, that is, a sense of self-worth that is not overly dependent on a narrow range of forms of social recognition and that is not overly invested in a narrow range of attributes, capacities, relationships, and so on. For example, the discovery of infertility, at least in our society, is commonly extremely devastating to a woman's general sense of self-worth. But just how far-reaching and generally debilitating this feeling is depends on the extent to which a woman has invested her sense of self-worth in maternity. This in turn will depend on the importance of maternity within the central social spheres of her life, on what other social opportunities are available to her, and on whether there are other meaningful spheres of activity in her life from which she can gain social recognition.[43]

A diversity of forms of social recognition is typically absent in contexts of oppressive socialization. In such contexts, only certain aspects of the identities of agents are afforded recognition. Furthermore, their scope for self-defining agency is restricted to a limited range of social spheres. Given the connection between self-worth and social recognition, the effects are obvious. One effect is that the achievement of self-worth will be overly invested in certain aspects of the self and in certain social relationships, namely, those that conform to social norms and seriously restricted social roles, with the result that other aspects of the self are repressed or stunted. Some agents who are able to conform their self-conceptions to these restricted norms and roles may in fact be quite integrated as agents and have a reasonably strong sense of self-worth—which is why integration is a necessary, but not a sufficient, condition for autonomy.[44] More commonly, however, the effect will be some degree of internal conflict, alienation, or fragmentation of the self, as agents struggle to achieve a sense of the worthiness of their capacities in social contexts where there is restricted scope for their expression and where these are afforded little social recognition. In this kind of context it is not surprising that agents may voluntarily and apparently rationally make choices, like the choice to be a surrogate mother or to have a nose job or to undergo a sex-change operation, that promise to resolve these conflicts and provide them with greater social recognition. It should also not be surprising that the attempt to achieve integration by such means does not always succeed or enhance the agent's autonomy.

Social Recognition and the Cultural Imaginary

For the remainder of this article, I sketch an explanation of how a restricted or oppressive cultural imaginary may limit an agent's capacities for imaginative projection, and in so doing impair her capacities for self-definition, self-transformation, and autonomy. Previously, I suggested that in imagining from someone else's point of view we assume someone else's repertoire. In imagining from our own point of view, we draw on our own repertoire—that is, on our beliefs and desires and our own experiences as these have been sedimented in memories, mental and bodily dispositions, and habits. Imagining involves elaborating from this repertoire. I have also argued that our points of view and those of others are developed in the context of particular social relationships and particular social contexts. Furthermore, our sense of self-worth and our self-conceptions are shaped by, and responsive to, social recognition. One of the most important ways in which social recognition is expressed or withheld is through cultural images, representations, symbols, and metaphors. These representations reflect, incorporate, and instantiate, often in subliminal but nevertheless powerful ways, social and cultural understandings of agents' worth, especially understandings of the significance and worth of various kinds of identities—such as gender, ethnic, racial, and religious identities.[45] Drawing these points together, I want to make three suggestions to explain the connections among the cultural imaginary, an agent's imaginative projections, and the impairment of autonomy in oppressive social contexts.

First, the repertoire on which we draw in our imaginary self-representations is mediated by the available cultural repertoire of images and representations. The social psychic force of this imagery mirrors the psychic force of mental imagery; it shapes our emotions, our desires, and our beliefs. So the medium by which the cultural imaginary informs our beliefs and shapes our desires is through our own representations; cultural imagery latches on to the individual psyche, as it were, by gripping the imagination.

Second, the ambivalent role of cultural imagery vis-à-vis our imaginations mirrors the ambivalent role of imagining in self-understanding. On the one hand, I have argued that the activity of imagining can abstract us from our habitual modes of understanding and open up a space within which to envisage new possibilities of self-definition and self-understanding. Imagining can do this because we are not restricted to representing only what we actually are or what we think is actually possible. We can represent what we might want to be, what we wish to be possible, or just what might be or might have been possible. This is what is liberating about imagining. Innovative cultural imagery plays a similarly liberating role. In representing what might be possible, it abstracts us from our habitual understandings of ourselves and others and so begins to loosen the grip of dominant imagery—which is why alternative representations of gender relations and sexual difference have been so vital to feminist efforts to restructure our social understandings. On the other hand, representations can act like compulsions to constrain the imagination, enforce habitual patterns of thought, and stymy self-understanding and self-definition. I suggested earlier that imaginative projects that are initiated in the service of desire can have this effect. The imaginer deliberately rules out beliefs, emotions, and desires that might conflict with the desire that seeks satisfaction in the imagining or that might conflict with her self-conception, and in so doing narrows the window that the imagination can open into the self. Similarly, cultural imagery enlisted, consciously or unconsciously, in the service of the desire for domination or the desire to perpetuate the status quo draws on a curtailed cultural point of view to restrict the repertoire in terms of which the culture can represent itself.[46] When these restricted cultural representations grip the imaginations of individuals, the effect is to narrow the range of the repertoires on which we can draw in our imaginative projects and so to curtail our imaginative explorations of alternative possibilities of action, emotion, belief, and desire. Having a restricted repertoire is, of course, quite consistent with having a vivid imagination. There are all sorts of tediously repetitious imaginative permutations and combinations that can be elaborated from a single theme, as Hollywood knows all too well.

Third, given the connection between an agent's sense of self-worth and social recognition, there is a strong incentive for agents to identify with those cultural representations of their identities that seem to afford greater social recognition and to incorporate these representations into their self-conceptions and their imaginative projections. Even if these representations are oppressive, in the sense that they present agents with severely curtailed avenues for achieving social recognition, the fact that these avenues afford the main means of achieving social recognition nevertheless provides agents with a strong incentive for identifying with them. It may also provide them with a strong incentive for resisting innovative cultural imagery. Thus, whereas oppressed agents may have more or less rich fantasy lives within a restricted repertoire, their desires and capacities to *seriously* imagine alternative possibilities for action, emotion, and desire, that is, to *seriously* imagine alternative lives, are likely to be underdeveloped.

There are three different but interrelated levels at which socialization can impede autonomy: first, at the level of the processes of formation of our beliefs, desires, patterns of emotional interaction, and self-conceptions; second, at the level of the development of the skills and abilities that constitute what Diana Meyers calls autonomy competence; third, by frustrating a person's ability or freedom to act upon or realize her autonomous desires or an autonomously conceived life plan. For good reason, feminists have had a lot to say about how restricted social opportunities curtail autonomy at the third level, and Meyers has investigated the way in which socialization can hamper the realization of autonomy at the second level— by hampering the development of autonomy competence. Understanding the role played by imaginative representation in self-definition and understanding the relationships among our individual imaginative projects, social recognition, and the cultural imaginary are crucial parts of understanding how socialization can impede autonomy at the first level—at the level of the processes of formation of our beliefs, desires, patterns of emotional interaction, and self-conceptions. What it can help explain is why, in oppressive social contexts, the capacities of agents for autonomous action can be impaired by their own inabilities to imagine themselves otherwise.

Notes

1. My thanks to Sarah Bachelard, Peter Menzies, Diana Meyers, and especially Natalie Stoljar for helpful comments on earlier drafts of this article.

2. Diana Meyers, *Self, Society, and Personal Choice* (New York: Columbia University Press, 1989), part 2, section 4. In this book, Diana Meyers develops the notion of autonomy as a competence that comprises an array of skills and capacities. She provides a useful summary of her account in "Personal Autonomy and the Paradox of Feminine Socialization," *Journal of Philosophy* 84 (1987): 619–628. See also the discussion of autonomy competency in the introduction to this volume.

3. Paul Benson, "Autonomy and Oppressive Socialization," *Social Theory and Practice* 17 (1991): 385–408, 396–397.

4. Richard Wollheim, *The Thread of Life* (Cambridge: Cambridge University Press, 1984).

5. A number of feminist philosophers, for example, have analyzed the alignments between philosophical conceptual structures and symbolic or metaphorical cultural representations of masculinity and femininity. In *The Man of Reason*, 2nd ed.(London: Routledge, 1992), Genevieve Lloyd analyzes the historically variant symbolic associations between reason and masculinity in the history of philosophy; in *The Philosophical Imaginary*, trans. Colin Gordon (Stanford, Cal.: Stanford University Press, 1989), Michele Le Doeuff analyzes the conceptual role played by a range of different philosophical metaphors, including metaphors of the masculine-feminine distinction; in *Speculum of the Other Woman*, trans. Gilligan C. Gill (Ithaca, N.Y.: Cornell University Press, 1985), Luce Irigaray focuses on certain textual metaphors, for example, in the work of Plato, Hegel, and Freud, among others, to suggest that Western theoretical discourse is structured by a phallocentric representation of sexual difference in which the feminine is always represented in relation to masculinity as lack or complement. In "Gendered Reason: Sex, Metaphor and Conceptions of Reason," *Hypatia* 6 (1991): 77–103, Phyllis Rooney locates feminist concern with metaphorical and symbolic representations of reason and femininity in the context of theories of metaphor, such as those of Max Black, that argue for the view that metaphor has conceptual force. See Black, "Metaphor," in *Models and Metaphors* (Ithaca, N.Y.: Cornell University Press, 1962). For different developments of Black's account, see also Paul Ricoeur, *The Rule of Metaphor*, trans. Robert Czerny (London: Routledge & Kegan Paul, 1978), and Eva Kittay, *Metaphor: Its Cognitive Force and Linguistic Structure* (Oxford: Clarendon Press, 1987).

6. In "Imagination and the Self," Bernard Williams makes a similar distinction between "simple visualing," in which a scene is visualized from no particular point of view, and "participant imagery," in which the imaginer is a participant in the visualized scene. Williams, "Imagination and the Self," in *Problems of the Self* (Cambridge: Cambridge University Press, 1973). Although Wollheim does not explicitly discuss Williams, his analysis is clearly an engagement with the issues raised by Williams.

7. Here Wollheim's analysis disagrees with Williams, who argues that one cannot coherently imagine being someone else. Williams's argument centers on the analysis of imagining being Napoleon.

8. Wollheim, *Thread of Life*, p. 71.

9. Ibid., p. 87.

10. Wollheim's concern with analyzing what he calls the process of life, or what it means to live the life of a person, seems to be a response to reductive accounts of personal identity, such as that proposed by Derek Parfit in *Reasons and Persons* (Oxford: Oxford University Press, 1984). Parfit claims that a person is no more than a brain, a body, and a series of interrelated mental and physical events and that a person's life can be described, without omission, in purely impersonal terms. For critiques of Parfit that provide different but related

accounts of exactly what is omitted by an impersonal description, see Christine Korsgaard, "Personal Identity and the Unity of Agency: A Kantian Response to Parfit," *Philosophy and Public Affairs* 18 (1989): 101–132, reprinted as chap. 13 of Korsgaard, *Creating the Kingdom of Ends* (Cambridge: Cambridge University Press, 1996); also Paul Ricoeur, *Oneself as Another,* trans. Kathleen Blamey (Chicago: University of Chicago Press, 1992), studies 5 and 6.

11. The temporal dimensions of selfhood are also discussed by Genevieve Lloyd in "Individuals, Responsibility, and the Philosophical Imagination" in this volume.

12. Wollheim, *Thread of Life,* p. 31.

13. Ibid., p. 98.

14. Ibid., p. 100.

15. Again the target here seems to be a view of memory like that of Parfit. Parfit provides an account of ordinary memory as a subclass of quasi memories. Ordinary memories are quasi memories of our own past experiences, as opposed to other people's past experiences. The argument hinges on viewing memories as memory traces, raising the theoretical possibility that one person's memory traces might be copied from one person's brain and transplanted into another person's brain. The argument centers on the example of Jane's quasi memories of Paul's memories of Venice, as a result of an operation that involves copying and transplanting a discrete section of Paul's memory traces into Jane's brain. Parfit argues that Jane quasi-remembers Paul's memories of Venice from Paul's point of view, that is, in the first-person mode of presentation. However, where these quasi memories differ from ordinary memories is that whereas the latter involve the first-person mode of presentation accompanied by a belief that these memories are memories of one's own experiences, Jane's quasi memories are not accompanied by this belief (Parfit, *Reasons and Persons,* pp. 220–222). On Wollheim's account of memory, the idea that one could quasi-remember somebody else's experience from their first-personal point of view is incoherent because it violates the necessarily dispositional character of memory. Wollheim's discussion centers on an example that is similar to Parfit's, the example of quasi-remembering being his own father as a boy walking to school through the streets of Breslau (*Thread of Life,* pp. 112–115). In his discussion of Parfit in *Oneself as Another,* Ricoeur is also critical of Parfit's notion of quasi memory, claiming that in reducing memory to the memory trace, Parfit has stripped memories of their distinctive phenomenological character of always being someone's memories. Like Wollheim, Ricoeur connects this phenomenological character with temporality.

16. Susan Brison makes a similar point about memory in "Outliving Oneself: Trauma, Memory and Personal Identity," in *Feminists Rethink the Self,* ed. Diana Tietjens Meyers (Boulder, CO: Westview, 1997). Her discussion of the effects of traumatic memory brings out the way in which memories shape our points of view. A central feature of traumatic memories is that they block agents' abilities to project themselves into the future, hence giving rise to the feeling among trauma survivors of having outlived themselves, a feeling captured in the metaphor of having stayed on the train one station past one's destination. In Brison's analysis, this blockage arises from the way in which traumatic memories invade the present, dominating the person's point of view and disconnecting her from her memories of her past before the traumatic event. My analysis of self-formation suggests that traumatic memories form part of a person's point of view that cannot be integrated into the person's self-conception. The process of recovery involves the attempt to achieve some measure of integration. Two recent novels that powerfully evoke and reflect on the interweaving of memory and the present in the aftermath of trauma are the three novels forming Pat Barker's *The Regeneration Trilogy* (London: Viking, 1996) and Anne Michaels, *Fugitive Pieces* (London: Bloomsbury, 1997).

17. Meyers, *Self, Society, and Personal Choice.*

18. Amélie Rorty and Richard Wong use the notion of "reflective equilibrium" to char-

acterize the process whereby agents shape their self-identities. I am adopting their usage of this term. Rorty and Wong, "Aspects of Identity and Agency," in *Identity, Character, and Morality: Essays in Moral Psychology*, ed. Amélie Rorty and Owen Flanagan (Cambridge, Mass.: MIT Press, 1990).

19. Many theorists of autonomy see some kind of intrapsychic integration as a necessary condition for autonomy (for a fuller discussion see the introduction to this volume). I concur with this view, although I do not provide an argument for it here. However, for reasons that are now familiar in the literature and that I discuss later, although I regard integration as I characterize it in this section as a necessary condition for autonomy, it is not a sufficient condition. My account of integration is probably closest to Marilyn Friedman's in that, like her, I resist a hierarchical account of the different elements of the self and see integration as involving a mutual process of reflection among these different elements. Friedman, "Autonomy: A Critique of the Split-Level Self," *Southern Journal of Philosophy* 24 (1986): 19–35. Where my account differs from Friedman's is in its characterization of the different elements of the self. My account also shares similarities with the accounts of Diana Meyers, who stresses the importance of conceptualizing integration within the context of a conception of the self as dynamic and capable of self-transformation. Meyers, *Self, Society, and Personal Choice*, part 2, sect. 2, and "Intersectional Identity and the Authentic Self?: Opposites Attract" in this volume.) What makes the self dynamic, in my view, is first, the fact that the self is internally differentiated and not a seamless unity and, second, the fact that the self is formed and continually transformed in the context of relations with others, relations of connection and differentiation. I discuss these points more fully later.

20. It is important not to read the metaphors of the internal audience and an internal observer too literally, as implying different entities within the self. The point of the metaphors is to capture the idea that we can take up different attitudes toward ourselves and toward our own emotional states and to show that these different attitudes are characterized by different degrees of involvement.

21. Because I stress the importance of both point of view and self-conception to an agent's identity, my view is not vulnerable to the charges made against hierarchical accounts by Irving Thalberg, for example, that they give privilege to only the "higher-level" aspects of the self and so beg the question against Freudian accounts of our psychic structure. Thalberg, "Hierarchical Analyses of Unfree Action," *Canadian Journal of Philosophy* 8 (1978): 211–225. On my account, unconscious desires form part of a person's point of view.

22. My account of externalization recalls Frankfurt's notion of externality in "Identification and Externality," in *The Identities of Persons*, ed. Amélie Rorty (Berkeley: University of California Press, 1977), and "Identification and Wholeheartedness," in *Responsibility, Character and the Emotions*, ed. Ferdinand Schoeman (New York: Cambridge University Press, 1987). Both essays are reprinted in Frankfurt, *The Importance of What We Care About* (New York: Cambridge University Press, 1988).

23. See especially his critique of utilitarianism in "A Critique of Utilitarianism," in J. J. C. Smart and Bernard Williams, *Utilitarianism: For and Against* (Cambridge: Cambridge University Press, 1973).

24. Dworkin's distinction between critical and experiential interests arises in the context of his discussion of euthanasia in *Life's Dominion: An Argument about Abortion and Euthanasia* (London: Harper Collins, 1993), chap. 7.

25. See especially "Identification and Externality," "The importance of what we care about," "Identification and wholeheartedness," and "Rationality and the unthinkable," in Frankfurt, *The Importance of What We Care About*. See also "The Necessity of Ideals," in *The Moral Self*, ed. G. Noam and T. Wren (Cambridge, Mass.: MIT Press, 1993).

26. It is important to note the difference between dissociation and disavowal. Whereas

disavowal involves denial, dissociation can involve accepting a desire or a character trait as an element of one's makeup, without endorsing it. The process of acceptance, without endorsement, can sometimes be very important to our ability to achieve a relatively stable integration among the different elements of the self since a disavowed desire is very likely to lead to serious internal conflict and self-divison. A similar point is made by Jean Grimshaw, who argues for the importance of conceptualizing autonomy in such a way that it does not require agents to disown or disavow their desires. As Grimshaw points out, in many cases acceptance of aspects of oneself that one may not particularly like or endorse is more likely to promote autonomy than disavowal. Grimshaw, "Autonomy and Identity in Feminist Thought," in *Feminist Perspectives in Philosophy*, ed. Morwenna Griffiths and Margaret Whitford (Bloomington: Indiana Uuniversity Press, 1988). Susan Brison's discussion of coming to terms with traumatic memories is an example of the difference between dissociaton and disavowal and highlights the importance of the former to self-formation. Brison, in "Outliving Oneself," suggests that an important part of remaking herself in the aftermath of trauma involved dissociating herself from her traumatic memories. This dissociation was not a matter of denying that the remembered traumatic event happened to her and was part of her subjective history but rather a matter of dissociating her self-conception from the event and her memories of it.

27. It is because I see this process of reflection as involving a three-way process of negotiation among our points of view, self-conceptions and cares, values and ideals, with no particular element of the self given primacy, that I regard this account as non-hierarchical.

28. Anne Donchin's article in this volume, "Autonomy and Interdependence: Quandaries in Genetic Decision Making," draws attention to the nonvoluntary nature of biological and genetic ties and focuses on their implications for conceptions of autonomous decision making in genetic contexts.

29. For further discussion of the way in which the kind of fragmentation of the self that is a consequence of trauma can change a person's sense of what matters, see Brison, "Outliving Oneself," and "Surviving Sexual Violence: A Philosophical Perspective," *Journal of Social Philosophy* 24 (1993): 5–22.

30. Amy Mullin argues for a related account of integration as involving a process of negotation between diverse aspects of the self. Mullin, "Selves, Diverse and Divided: Can Feminists Have Diversity without Multiplicity?" *Hypatia* 10 (1995): 1–31.

31. The importance of this kind of intrapsychic integration to agency is made particularly clear by the effects of trauma, which is often characterized as involving loss, fragmentation, or "dismemberment" of the self, sometimes to the point of feeling that one's former self has died.

32. The notion that unified agency is a practical, not a metaphysical, matter is discussed by Korsgaard in "Personal Identity and the Unity of Agency."

33. For a detailed discussion of this issue see Brison, "Outliving Oneself."

34. As Annette Baier points out, persons are "second persons," in a number of senses: in the sense that we only become persons after a long period of dependency on other persons from whom we learn what it is to be a person; in the sense that we can only acquire and sustain self-consciousness because we know ourselves as persons among other persons; in the sense that we each only learn to distinguish ourselves as an "I" in the context of being addressed by another as a "you" and addressing another as a "you"; and in the sense that our self-consciousness is a historical, narrative consciousness, which emerges through the "acquisition of a sense of ourselves as occupying a place in an historical and social order of persons, each of whom has a personal history interwoven with the history of a community." Baier, "Cartesian Persons," in *Postures of the Mind: Essays on Mind and Morals* (Minneapolis: University of Minnesota Press, 1985), p. 90. Baier's notion of second persons thus connects the social or relational dimensions of personhood with its historical dimensions through the notion of

memory as recollection or narrative self-consciousness. These connections are also central to Genevieve Lloyd's reading of the narrative self in *Being in Time: Selves and Narrators in Literature and Philosophy* (New York: Routledge, 1993) and to her account of the social dimensions of responsibility in "Individuals, Responsibility, and the Philosophical Imagination," in this volume.

35. Susan Brison's reflections on trauma suggest that when one's sense of self has been "dismembered," and the various elements of the self are in disequilibrium, this tacit self-knowledge is also disrupted. The survivor of trauma no longer knows who she is, what she feels, or what aspects of her former self she can continue to identify with—which is why she is unable to integrate the various aspects of her identity.

36. Diana Meyers also argues that persistent regret is a good indicator that a decision or choice was not autonomous. See *Self, Society, and Personal Choice*, part 2, sect. 1. As Bernard Williams makes clear, however, this kind of "agent-regret" may be the result not only of failures of self-knowledge but also of bad luck. Thus, achieving an equilibrium between the different aspects of the self might be more a matter of luck than we find comfortable. Williams, "Moral Luck," in *Moral Luck* (Cambridge: Cambridge University Press, 1981).

37. This is, of course, a central theme in Hume's moral psychology, a theme emphasized in Annette Baier's interpretation of Hume. David Hume, *A Treatise of Human Nature*, ed. L. A. Selby-Bigge, rev. P. H. Nidditch (Oxford: Clarendon Press, 1978), books 2 and 3; Baier, *A Progress of Sentiments: Reflections on Hume's Treatise* (Cambridge, Mass.: Harvard University Press, 1991).

38. Once again, the experience of trauma illuminates the role played by social relationships and social recognition in intrapsychic integration. Trauma is characterized not only by self-alienation but also by a sense of loss of connection with intimate and nonintimate others. One symptom of this is that the agent's usual trust that others are not disposed to harm her has been shattered; another is that the agent feels that her experience of trauma puts a gulf between her and others who have not undergone the same experience. This gulf leads to the feeling, on the part of the agent, that she cannot be herself with other people. This feeling is a persistent emotion for Billy Prior, one of the central characters in Pat Barker's *The Regeneration Trilogy*, whose sense of alienation from civilians who have not experienced the horrors of the trenches sometimes manifests itself in an overwhelming violent hatred of them. For many of the characters in Barker's novels, including Prior, the only way to escape this sense of alienation is to go back to the trenches and to the solidarity in the face of horror that unites the soldiers there. For Brison, being able to overcome the feeling of alienation from others and to reconnect with them was one of the most important factors in regaining her sense of self, or rather remaking herself. Constructing a narrative of the experience and having others listen to it and, in doing so, acknowledge the pain she had undergone were essential to being able to reconnect with others and, through them, with her self.

39. My discussion at this point is indebted to Paul Benson's analysis of self-worth in "Free Agency and Self-Worth," *Journal of Philosophy* 91 (1994): 599–618.

40. Benson makes a similar point in "Autonomy and Oppressive Socialization."

41. Brison, "Outliving Oneself," p. 30.

42. On the notion of intersectional identity, see Kimberlé Crenshaw, "Demarginalizing the Intersection of Race and Sex: A Black Feminist Critique of Antidiscrimination Doctrine, Feminist Theory, and Antiracist Politics," in *Feminist Legal Theory*, ed. Katharine T. Bartlett and Rosanne Kennedy (Boulder, Colo.: Westview, 1991).

43. Natalie Stoljar's discussion of autonomy and contraceptive risk taking in "Autonomy and the Feminist Intuition," in this volume, provides another example of the way in which an agent's capacities for autonomous decision may be compromised if her sense of self-worth is overly dependent on a narrow range of forms of social recognition.

44. As Benson remarks, in raising this objection against Marilyn Friedman's integration account of autonomy, "An integration view detects threats to autonomy only when the total internalization of autonomy-inhibiting socialization fails to take hold or begins to break down" ("Autonomy and Oppressive Socialization," p. 95).

45. For a recent discussion of the role played by cultural imagery in shaping identities, see Diana Meyers, *Subjection and Subjectity: Psychoanalytic Feminism and Moral Philosophy* (New York: Routledge, 1994).

46. In *Wild Swans* (London: Harper Collins, 1991), a personal and cultural autobiography of life in Mao's China, Jung Chang vividly describes how a whole country can be in the grip of such imagery.

7

INTERSECTIONAL IDENTITY AND THE AUTHENTIC SELF?

Opposites Attract![1]

Diana Tietjens Meyers

I start from the conviction that autonomy is not a figment of the philosophical imagination; rather it is a phenomenon that most people have some experience of and that they commonly value (in my opinion, rightly so). Nevertheless, the term "autonomy" is not in everyday usage, and, it must be admitted, it is a philosophical term of art. Still, it does not follow that people have no way of talking about autonomy or that they don't talk about it. Colloquially, the exhortations "Be true to yourself!" and "Don't cave in!" express the value people place on autonomy, and the declarations "She lives by her own lights," "Now I know what I really want," and "I feel solid [right in my skin, at one with myself] about this" voice their achievement of autonomy. Think, too, of the soaring refrain of the Sinatra tune, "I did it my way" —a paean to autonomy. Likewise, there are idiomatic expressions associated with heteronomy. People may bemoan their lack of autonomy—"I feel at sea [adrift]," "I'm at odds with myself," or "How could I have given in?" And they may stand up for their autonomy and claim it as a right—"Mind your own business!" or "Butt out!" When people feel confused, irresolute, pressured, and so on, they may lament their lack of autonomy or protest incursions on it. When people are clear about what they truly want, who they deeply care about, what they genuinely believe in, and so forth, and when they are able to act on these desires, affections, and values, they may attest to their own autonomy.

In philosophical treatments of autonomy, this satisfying, sometimes exhilarating, experience of self-understanding and self-realization has been crystallized in the ideas of authenticity and self-governance. This way of conceptualizing the phenomenon of autonomy has, alas, proved susceptible to hyperbolic distortion. Self-understanding has been taken to presuppose a transparent self; congruence of self and action has been taken to presuppose a unitary, homogeneous self; self-governance has been taken to presuppose unfettered independence from other individuals, as well as from the larger society.

To the extent that this caricature has seized the philosophical imagination, feminists have charged, the autonomous individual has been reduced to an androcentric phantasm.[2] Yet, despite feminist objections to the self-originating, self-sufficient, coldly rational, shrewdly calculating, self-interest maximizing, male paragon of autonomy, and despite feminist wariness that reclaiming autonomy will prove antithetical to the project of revaluing interpersonal capacities that are conventionally coded feminine, many feminist writers continue to invoke ostensibly discredited values like self-determination in unguarded writing about the needs of women and the aims of feminism.[3] It is notable, too, that other feminists have rallied to the explicit defense of autonomy.[4] This revival is by no means surprising, for feminists must account for the control women exert over their lives under patriarchy, for their opposition to subordinating social norms and institutions, and for their capacity to bring about emancipatory social change. The concept of autonomy promises to be helpful in these endeavors.

The philosophical problem of autonomy takes on texture and depth when it is situated in a realistic context. The reality I propose to inject into my discussion of autonomy is the fact that enormous numbers of people are assigned to social groups that are systematically subordinated. The wonder is that despite this subordination, some of these individuals are exemplars of autonomy, and few of them altogether lack autonomy. There are autonomous dissenters and revolutionaries and legions of individuals who autonomously craft private lives within the confines of oppressive regimes.[5] That this is so belies two prominent, seemingly incontrovertible assumptions about autonomy. First, although it seems undeniable that an autonomy-friendly environment is necessary for autonomy, this is not the case. Horrible as they are, social and economic structures that funnel individuals into a preordained status, that regiment their life trajectories, and that penalize nonconformity need not defeat autonomy. A social and economic environment that makes a wide range of attractive options available to all individuals is conducive to, not necessary for, autonomy. Second, intuitively it seems that psychic fragmentation would preclude autonomy. Yet, recent work on the social positioning, vulnerability, and subjectivity of subordinated people suggests that as long as oppressive social structures and discourses survive, which is to say, for the foreseeable future, their identities will not be unified and coherent. Still, many of these individuals enjoy autonomy in at least some parts of their lives. Indeed, one implication of the line of thought I develop is that multiply oppressed individuals are in some respects better positioned to make autonomous judgments concerning issues of social justice and policy, and hence are better positioned to exercise autonomous moral and political agency, than multiply privileged individuals are.

Of course, recognizing that autonomy is possible despite structures of domination and subordination is no reason for complacency. On the contrary, to advocate expanded opportunities for autonomy is to endorse significant social and economic change. Nevertheless, I leave this aspect of autonomy aside and focus on the question of how autonomy is possible for individuals whose identities are shaped by structures of domination and subordination.

Specifically, I take my cue from work by feminists and critical race theorists on women's diversity and intersectional identity. The idea of intersectional identity is premised on the general philosophical thesis that who one is depends on one's social experience. However, the intersectional conception is specific to societies that exhibit certain kinds of social stratification, for it derives from a social-psychological view about how individuals internalize gender, sexual orientation, race, class, and ethnicity in sexist, homophobic, racist, classist, and xenophobic societies. This view does not purport to capture the whole of personal identity but rather those aspects that are conditioned by membership in subordinated or privileged social groups. It emphasizes that people are categorized according to gender, sexual orientation, race, class, and ethnicity and that these multiple ascriptions interact—sometimes compounding one another's effects and sometimes creating inner divisions and conflicts.[6] On this view, who we are—what we are like and how we think and act—is significantly influenced by social systems of domination and subordination. Of course, intersectionally constituted subjects may or may not notice attributes that stem from crosscutting systems of domination and subordination, and when they notice such attributes, they may or may not understand them as consequences of these social structures. People are not introspectively clairvoyant, but to the extent that they fail to make these connections, their self-concepts are incomplete and possibly distorted.

Although Lacan originated the intersectional view of the self, I take the liberty of ignoring Lacanian doctrine. Instead, I draw attention to the tropes feminists and critical race theorists are currently using to articulate the concept of intersectionality. This approach is justified, in my view, because the impulse to fashion novel imagery hints at points of dissatisfaction with Lacan's theory and because these theorists' imagery is suggestive of heretofore buried agentic potential. After reviewing in the first section a number of tropes of intersectional identity and characterizing the experiences and capacities they symbolize, I take up the topic of autonomy, and I seek to capitalize on the richness of these intersectional tropes.

To clarify the problem of autonomy once it is placed in an intersectional framework, I set out several obstacles to achieving autonomy as an intersectional subject (in the second section). I then focus on two aspects of autonomy—self-knowledge and self-definition—and argue that intersectional identity obliges us to rethink the concept of authenticity (in the third section). If ignorance of one's intersectional identity impairs autonomy, intersectional identity and hence the internalized norms of the groups to which one is assigned are attributes of the authentic self. But since intersectional identity is constituted in part through a process of self-definition, the authentic self is an evolving self that is not chained to conventional group norms. Although it is easy to discard concepts of authenticity that exclude the influence of social experience or that rule out personal transformation, it is extremely difficult to furnish an account of authenticity that does not succumb to these pitfalls. To bring out the nature of this difficulty, I examine Harry Frankfurt's well-known views. Although Frankfurt's account of the authentic self accommodates intersectional identity in some respects, I argue that its reliance on organizing identity constituents into an integrated order ultimately defeats it (in the fourth section). I propose, then, that we redirect our attention—away from the internal structure of the authentic self and toward the process of constituting an authentic self. Thus, I recommend viewing the authentic self as the collocation of attributes that emerges as an individual exercises self-discovery and self-definition skills (in the fifth section). Applying the skills that comprise autonomy competency, intersectional subjects analyze their position in social hierarchies, interpret the psychic impact of their social experience, and reconfigure their identities as members of social groups. In so doing, they constitute authentic intersectional identities.

The Trope of Intersectionality

Intersectionality is currently the reigning feminist metaphor for complex identities insofar as they are constituted by race, ethnicity, class, and sexual orientation together with gender.[7] The trope of intersectionality has numerous variants taken from a wide assortment of domains, including mathematics, cartography, anatomy, and botany. While all of these images share the aim of symbolizing an identity drawn from diverse sources that may give rise to conflicting desires and rival allegiances, they highlight different potentialities and liabilities of such identities.

Kimberlé Crenshaw's primary image of intersectionality may seem antiseptically mathematical. She pictures intersectional identities as points on a plane plotted in relation to axes which represent practices of oppression such as sexism and racism.[8] Invoking social scientific quantification, this image desubjectivizes gender and race and accents baleful social realities. But by declaring that the social scientific apparatus of variables, equations, and graphs is itself a metaphor, Crenshaw punctures the objectivist pretensions of social scientific analysis and resubjectivizes her image. The axes and plotted points translate into palpable experience.

Crenshaw does not confine herself to a single static, figurative interpretation of intersectionality. She also dramatizes it. Sexism and racism are vehicles on a collision course. The vehicles are hurtling down highways that converge at an intersection, where a pedestrian who is crossing cannot get out of the way before the two vehicles speed into the intersection and crash.[9] Struck simultaneously from two directions, the pedestrian's injuries are severe. But since it is almost impossible to trace them to their respective causes, responsibility cannot be apportioned between the drivers. Consequently, neither is blamed, and both go free. Crenshaw states that subordinating practices operate synergistically, but plainly she has in mind a sinister synergy—sinister both because of the devastating harm inflicted and because of the unwarranted privilege condoned.[10]

Crenshaw's crash metaphor vividly symbolizes the victimization brought about by patterns of oppression. However, it misses a contrary feature of group-based identity. The targets of oppression seldom experience themselves solely as victims. They often defy others' bigotry by valuing their association with the group that others systematically penalize and by upholding its traditions. The most common vernacular trope for group-based identity, namely, group membership, expresses this positive identification. Appropriating and adapting this locution, Kirstie McClure writes of intersecting group memberships.[11] If visualized as lifeless Venn diagrams, her trope merely represents inert items sorted into various overlapping categories. But it doesn't take much imagination to animate the trope. Since the items referred to are people, it is natural enough to construe membership in a group as belonging to a group and to associate belonging to a group with joining it. Thus, membership imagery introduces connotations of feeling at home in a community and of voluntary participation in it—that is, of willed and willing identification with a social group.

Important as these dimensions of group-based identity are, it might be countered that group membership should not be portrayed in overly rosy terms. As Crenshaw observes, African-American women may find themselves "situated between categories of race and gender" since these categories are sometimes regarded as mutually exclusive.[12] Thus, they may experience ambivalence toward, even alienation from, their race or their gender. María Lugones's cartographic imagery perspicuously captures the complex group-based identities that may give rise to this sort of experience. Intersections of geopolitical entities—that is, borders—symbolize identity-constituting regimes of stratifying social classifications, and the border dweller personifies intersectional positioning and experience.[13] Although familiar with and drawn to both sides of the boundary line, border dwellers are not completely welcome and comfortable in either territory. Despite the awkwardness of this position, Lugones recommends inhabiting frontiers. In her view, border dwellers occupy an epistemically favorable vantage point, for the virtues and the defects of each community are easier to spot from the border.

Lugones assigns border dwellers the role of emissaries who maintain diplomatic relations between mutually suspicious (in some cases, hostile) polities. Chantal Mouffe's construal of intersectional identities as articulations elaborates this mediational theme.[14] On the one hand, her metaphor calls to mind anatomical and botanical intersections. Articulations are joints or nodes, organic mechanisms of juncture and mobility. On the other hand, there are articulations that function as social intersections—utterances that demarcate and communicate positions; that invite others to reply; that may be refined, amended, or renounced. Deemphasizing the harms wrought by group-based domination and subordination and playing on this double entendre, Mouffe's image symbolizes both the fixity of group classifications and their amenability to renegotiation and modification.

This sample of tropes of group-based identity highlights two claims about personal identity and groups. First, these images put a spectrum of identity determinants on a par. Gender is not portrayed as more fundamental or more pervasive than race, class, ethnicity, or sexual orientation, nor is gender portrayed as secondary to any of these other group categories. Insofar as identity is shaped by these social structures, it is characterized as a commingling of equally robust, equally decisive identity determinants. Second, the notion of intersectional identity is paradoxical. Ties to groups are commonly experienced as emotionally gripping and integral to one's sense of self, yet these ties may be experienced as imposed and confining, even wounding. Likewise, the divergent demands entailed by ties to different groups can lead to estrangement from oneself and from others, yet they endow individuals with opportunities for agency, both for self-definition and for affiliation with others.

Barriers to the Autonomy of Intersectional Subjects

Intersectional subjects are not at all promising material for autonomy, for it is difficult for them to achieve self-knowledge, self-definition, and self-direction. If doing what one "really wants" is a hallmark of autonomy, one must know who one is— one's capabilities and weaknesses; one's values, commitments, and goals; and so on —so that one can make choices that express one's "true self," that is, one's "genuine desires." Unfortunately, everyday discourses of selfhood conspire against discerning the ways in which one's identity is codetermined by gender, sexual orientation, race, class, and ethnicity. Thus, intersectional subjects may be too opaque to themselves to be autonomous. Even supposing that this obstacle to self-knowledge could be overcome, however, intersectional codetermination would itself pose further obstacles to autonomy. When autonomous individuals are dissatisfied with themselves, they must be able to make needed changes, and when they have decided upon a course of action, they must be able to carry it out. But since group ascriptions constrain intersectional subjects and since codetermination unsettles them, self-definition and self-direction are impeded. Again, intersectional identity jeopardizes autonomy.

In the United States today, intersectionality is not a default conception of personal identity. Indeed, most people are not even acquainted with this conception. No doubt, American society's inveterate denial of social stratification and pervasive injustice combines with its creed of equal opportunity and upward mobility to militate against admitting relations of domination and subordination as sources of identity. On those occasions when we need a conception of identity that acknowledges inner heterogeneity, for example, to make excuses, Freud's privatized divided self can be pressed into service without bringing issues of social justice to the fore. Likewise, the idealization that is homo economicus or the liberal bearer of rights valorizes unity, coherence, and constancy, and the ubiquity of this idealization casts suspicion on the conflicts endemic to intersectional subjectivity. These default conceptions of identity leave little room for alternative conceptions to gain proponents, for the very familiarity of these discourses of selfhood induces us to articulate our self-concepts by using these models. Without a discourse that is conducive to articulating an intersectional identity, few people will view themselves as intersectional subjects.

Current ordinary American English does not furnish language for use in first-person singular identity avowals that gives equal weight to diverse group determinants of identity and that prompts individuals to consider how these identity determinants interact.[15] Colloquial language that demarcates class identities does not exist—according to our social mythology, almost everyone is middle class. Racial categories are conceptually muddled, and affirmations of racial identity are so fraught with emotional uneasiness that they are often perceived as inflammatory.[16] Yet, the ethnicities of racial "minorities" are sidelined, so their race remains on center stage.

For example, outside the Haitian and Korean communities, these ethnicities are subsumed by racial classifications. In contrast, for whites, ascriptions of ethnicity take precedence over race. Since the ethnicities of Euro-Americans are racialized— to be Swedish American or Italian American is by definition to be white—their race is ever-present yet pushed into the wings. The conventions of self-ascriptions of gender and sexual orientation are asymmetrical, too. Equated with humanity itself, maleness and heterosexuality go unmentioned, whereas womanhood, homosexuality, and bisexuality are mandatory and salient categories of self-description.[17] Although people are intersectional subjects, many of them do not know it, for our discourse exaggerates the significance of some group memberships while discounting the significance of others. But to lack self-knowledge is to lack autonomy.

An additional obstacle to autonomy for intersectional subjects stems from the fact that gender, sexual orientation, race, class, and ethnicity are categories that divide people into dominant and subordinate groups and that prescribe personality types and behavioral norms for each. In a society that is historically divided along harsh, unyielding axes of dominance and subordination, individuals cannot escape the influence of cultural stereotypes and other prescriptive representations of the groups they belong to, nor can they escape the influence of the social and economic advantages and disadvantages that institutions confer on these groups. As Anthony Appiah remarks, "I don't recall ever choosing to identify as a male; but being male has shaped many of my plans and actions."[18] Group ascriptions are not the sole determinants of who we are, nor do members of the same social group have identical identities or, for that matter, a subset of identical identity components. Nevertheless, individuals who belong to different groups have different social experience, and this targeted and lifelong socialization shapes individualized identities.[19] Whether they know it or not, people have intersectional identities, and these identities influence what they believe, how they deliberate, and how they conduct their lives.

Many individuals in privileged categories do not experience their group ties as constraints, but many individuals in disvalued categories experience theirs as subjugating. Whether one is assigned to a dominant or a subordinate group, though, one is inducted into its distinguishing paradigms and norms. Most men never seriously consider using their right to family leave to spend time with a newborn or newly adopted child, and a man who does so is likely to have as hard a time climbing the corporate ladder as a woman who wants to be CEO (chief executive officer). Thus, to have an intersectional identity is to be culturally defined and directed. But since self-definition and self-direction are necessary for autonomy, group-targeted cultural norms put autonomy at risk.

Finally, tensions often arise between the demands of gender, sexual orientation, race, class, and ethnicity—for example, for an African-American man, the norms of gender prescribe authority, whereas the norms of race prescribe deference; for a lesbian, the norms of gender mandate motherhood, whereas the norms of sexual orientation prohibit it. Likewise, the diversity of the individuals assigned to these categories and their divergent interests may present political conundrums. For African-American women, commitment to antiracist politics may entail tolerating sexism, and commitment to feminist politics may entail tolerating racism. As a result, intersectional identities often leave individuals torn by conflicting self-understandings and conflicting social and political loyalties. But if one cannot decide what one really wants, one cannot do what one really wants—one cannot be "true to oneself." To the extent that intersectional identity prevents one from translating one's identity into action, it thwarts self-direction and hence autonomy.

Authenticity as an Intersectional Subject

Observations along the lines just sketched lead some theorists to jettison the idea of intersectional *identity*. Some hold that group ascriptions have profound effects on individuals but that the impact of these classifications is so variable, so contradictory, and so volatile that no consolidation of identity is possible. In this view, intersectionality provides an argument against the very idea of personal identity and a compelling reason to join with postmodernists in declaring personal identity an anachronistic modernist sham.[20] Call this the *contrarian* view of identity. Others deny that individuals inevitably internalize group paradigms and norms and conclude that there are only unique individuals and individual identities. Whether an individual's identity is constituted by ties to any social group depends on that individual's choices. When externalized and lodged in oppressive social structures that place some individuals in "multiple jeopardy,"[21] intersectionality clears the way for resurrecting a curiously voluntarist, individualist—that is, modernist—conception of identity. Call this the *personalist* view of identity.[22]

I urge that these two challenges to intersectional identity stem from opposite misunderstandings of the self and agency, and I take the occasion of examining these misunderstandings to rethink the concept of the authentic self. For the purposes of this discussion, I base my conception of authenticity on two ideas that are implicit in the following autonomy idioms: "Now I know what I *really* want" and "Be true to yourself." The former expression distinguishes desires that one happens to have from one's real or genuine desires—that is, the desires of the authentic self. The latter voices the conviction that it is good for people to act on their authentic desires and so presumes that doing so falls within the bounds of social acceptability—that is, that one's authentic desires are morally creditable. One's authentic self points to a way of living that is both distinctively one's own and socially decent. Thus, I consider the relation between intersectional identity and the authentic self from the standpoint of three domains of autonomous choice and action—personal, moral, and political autonomy.[23]

Self-Knowledge

Proponents of the personalist view of identity—those who do not deny that each individual has an identity but who do deny that group ascriptions play a key role in shaping it—overestimate the degree to which individuals are immune to their social context and overlook a major threat to autonomous choice and action by oversimplifying the task of self-discovery. Self-ignorance is one of the principal enemies of autonomy, and self-knowledge requires being honest with oneself about who one is—owning up to and owning one's identity. In what follows, I urge that understanding the impact of group memberships on one's identity is necessary not only for personal autonomy but also for moral and political autonomy. In view of the interconnections between owning up to and owning one's intersectional identity and leading an autonomous life, intersectional identity should be considered a feature of the authentic self.

Now, let me forestall the objection that this view of authenticity posits a dangerously static conception of the self with retrograde social consequences by noting that owning up to and owning one's intersectional identity is an accomplishment not merely of self-discovery but also of self-definition (see the following sub-section).[24] Thus, accepting intersectional identity as a feature of one's authentic self does not entail clinging to a community of origin or capitulating to stereotypical group norms. Rather, it entails analyzing the social significance of one's community of origin, disclosing to oneself the ways in which associated norms have become embedded in one's own cognitive and motivational structure, appreciating how entrenched they are, and assuming responsibility for the ways in which one may enact them. Autonomy unfolds in situ, and autonomous individuals must work with whatever material is at hand. Since part of what is at hand in historically stratified societies is an endowment of intersecting group-identity determinants, individuals who seek autonomy are well advised to candidly appraise where they stand in society's hierarchies and to make as complete an inventory as they can of what they have internalized as a result of being assigned to certain social groups. I stress that this advice applies differently but with equal force to individuals who identify primarily with dominant social groups and to individuals who identify primarily with subordinate social groups. Whatever one's social position, intersectional identity serves as a platform for autonomy.

One reason to regard intersectional identity as a feature of the authentic self is that it is a starting point for leading an autonomous life. Moreover, as I now argue, impoverished, mistaken, or deluded views about one's group memberships and their psychic influence—that is, failure to own up to and to own one's intersectional identity—undermines autonomy. Self-knowledge of intersectional identity is not merely a possible point of departure for autonomy, it is a portal autonomous individuals in invidiously stratified societies cannot avoid passing through. Since the self-knowledge that is necessary for autonomy in unjust societies includes knowledge of one's intersectional identity, intersectional identity should be regarded as a feature of the authentic self as long as social injustice persists.

Since intersectional identity is not among our default self-concepts, unacknowledged group memberships commonly structure people's feelings, thoughts, and actions. Poor understanding of the implications of gender, sexual orientation, race, class, and ethnicity ascriptions may have damaging repercussions. Ideologies of social stratification value or disvalue attributes depending on what "sort" of person bears them—ambitious white men are admirable, whereas ambitious women are distasteful; boisterous Irish Americans are lively, whereas boisterous Jews are loud; and so forth.[25] Self-interpretations are filtered through this noxious fog of bigotry.[26] As a result, individuals whose self-esteem is enhanced may be emboldened to hope for more out of life, whereas those whose self-esteem is diminished may be dissuaded from hoping for much of anything. Plainly, individuals' voluntarily elected, identity-constituting goals and plans often echo the mandates of hierarchy-enforcing institutions and practices. A talented, ambitious woman may reproach herself for immodesty, pare down her aspirations, and reconcile herself to being the CEO's wife and unsalaried business hostess. To the extent that the unconscious influence of intersectional identity leads people to misjudge their potential and pursue plans that either stunt their development or exceed their capacities, and to the extent that this unconscious influence disrupts relationships or sabotages undertakings that matter to them, self-ignorance undercuts their personal autonomy.

I take it to be axiomatic that desires, attitudes, and the like are enigmatic and subject to interpretation and reinterpretation because indefinitely many factors converge in their genesis. The origins of a person's overall moral outlook and specific political preferences are especially baffling. Fueled by one's social context—the opinions of friends, family, and respected public figures, as well as the opinions of people whom one detests or dislikes—and by one's prognostications about how social policy may further or hinder personal objectives and plans, a person's moral views and politics defy easy, linear explanation. Still, if the intelligibility of desires and attitudes requires that they be autobiographically situated, and if gender, sexual orientation, race, class, and ethnicity are important autobiographical strands, tracing the relations between one's moral convictions and political stance, on the one hand, and one's membership in these groups, on the other hand, will be necessary to autonomous moral judgment and autonomous political action.

Crenshaw's crash metaphor draws attention to a dimension of intersectional identity that is particularly germane to the issue of moral and political autonomy. The crash metaphor represents those subordinated by group-based injustice as suffering from multiple injuries and those enforcing the subordination as exempted from harm and exonerated of all responsibility. Although Crenshaw's focus is on the fate of the victims, the concept of intersectional identity reminds us that many people are reckless automobile drivers in some respects and pedestrian fatalities in others. Many members of subordinated social groups occupy some dominant social positions as well. Their identities fuse axes of harm with axes of advantage. Likewise, it is not unusual for individuals who belong to privileged social groups to belong to one or more subordinated groups as well. Thus, the trope of intersectional identity dismantles the stark opposition between dominant and subordinate positions. Very few people have wholly privileged identities. Very few people have wholly subordinated identities. Most people's identities blend socially disvalued and socially valued group-identity determinants. To many people, this is news. But, I urge, this self-ignorance compromises autonomy.

Members of subordinated social groups face a cruel dilemma: they have very good reason to dwell on the proportions, the frequency, and the irreparability of the iniquities they suffer, and they also have very good reason to forget all about it. As long as there is group-based disenfranchisement, many people will find their need to pursue their own projects and fulfill personal goals on a collision course with a commitment to social justice. Thus, some highly successful professional women denounce feminism and dismiss (even despise) women who blame their career setbacks on discrimination or family responsibilities—"If I could make it," goes their refrain, "why can't you?" Moral equilibrium is elusive when social structures and customary practices are stacked against you. Still, if individuals routinely framed their self-portraits by using the intersectional model, disavowal of group-identity determinants would be a less feasible, less tempting defense—less feasible because locating oneself in gender, sexual orientation, race, class, and ethnicity hierarchies would be regarded as a minimal condition of self-knowledge; less tempting because avowing member-ship in a subordinate group would not reduce individuals to victimhood since mem-bership in subordinate social groups is usually coupled with membership in one or more privileged social groups. In reconnecting people to *all* of their group-identity determinants, intersectional identity works as an antidote to shame, self-contempt, and self-limitation and therefore as a support for personal autonomy.[27] It may enrich the individual's moral and political outlook as well, for in counteracting the deraci-nation of denying one's membership in a subordinated social group, it would coun-teract moral anesthesia and motivate people to overcome cooptation and anomie.[28] Apprehending one's intersectional identity—that is, knowing who one is—may prompt resistance to unjust treatment—that is, moral and political autonomy.

Intersectional subjectivity also broadens people's moral purview in other re-spects. Members of subordinated social groups sometimes become fixated on the subset of hardships that they themselves suffer, thereby losing sight of other grievous wrongs. Middle-class women who ardently object to sexist discrimination are no-torious for exploiting the poor, uneducated women they employ as nannies. But greater awareness of how group identities are amalgamated in individual identities can alleviate this problem, for intersectional identity obliges many individuals to admit to some social privileges, such as the advantage of affluence in a sexist society or the advantage of heterosexuality in a homophobic society, at the same time as they fight the injustices that afflict them as members of subordinated social groups. The point, of course, is not to pacify people into thankfulness for small blessings, nor is it to condemn strategic prioritization of one group identity over others. Rather, the point is to mobilize the resources of intersectional identity to temper the morally untenable zealotry that may accompany a monolithic group identification. Acute sensitivity to injustice is no threat to moral insight unless one group-identity determinant is split off from others or gains superordinate status in relation to oth-ers. Ignorance of one's intersectional identity—that is, ignorance of who one is— is a major threat to nuanced social critique, and knowledge of one's intersectional identity is needed for autonomous moral judgment and autonomous political agency.

For people who are identified primarily with dominant social groups, moral in-tegrity may become a casualty when intersectional identity is suppressed and dis-creditable political views are displaced onto universalistic moral principles. Failing to make connections between one's socially valued group memberships and one's po-litical views leads to self-deception, rationalization, and corruption of principles— in short, to moral heteronomy.[29] If people fail to acknowledge their reliance on and eagerness to keep advantages conferred by maleness, heterosexuality, wealth, white-ness, or ethnic privilege, impartiality is liable to be perverted into a self-serving ex-cuse for dismissing morally warranted, urgent political demands.[30] In camouflaging the nefarious instrumental purposes served by steadfast adherence to ostensibly fair principles and the nature of people's emotional investment in the status quo, the "high ground" of moral scruple becomes an unassailable refuge for the beneficiaries of social stratification and elitism.[31] In societies in which gender, sexual orientation, class, race, and ethnicity matter enormously to individuals, it strains credulity to conduct social life as if venerated moral theories were insulated from these patterns of domination and subordination. Again, intersectional self-knowledge is indispensable to autonomous moral judgment and autonomous political agency.

In urging people to analyze their intersectional identities, what I am endorsing is maximum transparency of group-identity determinants together with unsparing honesty about the ways in which group identities are replicated in people's moral and political thinking. It is as important to autonomy that self-concepts based on the trope of intersectionality would expose privileged identity determinants and the conservative views they undergird as it is that such self-concepts would expose devalued identity determinants (or combinations of valued and devalued identity determinants) and the social critiques they spark. Without intersectional identity, self-knowledge is, at best, incomplete and inaccurate. Without self-knowledge, moral and political autonomy are imperiled.

Now, according to feminist standpoint epistemology, the social analyses generated by oppressed social groups are more reliable. If the moral psychology I have sketched is correct, my account of the relation between intersectional identity and autonomy lends support to this claim. Since it is probably less threatening for a person identified primarily with a subordinate social group (or groups) to acknowledge previously unnoticed ties to a privileged social group (or groups) than it is for a person identified primarily with a privileged social group (or groups) to acknowledge dependency on undeserved advantages, autonomous moral judgment and autonomous political agency may be more accessible to oppressed individuals.

Still, it might seem that to accept the view I have presented is to despair of autonomy, for it seems unlikely that anyone who was not already autonomous could gain the self-knowledge that autonomy presupposes. As I pointed out before, the grammar of identity self-ascription in current American English downplays some group-identity determinants while spotlighting others. Since vernacular discourse does not invite people to articulate intersectional identities, it is no accident that relatively few people see themselves intersectionally. Indeed, owning up to and owning an intersectional identity involves a struggle to overcome these very cultural constraints—that is, a program of autonomous self-examination and interpretation. I turn in the next subsection to the question of how this struggle can be conducted, and I offer in the last section a theory of the nature of authenticity that dissolves the paradox that one needs to be autonomous to become autonomous. At this point, I confine myself to suggesting that if owning up to and owning an intersectional identity is an act of autonomy, we have a further reason to regard intersectional identity as a feature of the authentic self. If authentic attributes are neither innate nor transcendent, if authentic attributes are those that are autonomously discovered or defined, the codeterminants of intersectional identity are authentic.

Self-Definition

According to proponents of the contrarian view of identity—theorists who repudiate the possibility of personal identity of any sort—individuals are at the mercy of the ebb and flow of incoherent group discourses. Wafted about by these crosscutting discursive currents, individuals have no stable traits and therefore no personal identity (never mind authentic identity). Plainly, this view flies in the face of most people's experience. People have reflexive experience of their own continuities. Some of these continuities are conspicuous because they are aggravating, frustrating vices, faults, weaknesses, or foibles that just won't go away. Others may be less attention grabbing, perhaps because they are not troublesome, but nonetheless real—for example, gratifying emotional bonds, beneficial capabilities, pleasing personality traits, and rewarding interests. Likewise, people have interpersonal experience of others' continuities and rely on their associates to react in characteristic and hence fairly predictable ways.

The experience of personal identity that I am invoking does not require an immutable or a monotonously consistent core self. Decentered, processual subjectivity is compatible with a sense of personal identity. Indeed, to lose all sense of personal identity (or to find oneself split into multiple identity fragments) is not to advance to the postmodernist condition with winning verve. Nor is experiencing oneself as a tight identity knot cleansed of social taint to regress to the modernist condition in pitiable trepidation. Both are symptomatic of a dire need for the services of a psychotherapist. There is no doubt that continuities stemming from group membership have sometimes been portrayed as if they were trait nuggets implanted in individuals. I suspect that the metaphor of internalization fosters a proclivity for reading theories that report group-specific patterns of attributes or conduct in this simplistic way—as if our psyches swallowed social inputs whole and never metabolized them.[32] But it is also true that the contrarian view of identity exaggerates the flux of subjectivity and, more important, overlooks faculties of self-definition.

Reprising some of the tropes of intersectionality highlights the intersectional subject's capacity for self-definition. Crenshaw's crash metaphor polarizes groups into axes of harm or axes of benefit. But McClure's image of group membership complicates this picture by suggesting that axes of harm are not exclusively harmful. Despite long histories of oppression, subordinated social groups have sustained traditions that are worthy of respect and that many group members willingly uphold. Thus, belonging to a group is often a source of sustenance and guidance. Still, as Lugones's trope of border habitation implies, belonging to a group does not entail total immersion in that group's culture and norms. To have an intersectional identity is to belong to a number of groups and not to belong wholly to any. Thus, group members can use their experience of alienation to gain critical insights into the norms and values of different social groups.[33] Responding to the concern that a purely negative critique condemns people to unchanneled rage or unavailing despair, Mouffe's trope of articulation endows people with a capacity for piecemeal synthesis and provisional reconstruction. Although group-based identity is neither expungible at will nor free of liabilities, persons with intersectional identities are plainly not helpless captives of social groups.

To clarify the view of self-definition these identity tropes adumbrate, I begin by sketching an example. Worldwide, almost all women want to have children, and most of them become mothers. Yet, studies of U.S. women provide abundant evidence that few of these women autonomously choose to become mothers; most regard motherhood as their destiny and proceed automatically to fulfill it.[34] I submit, however, that reflecting on this undertaking from the standpoint of intersectional identity would provide one route through which autonomous motherhood might be achieved.

Consider a young, white, middle-class, heterosexual (let us suppose, recently married), Italian-American woman. What perspectives on motherhood do her various group memberships afford her? Her gender, sexual orientation, and ethnicity collude in propelling her toward pregnancy and motherhood. "Woman," as Simone de Beauvoir reminds us, "is a womb";[35] the telos of female heterosexuality is childbearing; Catholicism-infused Italian-American culture reveres motherhood. Plainly, these identity codeterminants—the ones she is most likely to be conscious of— converge on and affirm her becoming a mother.

What about her race and class identities? They, too, support this choice, but not quite so unambiguously. The ubiquitous (albeit more and more outdated) image of U.S. middle-class life—the happy, prosperous suburban family—includes a heterosexual couple and a pair of kids. It is less obvious, though no less sure, that her white racial identity reinforces the motherhood norm. A century ago, it was still respectable for American public figures to urge white women to procreate to maintain white racial dominance.[36] Such blatantly racist doctrines are no longer proclaimed publicly, but they contaminate white racial heritage and surface occasionally in the fulminations of right-wing fanatics. Notice, though, that if my hypothetical woman attended to her racial identity and exposed the nature of the support it proffered for motherhood, it might give her pause. Unconscious racism remains common among white middle-class Americans, but naked racism is hard for most of them to stomach. Likewise, inspection of the class backing for maternity might raise an alarm. That every baby born into the American middle class can be expected to consume a colossal chunk of the planet's resources might prompt her to consider abstaining from bringing another resource glutton into the world.

I am not suggesting that attention to intersectional identity would convince women to stop having children. On the contrary, many women, including quite a few feminists, see mothering as a practice worthy of celebration and as a legacy that ought to be self-consciously and joyously perpetuated. What I am suggesting is that intersectional identity both reinforces conventional gender expectations and affords opportunities to reassess those norms. Linking oneself to white racial status or to middle-class economic status exposes reasons militating against conformity. Most important, perhaps, the tensions between the different dimensions of intersectional identity introduce a wedge of optionality that authorizes *individualized* reflection and choice. In the end, a woman might refuse on principle (antiracist or ecological) to reenact the feminine maternal norm, but alternatively she might conclude that the satisfactions of motherhood would probably outweigh the negatives and decide to have children.

I have not attempted to canvass every conceivable way in which intersectional identity might figure in an autonomous decision about becoming a mother. However, the selection of factors I have presented suffices to demonstrate that intersectional identity contributes to autonomy by connecting individuals to systemic social relations and to the social meanings of those structures. The light social interpretation sheds on seemingly personal conduct makes room for autonomous self-definition—thoughtful clarification or reshaping of one's desires, personal traits, values, interests, and goals—and thus for autonomous self-direction—plotting a course of action that enacts those attributes as fully as possible.

As members of social groups with worthy traditions, individuals may find inspiration and guidance; as border dwellers between social groups, they may find critical tools in one tradition to apply to another; as articulators linking diverse groups, they may find ways to synthesize and reconstruct familiar traditions. But how do they do this? And what does this say about authenticity?

First, it is important to underscore the fact that in the example I sketched the most promising springboards for critical reflection are the dimensions of intersectional identity that are most suppressed and least likely to be taken into account—in this case, race and class. Most U.S. whites do not think of themselves as having any racial identity, and they regard middle-class status as virtually universal and therefore nothing special. Thus, avowing an intersectional identity with race and class as codeterminants itself requires an initial process of autonomous self-definition.

Second, embracing such an intersectional identity would not necessarily lead a woman to the critical levers I have described. She might perceive her race as neutral and her class as an unalloyed blessing. Thus, gaining access to the critical potential of group-identity determinants requires scrutinizing and analyzing the history and current position of the social groups to which one belongs—another process of autonomous self-definition.

Finally, consider a woman who has engaged in the first two forms of self-definition and who has decided against motherhood but who is beset by residual conflicts between that choice and her identity as a woman, a heterosexual, and an Italian American. Her independence of mind and will notwithstanding, her gender, sexual orientation, and ethnicity continue to construct her as a mother and thus wage a psychic guerrilla campaign against her commitment to her chosen course. Let us suppose that she confronts these challenges to her decision and, defying them, renews it. Let us suppose further that she resents the rigidity of the reproductive norms correlated with her gender, sexual orientation, and ethnicity and that she resolves to put a stop to these attacks on her autonomy.[37] To do this, she needs to redefine herself as a woman, a heterosexual, and an Italian American. But, of course, she lacks the cultural and linguistic authority to redefine these categories as she pleases. She can vow to ignore well-intentioned associates' efforts to induce her to reconsider; she can terminate relationships with those who cannot resist menacing her with disparaging comments about her barrenness; she can boycott the pronatalist media onslaught; and so on. But since she has already internalized the motherhood imperative and since extirpating this message is tantamount to repudiating femininity as it is defined by or for these groups, individualistic strategies of self-definition have serious drawbacks, and moreover, they are unlikely to be entirely successful. To address this problem, a nonconformist woman would be well advised to join with other group members and embark on a project of cultural critique aimed at reconfiguring the social identity of their group—a project of autonomous collective self-definition.[38]

For individuals, self-definition involves addressing questions along the following lines: What sort of person am I? What groups do I belong to? What is the significance of belonging to these particular groups? What sort of person do I aspire to be? How do the groups I belong to hold me back? How do they help me? What really matters to me? What desires, personal traits, values, interests, and aims should I seek to enact?

At the collective level, self-definition focuses on social groups, people's attitudes toward them, and their expectations of group members: What are the social meanings of being, say, a woman? What is worth preserving from traditional feminine norms? What should be scrapped? How can we build solidarity among women despite our diversity and disparate needs? What objectives should we pursue as a group? How do we want our group to be symbolized in the popular imagination?

To accomplish self-definition, individuals must exercise a repertory of skills.[39] The competency needed for self-definition includes, but is not limited to, the following:

1. Introspective skills that sensitize individuals to their own feelings and desires, that enable them to interpret their subjective experience, and that help them judge how good a likeness a self-portrait is

2. Imaginative skills that enable individuals to envisage a range of self-concepts they might adopt

3. Memory skills that enable individuals to recall relevant experiences not only from their own lives but also experiences that associates have recounted or that they have encountered in literature or other artforms

4. Communication skills that enable individuals to get the benefit of others' perceptions, background knowledge, insights, advice, and support

5. Analytical and reasoning skills that enable individuals to compare different self-concepts and to assess the relative merits of these alternatives

6. Volitional skills that enable individuals to resist pressure from others to embrace a conventional self-concept and that enable them to maintain their commitment to the self-portrait that they consider genuinely their own, that is, authentic

7. Interpersonal skills that enable individuals to join forces to challenge and change social norms

It is important to recognize that intersectional self-definition poses unusually exiguous problems. A gesture of cultural dissidence, intersectional self-definition involves seeking out heterodox resources within one's culture, perhaps borrowing from other cultures, and synthesizing these materials in novel ways. Individuals who define themselves as intersectional subjects are exceptionally dedicated and intrepid, and they need proficiencies that are sadly uncommon.

It cannot be emphasized enough how difficult intersectional self-definition is. Indeed, I would venture that one reason why the contrarian view of intersectional identity is so attractive is that the obstacles to intersectional self-definition are so formidable. As I have said before, there is no convenient terminology—no shorthand, as it were—for articulating intersectional identities, nor, I would add, are there narrative templates that are conducive to intersectional autobiographies. For the most part, then, people's interpretations of their psychological development, character formation, and desire arousal sideline intersectional identity. Indeed, stories that feature intersectional subjects can seem precious and overcomplicated, if not downright weird. People cannot be expected to cast their gaze inward, behold their intersectional identity, and intuit its import, for culturally transmitted cognitive schemas and emotional scripts organize introspection, and these frameworks are not hospitable to intersectional self-definition. To define oneself intersectionally, one must activate competencies that mesh intellect and feeling in order to seek out and assimilate nonstandard interpretive frameworks. One must be introspectively vigilant, attuned to signs of frustration and dissatisfaction, attentive to baffling subjective anomalies, and willing to puzzle out gaps in one's self-understanding. One must be equipped to tap into oppositional intellectual currents. Curiosity about other people and their cultures is invaluable, and so is a passion for ideas. But it would be disastrous to sponge up whatever one comes across, for neo-Nazis are publicizing their views on the internet alongside benign political movements. Although one cannot learn anything new unless one approaches unfamiliar material in a receptive and charitable spirit, one must command critical thinking skills. Not only must one be alert for errors of fact and fallacies in reasoning, but one must also register emotional cues that signal confusion or danger. Still, extracting what is worthwhile from newly encountered material is the key to enriching one's self-knowledge and to redefining oneself.[40] Thus, one must be able to identify such ideas, incorporate them into one's own cognitive and emotional viewpoint, and apply them as one defines oneself. Yet, since securing an intersectional self-portrait ultimately requires cultural transformation, one must have a way to displace conventional tropes of the self and stereotypes of social groups, as well as a way to replace them with intersectional tropes and emancipatory group images.

Now, individuals with different temperaments, talents, priorities, and personal styles exhibit autonomy competency in distinctive ways. Some rely on reading or exposure to other media to acquaint themselves with heterodox perspectives; others rely mainly on social exchanges.[41] Neither is superior. Some rely on informal support networks to help them develop and sustain intersectional self-definitions; some seek out professional psychological counseling.[42] Both can be effective. To catalyze needed cultural change, some people become journalists, scholars, novelists, or artists and publish books or articles, create artworks or advertizing, or mount dramatic productions; others form political groups within which intersectional identities are reaffirmed and through which social structures that reinforce monistic conceptions of identity and repressive group identities are opposed; others become lawyers, politicians, or business leaders and work through the system to bring about such change.[43] All of these strategies are needed. There is no universal formula or step-by-step procedure for intersectional self-definition.

I have emphasized that intersectional self-definition takes place at both the individual level and the collective level and that self-definition at one level interacts with self-definition at the other. The concerns that individuals identify as central to their lives will shape a group's self-understanding, and a group's interpretation of its social position together with the political agenda it sets for itself will have an impact on the options that are psychologically and materially available to (or beyond the reach of) individuals. These reciprocal effects suggest that self-definition has no terminus. Groups must modify their self-concepts in response to individual needs and initiatives, and individuals must adjust their self-concepts as collectivities reconstruct the meaning of group membership and gain expanded opportunities for members of subordinated groups.[44] Self-definition is best viewed, then, as an open-ended process of reflection, reconsideration, revision, and refinement, and self-portraits are best viewed as works in progress. Authentic intersectional selves are never finalized.

The Authentic Self as an Integrated Self

Lately, there has been quite a vogue in commending play as the prime mode of personal and political agency.[45] The values of insouciance and fun are surely needed as a counterweight to the image of the autonomous individual as an isolated, plodding planner, wholly lacking in panache and merriment, and also as a corrective to the image of leftist activism as a deadening drill of solemnity and stalwartness. Playfulness calls to mind relaxing with friends, as well as casual fooling around that breaks the ice with strangers or eases strained relationships. Likewise, this mode conjures up the frisson of dreaming up outré schemes, the allure of trying on outlandish personas, the kick of bashing the establishment, and the puckish sport of tweaking convention. These gambits connect play with a key strategy for achieving autonomy —namely, improvisation—and also with an important subjective dimension of autonomy—that is, the exhilaration that stems from hitting on just the right enactment of one's desires and values, especially when circumstances are not conducive to expressing them at all.

Playfulness contributes to self-discovery and self-definition when it helps intersectional subjects maintain intimate interpersonal bonds and forge connections across social barriers. Moreover, unlocking one's imagination and freeing up one's will are plainly necessary for self-definition—particularly for members of subordinated groups who have been tyrannized by severely restricted opportunities and repressive norms, but also for members of privileged groups who need to divorce their picture of egalitarian social relations from their fears of loss and fantasies of subjugation. Yet, conflating agency with play threatens to reduce agency to the randomness and arbitrariness of acting on impulse. Members of subordinated groups cannot afford to be seen this way (or, for that matter, to see themselves this way), for being cast as a "playmate" is infantilizing (all too reminiscent of being cast as a plaything), and this belittlement allows others to decline to take their grievances seriously. Nor can members of subordinated groups afford to see members of privileged groups who are mobilizing to defend their dominant status as playmates, for construing their retrograde politics as play would exempt them from accountability. The trait of playfulness is an asset for intersectional subjects, but play is only part of autonomous agency.

Members of subordinated groups should not stake their future on serendipity. The compass of authentic individual identity is needed to guide individuals' choices and to chart a progressive political course. If severing agency from identity is misguided, though, it is necessary to clarify what it is like to have an authentic identity. I begin by considering Harry Frankfurt's influential account of the authentic self. In my view, Frankfurt's treatment of personal integration illustrates how the exigencies of addressing a traditional philosophical problem can supersede awareness of human psychological frailty and the confounding complexity of leading a life in the real world to yield an excessively rigid conception of integration. Indeed, Frankfurt's account shows how very difficult it is to explicate integration without appearing to recommend personal ossification.

Harkening to the classic problem of freedom and determinism, Frankfurt treats the authentic self as a psychic state that ensures free will once a person achieves it. For Frankfurt, one knows what one really wants when one has a "second-order volition" that a first-order desire be effective—that is, when one identifies oneself "decisively" with a first-order desire.[46] Identification is an act of self-constitution, which is accomplished through two types of decision: (1) demarcating the boundaries of the self, that is, separating oneself from desires one does not want to satisfy at all; and (2) internally organizing the self, that is, integrating one's competing desires into a "single ordering" that establishes one's priorities.[47] When one makes such decisions "without reservation" and thus "wholeheartedly," the first-order desires with which one identifies are "authoritative for the self."[48] To have an authentic self is to be wholeheartedly committed to a rank ordering of the desires one has decided to satisfy and to be wholeheartedly disassociated from those of one's desires that one has decided against satisfying. Autonomous individuals act only on their authentic desires; hence they have free will.

On Frankfurt's view, an authentic self is integrated in two respects: (1) one's endorsed first-order desires have been rank ordered so that one knows what is most important, and (2) one does not feel ambivalent about any of these desires or about the priorities one has set for oneself. Integration eliminates conflict, and wholeheartedness complements and completes integration.

Frankfurt accounts for some key phenomena associated with autonomy. At the beginning of this article, I listed some of the colloquial expressions people use to affirm their autonomy—"I feel solid," "I feel right in my skin," and "I feel at one with myself." Frankfurt's conception of wholeheartedness nicely captures the flavor of these expressions and the general sense of resolution, equanimity, and confidence they evoke. In addition, theories of intersectional identity implicitly endorse one form of integration, for they stress the urgency of opening lines of communication between differently situated group members to prevent one segment of the group from undertaking political initiatives that would be detrimental to another. Likewise, they call on group members to find shared interests that can serve as a basis for solidarity. Thus, these theorists underscore the need for intersectional subjects to conceptualize their group-identity determinants in inclusive terms and to integrate this enlarged understanding of the diversity of social groups with their political views. Frankfurt's emphasis on evaluating the worthiness of one's desires and on sorting out one's priorities is consonant with this view of the intersectional subject's political task.

Frankfurt's account of self-constitution through identification also seems promising for intersectional subjects. As the crash trope suggests, members of subordinated groups are victimized by their group identities, although as the membership trope suggests, they also find sustenance in their group identities. Now, it might seem that Frankfurt's idea of identification and integration gives these individuals a technique for coping with this predicament. They can disidentify with the harmful attributes they have internalized, for example, self-doubt, servility, or submissiveness, and they can identify with the empowering attributes they have internalized, for example, a mordant sense of humor, persistence in the face of adversity, or a love of convivial gatherings.[49]

Unfortunately, the strategy of identification and disidentification breaks down when faced with a core feature of subordination, namely, victimization. To disidentify wholeheartedly with one's victimization when one is in fact a victim of systemic injustice is to deny social reality and to foreclose resistance. Such disidentification may redouble the individual's vulnerability to injustice, or it may draw individuals into complicity in their own subordination or the subordination of other group members. Only if individuals can disavow harmful group-linked attributes, while identifying with their position as members of a wrongfully subordinated group and retaining their compassion for group members who have not succeeded in ridding themselves of disabling and disfiguring group-linked attributes, is the strategy of disidentification feasible for autonomous intersectional subjects. But since it is doubtful that one can decisively or wholeheartedly identify with being a victim without succumbing to self-pity or self-annihilation, it is doubtful that such an identification could be integrated into an empowering and coherent hierarchy of desires and values.[50] Indeed, ambivalence toward one's victimization seems a better attitude to strike. Neither wholeheartedly embracing it nor eschewing it, one seems more likely to preserve one's balance *and* one's autonomy.

Whereas theorizing agency as play underrates the intersectional subject's capacities for self-discovery and self-definition, in my judgment Frankfurt's account of authenticity and autonomy demands more self-mastery than intersectional subjects can (or should try to) deliver. Intersectional identity resists wholehearted integration. As the trope of border dwelling suggests, tensions between one's various group-identity determinants are bound to occur. Moreover, since these tensions fuel critique and social innovation, it would be dangerous to eradicate them.[51] For intersectional subjects, then, to attain integration would be to betray one's authentic self. Moreover, I have argued that the intersectional subject's need for ongoing self-definition precludes finalizing one's authentic self. Again, wholeheartedly settling into an ordering of one's desires seems incompatible with authentic intersectional identity.

The root difficulty here is Frankfurt's conception of integration. Recall that according to Frankfurt, conflicting desires with which one identifies must be integrated into a "single ordering."[52] At first, this might seem unexceptionable, for it seems that when people have conflicting desires, either they must set priorities, or events will decide for them. But setting priorities can short-circuit autonomy. Presumably, an autonomous individual would brainstorm and try to come up with a way to satisfy both desires before sacrificing either of them. If this is so, Frankfurt's emphasis on linear rank ordering deflects attention from the skills that enable people to reconcile apparently competing desires—whether by figuring out how both can be enacted after all or by working to change the social context that brings them into irresolvable conflict. Thus, Frankfurt discounts the activity of exercising those skills and inflates the importance of imposing order on one's identity constituents.

It becomes apparent how grave this preoccupation with order is when one recalls that Frankfurt's account is not limited to situation-specific autonomy. He speaks of identifying with characteristics that endure, and he avers that integration "provides . . . for coherence and unity of purpose over time."[53] In this broader context, whole-heartedly committing oneself to a "single ordering" would be self-defeating. There are no desires or characteristics that should always take precedence in any individual's life. Insofar as intersectional subjects are subordinated, they need to be on the qui vive for unanticipated opportunities. Insofar as intersectional subjects are both privileged and subordinated, they need to be ready to extend their social critique and build political coalitions with people whose interests are somewhat at variance with their own. If integration is understood as a wholehearted and lasting commitment to a self-chosen hierarchy of desires, personal traits, values, interests, and goals, and if an integrated self is an authentic self, integration and authenticity are often inimical to autonomy.[54]

Frankfurt might reply, however, that I am fastening on his phrases "single ordering" and "wholehearted commitment" and that I am reading him too literally. When Frankfurt shifts, as he often does, from propounding an account of free will to exploring the byways of moral psychology, it is clear that he regards the process of achieving integration as a gradual one and that he is well aware that intrapersonal conflict may persist despite one's second-order volitions. Nevertheless, we are left with the question of how to understand his claims about integration.

Maybe the right geometrical image for his conception of integration is not the vertical line but rather the pyramid. If integration has a pyramidal structure, an authentic self could have quite a few desires, personal traits, values, interests, and goals on the same level, but as one ascended toward the top of the pyramid, the levels would accommodate fewer and fewer identity constituents. This model would give the autonomous individual the multidimensionality and flexibility needed to respond appropriately to a wide range of situations, for individuals could pick and choose among identity constituents that they have placed on the same level, depending on circumstances. Indeed, the pyramid could be flat-topped, which would allow for the possibility that two or more projects could be of paramount importance. I submit, however, that anyone who tried to decide in advance which sets of desires, personal traits, values, interests, and goals should always take precedence over other sets would either give up, reverse him- or herself in the face of real situations, or live to regret sticking to his or her decisions. Moreover, if part of the point of making decisions and becoming integrated is to eliminate conflict, as Frankfurt claims it is,[55] this model of integration would fail. Suppose an individual puts her career and her family on the same level of her pyramid. The chances are slim indeed —even in a postpatriarchal world—that she will never face conflicts between them.

It seems to me that the geometry of integration is rapidly leveling down to a planar array of multifarious desires, sundry personal traits, plural values, and multiple overarching interests and goals. Yet, it is not true that autonomous people have no idea what is more important to them or that they have no guiding ideals. The trouble with theories of autonomy like Frankfurt's is that there is no way to codify their self-knowledge without forcing it into a mold that falsifies it and that turns autonomous individuals into cartoon figures, mechanically executing their previously elected plans. To be sure, autonomous people think prospectively about how much weight to give to different identity constituents, but they are prepared to adjust their plans, even to alter them radically, in light of new experience or unforeseen circumstances. If a neo-Nazi party made an unexpectedly strong showing in the next congressional elections, many reclusive intellectuals who are deeply committed to scholarship would autonomously set aside book manuscripts to join the battle against this threat.

Frankfurt is right that autonomous people are not incessantly besieged by wrenching conflicts and that they do have a sense of being integrated. I hesitate to call it a feeling of wholeness, but that is the sort of thing nonphilosophers (including many clinical psychologists) say. I think, however, that this sense derives from their powers of insight and judgment and their ingenuity at devising enactments of their desires, personality traits, values, interests, and goals that usually satisfy them; that their associates by and large respect; and that do not regularly antagonize people they need and care about. Although it is important to salvage the idea of personal integration, the quest for a blueprint for personal integration is futile.

Authenticity and Autonomy Competency

We need to reinterpret authenticity and to reconceive the relationship between authenticity and integration. It is a mistake to conflate authenticity with personal integration and to regard integration as a state persons must achieve as a precondition for autonomy. Instead, we should understand personal integration as the emergent intelligibility of an individual's autonomous self-discovery and self-definition. Moreover, since authenticity relies on intrapsychic tensions to spark personal development and social dissent, since it is compatible with ambivalence, and since it languishes if an individual cannot tolerate provisionality and rushes to closure, having an authentic self is best understood as the result of an ongoing activity of persons. By exercising autonomy skills, such as the ones I enumerated previously, people take charge of their identity and gain authenticity.

What autonomous people do to understand and define themselves is not aptly figured by any Euclidean shape or formal reasoning pattern. It is akin to improvisational orchestration.[56] Different instruments take solos; different instruments join in as backup; some instruments may fall silent for awhile. A tune sets the themes of the performance. But the rendition is not preplanned, nor will it ever be repeated in quite the same way. Still, the qualities of the instruments in the ensemble, the musicians' idiosyncratic playing styles, and the melody coalesce into a discernible logic —an integrated dynamic, if you will. Moreover, although the group will never duplicate a performance, their sound—their musical identity—will be recognizable whenever they play together.

I have shifted the accent from "integration" to "dynamic"—that is, from a psychic state, instantiating a prescribed infrastructure, to an intelligible process constituted by skillful but unregimented activity. The capability behind improvisational orchestration is musicianship; the capability behind self-discovery and self-definition is autonomy competency. The authentic self is nothing but the evolving collocation of attributes—analogous to a musical ensemble's sound—that issues from ongoing exercise of this repertory of skills. And an authentic self-portrait is an interpretation of that evolving collocation—analogous to an astute band member's commentary on the group's performance career.

This reorientation makes sense both of the intersectional subject's capacity for authentic identity and of some major obstacles to intersectional authenticity. It is evident that most people have acquired some degree of facility with most of the skills needed for self-discovery and self-definition. Thus, there is hardly anyone who has no authentic identity whatsoever. However, some individuals' circumstances in life strongly discourage them from acquiring this competency and virtually prohibit them from exercising it, whereas a few lucky individuals find themselves in environments that cultivate their autonomy skills and that shower them with opportunities to exercise their competency. Consequently, different people are more or less proficient at exercising these skills, more or less inclined to exercise them, and more or less successful at coordinating their skills into a smoothly functioning competency. Not surprisingly, then, intersectional subjects occasionally feel somewhat estranged from themselves or even thoroughly alienated from themselves. Yet, there are also moments when they are able to summon their skills and make enormous strides in self-discovery or self-definition.[57] Exposure to the concept of intersectional identity itself might precipitate a consolidation of authentic identity. So might discovering an unrealized potential or entering a new social milieu. Still, it must be emphasized that these advances are gains in authenticity, not because some core trait has been disclosed and not because the individual's priorities have been decisively set, but rather because exercising autonomy skills has drawn these attributes into the orbit of the authentic self and "authenticated" this self-portrait.

It might seem that what happens when people exercise these skills well is that they come to have a special feeling about the attributes they include in their self-portrait. As I said earlier, wholeheartedness is not an implausible candidate for this special feeling. But to resort to wholeheartedness would be to revert to a managerial-clerical view of integration, and as we have seen, intersectional identity rules that out. Furthermore, given the complexity of authenticity—the many different sorts of attributes that can be authentic identity constituents, as well as the multitude of ways any one of them can be enacted—it would be astonishing if authenticity were correlated with a single emotion. Thus, I recommend a multipronged account of the subjective sense of authenticity that is linked to exercising autonomy skills. When one is adept and does not need to struggle to exercise a repertory of skills, the activity itself is often absorbing, enjoyable, and satisfying in itself. Moreover, demonstrated competence produces reinforcing feelings of confidence and security. We have seen that self-definition involves self-exploration and self-discovery. Finding an undeveloped aptitude or a hidden virtue can be heartening; it might even spark elation and excitement. It is important to remember, too, that autonomy competency cushions the blow of discovering a limitation or a fault, for it enables people to change and to minimize the ill effects of what they cannot change. Thus, a disappointing revelation about themselves is not likely to plunge them into frustration or despondency. Ideally, it will be perceived as a fascinating puzzle or a revitalizing challenge. Sometimes self-definition reconciles seemingly opposed desires, personal traits, values, interests, or goals. Such resolutions may bring welcome feelings of relief and repose, short-lived though they may be. Finally, it is important to bear in mind the social skills that are enlisted in self-discovery and self-definition—autonomous individuals are equipped both to benefit from others' input and to recruit others to their point of view. This interaction is interesting and gratifying, and the resulting interpersonal backing for self-knowledge is reassuring.

Of course, the emotions I have mentioned do not exhaust the subjective experience of self-discovery and self-definition. Nevertheless, I think I have filled in this constellation of emotions sufficiently to show that it does justice to the idiomatic affirmations of autonomy that I have cited, as well as the sense of wholeness that autonomous individuals report feeling. I would add that since these emotions are tied to the exercise of particular skills, they seem less arbitrary and hence less mysterious than Frankfurt's conception of wholeheartedness.

The competency-based view of the authentic self that I am recommending dissolves the air of paradox around the conjunction of intersectional identity and autonomy. If there is no pattern that an authentic self must fit into, there is nothing troubling about an authentic self that harbors ambivalence about some matters and unresolved tensions between some identity constituents. Inasmuch as unresolved tensions can spur individuals to exercise their self-definition skills in more sophisticated and creative ways, these tensions may prove to be invaluable resources for authenticity. When circumstances are such that ambivalence is a reasonable response, as I have argued it is when individuals are victimized as members of a social group, viewing this attitude as an authentic identity constituent need not defeat autonomy. On a competency-based view of autonomy, it is not necessary to plot out every detail of one's life in advance, for one's autonomy skills enable one to address situations on a case-by-case basis. To be sure, mixed feelings about an identity constituent necessitate skillful deliberation each time it becomes an issue. But that hardly seems a liability if one commands autonomy competency and if no preprogrammed response is appropriate to every occasion. Ambivalence, when coupled with autonomy competency, may ensure supple and subtle responses.

Neither does the evolving, unfinished status of the authentic intersectional self pose a problem for this view of autonomy. Once again, if there is no pattern that an authentic self must instantiate, and if authenticity is not an all-or-nothing matter but allows for degrees, the loose ends of the intersectional subject—gaps and lags in self-knowledge, as well as approximate or incomplete self-definition—need not be problematic. Provided that individuals are able to exercise autonomy competency and are disposed to do so, they will gradually gain authenticity. Piecemeal authenticity, I would urge, is the best that we murky, fallible human beings can hope for.

Correlatively, the competency view makes sense of the fact that intersectional subjects need autonomy to gain the self-knowledge that they need to become authentic. If the autonomy they need to gain self-knowledge is autonomy competency—not a particular configuration of the self achieved through higher-order volitions about the self but rather the repertory of skills through which self-discovery, self-definition, and self-direction are achieved—there is no vicious circularity and no reason to be baffled. As with other competencies, one learns through practice, and practice augments proficiency. Children learn a language by hearing it spoken and by speaking. As they incrementally gain linguistic competency, they express more and more complex and interesting ideas. So, too, with autonomy competency. As one gains proficiency, one's authentic self develops, and one's self-portrait becomes more and more nuanced and rich. On this competency view of autonomy, authenticity is a lifelong project, yet it is attainable, as well as desirable, for intersectional subjects—that is, for us.

Notes

1. I am grateful to the editors of this volume, Catriona Mackenzie and Natalie Stoljar, for their extraordinarily helpful comments on earlier drafts of this article. Also I have presented different versions of this article at the Conference on Feminist Perspectives on Autonomy and Agency at the Australian National University, at a meeting of AMINTAPHIL at the University of Kentucky, at a colloquium of the Philosophy Department at the University of Illinois, Chicago, at the 1998 World Congress of Philosophy, and at sessions sponsored by the Society for Analytic Feminism at the Central Division APA and by the Society for Women in Philosophy at the Pacific Division APA. I am grateful to the audiences at all of those presentations for their responses to my work.

2. For skepticism about this feminist critique, see Marilyn Friedman, "Autonomy and Social Relationships: Rethinking the Feminist Critique," in *Feminists Rethink the Self*, ed. Diana Tietjens Meyers (Boulder, Colo.: Westview, 1997).

3. See, for example, Teresa de Lauretis, "Feminist Studies/Critical Studies: Issues, Terms, and Contexts," in *Feminist Studies/Critical Studies*, ed. Teresa de Lauretis (Bloomington: Indiana University Press, 1986), p. 10; Deborah K. King, "Multiple Jeopardy, Multiple Consciousness: The Context of Black Feminist Ideology," *Signs* 14 (1988): 42–72, 72; Maria Lugones and Elizabeth V. Spelman, "Have We Got a Theory for You! Feminist Theory, Cultural Imperialism and the Demand for 'The Woman's Voice'" in *Women and Values*, ed. Marilyn Pearsall (Belmont, Cal.: Wadsworth, 1986), p. 19.

4. See, for example, Jennifer Nedelsky, "Reconceiving Autonomy: Sources, Thoughts, and Possibilities," *Yale Journal of Law and Feminism* 1 (1989): 7–36, 7; Diana Tietjens Meyers, *Self, Society, and Personal Choice* (New York: Columbia University Press, 1989); Trudy Govier, "Self-Trust, Autonomy, and Self-Esteem," *Hypatia* 8 (1993): 99–120, 103–104; Seyla Benhabib, "Feminism and Postmodernism," in *Feminist Contentions*, eds. Seyla Benhabib et al. (New York: Routledge, 1995), p. 21; and, Alison Weir, "Toward a Model of Self-Identity: Habermas and Kristeva," in *Feminists Read Habermas*, ed. Johanna Meehan (New York: Routledge, 1995), p. 263.

5. For examples, see Meyers, *Self, Society, and Personal Choice*, pp. 3–8.

6. I should note before proceeding any further that I do not regard gender, race, ethnicity, class, and sexual orientation as an exhaustive and final list of group-identity determinants. However, there is wide consensus about the importance of these identity determinants, and these are the ones that the scholars who have developed the concept of intersectionality have stressed. Therefore, although I draw my examples from these sources, I do not foreclose the possibility that there are additional group categories that function intersectionally as codeterminants of identity.

7. The other major contender is multiplicity. See Naomi Scheman, *Engenderings: Con-*

structions of Knowledge, Authority, and Privilege (New York: Routledge, 1993), 102–104. However, I agree with Amy Mullin that in representing complex group-based identity as an internal population of personlike entities, this trope misrepresents complex group-based identity in serious ways. See Mullin, "Selves, Diverse and Divided: Can Feminists Have Diversity without Multiplicity?" *Hypatia* 10 (1995): 1–31. Moreover, I would urge that its associations with the pathology of multiple personality disorder make it an unfortunate choice. See my "The Family Romance: A Fin-de-Siecle Tragedy," in *Feminism and Families*, ed. Hilde Nelson (New York: Routledge, 1996).

8. Kimberlé Crenshaw, "Demarginalizing the Intersection of Race and Sex: A Black Feminist Critique of Antidiscrimination Doctrine, Feminist Theory, and Antiracist Politics," in *Feminist Legal Theory*, ed. Katharine T. Bartlett and Rosanne Kennedy (Boulder, CO: Westview Press, 1991), pp. 57–58.

9. Ibid., p. 63.

10. Ibid., p. 58. For a related discussion of multiple jeopardy, see King, "Multiple Jeopardy," p. 47.

11. Kirstie McClure, "On the Subject of Rights: Pluralism, Plurality, and Political Identity," in *Dimensions of Radical Democracy*, ed. Chantal Mouffe (London: Verso, 1992), p. 115.

12. Kimberlé Crenshaw, "Beyond Racism and Misogyny: Black Feminism and 2 Live Crew," in *Words that Wound*, ed. Mari J. Matsuda et al. (Boulder, Colo.: Westview Press, 1993), p. 114.

13. María Lugones, "On Borderlands/la frontera: An Interpretative Essay," *Hypatia* 7 (1992): 31–37, 34.

14. Chantal Mouffe, "Feminism, Citizenship, and Radical Politics," in *Feminists Theorize the Political*, ed. Judith Butler and Joan W. Scott (New York: Routledge, 1992), pp. 373–374, 381.

15. I confine my observations to current American English. Obviously, other linguistic communities, including other English-speaking communities, may furnish richer resources for articulating intersectional identities

16. Anticipating the next U.S. census, some antirace theorists are stressing the frequency of mixed-race ancestry and are challenging government reliance on familiar racial categories.

17. This is only one of many reasons why the U.S. military's "don't ask; don't tell" policy is bizarre, as well as unfair.

18. K. Anthony Appiah and Amy Guttman, *Color Consciousness* (Princeton, N.J.: Princeton University Press, 1996), p. 80.

19. For discussion of individualized gender identities, see Nancy Chodorow, "Gender as a Personal and Cultural Construction," *Signs* 20, no. 3 (1995): 516–544.

20. See Judith Butler, *Gender Trouble* (New York: Routledge, 1990), and Patricia Mann, *Micro-Politics: Agency in a Postfeminist Era* (Minneapolis: University of Minnesota Press, 1994).

21. I borrow this expression from King, "Multiple Jeopardy."

22. See, for example, Naomi Zack, *Race and Mixed Race* (Philadelphia: Temple University Press, 1993), and Iris Marion Young, "Gender as Seriality: Thinking about Women as a Social Collective," *Signs* 19 (1994): 713–738.

23. For discussion of different varieties of autonomy, see my *Self, Society, and Personal Choice*, pp. 8–19. As will become evident, it is impossible to sharply distinguish one kind of autonomy from another because different domains of autonomous choice and action overlap.

24. It is ironic that some advocates of the intersectional trope hold that just the reverse is true—that an intersectional self is too fluid, too indeterminate to have an identity, let alone an authentic identity. I take up this view in a later section.

25. See Adrian M. S. Piper, "Higher Order Discrimination," in *Identity, Character, and Morality*, ed. Owen Flanagan and Amelie Oksenberg Rorty (Cambridge, Mass.: MIT Press, 1990).

26. If this is so, it blurs Anthony Appiah's distinction between the collective dimension of individual identity and its personal dimension. See Appiah and Guttman, *Color Consciousness*, p. 93. Intelligence, charm, wit, and cupidity—these are Appiah's examples of personal attributes—take on different meanings according to what social groups an individual belongs to. In an anti-Semitic culture, "cupidity" has distinctive connotations when a Jew is being described; in a sexist culture, "charm" has distinctive connotations when a woman is being described; in a racist culture, "intelligence" has distinctive connotations when an African American is being described; and so forth. Thus, stereotypes infect the personal dimension of individual identity.

27. I should stress here that membership in subordinated social groups—indeed, membership in every major subordinated social group—does not necessarily lead to shame and self-contempt. I have more to say about subordinated social groups as sources of heterodox values and personal pride in my discussion of self-definition below. Also, although I do not have space to pursue this related point, it is worth mentioning that intersectional identity could play a key role in an account of transformative experience and retrospective ratification of political conversions. For discussion of this important and difficult topic, see Susan Babbitt, "Feminism and Objective Interests: The Role of Transformation Experiences in Rational Deliberation," in *Feminist Epistemologies*, ed. Linda Alcoff and Elizabeth Potter (New York: Routledge, 1993), and Claudia Card, *The Unnatural Lottery* (Philadelphia, Penn.: Temple University Press, 1996), chap. 2.

28. I do not mean to insist that every member of a subordinated social group is obligated to dedicate himself or herself to resisting injustice. Some people are drawn to politics, and others are not. Still, to ignore injustice may be to dissociate from oneself or to debase oneself. Moreover, ignoring injustice can betray other group members. While there is nothing wrong with choosing not to devote oneself to politics, denying or falsifying one's own background and social position is problematic, and there is a great deal wrong with thwarting others' efforts to overcome group-based subordination.

29. Piper, "Higher Order Discrimination," pp. 296, 305; for related discussion of culturally normative prejudice, see Diana Tietjens Meyers, *Subjection and Subjectivity: Psychoanalytic Feminism and Moral Philosophy* (New York: Routledge, 1994), pp. 51–56.

30. Martha Minow, *Making All the Difference* (Ithaca, N.Y.: Cornell University Press, 1990).

31. Implementing liberal principles without the insights furnished by intersectional identity often amounts to feigning impartiality. Since impartiality is the centerpiece of the liberal democratic ideal, proponents of traditional liberal precepts have good reason to endorse intersectional identity.

32. For good measure, I have used the plural "continuities" to stress that awareness of personal identity is not awareness of an enduring, invariant unit (who would think it is?). I also want to stress that continuities are not uniformities and that continuities can exist along with discontinuities.

33. If members of subordinate social groups are more likely to experience alienation from some of their group identities than members of privileged social groups, they may be more disposed to critically assess the values and practices of different social groups. Although other factors may counteract this disposition and neutralize this advantage, alienation may give individuals from subordinated social groups both a psychological incentive and an epistemic boost in seeking autonomy.

34. See, for example, J. E. Veevers, *Childless by Choice* (Toronto: Butterworths, 1980),

pp. 15, 40–42; Lisa Kay Rogers and Jeffrey H. Larson, "Voluntary Childlessness: A Review of the Literature and a Model of the Childlessness Decision," *Family Perspective* 22, no. 1 (1988): 43–58, 48; and Judith N. Lasker and Susan Borg, *In Search of Parenthood: Coping with Infertility and High-Tech Conception* (Philadelphia: Temple University Press, 1994), p. 11.

35. Simone de Beauvoir, *The Second Sex*, trans. H. M. Parshley (New York: Vintage, 1989).

36. Actually, at that time her Italian immigrant forebears were deemed as much a threat to white racial purity as the recently "emancipated" African-American slaves. In 1999, Italian Americans are fully assimilated whites.

37. It is worth noting that even if she herself capitulates to these reproductive norms and starts trying to get pregnant, she may resent this impingement on her autonomy, and she may dedicate herself to working to overturn these norms for the sake of future generations of women.

38. Nancy Fraser sketches a complementary conception of autonomy as being "a member of a group or groups which have achieved a degree of collective control over the means of interpretation and communication sufficient to enable one to participate on a par with members of other groups in moral and political deliberation; that is, to speak and be heard, to tell one's own life-story, to press one's claims and point of view in one's own voice." See Fraser, "Toward a Discourse Ethic of Solidarity," *Praxis International* 5 (1986): 425–429, 428. In a discussion of group memberships as affinities, Iris Young stresses the emancipatory potential of asserting group difference when doing so "reclaims the definition of the group by the group." See Iris Marion Young, *Justice and the Politics of Difference* (Princeton, N.J.: Princeton University Press, 1990), p. 172. Likewise, Linda Alcoff locates agentic possibilities of collective self-definition in viewing gender as a "construct, formalizable in a nonarbitrary way through a matrix of habits, practices, and discourses." See Alcoff, "Cultural Feminism versus Post-Structuralism: The Identity Crisis in Feminist Theory," in *Culture/Power/History*, ed. Nicholas Dirks, Geoff Eley, and Sherry Ortner (Princeton, N.J.: Princeton University Press, 1994), p. 114. In a similar vein, I have defended a discursive politics of collective self-definition through self-figuration in *Subjection and Subjectivity*, pp. 103–115.

39. For a detailed discussion of these skills and the ways in which they must be coordinated, see Meyers, *Self, Society, and Personal Choice*, pp. 76–91. I would like to refer readers to an intriguing psychological discussion of the experience of control that lends support to my competency-based approach to autonomy. Ellen J. Langer and Justin Pugh Brown observe that psychologists have generally identified experiences of control with the ability to dictate or predict an outcome, and they argue that this conception is misguided. Reflecting on the problematics of control and self-blame in the psychology of victims of sexual violence, they maintain instead that one experiences control when one is "mindful of the choice one was making," that is, when one regards oneself as an able decision maker and has made one's decision in a thoughtful way. See Langer and Brown, "Control from the Actor's Perspective," *Canadian Journal of Behavioral Science* 24 (1992): 267–275, 269, 273. Presumably, individuals who have autonomy competency are more likely to view themselves as good decision makers, more likely to exercise those skills when confronted with choices, and therefore more likely to feel in control of their lives.

40. I can't resist putting in a plug for liberal education here, for it seems to me that education designed to ensure knowledgeability about history and contemporary society and to nurture subtle readings of fiction and biography has a pivotal role to play in strengthening self-definition skills and thus in securing autonomy. I would stress, moreover, that liberal education should not be confined to colleges and universities; grade schools and high schools should also see liberal education as their mission. Neither can I resist lamenting the vacuity of

popular entertainment. The media could be doing a far better job of broadcasting information and innovative ideas for people to reflect on and possibly to appropriate.

41. I owe the inception of my feminist consciousness and feminist sense of gender identity to a friend who would not let me deny the gender bias in a Fellini movie we had just seen, and I owe a great deal of my limited grasp of my racial identity to the work of critical race theorists.

42. I regard myself as lucky to have been associated with women's studies programs throughout most of my professional career, for in addition to their academic contributions, these programs constitute dissident cultural communities in which nonconformist views of personal identity flourish.

43. Despite the relatively small audience for scholarly articles like this one, I cannot help hoping that my writing will have an impact, however small.

44. It is perhaps advisable to issue a caveat at this point. Intersectional identity does not, in my view, suffice to account for social critique and emancipatory politics. Intersectionality is an invaluable trope, but no single figuration of the self can symbolize all identity determinants together with the extensive repertory of intellectual, emotional, and social capabilities that contribute to social critique and emancipatory politics. Since there are different ways in which views of the self can be monistic, monistic views of the self can be misguided for different reasons. Not only do we need to recognize each individual's multiple group memberships, but we also need to draw on multiple figurations of the self (for extended discussion of the virtues of the tropes of heterogeneity and relationality, see my *Subjection and Subjectivity*). Although I endorse the intersectional view of the relation between individual identity and social groups, I do not believe that this relation exhausts individual identity, and I do not favor a monotropic view of individual identity.

45. For example, Butler, *Gender Trouble*; Appiah and Guttman, *Color Consciousness*; Susan Rubin Suleiman, "Playing and Motherhood: Or, How to Get the Most Out of the Avant-Garde," in *Representations of Motherhood*, ed. Donna Bassin, Margaret Honey, and Meryle Mahrer Kaplin (New Haven, Conn.: Yale University Press, 1994); and María Lugones, "Playfulness, "World"-Travelling, and Loving Perception," *Hypatia* 2 (1987): 3–19.

46. Harry Frankfurt, "Freedom of the Will and the Concept of a Person," *The Journal of Philosophy* 68 (1971): 5–20, 10–13, 16.

47. Harry Frankfurt, *The Importance of What We Care About* (Cambridge: Cambridge University Press, 1988), p. 170.

48. Ibid., pp. 170, 174–175.

49. Members of privileged social groups might disidentify with attributes that reinforce their dominant social position and identify with attributes that foster egalitarian social relations.

50. This is not to say that one should never temporarily and strategically identify or disidentify with one's own victimization. Such identification can strengthen bonds of solidarity with other victims, and such disidentification can make psychic space for renewing one's sense of self after a bruising experience. However, such tactical identification and disidentification is not decisive, wholehearted, or identity defining, and it is not the sort of thing Frankfurt is talking about.

51. It is sometimes argued that thoroughgoing integration—the convergence of one's group identities into a smooth blend—is a privilege of the totally privileged. See Naomi Scheman, "Queering the Center by Centering the Queer," in Meyers, *Feminists Rethink the Self*, p. 125. Although I agree that social structures and cultural norms confer "easy" integrity on some privileged individuals, I suspect that this outsider's picture of privilege is not altogether accurate. There are sources of conflict within any group identity; I noted a case in point with respect to white racial identity in an earlier section. The difference between so-

cially esteemed group identities and socially ostracized group identities is that the conflicts are well camouflaged and therefore are difficult to discern in the former. Also, members of privileged social groups have little incentive to uncover them. Ironically, then, in this respect privilege makes it harder to be autonomous. Pure privilege is no panacea for heteronomy.

52. Frankfurt, *Importance of What We Care About*, p. 170.

53. Ibid., pp. 171–172, 175.

54. For related discussion of Frankfurt's account of integration and the virtue of integrity, see Cheshire Calhoun, "Standing for Something," *The Journal of Philosophy* 92 (1995): 235–260, 236–241.

55. Frankfurt, *Importance of What We Care About*, p. 175.

56. In a somewhat different context, Martha Nussbaum invokes jazz improvisation to figure deliberation. See Nussbaum, *Love's Knowledge* (New York: Oxford University Press, 1990). I would also like to mention that the view of personal integration I propose in an earlier work depicts integration as a very loose weave—"a personality marked by characterological strands that are amenable to combination and recombination both amongst themselves and also with various evanescent traits." See my *Self, Society, and Personal Choice*, p. 73. Construed in this way, the concept of integration functions as a beacon for self-definition. Since integration enables autonomous spontaneity and minimizes self-reproach, exercising autonomy skills moves self-definition in this direction (pp. 59–75). But notice that getting carried away and trying to achieve a tight, sharply patterned weave is counterproductive, for people with rigid personalities cannot adjust to changing circumstances and consequently their efforts to realize their values and fulfill their goals are likely to be thwarted. In short, hyperintegration impedes self-direction. Finally, I want to emphasize that, in this view, integration does not dictate the outcome of self-definition. Integrated personalities are unique, individualized personalities.

57. Elsewhere I have discussed the possibility that there might be threads and pockets of autonomy in a life that is not globally autonomous. See *Self, Society, and Personal Choice*, pp. 160–162.

8

THE PERVERSION OF AUTONOMY
AND THE SUBJECTION OF WOMEN
Discourses of Social Advocacy at Century's End[1]

Lorraine Code

> What have I to say about freedom and the self?
> I wondered whether I should not point out that *all* the components of the
> philosophy of the self in the West have . . . had a liberating effect . . . but
> point out, too, that this philosophy was undermined by aspects unfore-
> seen and at the time unforeseeable, repressive aspects having to do with
> phallocentric and colonial patterns of speech. . . . Might it not be neces-
> sary to do two things at once: to emphasize both the permanent value of
> the philosophy of rights, and, simultaneously, the inadequacy, the limits
> of the breakthrough it represented?
>
> (Helene Cixous)[2]

Autonomy

Autonomy has figured prominently as an emancipatory ideal in the feminist, antiracist, and postcolonial analyses of oppression, subjection, subjectivity, and agency
that are the inheritors of the philosophy of rights, as well as in the activism informed by these theories. Yet while recognizing autonomy's effectiveness and its persistent appeal, my entry into this discussion originates in a profound unease with
the autonomy-saturated theories and rhetorics that infuse affluent Western social-
political spaces in the late twentieth century, holding in place a regulative autonomy
ideal that, paradoxically, underpins patterns of oppression and subjection. At the
same time, and aware that in so doing it produces a contradiction, my engagement
with these issues acknowledges the point it challenges: namely, autonomy's liberatory promise for women and other Others, whose marginality is marked and perpetuated by a lack of the very autonomy that many members of advantaged social

groups take unthinkingly for granted and that some feminists—I among them—represent as a contestable value.[3] This discussion thus works within a tension, which it does not seek to resolve. Its aim is less to reconfigure autonomy "relationally" than to think through some enactments of autonomy within relations that are as complicit with larger oppressive structures as they are subversive of them, as constraining of autonomy-realizing potential as enabling of it. Here I focus on *advocacy relations*. But my analysis does not suppose that autonomy can easily be disencumbered of the individualistic baggage it now carries, any more than "care" can be extracted from its feminine associations with a private realm of intimacy to become a value neutrally appropriate for all.[4] Rather it engages with autonomy's ongoing aspirational-inspirational appeal while attempting to disentangle its residual promise from some of the "perversions" of its capitalist patriarchal effects to which my title alludes.

The tension is generated, in part, out of a rift between sedimented Kantian-derived conceptions of unified subjectivity and late twentieth-century "decenter-ings" of the human subject, which destabilize many of the founding assumptions of Enlightenment-liberal autonomy.[5] Modern, often hyperbolized, variations on (Kantian) self-transparency and self-determination frame the picture of human selves that operates regulatively within the dominant social-political imaginary of liberal democratic societies. That picture is remarkably impervious to contestations variously supported in social scientific inquiry and in twentieth-century social-political theory of the very conceptions of subjectivity and agency on which it tacitly relies.[6]

Such contestations suggest that the self with its attendant-constitutive responses and responsibilities, both epistemic and moral, can (historically) no longer be the self and (anthropologically and geographically) never was uniformly the same self for whom classical autonomy ideals were imagined. Twentieth-century psychological, linguistic-philosophical, and historical-material evidence radically unsettles the ideal of unified, self-determining subjectivity. Informed by Freudian theory, Nietzschean genealogy, and postcolonial, post–World War II, and post-1968 political upheavals, it contests the very idea that the subject can be as self-consciously transparent to herself or himself as classical autonomy assumes, thus casting in doubt the "controllability of our own doing" that makes self-determination a plausible goal. Conjoined with a post-Wittgensteinian and post-Saussurean linguistic turn that puts in question the human subject's presumed capacities to "constitute or exhaust meaning" to the extent that it can claim authorship of its own being,[7] these challenges to humanistic ontologies of the self destabilize beliefs in the subject's "mastery" of herself or himself that classical liberal theories require. Intersecting with historical-material refutations of classical autonomy's founding belief in circumstantial homogeneity, whose untenability feminist, antiracist, and postcolonial theorists have amply demonstrated, these lines of thought culminate in a presumption *against* the plausibility of the conception of the self that orthodox autonomy theories presuppose. They delineate a tension between, on one side, an entrenched and indeed escalating adherence to the core assumptions of the classical ideal in the social rhetorics of affluent liberal societies and, on the other side, theoretical and practical-empirical demonstrations, particularly from postpositivistic social science, that the ideal cannot hold.

Mainstream Anglo-American philosophy is not impervious to these upheavals;

conceptions of self, society, subjectivity, and agency are hotly debated issues at century's end. To mention just two loci of contest that are germane to this inquiry: communitarians take issue with the atomistic picture of the moral and political subject they find in John Rawls's theory of justice, arguing that it neglects the significance of communal values in shaping moral-political lives;[8] and many feminists (especially in the United States), indebted to Nancy Chodorow's work in object-relations psychology, have adopted her terminology of "relational individualism" to elaborate a conception of selves embedded in and defined from within intersubjective relations.[9] These critical projects notwithstanding, a hyperbolized version of that presumably supplanted ideal tenaciously dominates the social imaginary—the common sense—of white, Western societies. It descriptively configures and prescriptively animates the discourses of self-sufficient individualism in which "autonomous man" retains his place as an iconic figure, emblematic of an unrealistic imperative toward self-reliant self-making.[10] Exhortations about "being one's own person" and having a coherent "life plan," which infuse twentieth-century social-political discourse, continue to promote self-determination both descriptively and normatively, as though its possibility and desirability were *hors de question*.[11] This rift between theoretical interrogations of autonomy and social practices that assume and uphold it as an old-style universal entitlement perpetuates a discontinuity between philosophical analyses and the politics of autonomy, in an era when many philosophers are as fully committed to addressing the exigencies of everyday lives as to achieving analytic clarity. It maintains a division between theory and practice that amounts, for most feminists, to a false dichotomy.

In its Kantian origins, autonomy is an achievement of Enlightenment, understood as man's "*emergence from . . . self-incurred immaturity*," where the immaturity endemic to heteronomy manifests itself in an "inability to use one's own understanding without the guidance of another." Emancipation is a task "for each separate individual," as the Kantian motto "*sapere aude!*—have the courage to use your *own* understanding!"—signals. It requires people to cultivate "their own minds," making it the "duty of all men to think for themselves"[12] in order to escape the shackles of heteronomy. Yet in his 1984 reading of Kant's essay, Michel Foucault urges twentieth-century readers to notice the limited scope of Kant's "all." He asks: "Are we to understand that the entire human race is caught up in the process of Enlightenment?"[13] The negative answer Foucault expects is anticipated in Kant's assertion that the majority of people "*including the entire fair sex*" will find the move to maturity too difficult and dangerous.[14] Kant's emphasis on the "freedom to make *public use* of one's reason in all matters"[15] confirms the circumscribed scope of this emancipation in societies marked by hierarchical divisions that determine *whose* rational utterances merit public acknowledgement, preserving areas of heteronomy even where autonomy is heralded as a universal possibility. Such exclusions are differently configured in diverse cultural-historical circumstances; they run as much along class, race, and other lines of power and privilege as along lines drawn by membership in "the fair sex." Yet autonomy's defenders tend to read these exclusions as inconsequential to a "universal" release from thraldom, which nurtures a stark individualism fueled by the silent assumption that autonomous man is free to sidestep the constraints of materiality and the power of social-political structures in his projects of radical self-making.

In *The Unnatural Lottery*, Claudia Card articulates feminist hesitations about endorsing this Kantian—and latterly, Rawlsian—conviction that "we can all act as duty requires, come what may," that "our goodness (or badness) is entirely up to us," a conviction that minimizes the extent to which the ordinary lives of many ordinary people are lived within circumstances so oppressive and damaging as to block all routes to autonomous agency. She is "sceptical of Kant's apparent assumption that the same basic character development is accessible to everyone."[16] Guiding her project, Card explains, is a belief that

> it is not enough to confront the inequities of the "natural lottery" from which we
> inherit various physical and psychological assets and liabilities. It is important also
> to reflect on the *unnatural* lottery created by networks of unjust institutions and
> histories that bequeath to us further inequities in our starting positions and that
> violate principles that would have addressed, if not redressed, inequities of
> nature.[17]

The "perversion of autonomy" I name in my title renders these circumstances not merely descriptive but prescriptively coercive in societies permeated by the imperatives of a hyperbolized autonomy conjoined with individualistic conceptions of subjectivity and agency. In what follows, I begin to think through the immobilizing, ultimately autonomy-contesting effects of some of these injustices and coercions. Autonomy in its hegemonic articulations, I am suggesting, is a locally specific value and ideal that is prone to exceed its reach. As Margaret Walker aptly puts it: "A certain kind of society holds out to us, and gives some of us, to varying degrees and at different costs, the gift of (roughly) autonomous lives."[18] Because the scope of its easy realization seems to encompass most of the social spaces inhabited by the upholders of individualistic autonomy—those Sabina Lovibond aptly dubs "worshippers of the individual"[19]— its local specificity often disappears from view.

My discussion therefore traces a curious rhetorical genealogy by which a hyperbolized conception of autonomy has become a controlling, even a distopian, ideal, particularly in the United States and, derivatively, in Canada. This powerful (regional) confluence of autonomy with individualism has issued in a cluster of regulative principles whose effects are as negative as they are positive for people hitherto marginalized. It has generated a social-political-epistemic imaginary visibly peopled by the self-reliant rational maximizer, the autonomous moral agent, the disinterested abstract knower, and the rational economic man of late capitalism, to mention the most familiar tropes; and *invisibly* peopled by less consequential, because less perfectly autonomous, Others. Thus my autonomy skepticism finds echoes in the title of Willard Graylin and Bruce Jennings's book, *The Perversion of Autonomy* (which supplies part of my title). Here Graylin and Jennings contend that "autonomy's success in the struggle for the American moral imagination has made it overbearing and overweening"; that "the imperialism and arrogance of autonomy must be bridled."[20] This "imperialism" fuels the tension between women's (and other Others') legitimate struggles to claim an autonomy that has never been theirs, as these struggles confront *perversions* of autonomy in the affluent parts of the Western world.

The terms of the tension are writ large in an opposition between stark autonomy and a cluster of epistemic and moral practices I call "advocacy," which include representing, arguing for, recommending, acting, and engaging in projects of inquiry in support or on behalf of someone or some group of people, whether epistemologically or morally. My interest is in how advocacy plays into the politics of knowledge, where "advocacy research" becomes a denigratory slogan with which to dismiss research that appears to serve "special" as opposed to universal (read: "dominant") interests and where credibility is conferred in unevenly distributed practices of acknowledgement that claim the power to recognize the experiences of would-be knowers as knowledgeable, grant their testimony fair hearing, and enable their participation in authoritative and emancipatory epistemic practices. Nonstandard (nonmale, nonaffluent, nonwhite) members of epistemic communities often occupy "starting positions" from which they cannot achieve those outcomes "without the guidance of another."

Advocacy and autonomy emerge as oppositional in this "speaking for" sense in the individualistic discourse that shapes the social welfare debates of the 1990s, in which the mythologized "individual" achievements of autonomous man produce as their foil and negative counterexample a reinstituted *subjection* of women. Women come to be judged as unreliable knowers, women on welfare as failing to meet a standard of civic self-sufficiency, women seeking child care as inadequately autonomous in assuming responsibility for their "own" choices, all represented as "entirely up to them." Structurally, the process recapitulates the subjection to paternalistic tutelage John Stuart Mill sought to counter more than a century ago.[21] Against this autonomy-advocacy opposition, I am working to construct an ecologically modeled conceptual apparatus that will counter autonomy's hyperbolic excesses. My project is both diagnostic and prescriptive. Locating itself "down on the ground," it is informed as much by the rhetorical effects of autonomy imperatives in people's lives and situations—what I call their "habitat"[22]—as by philosophical-conceptual analyses of autonomy "as such."

Epistemology

In Anglo-American mainstream theories of knowledge, this hyperbolized autonomy ideal permeates and legitimates the discourses of impersonal mastery that trade on an image of autonomous man as a ubiquitous, invisible expert-authority, who stands above the fray to view "from nowhere" the truths the world reveals to a mind prepared. Epistemic autonomy is a multifaceted ideal, which I paint here with broad strokes. I discern it also where "autonomy" was not the term of art that the philosopher(s) used, yet where the effects of the ideals that animate the theory justify the translation. The autonomous knower escapes the governance of the body, transcends reliance on the senses, to cultivate reason freed from every distracting influence. Neither for a Cartesian disembodied reasoner nor for a merely incidentally embodied empiricist knower do knowledge-productive effects flow from the specificities of embodiment. Epistemic autonomy celebrates an escape from the influences of Bacon's "Idols,"[23] and latterly, too, from the influences—the governance —of *location* and the particularities of experience and identity. Hyperbolized, this facet of autonomy becomes the stark objectivism that is the keystone of twentieth-century scientistic positivism, in which it is abstract individuals who know, each a potential surrogate for every other because they are never individuated. Continuous with Kant's injunctions, autonomy is also about thinking for oneself, having the courage to use one's own understanding. Epistemic self-reliance is its watchword: freedom from dogma, opinion, or hearsay and from subjection to the heteronomy of higher authority, be it sacred or secular.

The appeal of epistemic autonomy is clear. Transcending the confusion of sensory, social, emotional, and locational particularity is the Holy Grail that inspires the epistemological project, promising the certain knowledge that only objective detachment can yield. And within controlled circumstances, success has seemed to be possible. As physical and technological science extend "man's" knowledgeable control of his environment, they fuel this autonomous dream, perpetuating the social imaginary that sustains it and disqualifying more frankly *situated* contenders from recognition as knowers.[24] Epistemic autonomy legitimates mastery over the "external" world, generating structures of authority and expertise, as the power to predict, manipulate, and control objects of knowledge—both human and nonhuman—informs and guides inquiry. It is but a short step to the place where autonomous man in his epistemic robes claims a responsibility to think and know for Others too immature to escape the constraints of heteronomy—to know "their own" interests or to understand their experiences—even as he separates responsibility for the uses to which his knowledge is put from a quest for knowledge that speaks for itself and is good for its own sake.

Yet the tension holds. Successor epistemology projects committed to destabilizing power-infused patterns of epistemic authority often incorporate campaigns for epistemic autonomy by or on behalf of those who continue to dwell in (enforced) tutelage: autonomy as the "freedom to make public use of one's reason," the "courage to use [one's] own understanding." Epistemic heteronomy has consistently been women's lot under patriarchy, manifested at its most outrageous in a conviction that women cannot even know the truth of their own experiences. Small wonder, then, that autonomy persists as a feminist goal, despite the often antifeminist consequences of its hyperbolic invocations.

Testimony's uneven successes in claiming acknowledgement are at the heart of the issue. Of the classical sources of empirical knowledge—perception, memory, and testimony—testimony ranks a distant third on a scale of epistemic respectability. Greater esteem accrues to the putatively more direct, more self-reliant processes of perception and memory. Testimony's *situatedness*, its inescapable positioning as *someone's* speech act, locates it closer to opinion, to hearsay rather than to sanitized —thus presumably more trustworthy—sources of knowledge in controlled observation conditions. Its source in the specificities of experience puts testimony's detachment and replicability in question. Hence denigrations of testimony persist in epistemology and the politics of knowledge, insisting on and reinforcing the illusion of cognitive autonomy. Testimony challenges that illusion; it stands as a constant reminder of how little of anyone's knowledge, apart from occurrent sensory input, is *or could be* acquired independently, without reliance on others. Testimony—in the elaborated sense of learning from other people; from the cultural wisdom embedded in everyday language; and from books, media, conversation, journals, and standard academic and secular sources of the information—makes knowledgeable living possible. Thus it is curious to discredit testimony because it offers evidence *not* achieved "independently" and "at first hand." Most epistemic negotiations and many justificatory strategies take testimony as their starting point, as they engage questions about who knows and how. Their resolutions have as much to do with testimony's variable credibility as with perception and/or memory singly conceived. Yet despite overwhelming everyday evidence, showing that people are fundamentally reliant on testimony and advocacy, the image of the self-reliant knower confronting the world directly remains integral to and constitutive of the dominant model of knowledge in mainstream epistemology. Indeed, if that image could not be held intact, the basic tenets of the system would also fail to hold. With other feminist epistemologists, my purpose is to contribute to the evidence that they cannot.

In standard epistemologies, it is in its "flattened" moments, when it reports on —replicates—simple (*S* knows that *p*) knowledge claims and can be assimilated to aural perceptual-observational knowledge, that testimony is most amenable to formal analysis: "Jane said that she knew Dick had fed Spot."[25] Here it claims its greatest credibility, at scant remove from perception and memory. But when it moves closer to concrete and frankly personal reporting, testimony no longer claims the replicability required of orthodox empirical knowledge, and thus its credibility diminishes.

Yet testimony is seldom concerned with generalities, with universals. It is about particularity, about concrete things that "merely happen," a feature that exacerbates its uneasy relations with objectivist theories of knowledge. Thomas Nagel puts the problem well: "Something in the ordinary idea of knowledge must explain why it seems to be undermined by any influences on belief not within control of the subject—so that knowledge seems impossible without an impossible foundation in autonomous reason."[26] Because a morally sensitive epistemology of particularity that pays responsible attention to testimony cannot claim such a foundation, it appears to face two choices. Either it must relinquish its claims to count as epistemological inquiry, or it must push against the boundaries of the orthodoxy to demonstrate its effectiveness in addressing issues on which moral and epistemic agents require guidance. Here I opt for the second alternative: for an epistemology-morality that (borrowing Margaret Walker's words) "bears a far greater *descriptive* and *empirical* burden, in pursuing details of actual moral [and epistemic] arrangements, than it is commonly thought to entail."[27] In so doing, I challenge a philosophical assumption that beginning in particularity entails remaining stuck there, enmeshed in the minutiae of the concrete and unable to escape the merely experiential.

Anne Seller's claim that "as an isolated individual, I often do not know what my experiences are" and Ludwig Wittgenstein's claim that "knowledge is in the end based on acknowledgement" capture the limitations of the autonomy-of-knowledge credo as it discredits the testimony that makes experiential knowledge possible.[28] Gaining acknowledgement requires more than the courage "to use one's own understanding," more than an individual resolve to make free "public use of [one's] reason," in a hegemonic social imaginary that discounts testimony because of the testifier's failure of self-reliance or of her or his disenfranchised position in the social order. Membership in "the fair sex" is but one such position: a sex whose very "fairness" annuls expectations of fair acknowledgment.

Advocacy

Modern science and orthodox epistemologies established themselves in a founding gesture in which, as Lynette Hunter observes,

> neutral logic and pure language replaced "rhetoric." [And science assumed] a rhetorical stance that denied that the rhetoric of social persuasion in historical context was needed, even denied that it existed . . . built upon the concept of the "universal autonomous man," able to communicate infinitely replicable experience [and] isolation from the social world, which might contaminate the purity or challenge the totality of explanation. . . . *Its rhetoric claims that there is no need for rhetoric.*[29]

With testimony at its epistemic core, advocacy defies these assumptions. Hence, transgressing the boundaries that claim to separate objective knowledge claims from rhetoric, it moves to the margins of epistemic legitimacy.

Like testimony, advocacy bears the taint of the Kantian claim that emergence from heteronomous immaturity requires using "*one's own* understanding without the guidance of another." To the media-informed eye, legal contests, where the aim is to ensure that advocacy triumphs, confirm the mutually antithetical character of advocacy and truth. Despite legal limitations on misrepresentation, lawyers' well-known commitments to advocating *for* their clients reinforce the belief that advocacy, by definition, abdicates respect for truth. Analogously, in medical discourse a sharp distinction between measurable, diagnosable symptoms and context-providing narratives proclaims a connection with advocacy that disqualifies narratives from contributing truth-producing evidence to a physician's medical knowledge.[30] In moral-political discourse, advocacy is cast as the villain behind conflicts of interest and ideologically driven lobbying, evoking the "interest group" label that invites condemnation in the social rhetorics of equal (impartial) treatment for all, in which impartiality is objectivity's analogue.

Empiricist epistemologists, for whom facts are self-presenting—they need no one to speak (advocate) for them—confirm that advocacy obstructs objectivity. There is no need to see facts through anyone else's eyes, and an autonomous knower will refuse such (heteronomous) dependency. Such assumptions fuel charges that represent "advocacy research" as inquiry in the service of "special interests," which sacrifices objectivity to those interests. Peter Novick, writing of historical knowledge, summarizes the position well: "The objective historian's role is that of a neutral, or disinterested, judge: it must never degenerate into that of an advocate or, even worse, propagandist."[31] The juxtapositions he invokes display advocacy's presumed proximity, for epistemologists, to the worst rhetorical excesses.

Nor are such worries unfounded. Advocacy operates variously; sometimes, undoubtedly, it "shapes the truth" to serve specific ends, truth becomes subservient to those ends (which are themselves often nefarious), and "propaganda" is the appropriate label; exposure and censure the required responses. Yet this is neither advocacy's only nor even its principal function. In the examples I address, advocacy practices endeavor to *get at* truths that operate imperceptibly and implicitly, below the surface of the assumed self-transparency of evidence. They are strategically effective in claiming discursive space for "subjugated knowledges," putting knowledge into circulation where it can claim acknowledgment and working to ensure informed, emancipatory moral-political effects.[32] Because advocacy's epistemic and moral-political aspects are intertwined, *responsibility* is central to its respectable functioning. Advocacy is at once dependent on the quality of knowledge that informs it and on the level of epistemic responsibility and the climate of trust in which it circulates. Just and fair interpretive judgment of testimonial claims is at issue. Advocacy practices rely for their "goodness" on the expertise of the advocate(s) and their responsiveness to testifiers, who in their isolation, often require the guidance of others to know what their experiences are. It makes truths available for negotiation with, by, and for people diversely positioned in an epistemic hierarchy that erroneously assumes universal, autonomous access to the evidence and the acknowledgement on which knowledge depends. At its best, then, advocacy can counterbalance the patterns of incredulity into which the testimony of marginalized knowers tends to fall.

My interest, specifically, is in women's and other Others' positionings within advocacy relations that promote or thwart autonomous epistemic stances. But this is a collective, collaborative autonomy; it is not "relational" in the more enclosed sense that derives from object-relations theory. It is enacted in interpretive, "advocative" communities of which one-one dyadic relations are only one minor example. Democratically engaged, advocacy relations foster negotiations aimed at countering the isolation that inhibits the experiential knowledge of which Anne Seller writes and promoting the acknowledgement that Wittgenstein declares the sine qua non for establishing knowledge.

At the confluence of ideal autonomy and individualism, the epistemic dichotomy between autonomy and advocacy is sustained and runs parallel to two further regulative dichotomies: the fact-value dichotomy and the justification-discovery dichotomy. Within their confines, bona fide knowers stand judiciously and impartially outside processes of discovery, which are represented as temporally prior to and substantively distinct from knowledge and knowing proper. These knowers distance themselves from the guesses, trials and errors, persuasions, and negotiations integral to "contexts of discovery." Discovery is conceived as a messy, value-infected process whose planned obsolescence ensures its invisibility in "contexts of justification": the evaluation, adjudication, verification, and/or falsification that are the proper business of epistemology. Here values and human interests are rigorously expunged to allow facts to stand forth in their crystalline purity. Thus even though values indeed permeate processes of discovery, knowledge as product can be cleansed of their distorting influence in autonomous, impartial justification.

Feminist epistemologists, together with naturalistic and other successor epistemologists, however, have reclaimed the epistemic centrality of practices of discovery, both institutional and everyday, moving them back into focus as places where situational specificities shape knowledge-producing projects at every level. Demonstrating that politically infused assumptions structure most research projects from the bottom up, if often tacitly, feminists expose the elusiveness of value neutrality, even as they show that mainstream epistemology is itself as value-laden as the "special interest" projects it denigrates for their explicit commitment to values and interests. As

Donna Haraway, with characteristic irony, notes: "the messy political does not go away because we think we are cleanly in the zone of the technical."[33]

These feminist arguments contest the emotivism that represents values and interests as merely noncognitive expressions of feeling. Values, background assumptions, and locational specificities that inevitably inspire and inform inquiry are as open to critical evaluation as are its "products." Indeed, as Sandra Harding puts it, the "strong objectivity" that characterizes many feminist projects refuses to allow inquirers "to be unconcerned with the origins or consequences of their problematics and practices or with the social values and interests that these problematics and practices support."[34] Strong objectivity demands a breadth of scrutiny that encompasses both the specificities of the standpoint of the knower and the "nature" of the known in order to fulfill its claims that avowedly engaged, politically committed investigations can yield well-warranted conclusions.

"Naturalized" epistemologists—even those who claim no political investment—are comparably committed to abandoning the quest for a priori necessary and sufficient conditions for knowledge in general in their studies of how epistemic agents actually produce knowledge, variously, within the scope and limits of human cognitive powers as these are revealed in the same projects of inquiry.[35] Naturalism (recalling Walker's words) takes on "a far greater *descriptive* and *empirical* burden, in pursuing details of actual [epistemic] arrangements" than standard Anglo-American epistemologies have tended to do. Contrary to some of its critics, it is not merely descriptive, for it aims to achieve good descriptions in order to bring its normative requirements within the range of human (natural) cognitive abilities.[36] Indebted to the work of W. V. O. Quine, many naturalists examine knowledge production within cognitive science laboratories to establish their conclusions. In my work, by contrast, I loosen the connections between naturalism and science (especially in its scientistic aspects) to propose that secular knowledge making supplies "more natural" sites for studying knowledge production in its local specificity and its global effects. Here, advocacy relations are those sites: exemplary of places and processes where knowledge is collaboratively negotiated.

I examine advocacy in two locations: first, in medicine, where philosophers often discuss it as a moral issue that either compromises or enhances autonomy, yet where I read it also as an epistemological issue; and second, in the discourses of social welfare that work from a presumption of individualistic self-reliance that generates coercive, regulative autonomy imperatives. These examples are about the functioning of advocacy in a relational nexus in which lines of epistemic power and privilege structure the constitutive relations.

Medicine

Advocacy tends to appear as an ethical issue in the literature of theoretical medicine, where the commonly named advocates are nurses, physicians, patient or lay advocacy groups, lawyers, and pharmacists.[37] Sometimes they—especially nurses—act as intermediaries, from patient to doctor or to the medical establishment, representing the patient's interests, which for structural reasons the patient is unable to represent autonomously (for herself or himself). Often (though less so in patient advocacy groups), the relationship is structured around assumptions of a patient's passivity, with autonomy as the preferred contrast and advocacy as the route toward achieving it. The language of "representing interests" may appear to contain the issues within a moral-political frame. But closer reading shows that they are as significantly about knowledge—experiential knowledge—about facilitating its passage through structures of public visibility and scientificity en route to claiming the acknowledgment that makes informed moral deliberation possible.

Of interest to feminists has been a path depicted as running from inarticulate patient to appropriately "experienced" nurse to scientifically knowledgeable doctor, following an ascending line of legitimation that culminates in and confirms the commonsense belief that "doctor knows best." Here the (presumptively) female nurse acts as an intermediary, advocating from patient to (presumptively) male doctor. Assuming that the nurse's "special understanding" enables her to promote the patient's "autonomy, dignity and best interests," this picture at once confirms the nurse's position within a care-giving sphere and contains her within gender-specific patterns of deference to the doctor's acknowledged expertise.[38] Peta Bowden's nuanced analysis shows how this capacity of sensitive nursing practice can perform what I call the *advocacy* that enables patients to "interpret their dependency as harmonious with an established context, yet free of conflict with celebrations of autonomy and independence in the wider culture."[39] From a feminist point of view, the politics of these discussions—of which Bowden is well aware, yet which I cannot discuss fully here—are contestable in their confirmation of the power structures of traditionally gendered divisions of labor. But the issue of how testimony-based knowledge can cross the threshold of acknowledgement is salient; clearly the autonomous knower—even of his or her "own" experiences—is a rare bird. Speaking from her experiences of physical disability, Susan Wendell observes: "My subjective descriptions of my bodily experience need the confirmation of medical descriptions to be accepted as accurate and truthful."[40] The question is how such experiential knowledge could achieve acknowledgment; the answer is not to be found in the autonomy-of-knowledge credo.

Wendell's observation thus invites the stronger claim that even with pain and suffering—experiences that are quintessentially "my own" and that form the cornerstone of epistemic "privileged access"—I cannot, as an autonomous knower, know what my experiences are. For people who are traditionally silenced, marginalized, and discredited—women, blacks, the poor, the disabled, the elderly—these problems are acute. Thus Elaine Scarry eloquently confirms the isolation of experiential certainty:

> For the person in pain, so incontestably and unnegotiably present is it that "having pain" may come to be thought of as the most vibrant example of what it is to "have certainty," while for the other person it is so elusive that "hearing about pain" may exist as the primary model of what it is "to have doubt."[41]

Acknowledgement is far more elusive than arguments from first-person privileged epistemic access can allow; here epistemic autonomy recedes to a vanishing point. Scarry observes:

> The success of the physician's work will often depend on the acuity with which he
> or she can *hear* the fragmentary language of pain, coax it into clarity, and inter-
> pret it . . . many people's experience . . . would bear out the . . . conclusion that
> physicians do not trust (hence, hear) the human voice, that they in effect perceive
> the voice of the patient as an "unreliable narrator" of bodily events, a voice which
> must be bypassed . . . so that they can get around and behind it to the physical
> events themselves.[42]

When that voice speaks from within stereotypically sustained patterns of incredulity that in the dominant social imaginary tell against the veracity of its tellings
because of the marginal status of the teller, it is no wonder that autonomously
knowing even one's own experiences can neither be taken for granted nor achieved
without advocacy.

In short, I am claiming that *practices of advocacy often make knowledge possible*
within the hierarchical distributions of autonomy and authority in Western societies. The point comes across clearly in a cardiac condition known as syndrome X
and in chronic neurological-muscular pain known as fibromyalgia: two afflictions
more common for women than for men.[43] Because neither pathology is readily de-
tectable in standard diagnostic procedures, patients who present their symptoms to
a physician—because they *know* that there is something wrong with them—are frequently dismissed as complaining of a pain that is "all in their minds," and therefore
not *real*.[44]

Advocacy is the epistemic (the politics-of-knowledge) issue. The point is not
that practitioners of "normal science" (normal medicine), where male experiences
silently establish the norm, *should* know that women's experiences might manifest
differently from men's, and thus that women *should not* merely receive instructions
to live with their symptoms. These are hollow "shoulds" when the authority of textual interpretation is confirmed by the best scientific standards, according to which
symptoms that do not "fit" count as aberrant and anomalous.[45] The force of the paradigms that govern medical knowledge is such that *individual* dissenting voices,
whether of patients or physicians, have scant hope of claiming a hearing.[46] Only a
substantial and authoritative chorus of interrogating voices can initiate research that
could dislodge an established procedure or check the inertia of established practice.
It is not enough for people *autonomously* (separately) to maintain the veracity of
"their own" experiences; nor is women's failure to gain autonomous acknowledgment a sign of their immaturity as members of the fair sex, dwelling still in tutelage.

Thus the stripped-down fiction of uniformly perceptive, autonomous knowers
confronting self-announcing facts has to yield to a picture of knowledge construction as a social-communal-political process, in which items of would-be knowledge
are embedded in discourses informed by interests, hierarchies of power and privilege, uneven credulity, and the pragmatics of giving or withholding trust. Such an
epistemic terrain becomes a fertile ground for advocacy to demonstrate its effectiveness in opening out rhetorical spaces prepared for *the insurrection of subjugated
knowledges*.[47]

Consider the following example. Speaking of syndrome X, Robin Henig notes
that in response to persistent and growing patient activism, once "a handful of car-

diologists" began to hear the hitherto muted voices of these "frustrated heart patients," a massive clinical trial was launched in the United States, all of whose 140,000 subjects are women.[48] Analogously, when *Harvard Women's Health Watch* corroborates these women's experiential reports, the credibility index of the syndrome X story rises.[49] The conclusion again suggests itself that advocacy research, empirically grounded, scientifically conducted, and politically enacted—but *advocacy* nonetheless—is necessary if such breakthroughs are to disrupt the sedimented knowledge that informs institutional power structures.

For feminism's detractors, however, any hint that research is advocacy-driven condemns it as deficient in objectivity and, therefore, in credibility. To cite just one example, Christina Hoff Sommers criticizes a study of rape in contemporary U.S. society with the claim that "High rape numbers serve gender feminists by promoting the belief that American Culture is sexist and misogynist." She contends: "We need the truth for policy to be fair and effective. If the feminist advocates would stop muddying the waters we could probably get at it."[50] The tacit contrast here is instructive: Sommers assumes that research that is not explicitly feminist operates from no preconceived agenda, hence, apparently, that objective inquiry amounts to random fact finding designed to serve no specific ends. Yet this assumption sits oddly with her belief that projects designed to show that the rape statistics are unrealistically high will, by contrast, be innocent of political commitments.[51] The contrast is an odd one, commonly drawn to distinguish research that implicitly confirms the status quo (and thus claims apolitical status) from research that contests received truths from an explicitly declared standpoint or situation. The rhetoric of "interest group advocacy" preserves the presumption of disinterestedness on the part of unmarked, dominant inquirers.

The issue is complex. Politically informed theorists are well aware of the advocacy research that promotes the interests of drug companies, governments, the arms industry, manufacturers, and multinational corporations with research designed to demonstrate the harmlessness of toxicity-producing practices too numerous to mention. On the basis of these examples alone, it is no wonder that advocacy research has a bad name. Yet advocacy research is multifaceted in its aims and agendas, as frequently benign as it is malign in its findings. Think, by way of contrast, of the advocacy research devoted to developing safer contraception, fighting to eradicate pollutants and toxic substances, studying environmental and workplace harms, and investigating scientifically worthy remedies for disease. The issue, then, is not about condemning advocacy *simpliciter* but about establishing deliberative communities where inquiry is subject to public scrutiny that evaluates agendas according to larger criteria of responsible epistemic practice.[52] Without advocacy, phenomena such as syndrome X could not achieve recognition as pathologies that require major reconfigurations in "normal medicine."

Advocacy is thus both an epistemic and a political issue. Without advocacy, few of "us" will become sufficiently expert to challenge the combined force of scientific paradigms and hegemonic social imaginaries that sustain the politics of knowledge. Nor is the problem about expertise and authori*tative* practice *tout court* but rather about specific instances when authori*tarian* expertise operates behind a screen of autonomous objectivity to paper over the gaps, the breaks in the putatively seamless imaginaries that legitimate it. Ignorance unacknowledged becomes the thematic issue; it takes an expert advocate to expose the gaps in the knowledge of the experts.

What was long seen as women's and other "underclass" knowers' failure to have the courage to use their own understanding (*sapere aude*) emerges as a universally unrealizable, even impossible demand. And (some, usually white) men's apparent successes recall Claudia Card's "unnatural lottery." The ease with which they fit text-book descriptions, with which their testimony receives acknowledgment and their experiential utterances are taken on faith, can only be explained in terms of the starting positions they occupy in "unjust institutions" such as those Card names.

Social Welfare

Graylin and Jennings's book referred to in my title does not engage with advocacy. It locates itself, still, within the autonomy versus coercion debates that originated in 1960s protests against paternalism, in medicine and elsewhere. Autonomy run wild, they suggest,[53] denies coercion's necessary function in promoting human well-being. Showing people what is best for them requires reclaiming a "community-oriented" version of paternalism, which they represent as a "softened" and therefore justifiable form of coercion.[54] The authors, however, offer no analysis of the power and privilege asymmetries in societies where patterns of incredulity prevail at a level well below the place at which their deliberations begin. In consequence, their analysis leaves open no space between "the perversion of autonomy"—about whose features I think they are often right—and "the proper uses of coercion"—where I think they misrepresent the social-political situation.

A false dichotomy between autonomy hyperbolized and reclaimed practices of social control that promote "the good of the individual" structures the analysis.[55] The authors are less concerned with the space between, where the interpretive, negotiative, and testimonial work of advocacy occurs, collectively and critically, in communities that resist the impossible demands that an autonomy obsession exerts. This is the space where open, responsible, and creatively critical democratic deliberation, both personal and social-political, can occur. By contrast, Graylin and Jennings's quest for the proper uses of coercion appears to start from a place where a stark condemnation of advocacy reinstates the iconic figure of autonomous man as a regulative exemplar. He reenters as the central figure in a discourse in which stereotypes short-circuit any need to know people and their circumstances well, posing as knowledge-achieved that renders unnecessary the very negotiations that could make more responsible knowing possible.

Examples abound in the politics and rhetorics of social welfare, in which an assumed equality of access to social goods, that requires no advocacy, underwrites the belief that failure to achieve autonomy is a social sin. Thus "public" measures are enacted to enforce self-sufficient autonomy after all, while reliance on social services slides rhetorically into a weakness, a dependence on social advocacy that, paradoxically, invites—and receives—judgments of moral turpitude. For example, in her poignantly titled essay, "The Unbearable Autonomy of Being," Patricia Williams shows how the entrenched stereotype of "the black single mother" in the United States is often invoked to disguise "the class problems of our supposedly classless society . . . by filtering them through certain kinds of discussion about race and the shiftless, undeserving, unemployable black 'underclass.' "[56] In consequence, single mothers (who are *not*, she notes, predominantly black or "teenaged") are left resolutely to their own devices, as the advocacy that might elicit more responsible responses from an affluent society is condemned as special pleading for members of "interest groups" who have not made the right choices, not exercised self-restraint and self-reliance, and not contributed "appropriately" to the society that demonizes them. Even arguments that ought to awaken the self-interest of the affluent in response to evidence that single mothers "now bear a greater responsibility than at any time in our history for raising the children of this society," and hence that everyone has a stake in the well-being of these children, are reconstructed as truth-ignoring advocacy for the "shiftless welfare queen who always gets more than she deserves."[57] The presumed autonomy of the affluent sex, class, and race that allows them to "know" her thus produces and condemns a new heteronomy of others who fail by its unexamined coercive standards.

Cornel West offers an analogous example:

> The new black conservatives claim that transfer payments to the black needy engender a mentality of dependence which undercuts the value of self-reliance and of the solidity of the black poor family. . . . [Yet] in the face of high black unemployment, these cutbacks will not promote self-reliance or strong black families but will only produce even more black cultural disorientation and more devastated black households.[58]

An ever vigilant individualistic and coercive imperative takes on a censorious demeanor that suppresses the possibility that such responsibilities are more collective than individual. A set of intransigent assumptions keeps in circulation the prescriptive consequences of hyperbolized autonomy, bypassing empirical evidence that demonstrates how the effects of "the unnatural lottery" count among the conditions that make knowledge possible or block its passage altogether.

Such rhetorical shifts reinforce the coercive power of an old-style autonomy that discredits the very advocacy practices that are integral to the idea of a society as a locus of mutual responsibility. Yet social welfare, in the United States and Canada as elsewhere, came into being because of *advocacy* (often by women) to privileged people who were themselves able to expect social benefits, as a matter of course, that in less affluent positions earned the label "welfare."[59] The rhetoric of self-reliance, sanctimoniously manipulated, enforces a stoic version of autonomy, separately and singly, on people thwarted in their efforts to achieve it by the very free-market society whose "just" distributions of power and privilege produce their deplored "inability." As Wendell notes, "When governments want to make cutbacks in social services, they may 'release' people from institutions without adequate support to enable them to live on their own . . . describing the changes they make as creating more 'independence.' "[60] Yet these perversions of autonomy enforce renewed patterns of subjection after all.

The rhetoric that encourages dismantling the welfare state reiterates the rhetorics of opposition to its creation. Martha Minow records that "to many observers, state-supported social welfare jeopardizes individual autonomy, independence and freedom."[61] Opposition to the infant and maternal health legislation (1927) deployed "communist" and "socialist" as terms of invective, inveighing against it because it "interfered . . . with the free-market economy" and voicing fears that "women would reject their traditional roles, *given the act's encouragement of women to seek information about their own bodies and health.*"[62] *Sapere aude* indeed. The voice of autonomy hyperbolized is as audible here as in the 1994 California repeal of welfare for single mothers, with arguments that welfare thwarts their autonomous self-reliance, and in Ontario's 1995–1996 conservative attacks on social welfare that "interferes" with personal autonomy. Welfare as a vehicle for a "free ride" is the guiding metaphor, an image that masks the extent to which welfare humiliates and coerces even as it "helps." Minow notes that "public assistance and social work interventions too often . . . controlled and restricted . . . people [in need] and subjected them to governmental regulation without protection against power imbalances."[63] Linda Gordon observes that welfare "humiliates its recipients by subjecting them to demeaning supervision and invasions of privacy."[64] What the discourse of autonomy initiates as an entitlement mutates into a disempowering gift that imposes obligations its recipient cannot honor, for the very reasons that led her to seek assistance in the first place.

Welfare issues, then, are about relations to and within an intransigent system informed by stereotyped "knowledge" of subjectivity and agency that continues to hold autonomous man in place as a regulative fiction while subjecting women and others who cannot measure up to the dictates of an impossible imperative. This putative knowledge legitimates policies, actions, and treatments modeled on *his* experiences and options and glosses over the extent to which autonomous man himself is dependent on patterns of invisible advocacy for "his own" putatively autonomous achievements.

In both of these relational complexes, it may appear that the point of advocacy is to secure the very autonomy that is lacking. Indeed, the empowering practices enjoined and engaged often name autonomy realization among their goals. But this is autonomy entirely remodeled: disindividuated, decentered, and reconfigured along patterns of mutual and crisscrossing recognitions and responsibilities. It does not define itself in opposition to a caricatured paternalism, as in Graylin and Jennings's account; it is multiply, relationally structured all the way down, eschewing the individualism around which twentieth-century hyperbolized autonomy defines itself. Jane Flax rightly observes that "the success of feminist projects does not depend on the acquisition of an autonomous agency some white men can pretend to exercise" noting that "the *appearance* of stability, autonomy, and identity is generated and sustained by relations of domination, denial of aspects of subjectivity, and projection of contradictory material onto marked others."[65]

Feminists are well aware that within the insider-outsider structures that frame the politics of public knowledge and the prestige of scientific knowledge, "ordinary" women's voices—like those of other disenfranchised knowers—often go unheard and rarely achieve autonomous acknowledgment. Their reports of violence, sexual assault, racism, and sexism in the workplace are as often discredited as acted on. Such patterns of incredulity prompt the uneasy suggestion I have elaborated in this section, that first-person experiential reports often require "expert" *advocacy* to claim a serious hearing. The suggestion is "uneasy" because of the delicacy of issues about who can or should speak for whom, in a long history of propertied white men speaking for, thinking for, voting for, and making decisions for "their" women and their alleged inferiors, while claiming to know women and other Others better than they can know themselves. Feminists have to be as wary of women speaking for one another as of men's presumptions to speak on women's behalf. And advocacy seems to erase women's hard-won capacity to speak in their own voices; it threatens a renewed silencing that would replicate oppressive patterns of hierarchical expertise.

Thus, as I note in the previous section, the politics of advocacy are among the most contested issues in present-day activism and research. The task, then, is to devise ways of distinguishing responsible advocacy from appropriation, acknowledging that we cannot always speak for ourselves, yet that people who speak for us, on our behalf or about us, are as often underinformed, self-interested, and imperialistic as they are supportive and empowering. Although I cannot spell out a finite set of rules for responsible advocacy, clear violations of the trust, sensitivity, and integrity on which it relies become visible in feminist-informed deliberation, indicating, by contrast, how responsibilities might differently be assumed. Thus, for example, the failures of "one policy, one diagnosis fits all" that are vividly apparent in my welfare and medical examples become catalysts for transformative advocacy. In guiding that effort, I propose that ecological thinking offers a more responsible approach than those mandated by the discourses of disinterested autonomy.

Ecology

> The decentering of the subject, gained by the labors of structuralism and poststructuralism, levelled hierarchies and shifted a vertical vision of the world toward a more horizontal one, so important for feminism, that places on the same surface both multiculturalism *and* ecology. (Verena Conley)[66]

> When I do not see plurality stressed in the very structure of a theory, I know that I will have to do lots of acrobatics—like a contortionist or tight-rope walker—to have this theory speak to me without allowing the theory to distort me *in my complexity.*
>
> (María Lugones)[67]

Revisionary projects of thinking through the renewed subjections consequent on "perversion[s] of autonomy" can only be minimally transformative while they remain framed within the confines of individualistic conceptions of knowledge, subjectivity, and agency, where, as Val Plumwood persuasively observes, the subject "loses a sense of itself not only as an organic but as a social being, as an agent in and chooser of political, economic and technological frameworks."[68] Softening the coercive force of the social imperatives that individualistic autonomy generates by elaborating individualistic selfhood into intersubjective multiples of the Same, begins to contest the hegemony of the framework. Yet the discourses of *mastery* I refer to earlier, which are spawned and thrive at this confluence of individualism and hy-perbolic autonomy, permeate the instituted social imaginary of the affluent West-ern world so thoroughly that internal tinkering with their detail cannot achieve the transformative effects that revisionary politics require.

Ethical self-mastery, political mastery over unruly and aberrant Others, and epistemic mastery over the "external" world pose as the still-attainable goals of the Enlightenment legacy that maintains the tensions within the discourses of auton-omy and social advocacy I have discussed. They sustain hierarchical, generally ex-ploitative relations between members of privileged cultures and of nonaffluent, non-Western societies and cultures at home and abroad. These relations are config-ured into top-down (vertical) patterns of authority and expertise that legitimate domination in the name of an achieved *mastery of* the human and natural world and *mastery over* the personal idiosyncrasies of the masters.[69] They endorse exag-gerated proclamations of the "permanent value" (recall Cixous) of the abstract au-tonomous agency integral to the philosophy of rights, which reduces "plurality" to variations on the Same; substitutes instrumental policy decisions for open practices of deliberative democracy; and distorts the complexities of specific positionings and allegiances in the name of universal, impartial rights, obligations, and duties. These discourses underwrite an equivalently reductive picture of epistemic agents as isolated units on an indifferent landscape, to which their relation is one of dis-engaged indifference.

In contradistinction to discourses of mastery and domination, I propose to en-list the ethicopolitical potential of *ecological* thinking to reconfigure knowledge, so-ciality, and subjectivity.[70] This proposal does not recommend interjecting an alter-native social imaginary into the old-but-not-yet-tired hegemonic imaginary, thus merely offering a "choice." Ecological thinking reconceives human locations and re-lations all the way down. It infiltrates the interstices of the social order, where it ex-pands to undermine its intransigent structures, as the ice of the Canadian winter ex-pands to produce upheavals in the pavements and roads, working within and against these seemingly solid structures to disrupt their smooth surfaces.

The "decentering" that ecological thinking entails is enacted in its refusal to continue philosophy's tacit derivation from the white, affluent, Western, male ex-periences that also generate hyperbolic autonomy ideals. It displaces "man" from his central position in the world and "in" himself and disturbs the (often narcis-sistic) inwardness of autonomy. Ecological thinking's revolutionary potential recalls Kant's Copernican revolution, which moved "man" *to* the center of the philosophical-conceptual universe and whose effects were constitutive of human-istic, post-Enlightenment thought. Its picture of the physical and human world de-rived from and served the interests of a small class and race of people powerful enough to claim dominion over the rational and moral territory. Yet Kantian phi-losophy was parochial in the generic conception of "man" on which it turned—a recognition central to feminist, Marxist, postcolonial, and critical race theory. As humanism vied with theism in the seventeenth and eighteenth centuries, ecological thinking now vies with capitalism and its attendant discourses of autonomous mas-tery. Yet ecological thinking is not unilinear, for it emerges from and addresses so many interwoven, crisscrossing, often contradictory issues—feminist, classist, postcolonial, antiracist, environmental—that it requires multifaceted, multitextured chart-ings. It redirects the focus of theoretical analyses toward situated knowledges and situated ethicopolitics, in which situation is constitutive of, not just the "context" for, the backdrop against which enactments of subjectivity occur. (Donna Haraway comments: "I have a body and mind as much constructed by the post–Second World War arms race and cold war as by the women's movements."[71])

Ecological thinking—a peculiarly late twentieth-century phenomenon—examines the potential of epistemic and ethicopolitical practices to produce *habitats* where people can live well together, locally and globally, and respectfully within the physical and natural world.[72] This refocusing links ecological thinking's decen-tered aspects to its horizontal patternings. Both require conceptual and geographi-cal remappings of terrains where practices are engaged and theoretical conclusions constructed—mappings sensitive to detail and diversity and resistant to hasty trans-lation from situation to situation.

In these remappings, deductive (vertical) reasoning from overarching premise, principle, or governing law to conclusions systematically deduced and applied no longer claims solitary dominion over the epistemic terrain. Often it yields to and modifies its conclusions in concert with reasoning that traces evidential analogies and disanalogies horizontally, from situation to situation—"transversally," as Verena Conley puts it, "making a link between ecosystems that international capitalism seeks to polarize and ecological issues that pertain to local cultures."[73] Aware of the force of disanalogy, analogical reasoning is skeptical of universalizing conclusions and solutions: such skepticism is activated by syndrome X in my medical example. At its best, analogical thinking is interpretive, deliberative, and collaboratively ne-gotiated; it is usually more inductive than deductive, thus more modestly conjec-tural than arrogantly conclusive. Whereas it is often discredited for being subjective, "particularist," and situational rather than objective and universal, it can just as often be more fully empirical and responsible *to* its subject matter than conventionally re-spectable deductive-nomological reasoning.[74] Nor, in my rendition, is it only hori-zontal, for it also derives its understandings from genealogical analyses of the power that permeates and legitimates the instituted social imaginary.

The discourses of mastery enlist ready-made, easily applied categories to sum up and contain parts of the personal, social, and physical-natural world within a neatly manageable array of "kinds." Ecological thinking is more finely attuned to differences, as it resists the desire for unity that drives these practices—the desire to assemble the confusion of the human and natural world into maximally homoge-neous patterns. As the examples I have discussed show, such control legitimates ex-trapolation from the situations, symptoms, "needs," and goals of the powerful into diagnoses and policy decisions enacted on people who "must," if they are sufficiently enlightened, want to be just like them. By contrast, ecological thinking, in its com-mitment to complexity, urges sensitivity to detail, to minutiae, to what precisely—however apparently small—distinguishes this patient, this welfare recipient, from that; this practice, this locality, from that; as biologically based ecologists would dis-tinguish this plant, this species, from that. It investigates the meaning of these dif-ferences, and studies how they promote or thwart possibilities of living well.

Ecological thinking thus resists the epistemic practice common in science-venerating cultures of superimposing a grid on events and situations it needs to know, tucking in the bits that spill over the edges, and letting aberrations fall through the cracks. It is not an easy project, for it combines the careful attention to evidence that it finds in traditional versions of empiricism with investigations that locate symptoms, social issues, problems within wider patterns of power and privilege, oppression, and victimization. Thus, for example, in an analysis that displays many of the features I am describing as ecological, Lucy Candib argues against readings of medical symptoms that gloss over narrative issues derived from what I am calling the patient's "habitat" but are integral to responsible diagnosis. Connecting believability to advocacy, she writes: "Patients subject to abuses of power bring their stories of vulnerability to clinicians every day. . . . Advocacy means arguing for the believability of those stories."[75] She notes that women can experience chest pain, like many other symptoms, as a result of abusive practices that permeate their lives. Mapping the effects of these oppressions for this patient—abdicating the "disinterested posture" expected of family physicians, a posture that "corrupt[s] the idea of advocacy"[76]— a physician is able to cooperate with the patient in making sense of her symptoms, refusing to hold her autonomously responsible for their occurrence or to treat problems as merely mechanical failures, and doctors and patients are able to think differently about causes and cures. This is just one example of how ecological thinking can work.

In its respect for particularity, ecological thinking is committed to a methodological pluralism. Thus advocacy becomes neither a new paradigm nor a universally valid method simply to be "applied" across the places where ecological thinking can make a difference. Nor are all advocacy relations alike or all advocacy practices homogeneous. They produce multiple studies of (often linked) oppressions and generate multiple coalitions and forms of activism, where the trick is to understand the connections that grant the myriad oppressions of white, patriarchal, capitalist societies their mutually reinforcing power and to develop liberatory strategies.[77]

Being-in-the-world guided by ecological thinking differs radically from the masterful way of autonomous man, whose assumption that he can be master of all he surveys allows surveying to substitute for engaged participation and mastery to suppress diversity for the sake of instrumental simplicity. For Verena Conley (following Michel de Certeau), ecological thinking is "*a way of inhabiting the world*," "a social and natural concern aimed at measuring habitability."[78] These *structural* features inform ecological thinking through and through.

The sources in feminist and postcolonial theory of these features of ecological thinking will be apparent. Ecofeminism is a principal source, as are deep ecology and the "green" movement. All are contested and contestable positions, neither politically innocent nor able single-handedly to remake the world. All contain the seeds of "perversions" as inimical to "habitability" as the philosophy of rights, as capable of sowing renewed "subjections" as autonomy in its hyperbolized modes. Yet their intellectual-activist promise justifies the risks involved in drawing on them.

One such risk is in an alignment—indeed, an identification—in some ecofeminist writings of an essential "woman" with an equally essential "Nature": a practice which threatens to reconfirm the biological determinism that has kept women "in their place."[79] Thus, too, some ecofeminists affirm the naturalness of women's traditional care giving, extended now to include nature, while attending too little to how oppressive social structures exploit women's "natural" caring capacities and perpetuate their subjection. Equally conducive to wariness, for me, are the rehearsals of hypermasculinity enacted in romantic quests for a "return to nature," often as a place for male self-discovery; the spiritualism of some facets of environmentalism; and a tendency Plumwood finds in deep ecology "to focus exclusively on identification, interconnectedness, sameness and the overcoming of separation, treating nature as a dimension of self."[80]

Nonetheless, my position takes very seriously, and derives its guiding metaphorical apparatus from, the creative projects of ecological thinkers who are rethinking and reimagining social, epistemological, political, and economic philosophies of mastery by opening deliberative, discursive spaces in which to enter, critically and constructively, into a program such as Donna Haraway names in her injunction: "We must find another relationship to nature besides reification, possession, appropriation, and nostalgia."[81] As Haraway shows throughout her writings, reworking that relationship is vital to human survival at century's end.

The "situated knowledges" of Haraway's "modest witness" count as provocative models of ecological thinking. This modest witness

> insists on its situatedness, where location is itself always a complex construction
> as well as inheritance, and . . . casts its lot with the projects and needs of those
> who could not or would not inhabit the subject positions of the self-invisible and
> the discursive sites, the "laboratories," of the credible, civil man of science.[82]

Sandra Harding's "strong objectivity" figures prominently in the picture in its insistence on counting the circumstances of inquiring subjects as integral to the evidence from which knowledge is derived, as does Linda Alcoff's "real knowing" as enacted in the interpretive dimensions of coherence theory, and my "epistemic responsibility" as it dismantles boundaries between ethics and politics and between ethicopolitics and epistemology, reconfiguring patterns of accountability.[83]

Ecological thinking finds its point of departure in the natural dependence of knowledge production on interactive practices, such as the advocacy practices I have discussed, throughout human epistemic lives. Drawing critically on empirical evidence to determine how survival could be ensured and enhanced, not just quantitatively but qualitatively, it is wary of the power-infused racial, gender, and class stereotypes and essentialized conceptions of "science" and "nature" that become both self-fulfilling and self-perpetuating. Ecology (literally) looks to state-of-the-art natural science to supply some of the substance of its deliberations, yet it does not assume that science has a direct line to "the truth" nor merits uncontested licence to intervene where it pleases.[84] Ecology (metaphorically) draws the conclusions of situated inquiries together and maps their interrelations, and their consonances and contrasts, and their impoverishing and mutually sustaining effects.[85] Yet ecological thinking is not innocently benign, promising an unimpeded unfolding of epistemic and moral potential. Ecosystems are as competitive and unsentimentally destructive of their less viable members as they are cooperative and mutually sustaining; nor could ecological thinking in its metaphorical frame pose as a univocal good, free from critical and self-critical responsibilities. So if work within it is to avoid replicating the exclusions endemic to traditional epistemologies, it will often require advocacy engaged out of the vigilant monitoring on which transformative social movements always depend to preserve their fragile gains and counter the threat of renewed oppressions.

In the epistemically responsible and sensitive negotiations on which good advocacy depends, hyperbolized autonomy will have to yield space to a fuller recognition of *integrity*, a principle less individualistically based and more at home on this horizontally spread-out landscape. Claudia Card notes its connotations of "consistency, coherence, and commitment"; Margaret Walker connects it to "the sturdiness of structures people [especially socially subordinated people] have built, the property of holding up dependably under the weights and stresses these structures are apt to encounter,"[86] showing how remarkably even people wholly deprived of autonomy can yet preserve integrity. While refusing to romanticize nature, ecological thinking also assumes an integrity in natural processes and biodiversity that is worthy of respect if not of such fanatical preservation as principled refusals to swat a mosquito, innoculate against diphtheria, or restrain a dangerous offender might display.

In an analysis that links ecology and autonomy within an epistemological-ethical frame and is consonant with my discussion here, Cornelius Castoriadis notes how representations of scientific knowledge as disinterestedly neutral shape "the dominant social imaginary (*imaginaire social*) of our epoch," for which "the central aim of social life is the unlimited expansion of rational mastery."[87] This imaginary claims the assent of the social majority, as citizens are nurtured from infancy to ingest an unquestioned relationship to an "ensemble of needs" whose satisfaction becomes a life-long project. The discourse of needs "naturalizes" its referents and obscures their artifactuality.

For Castoriadis, genealogies of the *creation* of the "individual," complete with his needs, within this imaginary expose the contingency of the process and the interests it tacitly serves, thus making it possible to turn it against itself by utilizing that same scientific, technological, and social-psychological knowledge to reconstruct human relations to the social and natural world.[88] The ecological movement becomes a resource for addressing the "political problems of the reconstruction of autonomous society," which has posed as many problems for the women's movement and the youth movement as for the worker's movement. It offers a creatively inspired emancipatory conceptual apparatus within which to refuse ongoing colonization by an imaginary that requires relations of dominance and submission to sustain it, relies on concealed linkages between power and knowledge, and promotes the individual autonomy of a few through the heteronomy of the many.

Here I have discussed advocacy relations as micro practices that work within and for a commitment to ecological thinking by setting creative ethicopolitical changes in motion to disrupt the social imaginary governed by the rhetoric of autonomous individualism. They initiate disruption not for its own sake but for the sake of creating more habitable *habitats* in which to recognize, acknowledge, and thus make space (rhetorical, physical, and *agenda* space) for such subjugated knowledges as women's inexplicable medical disorders and for the kind of social being that affirms an ideal of citizenship in which the distortions that fuel the perversions of autonomy that animate renewed subjections of women and other socially marginalized Others can no longer claim a place. Such work opens spaces for a new, creatively interrogating, *instituting* social imaginary to undermine and displace the *instituted* imaginary that claims to represent the natural way of being and knowing.[89]

Whereas a relational autonomy drawn from the polite relations of ordinary liberal societies starts well above the bottom line of struggles for autonomous control even over one's body that sickness, poverty, malnutrition, and oppression erase or render impossible, in ecological thinking places of excess in the negative effects of the "unnatural lottery" become starting places for investigation, not for blame or for subjection within an illusory autonomous sameness. With its conception of materially situated subjectivity for which embodied locatedness and deliberative interdependence are constitutive of the very possibility of knowledge and action, ecological thinking opens the way to a renewed conception of responsible citizenship, as responsible in its knowing as in its doing.

Notes

1. I presented earlier versions of this chapter to the departments of philosophy at La Trobe University and SUNY Buffalo, at the Centre for Gender Studies at the University of Adelaide, and at the conference on Feminist Perspectives on Autonomy and Agency at the Australian National University. I have benefitted from the discussions on those occasions and from comments by Murray Code, Helen Connole, Pablo DeGrieff, Catriona Mackenzie, and Richard Schmitt.

2. Helene Cixous, "We Who Are Free, Are We Free?" trans. Chris Miller, in *Freedom and Interpretation: The Oxford Amnesty Lectures 1992*, ed. Barbara Johnson (New York: Harpercollins, 1993), p. 18 (emphasis in the original).

3. See, for example, Lorraine Code, *What Can She Know?: Feminist Theory and the Construction of Knowledge* (Ithaca, N.Y.: Cornell University Press, 1991), chaps. 3 and 4, and Jean Grimshaw, *Philosophy and Feminist Thinking* (Minneapolis: University of Minnesota Press, 1986), chap. 5.

4. For an analysis of care's associations with feminine values that stay too close to home, see Sarah Lucia Hoagland, "Some Thoughts about 'Caring,'" and for a discussion of its oppressively feminine associations, see Michele Moody-Adams, "Gender and the Complexity of Moral Voices," both in *Feminist Ethics*, ed. Claudia Card (Lawrence: University Press of Kansas, 1991). Joan Tronto analyzes care's "underclass" associations in "Beyond Gender Difference to a Theory of Care," *Signs: Journal of Women in Culture and Society* 12 (Summer 1987): 644–663.

5. Axel Honneth offers a succinct analysis in "Decentered Autonomy: The Subject after the Fall," trans. John Farrell, in Axel Honneth, *The Fragmented World of the Social: Essays in Social and Political Philosophy*, ed. Charles W. Wright (Albany: SUNY Press, 1995). David R. Hiley discusses analogous tensions between autonomy and community in *Philosophy in Question: Essays on a Pyrrhonian Theme* (Chicago: University of Chicago Press, 1988), especially chap. 2, "Progress against Ignorance." He writes: 'We [in the twentieth century] have retained eighteenth-century conceptions of freedom which have as their central feature the idea of individual self-determination, yet we seem no longer able . . . to support both our autonomy and genuine community" p. 63.

6. For a sampling of recent texts, see M. Jacqui Alexander and Chandra Talpade Mohanty, eds., *Feminist Genealogies, Colonial Legacies, Democratic Futures* (New York: Routledge,

1997); Diana T. Meyers, ed., *Feminists Rethink the Self* (Boulder, Colo.: Westview Press, 1997); Lewis R. Gordon, *Her Majesty's Other Children: Sketches of Racism from a Neocolonial Age* (Lanham, Md.: Rowman & Littlefield, 1997); Erica Burman, *Deconstructing Developmental Psychology* (London: Routledge, 1994); Debbora Battaglia, ed., *Rhetorics of Self-Making* (Berkeley: University of California Press, 1995); Marilyn Waring, *Three Masquerades: Essays on Equality, Work and Human Rights* (Toronto: University of Toronto Press, 1996); Kirsten Hastrup and Peter Hervik, eds., *Social Experience and Anthropological Knowledge* (London: Routledge, 1994); and Jennifer Radden, *Divided Minds and Successive Selves: Ethical Issues in Disorders of Identity and Personality* (Cambridge, Mass.: MIT Press, 1996).

7. These phrases are Honneth's, in "Decentered Autonomy," p. 261, to whom I am indebted in framing these issues.

8. See especially Michael Sandel's Introduction in *Liberalism and Its Critics*, ed. Michael Sandel (Oxford: Blackwell, 1984), p. 5; and for a critical analysis, see Honneth, "The Limits of Liberalism: On the Political-Ethical Discussion Concerning Communitarianism," in Honneth, *Fragmented World of the Social.*

9. See especially Nancy Chodorow, "Toward a Relational Individualism: The Mediation of Self through Psychoanalysis," in *Reconstructing Individualism: Autonomy, Individuality, and the Self in Western Thought*, ed. T. C. Heller, M. Sosna, and D. E. Wellbery (Stanford, Cal.: Stanford University Press, 1986).

10. Note that individual*istic* subjectivity and agency (and thus also individual*ism*) contrast with North American vernacular talk of "individuals" to mean "people." They contrast also with individual*ity*, which is not under threat in these contestations of its boundary claims.

11. Richard Schmitt discusses how "The Autonomy of the Philosophers" culminates in the importance of having a "rational life plan," in *Beyond Separateness: The Social Nature of Human Beings—Their Autonomy, Knowledge, and Power* (Boulder, Colo.: Westview Press, 1995), pp. 4–6. I discuss the class, race, and gender specificity of such "plans" in "Rational Imaginings, Responsible Knowings: How Far Can You See From Here?" in *EnGendering Rationalities*, ed. Nancy Tuana and Sandi Morgen (forthcoming). See also Margaret Walker, "Career Selves," in *Moral Understandings: A Feminist Study in Ethics* (New York: Routledge, 1998).

12. Immanuel Kant, "An Answer to the Question: 'What Is Enlightenment?'" (1784), trans. H. B. Nisbet, in *Kant's Political Writings*, ed. Hans Reiss (Cambridge: Cambridge University Press, 1970), pp. 54–55 (emphasis in the original).

13. Michel Foucault, "What Is Enlightenment?" trans. Catherine Porter, in *The Foucault Reader*, ed. Paul Rabinow (New York: Pantheon Books, 1984), p. 35. I discuss Foucault's reading of Kant's essay at greater length in "Critiques of Pure Reason," in Lorraine Code, *Rhetorical Spaces: Essays on (Gendered) Locations* (New York: Routledge, 1995).

14. Kant, "Answer to the Question," p. 54 (my emphasis).

15. Ibid., pp. 55 (emphasis in the original).

16. Claudia Card, *The Unnatural Lottery: Character and Moral Luck* (Philadelphia: Temple University Press, 1996), pp. 3, 4. The title plays on John Rawls's claim that the distribution of natural human assets is decided by a "natural lottery," which is "arbitrary from a moral perspective." See Rawls, *A Theory of Justice* (Cambridge, Mass.: Harvard University Press, 1971), p. 74. The members of a society who are "satisfying the principles of justice as fairness . . . are *autonomous* and the obligations they recognize self-imposed." Ibid., p. 13 (my emphasis).

17. Card, *Unnatural Lottery*, p. 20 (emphasis in the original).

18. Walker, *Career Selves*, p. 151.

19. Sabina Lovibond, *Realism and Imagination in Ethics* (Minneapolis: University of Minnesota Press, 1986), p. 169.

20. Willard Gaylin and Bruce Jennings, *The Perversion of Autonomy: The Proper Uses of Coercion and Constraints in a Liberal Society* (New York: Free Press, 1996), pp. 5, 24.

21. John Stuart Mill, *The Subjection of Women* (1869), in John Stuart Mill and Harriet Taylor Mill, *Essays on Sex Equality*, ed. Alice Rossi (Chicago: University of Chicago Press, 1970).

22. I use the term to capture the social-material-historical dimensions of situatedness. See also note 71.

23. Mary Tiles and Jim Tiles note that Bacon's four "Idols"—the idol of the tribe, the theater, the marketplace, and the cave—classify "the various false ideas which obscure and interfere with our grasping the true objects of knowledge," in Tiles and Tiles, *An Introduction to Historical Epistemology: The Authority of Knowledge* (Oxford: Blackwell, 1993), p. 37.

24. The reference is to Donna Haraway, "Situated Knowledges: The Science Question in Feminism and the Privilege of Partial Perspective," in *Simians, Cyborgs, and Women: The Reinvention of Nature* (New York: Routledge, 1991). Haraway denies that knowers can perform "the god trick" of extracting themselves from the world to perceive and know as if from nowhere. She refines and elaborates the conception of situated knowledges that eschew illusions of epistemic autonomy in *Modest_Witness@Second_Millennium.FemaleMan©_Meets_OncoMouse™: Feminism and Technoscience* (New York: Routledge, 1997).

25. For such analyses, see Elizabeth Fricker, "The Epistemology of Testimony," *Aristotelian Society Supplementary Volume* 61 (1987): 57–83, and C. A. J. Coady, "Testimony and Observation," *American Philosophical Quarterly* 10 (April 1973): 149–155.

26. Thomas Nagel, "Moral Luck," in *Mortal Questions* (Cambridge: Cambridge University Press, 1979), p. 36.

27. Walker, *Career Selves*, p. 13 (emphasis in the original).

28. Anne Seller, "Realism versus Relativism: Towards a Politically Adequate Epistemology," in *Feminist Perspectives in Philosophy*, ed. Morwenna Griffiths and Margaret Whitford (Bloomington: Indiana University Press, 1988), p. 180; Ludwig Wittgenstein, *On Certainty*, ed. G. E. M. Anscombe and G. H. von Wright, trans. Denis Paul and G. E. M. Anscombe (New York: Harper Torchbooks, 1971), § 378. See also Code, *What Can She Know?* chap. 5, and "Incredulity, Experientialism and the Politics of Knowledge," in *Rhetorical Spaces*.

29. Lynette Hunter, *Critiques of Knowing: Situated Textualities in Science, Computing and the Arts* (London: Routledge, 1999), pp. 30–31.

30. For instructive discussions of these issues, see Hilde Lindemann Nelson, ed., *Stories and Their Limits: Narrative Approaches to Bioethics* (New York: Routledge, 1997).

31. Peter Novick, *That Noble Dream: The "Objectivity Question" and the American Historical Profession* (Cambridge: Cambridge University Press, 1988), p. 2.

32. "Subjugated knowledges" is Michel Foucault's term in *Power/Knowledge: Selected Interviews and Other Writings, 1972–1977*, ed. Colin Gordon, trans. Colin Gordon, Leo Marshall, John Mepham, and Kate Soper (New York: Pantheon, 1980). I appeal here to Foucault's second sense of the term, in which it refers to "a whole set of knowledges that have been disqualified as inadequate to their task or insufficiently elaborated: naive knowledges located low down on the hierarchy, beneath the required level of cognition or scientificity." For Foucault, "It is through these . . . disqualified knowledges, that criticism performs its work." Ibid., p. 82.

33. Haraway, *Modest_Witness*, p. 68.

34. Sandra Harding, "Rethinking Standpoint Epistemology: What Is 'Strong Objectivity'?" in *Feminist Epistemologies*, ed. Linda Alcoff and Elizabeth Potter (New York: Routledge, 1993), p. 71. See also Nancy Hartsock, *Money, Sex and Power: Toward a Feminist Historical*

Materialism (Boston: Northeastern University Press, 1985); Helen Longino, *Science as Social Knowledge* (Princeton, N.J.: Princeton University Press, 1990); and Lorraine Code, "Taking Subjectivity into Account," in *Feminist Epistemologies.*

35. In Lorraine Code, "What Is Natural about Epistemology Naturalized?" *American Philosophical Quarterly* 33, no. 1 (January 1996): 1–22, I develop a critical analysis of these connections.

36. Prominent among these critics is Jaegwon Kim, "What Is 'Naturalized Epistemology'?" in *Naturalizing Epistemology*, ed. Hilary Kornblith (Cambridge, Mass.: MIT Press, 1994).

37. See, for example, Alice Herb, "The Hospital-based Attorney as Patient Advocate," *Hastings Center Report* 25, no. 2 (1995); American Medical Association Council, "Ethical Issues in Managed Care," *Journal of the American Medical Association* 273, no. 4 (1995); Leo T. Rosenberg, "Delaying Approval of a Critical Drug," *Journal of Medical Humanities* 15, no. 4 (1994); William May, "On Ethics and Advocacy," *Journal of the American Medical Association* 256, no. 13 (1986); Fredrick R. Abrams, "Patient Advocate or Secret Agent?" *Journal of the American Medical Association* 256 no. 13 (1986); Nancy S. Jecker, "Integrating Medical Ethics with Normative Theory: Patient Advocacy and Social Responsibility," *Theoretical Medicine* 11, no. 2 (1990).

38. The quoted phrases come from E. Charlotte Theis, "Ethical issues: A Nursing Perspective," *New England Journal of Medicine* 315, no. 19 (1986). See also Ellen M. Bernal, "The Nurse as Patient Advocate," *Hastings Center Report* 22, no. 4 (1992).

39. Peta Bowden, *Caring: Gender Sensitive Ethics* (London: Routledge, 1997), p. 124.

40. Susan Wendell, *The Rejected Body: Feminist Philosophical Reflections on Disability* (New York: Routledge, 1996), p. 122.

41. Elaine Scarry, *The Body in Pain: The Making and Unmaking of the World* (Oxford: Oxford University Press, 1985), p. 4.

42. Ibid., p. 6 (my emphasis).

43. I discuss the politics of knowledge of syndrome X in "How Do We Know? Questions of Method in Feminist Practice" in *Changing Methods: Feminists Transforming Practice*, ed. Sandra Burt and Lorraine Code (Peterborough, Ontario: Broadview Press, 1995).

44. Of syndrome X, Kathleen King notes: "Men often experience . . . 'textbook' cases of angina and other heart-disease symptoms because the textbooks are written to describe men's symptoms. . . . You're not going to think of heart disease unless the symptoms fit the classic picture. And . . . we don't know what the classic picture for women is." Quoted in Robin Marantz Henig, "Kind Hearts and Coronaries," *The Globe and Mail* (Toronto), 20 November 1993, D 8.

45. See Kirsti Malterud, "Women's Undefined Disorders—A Callenge for Clinical Communication," *Family Practice* 9 (1992): 299–303; "Strategies for Empowering Women's Voices in the Medical Culture," *Health Care for Women International* 14 (1993): 365–373; "The (Gendered) Construction of Medical Diagnosis. Interpretation of Symptoms and Signs in Female Patients," *Theoretical Medicine and Bioethics*, 1999 (in press).

46. I am referring to Thomas Kuhn's claims about the intransigence of paradigms. See Kuhn, *The Structure of Scientific Revolutions*, 2nd ed. (Chicago: University of Chicago Press, 1970).

47. Foucault, *Power/Knowledge*, p. 81 (emphasis in the original).

48. Henig, "Kind Hearts and Coronaries."

49. *Harvard Women's Health Watch* 1, no. 6 (February 1994).

50. Christina Hoff Sommers, *Who Stole Feminism?* (New York: Simon & Schuster, 1994), p. 103.

51. I am indebted in thinking about this example to Victoria Davion in "Listening to Women's Voices: Rape, Epistemic Privilege, and Objectivity," in *Daring to Be Good: Essays in Feminist Ethico-Politics*, ed. Bat-Ami Bar On and Ann Ferguson (New York: Routledge, 1998). The report under discussion is Mary Koss, "Hidden Rape: Sexual Aggression and Victimization in a National Sample in Higher Education," in *Rape and Sexual Assault*, Vol. 2, ed. Ann Wolpert Burgess (New York: Garland Press, 1988).

52. Donna Haraway's account of how Danish panels of citizen deliberation contribute to shaping democratic science and technology policies offers an impressive example of how such a process could work. It encourages a remarkable "degree of scientific and technical literacy . . . in ordinary people." *Modest_Witness*, pp. 95–96.

53. They call it "autonomy gone bonkers." Gaylin and Jennings, *Perversion of Autonomy*, chap. 10.

54. Ibid., chap. 9, "In Defense of Social Control: The Ethics of Coercion."

55. Ibid., p. 182.

56. Patricia J. Williams, "The Unbearable Autonomy of Being," in *The Rooster's Egg: On the Persistence of Prejudice* (Cambridge, Mass.: Harvard University Press, 1995), p. 177.

57. Ibid., pp. 174, 175.

58. Cornel West, *Race Matters* (New York: Vintage Books, 1994), p. 86.

59. Linda Gordon notes that "the meaning of 'welfare' has reversed itself. What once meant well-being now means ill-being." Gordon, *Pitied but Not Entitled: Single Mothers and the History of Welfare 1890–1935* (New York: Free Press, 1994), p. 1.

60. Wendell, *Rejected Body*, p. 148.

61. Martha Minow, *Making All the Difference: Inclusion, Exclusion and American Law* (Ithaca, N.Y.: Cornell University Press, 1990), p. 268.

62. Ibid., pp. 248, 249 (my emphasis).

63. Ibid., p. 267. See also Kathy Ferguson, *The Feminist Case against Bureaucracy* (Philadelphia: Temple University Press, 1984).

64. Gordon, *Pitied but Not Entitled*, p. 2.

65. Jane Flax, "Displacing Woman: Toward an Ethics of Multiplicity," in Bar On and Ferguson, *Daring to Be Good*, p. 152 (emphasis in the original).

66. Verena Andermatt Conley, *Ecopolitics: The Environment in Poststructuralist Thought* (New York: Routledge, 1997), p. 26. (emphasis in the original).

67. María C. Lugones, "On the Logic of Pluralist Feminism," in Card, *Feminist Ethics*, p. 43 (emphasis in the original).

68. Val Plumwood, *Feminism and the Mastery of Nature* (London: Routledge, 1993), p. 119.

69. Plumwood writes of "variations on the reason/nature story which develop in tandem with the emerging [capitalist] systems of individual appropriation and distribution [and] turn on a concept of . . . individual rationality, which denies both human and social others and earth others in its concept of the rational egoist subject of social and economic life" (ibid., p. 141).

70. I owe the term "ethicopolitical" to Bar On and Ferguson. In the introduction to *Daring to Be Good*, p. xiii, they pose "the central ethico-political question of feminism" thus: "*What is wrong with our current state, government, economy from a feminist perspective, and what ethical and political alternative values, visions, and strategies should feminists stand for and engage in?*" (emphasis in the original).

71. Donna Haraway, "A Cyborg Manifesto: Science, Technology, and Socialist-Feminism in the Late Twentieth Century," in *Simians, Cyborgs, and Women*, p. 173.

72. Raymond Williams connects "ecology" to "habitat" understood as "a characteristic

living place," in *Keywords: A Vocabulary of Culture and Society,* 2nd ed. (London: Harper-collins, 1983), p. 111, noting that the term enters everyday use in English in the mid-twentieth century, "though its scientific use . . . dates from the 1870s." It evolves into "the study of the relations of plants and animals with each other and with their habitat." Post-1960s ecology reinterprets economics, politics, and social theory "from a central concern with human relations to the physical world as the necessary basis for social and economic policy." I am claiming that in such reinterpretations, questions about the politics of knowledge claim an equally significant place.

73. Conley, *Ecopolitics,* p. 110.

74. For an analysis of analogy's low epistemic status, see Alison Wylie, "The Reaction against Analogy," *Advances in Archaeological Method and Theory* 8 (1985): 63–111.

75. Lucy Candib, *Medicine and the Family: A Feminist Perspective* (New York: Basic Books, 1995), p. 159.

76. Ibid., p. 76.

77. See also Chris J. Cuomo, *Feminism and Ecological Communities: An Ethic of Flour-ishing* (London: Routledge, 1998), especially chap. 7, "Activism That Is Not One."

78. Conley, *Ecopolitics,* pp. 110, 114 (emphasis in the original).

79. See, for example, Susan Griffin, *Woman and Nature: The Roaring inside Her* (New York: Harper & Row, 1978); Carolyn Merchant, *The Death of Nature: Women, Ecology, and the Scientific Revolution* (San Francisco: Harper & Row, 1980); Judith Plant, ed., *Healing the Wounds: The Promise of Ecofeminism* (Philadelphia: New Society Publishers, 1989); Irene Di-amond and Gloria Feman Orenstein, eds., *Reweaving the World: The Emergence of Ecofemi-nism* (San Francisco: Sierra Club Books, 1990); and Janet Biehl, *Rethinking Ecofeminist Pol-itics* (Boston: South End Press, 1991).

80. Plumwood, *Feminism and the Mastery of Nature,* p. 174. For discussions of deep ecology, see Bill Devall, "The Deep Ecology Movement," *Natural Resources Journal* 20 (April 1980); and Arne Naess, "The Deep Ecological Movement: Some Philosophical Aspects," *Philosophical Inquiry* 8 (1986): 10–31.

81. Donna Haraway, "Otherworldly Conversations, Terran Topics, Local Terms," in *Biopolitics: A Feminist and Ecological Reader on Biotechnology,* ed. Vandana Shiva and Ingunn Moser (London: Zed Books, 1995), p. 70.

82. Haraway, *Modest_Witness,* p. 270.

83. Harding, "Rethinking Standpoint Epistemology"; Linda Alcoff, *Real Knowing: New Versions of the Coherence Theory* (Ithaca, N.Y.: Cornell University Press, 1996); Lorraine Code, *Epistemic Responsibility* (Hanover, N.H.: University Press of New England, 1987).

84. Catriona Sandilands is eloquently critical of claims that the "voice of . . . science can 'see' nature for what it really is, and translate it into a form that can be readily perceived." See Sandilands, "From Natural Identity to Radical Democracy," *Environmental Ethics* 17 (Spring 1995): 75–91, 76.

85. For an example of such a mapping, see Chandra Talpade Mohanty, "Women Workers and Capitalist Scripts: Ideologies of Domination, Common Interests, and the Poli-tics of Solidarity," in *Feminist Genealogies.* I discuss Mohanty's essay as a sample of ecological thinking in "How to Think Globally: Stretching the Limits of Imagination," *Hypatia: A Jour-nal of Feminist Philosophy* 13, no. 3 (Spring 1998): 73–85.

86. Card, *Unnatural Lottery,* p. 32; Walker, *Career Selves,* pp. 115, 124.

87. Cornelius Castoriadis, "From Ecology to Autonomy," *Thesis Eleven,* no. 3 (1981): 8–22, 8. See also his *Philosophy, Politics, Autonomy: Essays in Political Philosophy,* ed. David Ames Curtis (New York: Oxford University Press, 1991).

88. Castoriadis is referring to technology, but his argument permits this expansion. He

writes: "The transformation of present technology . . . will have to seize part of what exists at present as technology and utilize it to create another technology" ("From Ecology to Autonomy," p. 20).

89. Castoriadis discusses the creative power of the "instituting imaginary" in "Radical imagination and the social instituting imaginary," in *Rethinking Imagination: Culture and Creativity*, ed. Gillian Robinson and John Rundell (London: Routledge, 1994).

II

RELATIONAL AUTONOMY
IN CONTEXT

9

CHOICE AND CONTROL IN FEMINIST BIOETHICS[1]

Susan Dodds

Within bioethics, respect for—and protection of—personal autonomy has been linked historically to the requirement that prior to invasive treatment, physicians obtain the informed consent of their patients. In placing a duty on physicians to inform patients adequately about their condition and the proposed treatment and to seek their patients' consent, the paternalism previously associated with medicine was thought to have been overturned in favor of respect for patients' autonomy. Over the past three decades, the effect has been to change the image of the doctor-patient relationship from the presumed beneficent paternalism of the doctor, acting on the best (medical) interests of the compliant patient, to a contract between patient-consumer and doctor–service provider. In this approach the physician has the role of expert adviser, providing information to the consumer, who then makes her or his health-care decisions free from paternalistic medical interference.

The narrow focus on consent as the sole locus for autonomy considerations in medicine has worked to constrain debate about autonomy in health care. This effect is similar to the way in which the protection of freedom of speech as the paramount expression of personal autonomy in social life constrains examination of the ways in which hate speech and other protected public expressions limit the capacity for some members of a society to develop and exercise personal autonomy.[2] Identifying autonomy with informed consent in health care makes it easy to overlook other limitations on autonomy in health care, just as the identification of autonomy with free speech in civil law facilitates a very narrow understanding of the effects of social institutions and practices on the development and exercise of personal autonomy. For example, the identification of respect for autonomy with informed consent presupposes that in the absence of pathology or extreme youth, all patients can be assumed to be fully autonomous agents; thus, those patients found not to be autonomous are presumed to be pathological or infantile and are treated appropriately in a paternalistic manner. Furthermore, identifying respect for autonomy with informed consent presupposes that ethical concern should be directed to the actions *of the physician* in obtaining consent (whether the physician gives full and adequate information, whether the physician has unduly influenced the decision of the patient, whether the physician explains the information clearly, etc.) and not to the decision-making process *of the patient*. Finally, the focus on informed consent ignores the ways in which health-care practices influence the development and demise of the capacity for personal autonomy.

Feminists who are working in the area of bioethics have written about their ambivalent attitude toward the ideal of autonomy as it is understood in that field.[3] Feminists are not alone in questioning the role of autonomy in bioethics, yet their concerns more readily draw out questions about the nature of autonomous agents and the social conditions conducive to the development of autonomy overlooked by this narrow "informed consent" approach. On the one hand, the dominant conception of autonomy used in the bioethical literature—autonomy understood as informed, rational, free choice—ill fits women's experience of medical intervention, especially in the area where feminist critiques have contributed most effectively, reproductive decision making. On the other hand, if women see themselves as lacking autonomy in these choices, it appears that the only alternative supported by bioethics is to treat women with beneficent medical paternalism, thereby denying women's agency.

Given the cost of relinquishing the ideal of autonomy, there are good grounds for reexamining the concept as it is employed in bioethics, asking how feminists have responded to it and whether an alternative conception of autonomy that is more applicable to health-care contexts could be developed. In this article I challenge the link, which is prevalent in the bioethical literature, between respect for autonomy and procedures for obtaining informed consent to medical treatment. I argue that an appropriate, relational approach will attend not just to health-care *choices* but also to the ways in which health-care practices can contribute to the development and shaping of people's capacity for autonomy. It will also attend to the role that medicine plays in socialization and the institutional factors that can impede or enhance both the development and continued exercise of autonomy.

The structure of this article is as follows. In the first section, I briefly recount the sources of the identification of personal autonomy with informed consent in bioethics. In the second section, I review the ways in which feminist bioethicists have problematized the focus on respect for autonomy that is understood as free, informed consent. In the third, I examine Susan Sherwin's approach to relational autonomy and her critique of the conception of autonomy employed in mainstream bioethical literature, and I identify limitations with that account of relational autonomy. In the fourth, I use Diana Meyers's procedural approach to personal autonomy to show that an adequate approach to respect, protection, and promotion of personal autonomy in health care is concerned with an array of health-care practices that move well beyond the narrow focus on choice in medical decision making. Whereas rational choice in health-care decision making may reflect personal autonomy, so that respecting those choices would constitute respect for that person's autonomy, autonomy and choice ought not be conflated.[4] In making a rational choice in a pressing health-care context, an individual would usually consider the currently available alternatives; her current understanding of her values, desires, and goals; and what action or choices she believes, based on the information she has, would be most likely to bring about their realization. Her rational choice, however, may reflect heteronomously acquired values, desires, and goals; her medical condition may affect her understanding of herself and her priorities; the available information and alternatives may be the result of autonomy-limiting policies and practices; and so on. Within health care there is a range of autonomy-influencing practices and policies to which those who wish to promote, protect, and respect autonomy ought to attend.

Bioethics

The discipline of bioethics grew out of a change in public attitude toward health care, which coincided with rapid changes in medical technology that affect both the beginning and end of life. Although these medical advances were hailed as breakthroughs, in many cases they failed to be cures. Rather, they made life possible when it might not otherwise have been so. Critics, including some in the medical profession and the families of those whose lives were extended, began to question whether the life thus saved was worth living, whether the opportunity offered was worth taking. In particular, people started questioning whether physicians ought to be left with the responsibility for making decisions of this kind.

As bioethics emerged as a discipline, Thomas Beauchamp and James Childress developed their very influential, principlist approach to bioethics. The approach is based on the application of four general moral principles to particular ethical problems. The four principles—autonomy, justice, nonmaleficence, and beneficence[5]— are grounded in Kantian deontology, Rawls's theory of justice, Mill's utilitarianism, Judeo-Christian morality and even a vestige of the Hippocratic oath. Beauchamp and Childress's metaethic shared some similarities with W. D. Ross's intuitionism, particularly his understanding of prima facie moral considerations.[6]

According to Beauchamp and Childress, the tetrad of principles are to be understood in the following way:

- Autonomy is to be understood as "personal rule of the self that is free from both controlling interferences by others and from personal limitations that prevent meaningful choice, such as inadequate understanding." The principle of respect for autonomy requires respecting those choices made by individuals whose decisions are free from external interference or personal limitations.[7]
- The principle of nonmaleficence is that one ought not to inflict evil or harm, and in general this principle has priority over the principle of beneficence.[8]

- The principle of beneficence covers three kinds of duties, all of which concern promoting the good of others: one ought to prevent evil or harm, one ought to remove evil or harm, and one ought to do or promote good.[9]
- The principle of justice requires fair or equitable distribution of benefits and burdens within a society.[10]

These principles are to be used as prima facie considerations in responding to an ethical problem. Beauchamp and Childress argue that the principles are sufficiently universalizable that any two careful ethical thinkers would apply them in the same way to similar cases, as well as flexible enough to respond to changing contexts, technology, and social concerns.[11] They are applicable to concrete incidents, avoiding the difficulty of applying a full-blown moral theory to specific cases. Despite Beauchamp and Childress's insistence that all four principles have a role to play in bioethics, the principle of autonomy has become elevated so that it is now, surely, the first among equals.[12]

The focus on autonomy has a good pedigree in both Kantian deontology and Millian utilitarianism. The conception of autonomy found in much of the literature in bioethics is more closely linked with Mill's understanding of personal liberty and the appropriate limitations of state authority[13] than with moral psychological accounts that question how and whether a self can be autonomous. Because bioethics is primarily concerned with the proper moral conduct of health-care providers, examination of the requirements of autonomy is directed at the actions that such providers ought to take to avoid *interference* with or *constraint* of patients' autonomy. Reflecting liberal political theory, respect for freedom (autonomy) is understood to require that the state, or health-care providers, do nothing that interferes with the self-regarding choices of rational adults. Thus within mainstream bioethics, the requirement to respect autonomy is understood as the duty of health-care providers to identify those patients who have the capacity for choice, in terms of developmental criteria and the absence of psychological pathology; to offer those patients choices concerning their health care and the information necessary to make an informed choice; and to respect the free, informed choices they make. As such, autonomy can be quite easily tied to the requirement of informed consent to medical procedures.[14]

I argue that the conception of autonomy that has emerged in bioethics is narrow and undertheorized. If we first think of autonomy in terms of the duties of health-care providers to autonomous agents and then link it with choice and consent, its scope is seriously constrained in a number of ways. Like the liberal political and theoretic conceptions of legal and political autonomy that have been roundly criticized by feminist political theorists, the conception of autonomy used in bioethics is rationalistic, atomistic, and individualistic. It assumes something like an atomistic individual, making a choice wholly for herself or himself. It assumes that, paradigmatically, individuals are equally rational and able to reflect on complicated choices once given adequate information. It ignores the social circumstances and power relations that affect choice contexts. Finally, it rules as out of order questions about any effects of the choice other than those selected by the chooser as significant. Because consent processes emphasize the responsibilities of health-care workers to offer information and avoid undue influence, informed consent can be understood as, at best, voluntary choice. Medical choices made in the absence of ignorance, coercion, or impediment to decision making capacity can be understood as voluntary. Whether those choices reflect what a person truly values, wants, or believes, however, is not something that can be determined simply by ensuring the absence of these impediments to choice.

In many ways it is astounding that this conception of autonomy, shorn from the self who chooses, has become the guiding light for so much of bioethics. It may be true that respect for autonomy can generate answers to bioethical problems, but this conception of autonomy seems particularly unsuited to the kind of decision making that goes on in health care. Many of the important, but by no means unusual, health-care decisions that individuals, friends, and families make are far removed from the cool, reflective, clear-headed decision making that is the paradigm of this view of autonomy. For many people, health-care decisions are made in a state of confusion, and the chooser is influenced by a number of internal and external pressures, including pain, discomfort, worry, and concern for others. In making decisions, patients may be primarily concerned with their relationships with others in several ways. Furthermore, their choices may affect people they have never met; and particular patients may, for the first time or for the umpteenth time, feel powerless and in a position of subordination to the health-care providers.

This conception of autonomy seriously constrains how we may conceptualize those who are not fully autonomous and how they are treated as a result. First, in this conception of autonomy, it is unclear how health-care workers ought to treat those who have some degree of autonomy but lack *full* autonomy. In practice those people whose capacity for choice might not be thought *fully* autonomous, for example, people in the early stages of Alzheimer's disease (who may have difficulty remembering some recent events but who may at the same time have a clear understanding of their settled preferences and central values), may be treated in one of two unacceptable ways. On the one hand, because autonomy is identified with informed consent, if a person in this situation is given adequate information and makes a choice that appears to reflect her or his stable preferences, that choice will be treated as autonomous, even if the person has failed to understand or retain salient features of the information required for a genuinely autonomous choice. Alternatively, the person might display some signs of incompetence, be diagnosed as suffering a mental illness, and thus have her or his authority to make self-determining decisions removed. In this latter case, even if the person has the capacity to make a specific health-care decision, her or his claim to make autonomous choices is undermined by the diagnosis of mental incapacity. At best, then, the person will be treated in a way that protects her or his "best interests," as understood by health-care professionals.

This lack of a middle ground, of an awareness that the capacity to make health-care decisions may admit of degrees, is one effect of the identification of autonomy with informed consent, which can be particularly harmful to women's interests. Given the effects of patriarchy, the kinds of medical choices women are asked to make, and the cultural association between "femininity" and "irrationality," women's options in health care are frequently constructed in ways that limit their autonomy.

Feminists attempting to challenge those conceptualizations and practices that inadequately respond to women's lives and experience often find themselves stuck with two unacceptable alternatives. They may choose to accept the limitations of the identification of personal autonomy with informed consent, and so preserve for women some, imperfect, control over their bodies; or they can attempt to reject those limitations, but in so doing risk having women conceptualized as, in general, incompetent to make health-care choices.

Feminist Bioethics

Given this unpalatable set of options, feminists working on bioethical issues have attempted to reshape the conceptual terrain on which women, and others subject to oppressive social conditions, are expected to make health-care decisions. Not surprisingly, there has been an array of different responses to these tensions.

Rosemarie Tong writes that there are three key approaches in feminist bioethics: (1) liberal feminism, focusing on autonomous choice; (2) radical feminism, which illuminates women's limited control over the institutions of health care, reproduction, and sexuality; and, (3) cultural feminism, sometimes identified with a feminine ethic of care.[15] Tong selects these three approaches to bioethics for special attention because "their different perspectives on the nature, form (embodied or disembodied), and value of the self's relationship to others explain liberal feminists' emphasis on issues of choice, radical feminists' emphasis on issues of control, and cultural feminists' emphasis on caring."[16]

I think that each of these three approaches contributes to a general critique of the conception of autonomy found in bioethics, and it can contribute to the development of an alternative conception of autonomy that better reflects our embodied existence and the concrete social context of health-care decision making. At the same time, all three contain significant limitations because they fail to adequately challenge the equation of autonomy with informed consent, thus failing to draw women out of the tension between accepting a conception of autonomy understood as choice, independent of the etiology of the choice, or rejecting the value and significance of personal autonomy for women.

Feminist writings on reproductive technology have highlighted the ways in which limited knowledge, power differences, interpersonal relationships, and the social meanings given to activities influence both autonomous decision making and the ethical landscape of health-care practice in certain contexts. The light shed by feminists on medical and social practices surrounding reproduction can be used to illuminate the limitations of the conception of autonomy in bioethics more generally.

Choice

Liberal feminists who are confronting ethical questions about reproduction argue that there is nothing special about women's reproductive capacity that justifies limiting their freedom to choose reproductive alternatives that are not inherently harmful to others. Laura Purdy's arguments concerning surrogate pregnancy, for example, use the language of contract and reproductive liberty to argue that women ought to be free to be or to use the services of surrogates.[17] Liberal feminists deny that "mere" biological difference is morally significant and emphasize the importance of expressing autonomy through choice. Purdy rejects the paternalism involved in protecting women from their own choices and questions whether the risk of harm that may follow choices about pregnancy or child rearing are so very different from other kinds of choice.

For liberal feminists, the fact that women have a different biological relation to procreation than men is not grounds for undermining women's autonomy, either through exclusive focus on the welfare of the fetus or future person or by attributing to women an inability to think clearly about reproduction because of their biological or social ties to gestation and motherhood. Liberal feminists have drawn attention to the ways in which women's autonomy has been trammeled by medical practice and research in reproduction, leaving women, on the one hand, resorting to dangerous treatments to avoid or achieve pregnancy because of poor information or limited alternatives and, on the other hand, subjecting women to massive intervention into and monitoring of pregnancy and birth.[18] Furthermore, liberal feminists show how choices are restricted by health-care policy, for example, through legislative or policy restrictions on access to donor insemination or in vitro fertilization (IVF) or by surrogacy practices that limit potential gestational mothers' access to information or legal advice.

Liberal feminists thus argue that the scope of personal choice ought not to be arbitrarily limited in a way that unjustifiably limits women's health-care alternatives, and that respect for personal choice in health care requires the provision of accurate, clear, and appropriate information. At the same time, liberal feminist bioethicists challenge assumptions about women's supposed inadequate competence to choose autonomously because of their gender. The liberal feminist approach is consistent with the bioethical focus on respecting autonomy through recognition of informed choice. Also, it forces the bioethicist to challenge social perceptions or prejudices that would limit the scope of women's choices and demands that bioethicists attend to the obstacles to effective communication of medical information.

Two kinds of criticisms can be raised about the adequacy of the liberal feminist conceptions of autonomy, women's embodiment, and decision making. First, the liberal feminist view assumes that health-care decision making occurs in a social vacuum. On the one hand, it assumes that the social factors that influence the availability of alternatives are neutral and, on the other hand, that all people are equally well placed to make health-care decisions because no competent person is unduly constrained by factors like oppressive social conditioning.

Second, the liberal feminist approach does not recognize the various ways in which women's embodiment can affect women's control in their decisions, particularly in regard to reproductive and child-rearing decisions. Menstruation, pregnancy, childbirth, and breast-feeding, for example, are not activities in which participation can be chosen or rejected in the same way that, for example, purchasing a book, deciding to practice the piano, or building a bookshelf are chosen or rejected. An adequate account of autonomy in health care must recognize the significant differences among kinds of choices. Different kinds of choices are affected by the degree

or extent to which bodily processes are involved and by the personal or social significance attributed to such processes. Although it is important to avoid equating
women's possibilities with their reproductive capacities, the differences between reproductive choices and other kinds of choices must be recognized. The liberal feminist approach, by failing to recognize adequately the role of human embodiment in
health-care decision making is unable to account for these differences.[19]

Control

Radical feminist approaches to bioethics emphasize the role that patriarchy has
played in the institutions of medical science, marriage, heterosexuality, and the family, arguing that women's reproductive capacity itself has been the source of their oppression and that the apparent choices they make about reproduction are not really
autonomous choices because the contexts are constructed by patriarchy.[20] The identity of woman, under patriarchy, is tied to her reproductive capacity, and this renders woman connected, dependent, and related to others in a manner that is both
damaging to her and that subordinates her to men. In this view, women lack control over reproductive technology and medical practice and thus should be wary of
being exploited by them.

In the radical feminist approach, the expression of a choice in a medical context should not be understood simply as an expression of autonomous choice because the social context within which women make reproductive decisions is both
exploitative and oppressive. Until women gain control over reproductive technologies and until the link is broken between being a woman and having an inferior social status, because of one's reproductive capacities, women ought to reject forms of
medical intervention that exploit this connection. For radical feminists like Robyn
Rowland and Janice Raymond, then, women's reproductive capacity, as understood
by patriarchy, is the source of women's oppression. For women to be free they must
not simply choose to use, or to be used by, the tools available to reinforce their oppressed state; rather they must seize the controls.[21]

Radical feminist contributions to bioethics demand an awareness of the effects
of race, class, gender, ability, and sexual orientation in the distribution of power in
a context of medical care, rather than a narrowly construed understanding of autonomous choice. The imbalance in power between physicians and patients, between husbands and wives, and between rich and poor become significant features
for understanding the ethical context of health-care decision making. A view that
focuses on purely formal criteria for autonomous choice and that overlooks the social and political context of health-care choices will be found inadequate by radical
feminism.

The radical feminist approach to bioethics challenges the presumption that the
rational choices of adults are autonomous in the absence of certain kinds of pathology. In this view, social conditions affect the development of personal autonomy
and the desirability of the alternatives among which a person rationally chooses. Although a physician may not have unduly influenced a patient's choice to seek a specific kind of treatment, that patient may not have sufficiently developed skills of
critical self-understanding to challenge, for example, the socialization of women

as mothers and wives, which leads her to seek medical reproductive assistance. The radical feminist approach queries the identification of respect for rational, well-informed, uncoerced choice with autonomous choice, in the absence of an examination of the significant social factors that shape decision making contexts.

The radical feminist approach to bioethics, however, contains some inconsistencies. For example, the account of patriarchy that supports the radical feminist mistrust of medical technology is not similarly applied to governmental institutions that are called on to protect women. In this account, women need to be protected from the harms that result from making nonautonomous decisions when they lack control over the context of the decision. In one version of the argument, for example, as put forward by Robyn Rowland, all interaction between women and medical professionals is regarded as necessarily exploitative, but state intervention seems to be viewed as nonproblematic.[22] Surely state institutions have sometimes been used to serve patriarchal interests, and some medical interactions have been nonexploitative.

An adequate account of the effects of patriarchal oppression on women's autonomy would need to explain the different ways in which the social contexts of health-care decision making influence women's choices, (including the reasons why these influences affect women as they do), and it would need to be sufficiently developed to distinguish among more and less exploitative medical interventions and practices. There is an inconsistency, however, between the view that women as a group may be exploited by unregulated access to reproductive technologies and the lack of a demand for similar regulation of other potentially exploitative practices. Even the weaker claim that women's choices in reproduction are likely to be influenced by internal and external factors that can cloud their judgment needs to be made consistent with the ways in which other significant health choices can be similarly clouded; reproductive decision making ought not be singled out for special treatment.

Care

Cultural feminism draws on the work of Carol Gilligan and focuses on caring relations among persons, rejecting the isolated atomism of justice-based ethical theories. Cultural feminism rejects the centrality of autonomy in bioethical principlism. Unlike those radical feminists who view women's interconnection with others as the source of oppression, cultural feminists positively value the activity of caring and responsibility for care. For cultural feminists, the proper focus of ethical concern is interrelationships, the connections between people.[23] Policies and practices are to be evaluated in terms of the degree to which they foster or dissolve caring relationships. Some versions of cultural feminism are not particularly feminist in approach; for example, Nel Noddings argues that ethical behavior involves putting oneself at the service of others and valuing the quality of relationships,[24] an approach that might well reinforce a traditional view of women as subservient, other-directed, and appropriately relegated to the role of carers rather than agents in the world.[25]

Some writers working within the care perspective, however, have articulated explicitly feminist versions of the approach, highlighting the need for a critical account of oppression to supplement any account of care, so that social practices that use care roles to exploit or oppress can be criticized. Joan Tronto, for example, does not simply argue that women's approach to ethical decision-making is better captured by the ideas of care and interconnection, but she also claims that a well-articulated ethical theory in which care has a central role to play can best challenge all forms of oppression.[26] Susan Sherwin, in *No Longer Patient*, shows how this kind of care approach, informed by an account of oppression, can be applied to bioethical issues.[27]

The care approach to bioethics highlights the many significant ways in which those facing decisions in health-care contexts do not make choices as isolated, rational atoms. Rather, their choices are very often affected by concern for a range of relationships that they value, relationships that tend to be discounted by the understanding of autonomous choice in mainstream bioethics. The care approach makes sense of the apparent altruism involved in many health-care choices, of parents,' patients,' and children's concern for the effects of different kinds of care on others, and of the responsibilities that go with certain kinds of choices. The care focus gives us an awareness of the relationships between people and the ways these relationships are affected by health care.

Both cultural feminist and radical feminist interventions in bioethics challenge the assumption that medical decision making is apolitical and asocial and that persons are best understood as independent, self-interested, atomistic choosers. The cultural feminist critique can be seen as the flip side to the radical feminist critique. The former account reminds us that social relationships are not wholly negative in their influence on people's lives. Relationships with others, including relationships founded on chance rather than choice, are central to human existence and can be valuable contributions to people's lives. Autonomy ought not to be conceived as independence or isolation from others; it ought to be conceived as a way to foster nonoppressive relationships of care. Health-care providers ought, therefore, to attend to the relationships involved in health care, that is, the significant relationships of patients that are affected by illness, health care, and health-care decision making. At the same time, bioethics ought not to presume that people will all share the same form of personal relationships; some relationships reflect and enhance the autonomy of those engaged in them, whereas others may not.

Although each of the three feminist approaches identified by Tong contributes to the critique of the narrow understanding of autonomy as rational choice within mainstream bioethics, each has been found to lack an adequate positive account of autonomy in health care. Liberal feminism's narrow attention to choice, independence, and freedom lacks a sufficiently well-developed understanding of the ways in which socialization and cultural contexts shape choices. Radical feminist accounts of social control over the circumstances of health-care choice are insufficient to offer any guide to developing a less oppressive health-care ethics. Finally, cultural feminist accounts have failed to provide a critical analysis of the relationships of care and dependence that could guide the identification of which relationships ought to be fostered in health-care contexts and which are inherently oppressive. Any adequate understanding of autonomy in health care will need to offer an alternative account of autonomy, one that incorporates the liberal, radical, and cultural feminist critiques.

Relational Autonomy

In her recent writings, Susan Sherwin presents an argument for a feminist perspective on bioethics and autonomy that develops an account of autonomy informed by these critiques. She argues for a richer, more complex understanding of autonomy than the one described in the mainstream bioethics literature.[28] Sherwin recognizes that respect for autonomy has an important role to play in health-care ethics, yet she challenges the standard assumptions made about the criteria for autonomous choice in health care. Her approach avoids the problems of those criticized in the previous section, as she does not overlook or oversimplify social relations; she provides a coherent account of oppression, and she recognizes that human dependency and relationships can be a double-edged sword in a patriarchal culture.

The account of autonomous choice in health care that Sherwin offers contextualizes health-care decision making. She gives due recognition to the ways in which health-care choices are shaped by a range of social values. For example, on the one hand, the scope of the decision is marked out by the institutional framework of health-care provision, including health-care resources, medical education, and community care. On the other hand, what people seek from health care is moderated by the social influences that shape their self-understanding to varying degrees. For example, women's demand for reproductive technology and cosmetic surgery are, at least in part, effects of the patriarchal association of femininity with childbearing and beauty understood as attractiveness to men. Through her contextualization of health-care decision making Sherwin begins to articulate an alternative understanding of autonomy in health-care ethics.

In Sherwin's view, feminist bioethics must be understood as an ethics of the oppressed:

> Feminists share a recognition that women are oppressed in our society and an understanding that their oppression takes many different forms, compounded often by other forms of oppression based on features such as race, ethnicity, sexual orientation, and economic class. Because feminists believe that oppression is objectionable on both moral and political grounds, most are committed to transforming society in ways that will ensure the elimination of oppression in all its forms.[29]

Feminist bioethics is focused, then, on identifying those features of health care that exacerbate or ameliorate oppression. Although feminists have appealed to autonomy to reject paternalistic treatment by the medical profession, there are good grounds for critically examining the ways in which the dominant conception of autonomy used in bioethics may contribute to systems of oppression.

According to Sherwin, autonomy is usually understood, in bioethics, as applying to particular decisions in particular contexts. A patient is thought of as autonomous with regard to a specific choice if the following criteria are met:

1. The patient is deemed to be rational with regard to the decision at hand.

2. The patient makes a choice from a set of available options.

3. The patient has adequate information and understanding.

4. The patient is free from explicit coercion toward or away from one of these options.[30]

Sherwin argues that each of these criteria raises problems for feminists concerned with the eradication of oppression.

First, if oppressed people are less likely to be thought of as autonomous agents —indeed, if the core of autonomy, rationality, has been conceptualized as antithetical to the characteristics identified with women—there is good reason to question the gender neutrality of autonomy as an ideal.[31] The rational competence of women and other oppressed groups is frequently questioned, insofar as they are thought to lack sufficient emotional distance and objectivity to act rationally.[32] Members of oppressed groups may lack sufficient autonomy for their choices to be accorded adequate respect by health-care providers—leaving them dependent on medical paternalism.

Second, the set of options a patient chooses from may already be constructed in a way that seriously limits the patient's autonomy. Decisions about medical research priorities and funding of the health-care system affect what alternatives are available for the physician to offer to the patient. These decisions may reflect discriminatory or biased practices that affect the particular patient's autonomy, and yet in most bioethical discussions these alternatives are thought of as a given set that does not require ethical scrutiny.[33]

Third, information made available to patients is inevitably that information deemed relevant by the health professionals who care for them; but the large gap between the life experience of health professionals, who are relatively privileged, and their sometimes seriously disadvantaged patients makes the likelihood that the former will provide information that meets the specific needs of their patients rather slim.[34]

Fourth, the forces that contribute to the coercion of the oppressed may be very difficult to identify. Drawing on Sandra Bartky's characterization of psychological oppression, Sherwin argues that those who experience this form of oppression may identify with their oppressed condition.[35] It is distorting, then, to describe as autonomous the choices made under circumstances of oppression. Echoing the views of radical feminists, Sherwin says that the absence of explicit coercion at the time of making a decision does not make that choice free.[36]

I agree with each of Sherwin's criticisms of the dominant bioethical conception of autonomy. However, I would take the criticisms further. In drawing out their implications, I think it is important to note that the inadequacies of the dominant conception of autonomy apply to *any* person who is in need of health-care and who must come to understand one's condition, make choices about one's care, and adapt to one's changed situation. While the dominant bioethical conception of autonomy serves to reinforce discriminatory attitudes toward women and other oppressed groups and their agency, I think that the problem with the dominant conception of autonomy is not simply one of oppression or gender.

The conception of autonomy that dominates bioethics, which identifies autonomy with informed consent, is inadequate for anyone in serious medical need, although the effects of its inadequacy may often be greater for those who have experienced oppression. The voluntary choice model is just as inadequate a tool for genuinely protecting and enhancing the autonomy of male patients in health-care situations as it is for women.

My first criticism of Sherwin, then, is that although she correctly identifies the kinds of features of the medical environment that limit people's decision-making capacity, she is wrong to assume that these limitations affect only those who have been subjected to oppression. A range of features about health-care crises and health-care institutions pose a threat to the capacity of anyone facing a health-care crisis, not just those oppressed by gender or social disadvantage.

Let us consider an example. A man (for the purpose of the argument, a white, able-bodied, tertiary-educated professional) who finds himself in a hospital, having had a heart attack, or a man who must make a decision about a prostate operation, after being diagnosed with prostate cancer, suddenly finds himself in a circumstance in which he is not fully in control of his life; he can no longer assume that his choice and consent will largely determine his future possibilities. Faced with his own mortality, his ability to engage in abstract reasoning may be clouded. The choices open to him are likely to be restricted by factors over which he has no control but which affect the quality of his care. Is he in a teaching hospital? Then he may be offered trial medication. Does his physician lean heavily toward leaving the prostate alone? The information given by his physician may not reflect his own set of priorities, and his socialization may make asking questions difficult. Will the bypass operation render him impotent? How can he avoid incontinence after the prostate operation? Finally, the factors that influence his decision, rendering it less free than the autonomy ideal presupposes, may be ones that have been inculcated in him as part of his enculturation. He may be pushed to accept invasive medical procedures because he believes that it would be weak or unmanly to accept his condition passively. He may be pushed to accept risky experimental treatment because he believes that it is the only way to avoid becoming dependent on others for care.

This example illuminates the ways in which even a bastion of patriarchy may find his autonomy threatened or undermined if his physician exclusively attends to information and choice in negotiating his health care, rather than understanding autonomy relationally. Even medical specialists find health care threatening and intimidating when they face medical emergencies as patients. Those who have been patients claim that it has changed "completely and forever" the way they practice medicine and has forced them to rethink the approach to informed consent by which the physician stands as dispassionate information provider rather than as a partner in medical decision making.[37] The point of the criticism is that the factors that Sherwin identifies as limiting health-care decision making affect most patients, not just those who are members of oppressed groups. It is quite true that our imagined white, male professional is likely to have readier access to wider alternatives in health care than relatively disadvantaged members of the community, but that does not mean that his autonomous health-care decision making is not open to limitation in a manner similar to theirs.

My second and more substantive criticism of Sherwin is that although her account challenges the connection between autonomy and informed consent familiar

in the bioethical literature, it still assumes that personal autonomy is correctly identified solely with medical choices. Whereas Sherwin wants health-care workers and
policymakers to examine more carefully the features of health-care decision making
that can constrain personal autonomy, her focus is still on autonomy understood as
choice. It may be that if health care practices were revised to acknowledge the effect
of the array of influences on choice that Sherwin identifies, patients would be able
to make not just voluntary choices but also rational choices. That is, their choices
would be made in accordance with principles of rational choice and deliberative rationality.[38] Sherwin's account encourages review of the processes of medical decision
making but does not require any reexamination of the process whereby a person develops the capacity for rational decision making. Her references to the effects of socialization and oppression indicate that she is aware that people's capacities for autonomy are influenced by the environment within which those capacities develop,
and yet she still identifies respect for autonomy in health-care with respect for rational medical choices.

   As I argue below, an adequate understanding of autonomy in health care must
not be restricted to an examination of the exercise of autonomy through choice but
must also encompass an understanding of the ways in which autonomy is developed
or, in Diana Meyers's terms, the ways in which the array of "autonomy competencies"[39] are fostered, shaped, and potentially thwarted. In the next section I look beyond patient decision making to other areas of health care in which autonomy can
be enhanced or limited by health-care providers or health-care systems.

Autonomy Competency and Health-Care Contexts

As I argued in the first section, the identification of personal autonomy with informed consent has meant that health-care workers concerned to respect autonomy
have understood their task as the improvement of processes for obtaining informed
consent and acting in accordance with the consent so obtained. Sherwin's argument
raises questions about the narrow focus on the relationship between the physician
and the patient in the consent process because factors external to that process, for
example, oppression, inadequate socialization, and limited health-care funding, affect the choices available to patients. These factors also influence the patient's (and
physician's) subjective understanding of those choices and shape the capacities of
patients to resist, inform, or control the process of obtaining information and making a decision. Sherwin thus pushes against an identification of autonomy with voluntary choice and toward an understanding of autonomy in health care as aligned
with contextualized rational choice.

   In this section I argue that an adequate understanding of respect for autonomy
in health care must extend to an understanding of the development and exercise of
the capacity for autonomous decision making, rather than focusing solely on informed consent or even rational choice of the kind that Sherwin supports. In arguing that the conception of autonomy appropriate to bioethics must include an understanding of the development of the capacity for autonomy, I am not arguing that
respect for the informed consent (voluntary choice) or rational choice of patients is
irrelevant to respect for autonomy. Rather, I am arguing that respect for autonomy is

not restricted to respect for choices of a certain kind but also requires promotion of the development of autonomous selves.

Procedural approaches to autonomy, such as those offered by Dworkin, Young, and Meyers,[40] require that autonomy be understood not merely in terms of the choices people make but also in terms of the relationships among the choices people make, their values, and the capacities they engage in making choices.[41] According to Meyers, "Autonomous people must be able to pose and answer the question 'What do I really want, need, care about, believe, value, etcetera?'; they must be able to act on the answer; and they must be able to correct themselves when they get the answer wrong."[42] To conduct this procedure, the autonomous person employs an array of skills that constitute "autonomy competency." An autonomous person asks and answers questions about her real wants, needs, concerns, and so on so that she can structure her life plan to secure personal integration.[43]

Autonomous self-direction occurs, according to Meyers, both episodically and programmatically:

> Autonomous episodic self-direction occurs when a person confronts a situation, asks what he or she can do with respect to it . . . and what he or she really wants to do with respect to it, and then executes the decision this deliberation yields. Autonomous programmatic self-direction has a broad sweep. Instead of posing the question "What do I really want to do now?" this form of autonomy addresses a question like "How do I really want to live my life?" To answer this latter question, people must consider what qualities they want to have, what sorts of interpersonal relations they want to be involved in, what talents they want to develop.[44]

Respecting the rational choices of a patient *may* also respect that person's autonomous episodic self-direction, assuming that the person's rational choice reflects her or his authentic desires, values, and so on. It is less clear, however, that these processes of respect for rational choices will be sufficient to recognize programmatic self-direction, although many significant health-care decisions affect programmatic self-direction. Furthermore, as was indicated by some of Sherwin's comments, many of the policies and practices that affect programmatic self-direction in the area of health may be outside the scope of individual patients' decision making (e.g., legal prohibitions on voluntary euthanasia, access to home-based care, availability of community-based support for people with disabilities, provision of universal access to health care, etc.). These features affect autonomy in a way that is not captured by the approach to autonomy that only concerns itself with specific medical choices.

According to Meyers, to exercise autonomous programmatic or episodic self-direction, autonomous people must develop an array of competency skills, those required for self-discovery (identifying what they want, value, care about, etc.), self-definition (acting on their desires, values, etc.), and self-direction (correcting their actions or understanding of their values when they misidentify them).[45] Exercising these skills constitutes autonomy competency. Rational choice, understood as choosing to act on that course of conduct that, of the available alternatives, best suits a person's desires, values, or life plan may or may not reflect a person's autonomy competency. Rational choices, choices made on the basis of principles of rational-

ity, display some of the skills of autonomy competency but do not constitute autonomy.[46] A person who is fully autonomous will make rational choices that reflect
their authentic desires or values. However, being able to make a rational choice does
not necessarily reflect full autonomy; rational choosers can make rational choices if
they have developed their capacity for rational deliberation in light of rational principles, even if they lack skills in self-direction. Even less should making rational
choices be understood as *constituting* autonomy in Meyers's account.

Applying Meyers's conception of autonomy to health care requires broadening
the focus from a narrow examination of the conditions for choice to an assessment
of the conditions for the development of the skills that encompass autonomy competency. Bioethicists concerned with protection, promotion, and respect for personal
autonomy in health care must direct their attention to the wide array of health-care
contexts that may impede the development of autonomy competency. The following
discussion sketches some implications of Meyers's approach to health-care ethics.

Autonomy Competency and Universal Access to Health Care

Meyers recognizes the interests that people are likely to have in those things necessary for the development and exercise of autonomy in a range of areas. She
writes that basic interests are to be understood as "generalized means to various
self-regarding ends." While Meyers does not wish the rational presumption that all
people share some basic interests, such as "health, strength, intelligence, power,
wealth, friendship, opportunities, and reputation,"[47] to override individual preferences and choices, it seems clear that in the provision of basic welfare services
(health, education, housing, etc.) a society can promote personal autonomy by enabling access to those things needed to develop autonomy competency and to pursue an autonomous life. Health-care systems are clearly part of this provisioning, insofar as good health and decent access to health-care facilities will be a precondition
for the pursuit of a very great range of autonomous projects. Thus, one initial implication of Meyers's account for bioethics is that the promotion and protection of
autonomy competency requires the provision of some level of universal access to
health care. Individual needs and wants with regard to services will vary, but it is reasonable to assume that all autonomous people will have an interest in health care
provision sufficient to provide for the basic health-care interests of the members of
the community (consistent with individual choice and preferences). Health-care systems that do not provide equitable access for all members of the community will not
promote and protect autonomy to the same degree as those that do.

Socialization and the Development of Autonomy Competency in Health-Care Settings

According to Meyers

> Someone is *minimally autonomous* when this person possesses at least some dispo-
> sition to consult his or her self and at least some ability to act on his or her own
> beliefs, desires, and so forth, but when this person lacks some other skills from the

repertory of autonomy skills, when the autonomy skills the person possesses are poorly developed and poorly coordinated, and when the person possesses few in-dependent competencies that could promote the exercise of available autonomy skills. I shall say that someone is *fully autonomous* when this person possesses a complete repertory of well developed and well coordinated autonomy skills cou-pled with many and varied independent competencies. *Medially autonomous* peo-ple range along a spectrum between these two poles.[48]

Meyers is particularly concerned to recognize the role of socialization in the devel-opment of autonomy competency. In her view the capacity for developing and ex-ercising full autonomy is affected by socialization, and given dominant influences in current child-rearing and educational practices, most socialization fails to develop the skills necessary for full autonomy. As a result, most women and men end up lacking full autonomy; they are minimally or medially autonomous.[49] Meyers dis-cusses the role of appropriate parenting and school education both in creating an en-vironment within which children can develop autonomy competency and in learn-ing some basic autonomy competency skills. What she says in this context is applicable to a number of health-care contexts.

Health-care settings are social environments that can play a socializing role in the development of autonomy competency. Some health-care settings can signifi-cantly inhibit the development of the skills that constitute autonomy competency, quite independently of the exercise of those skills in medical decision making. In particular, those people who receive long-term or residential care may be signifi-cantly socialized through the health-care environment. Three specific examples are (1) children born with severe disabilities or chronic serious illness and those who suffer trauma of various kinds while young, (2) adolescents and young adults with psychiatric illnesses, and (3) patients in nursing homes.

Health-care providers and policies can serve to promote full, medial, or mini-mal autonomy in children. For example, the future possibilities presented to chil-dren with disabilities or significant illnesses can come to dominate those children's self-understandings in ways that limit their ability to imagine other alternatives. In recent years there has been a revolution in the care of children with developmental disabilities that has given some children much greater opportunities to develop and exercise autonomy skills, within environments that both foster autonomy and pro-tect the child's welfare.

Provision of counseling and therapy to assist adolescents and young adults with psychiatric illnesses to better understand themselves, their illnesses, and their desires —rather than simply providing treatment to curb undesirable behavior—can en-hance the development of autonomy competency. Meyers argues that competency skills can be taught and recommends a range of educational practices to foster per-sonal autonomy in children.[50] These are also applicable to pediatric and adolescent health-care. Encouraging children with long-term illnesses to participate in decision making, to ask questions about their care, to voice their feelings and desires, and to take responsibility for aspects of their own care help them in the development of au-tonomy competency. On the other hand, uncritically treating such children as ill, needing total care, and unable to understand or accept their condition robs those children of the opportunity to develop the skills needed for autonomy competency.

Health-care workers can also assist parents and guardians to understand the child's concerns and condition and can challenge the preconceptions of parents and guardians that might stifle the child's autonomy development. Children who have experienced health-care institutions that foster rather than frustrate the development of autonomy competency will more likely become autonomous selves who can then make medical decisions that are autonomous. Those whose skills are frustrated or limited by health-care environments are less likely to develop the capacity for autonomous medical decision making and will be more likely to be minimally or medially autonomous, rather than fully autonomous.

Similarly, the autonomy competency of residents in nursing homes can be shaped by the health-care environment. Given that Meyers's account of autonomy recognizes stages or degrees of autonomy, the approach can be used to inform processes for preserving those autonomy skills that a person still retains when the person's autonomy has been compromised and he or she is dependent on others for care. Many elderly residents in nursing homes are physically very frail and ill, yet by no means do all such residents lack some degree of autonomy. Policies and practices in nursing homes designed to protect residents or to deal with limited resources very often have the effect of eroding lifelong dispositions to use an array of competency skills, leaving residents passive, atrophying their competence, and opening the way for rapid mental and physical deterioration.[51] Establishing nursing home practices that both recognize the limitations experienced by residents and seek to protect residents' remaining autonomy competency would require a significant reassessment of the role of nursing homes and health-care provision. Such a reassessment might well contribute to the breaking down of artificial barriers between health care and the rest of people's lives in a way that recognized the full significance of health care practices in the development, fostering, exercise, and protection of personal autonomy.

Health-Care Crises and Altered Self-Conceptions

Health-care emergencies very often require patients to confront new information that significantly alters their self-perception and future possibilities.[52] It may be appropriate, then, to treat these crises as inherently autonomy threatening. Although a fully autonomous person will have an array of skills that can be employed in coming to terms with major life changes, the suddenness and significance of some health-care crises force a radical reassessment of one's self-understanding, which may effectively derail a person's autonomy competency. The extent of the threat to a person's autonomy posed by these emergencies will depend on such features as the degree of autonomy competency the person has, the nature and circumstances of the crisis, and the various resources available to support the person through it (family, counselors, support groups, etc.).

To adapt the earlier example of the white, able-bodied, professional man, a man who has been brought to the hospital with a heart attack discovers that he requires immediate cardiac bypass surgery. This revelation could force him to completely reassess his self-understanding. His integrated life plan may have been built, in part, on the assumption that he was healthy, with a long professional career before him, and that he had the material and psychological resources to cope with whatever life might throw at him. The diagnosis and subsequent surgery may lead to a self-realization of the limits to his capacity to simply "will" himself to accommodate his changed circumstances. Although he may consent to the surgery and recuperative treatment, the impact of the events surrounding his hospitalization may well cause an enduring setback to his autonomy competency.[53] Any approach that emphasizes the significance of respect for autonomy at the front end (provision of information about treatment and respect for informed consent) will be unable to recognize the impact of trauma, terminal diagnosis, or personal medical emergencies on the self-understanding of patients and will, therefore, not be able to explain the importance of providing support for people in coming to terms with their altered circumstances as part of the protection and respect for autonomy.

Exercise of Autonomy: Information and Alternatives

The discussion of medical emergencies also raises the question about whether the presentation of more information and more alternatives in health care should be assumed to indicate greater respect for patients' autonomy. If we focus on the development and exercise of people's autonomy competency, rather than on the obligations of health-care workers to avoid interference with the informed consent or rational choice of patients, there are good reasons to doubt that more information and more alternatives being offered to patients will always enhance their autonomy. In both medical emergencies and cases in which a serious condition has been diagnosed, which will require a series of treatments with significant side effects, the provision of information and alternatives *may* enhance autonomous choice, but the provision of extensive information and alternatives, without some other form of support in decision making, may impede a person's decision-making capacity.

In these circumstances, being given vast amounts of information and opportunities to take full control of one's health-care is no guarantee that autonomy will be protected. Depending on the array of autonomy competencies that can be summoned to the task, a person may be better or less able to use information critically to determine how to choose authentically. In many cases, processes of counseling that help the person determine what it is he or she really wants in the context (and why) may better promote autonomy than greater information. That is, once it is recognized that significant medical decision making may confront a person with new information that challenges his or her self-understanding and capacity to exercise self-direction, processes that assist the person to reexamine, when possible, one's preferences, goals, values, and so on may better assist autonomous choice than clear information provision alone. There may not always be time or opportunity to realize this kind of support, yet when it is available to those who need it or want it, it would support patients' autonomy. For example, recognition of what a particular condition or treatment involves may be best understood by meeting with nonexpert sufferers, survivors, and carers, and it might better enable the patients to put the information they receive together with their own self-understanding.

Assisting patients to make choices through active understanding of their wants and expressed preferences may well better protect autonomy than detailing risk probabilities, especially when the alternatives are limited and one or other of the alternatives is clearly preferable in the circumstances. A full listing of all possible side effects, for example, may well do nothing but agitate a patient who is clear that she desires to be treated and understands that there are risks associated with achieving that goal.[54] The physician, standing as objective, neutral information source, is not necessarily an aide to autonomy. A health-care worker who has sufficient information; who can listen actively to the patients' identification of their concerns, desires, fears, and so on; and who can ask them how much they want to know and why will often better promote autonomy both in decision making and in the patient's capacity to learn to accommodate or respond to the changes in their health, so they can learn to live with, resist, or accommodate their altered circumstances.

By examining some feminist writings on bioethics and autonomy, I have shown that we need to break away from an understanding of autonomy that focuses narrowly on informed consent. In particular, I have extended both Sherwin's critique of the dominant conception of autonomy in bioethics and Meyers's procedural approach to autonomy to show the implications for health-care ethics of a relational account of autonomy modeled on Meyers's understanding of the development and exercise of autonomy competency. It is worth repeating that I am not arguing for doing away with some sort of improved consent process, of the kind that might be developed from Sherwin's insights. Rather I am arguing that in bioethics it is important not to restrict the scope of respect for personal autonomy to the consent process. The range of areas within health-care where the development, promotion, and exercise of autonomy competency can be influenced by health-care institutions, policies, and professionals must also be considered.

More work is needed in this area, however. At the practical level, the specification of the kinds of practices and policies in health care that need reexamination in light of the demands of autonomy must be elaborated in the context of existing health-care systems and an articulation of the likely autonomy-affecting features of different conditions and treatments. Finally, given the broader conception of autonomy articulated here, there is a need to reexamine the basis for assigning to health-care workers responsibility for patients' autonomy. The kinds of responsibilities and duties that individual health-care workers might have if this approach to autonomy is adopted need to be closely evaluated. For example, should all responsibility for respecting and promoting personal autonomy in health care fall into the hands of individual health professionals, or should there be state and institutional responsibility for some aspects of personal autonomy? Furthermore, there is the familiar issue of the importance of autonomy promotion, protection, and respect relative to other ethical considerations and legitimate demands on resources. Nonetheless, bioethicists who wish to respect autonomy should ensure, among other things, that they recognize autonomy in all its complexity.

Notes

1. This article has benefitted from comments from participants at conferences and seminars in 1996 and 1997, as well as from discussions with Rebecca Albury, Anne Donchin,

Catriona Mackenzie, Katherine Morgan, Barbara Secker, Susan Sherwin, and Natalie Stoljar, to whom I owe thanks.

2. See Susan Brison's article, "Relational Autonomy and Freedom of Expression," in this volume.

3. At least two, Susan Sherwin and Anne Donchin, have articulated relational conceptions of autonomy that they apply to health care: Susan Sherwin. "A Relational Approach to Autonomy in Health-care," in *The Politics of Women's Health: Exploring Agency and Autonomy*, The Feminist Health Care Ethics Research Nework, coordinator Susan Sherwin (Philadelphia: Temple University Press, 1998); Anne Donchin, "Understanding Autonomy Relationally," *Journal of Medicine and Philosophy* 23, no. 4 (1998).

4. See, for example, Diana Meyers's discussion of this distinction in *Self, Society, and Personal Choice* (New York: Columbia University Press, 1989), pp. 76–79, 101–102; see also Harry Frankfurt, "Freedom of the Will and the Concept of a Person," *The Journal of Philosophy* 68 (1971): 5–20; Gary Watson, *Free Will* (London: Oxford University Press, 1982); John Rawls, *A Theory of Justice* (Cambridge, Mass.: Harvard University Press, 1971).

5. Thomas L. Beauchamp and James Childress, *Principles of Biomedical Ethics*, 4th ed. (New York: Oxford University Press, 1994).

6. W. D. Ross, *The Right and the Good* (London: Oxford University Press, 1930).

7. Beauchamp and Childress, *Principles of Biomedical Ethics*, p. 121.

8. Ibid., pp. 190–91.

9. Ibid., p. 190.

10. Ibid., p. 327.

11. Ibid., pp. 14–26.

12. Sherwin, "Relational Approach to Autonomy"; Donchin, "Understanding Autonomy Relationally."

13. John Stuart Mill, *On Liberty* (1859); Joel Feinberg, "Legal Paternalism," *Canadian Journal of Philosophy* 1 (1971).

14. Indeed, in a recent article on the role of families in informed consent, Mark Kuczewski notes that it would not be much of an exaggeration to say that "all of medical ethics is but a footnote to informed consent." Kuczewski, "Reconceiving the Family: The Process of Consent in Medical Decision Making," *Hastings Center Report*, March–April 1996, pp. 30–37, 30.

15. Rosemarie Tong, "Feminist Approaches to Bioethics," in *Feminism and Bioethics: Beyond Reproduction*, ed. Susan M. Wolf (New York: Oxford University Press, 1996), p. 74.

16. Ibid.

17. Laura Purdy, "Surrogate Mothering: Exploitation of Empowerment," *Bioethics* 3 (1989): 18–39.

18. Susan Sherwin, "Feminism and Bioethics," in Wolf, *Feminism and Bioethics*.

19. See, for example, Catriona Mackenzie's critique of bioethical and feminist approaches to the ethics of abortion, in which she queries the adequacy of these approaches because of their narrow understanding of pregnancy as an event in the lives of women over which women lack control, in "Abortion and Embodiment," *Australasian Journal of Philosophy* 70 (1992): 136–155.

20. Tong, "Feminist Approaches to Bioethics," pp. 75–76.

21. Robyn Rowland, *Living Laboratories* (Sydney: Sun Books, 1992); Janice Raymond, *Women as Wombs: Reproductive Technologies and the Battle over Women's Freedom* (New York: HarperCollins, 1993).

22. Rowland, *Living Laboratories*; Raymond, *Women as Wombs*; Christine Overall, *Ethics and Human Reproduction: A Feminist Analysis* (Boston: Unwin Hyman, 1987).

23. Mary Jeanne Larrabee, *An Ethic of Care* (New York: Routledge, 1993).

24. Nel Noddings, *Caring: A Feminine Approach to Ethics and Moral Education* (Berkeley: University of California Press, 1994), p. 33.

25. See Susan Sherwin's critique of Noddings in Sherwin, *No Longer Patient* (Philadelphia: Temple University Press, 1992), p. 47. See also Virginia Held, who focuses on the mother-child relationship as the central ethical relationship, in *Feminist Morality: Transforming Culture, Society and Politics* (Chicago: University of Chicago Press, 1993).

26. Joan Tronto, "Beyond Gender Difference to a Theory of Care," *Signs,* 12 (1987): 644–663; Jennifer Nedelsky, "Reconceiving Autonomy: Sources, Thoughts and Possibilities," *Yale Journal of Law and Feminism* 1 (Spring 1989): 7–36.

27. Sherwin, *No Longer Patient.*

28. Sherwin, "Relational Approach to Autonomy."

29. Sherwin, "Feminism and Bioethics," p. 48.

30 Sherwin, "Relational Approach to Autonomy."

31. Genevieve Lloyd, *The Man of Reason: "Male" and "Female" in Western Philosophy* (London: Methuen, 1984).

32. Sherwin, "Relational Approach to Autonomy."

33. Ibid.

34. Ibid.

35. Sandra Bartky, *Femininity and Domination: Studies in the Phenomenology of Oppression* (New York: Routledge, 1990), chap. 2.

36. Sherwin, "Relational Approach to Autonomy."

37. Jan Bowen, "A Dose of Their Own Medicine," *Good Weekend,* 6 December 1997, pp. 30–34.

38. On the distinction between rational choice and autonomous choice, see Meyers, *Self, Society, and Personal Choice,* pp. 77–80; on the principles of rationality and deliberative rationality, see Rawls, *Theory of Justice,* pp. 410–423.

39. Meyers, *Self, Society, and Personal Choice,* p. 76.

40. Gerald Dworkin, *The Theory and Practice of Autonomy* (Cambridge: Cambridge University Press, 1988); Robert B. Young, *Personal Autonomy: Beyond Negative and Positive Liberty* (London: Croom Helm, 1986); Meyers, *Self, Society, and Personal Choice.*

41. In what follows I focus on Meyers's account because it draws on these earlier works and develops them in the light of feminist and further moral-psychological concerns. Meyers's account is particularly illuminating for developing an account of autonomy appropriate for feminist bioethics. She focuses on the role of socialization in the development of autonomy competency, on the importance for autonomy of one's understanding of one's emotions, and on the need to develop the capacity for self-definition.

42. Ibid., p. 76.

43. Ibid., p. 98.

44. Ibid., p. 48.

45. Ibid., 76.

46. Ibid., pp. 77–78.

47. Ibid., pp. 98–99.

48. Ibid., p. 170.

49. Ibid.

50. Ibid., pp. 195ff.

51. Jill A. Blakeslee, "Speaking Out: Untie the Elderly," *American Journal of Nursing* 88 (1988): 833–834; Susan Dodds, "Exercising Restraint: Autonomy, Welfare and Elderly Patients," *Journal of Medical Ethics* 22 (1996): 160–163.

52. Susan Brison reflects on the immediate and ongoing effects of sexual assault on a

person's self-understanding in "Outliving Oneself: Trauma, Memory, and Personal Identity," in *Feminists Rethink the Self,* ed. Diana T. Meyers (Boulder, Colo.: Westview, 1997).

53. The effect of medical crises need not all be damaging, however, as people may discover resilience they had not known themselves capable of, or they may come to reassess their self-understanding and their goals in positive rather than self-damaging ways.

54. Bowen, "Dose of Their Own Medicine," pp. 32–33.

10

AUTONOMY AND INTERDEPENDENCE

Quandaries in Genetic Decision Making[1]

Anne Donchin

Introduction

In 1996 a foundation funded by a British pharmaceutical company launched a project to allay public fears about the new genetic detection techniques under development in its industry.[2] The focal point of the project was a traveling road show, featuring performances of a play called *The Gift*, which focused on a family affected by an autosomal recessive genetic disorder (Friedreichs ataxia). The audience debate that followed was structured and circumscribed by a staff facilitator, who offered a preselected menu of options for resolving decisional quandaries dramatized by the play's characters. Included were such questions as these: when such techniques become feasible should they be available to individual parents, or should the state preclude individual exercise of options directed to genetic enhancement? Suppressed were questions involving the more subtle ambiguities suggested by the play's title and a perplexing array of further issues implicit in the drama, for example, should human choice supplant chance in the selection of genetic progeny? What stake does the society have collectively in the uses to which such newly emerging technologies are put? A complicated tangle of moral, social, and metaphysical issues was reduced to a few simple options: either the state reaches out to regulate genetic technologies or individuals are left free to select for their offspring whatever characteristics they prefer, limited only by the options available in the commercial marketplace and their individual purchasing power. Implicit in the debate's structure was a predisposition to leave individual family members free to make genetic decisions unencumbered by constraints that would limit the effects of their action on others.

The agenda was tailored around a conception of autonomy that idealizes the individual decision maker and abstracts options from both context and consequences. Its intended message, apparently, was that the new genetics would be problem-free if individuals would only utilize medical techniques to identify affected embryos. Guiding alternative resolutions of the dilemma presented in this well-meaning farce was a popular version of the individualistic conception of autonomy entrenched in bioethical theory. This theoretical structure stifled all other possible resolutions of the characters' dilemma and created the illusory expectation that social problems endemic to the new genetics would vanish if only affected embryos could be eliminated.

The project's deficiencies as a vehicle for public education helped crystallize my own uneasiness about the reigning conception of personal autonomy that motivates much health-care policy and practice. This conception bypasses concern about the particular situations of agents as long as formal informed consent requirements can be satisfied, ignores background conditions that shape options offered to patients, and regards decision makers in isolation from significant relations with surrounding others including health-care providers. My aim here is to show the need to reorder bioethical theory so that it incorporates a conception of autonomy that stimulates health-care professionals to respond appropriately to the social situation of patients and their families, including disparities in their power relationships.

Weak and Strong Relational Autonomy

The dominant framework of North American bioethics is structured around a set of cardinal moral principles, including autonomy, nonmaleficence, beneficence, and justice. Since publication of *The Belmont Report*[3] and Tom Beauchamp and James Childress's first edition of *Principles of Biomedical Ethics*,[4] this framework has dominated bioethics-oriented teaching, consultation, and scholarship, as well as the pronouncements of prestigious governmental ethics commissions. The prominence given to patient autonomy within this framework has been evident even in federal statutes such as the *Patient Self-Determination Act*.[5]

In subsequent editions of their text, Beauchamp and Childress have sought to adapt their version of this theoretical structure, now called "principlism," to address critical objections directed primarily to their ranking and representation of the principle of autonomy.[6] They now stress the *respect* due autonomous agents rather than an ideal image of fully autonomous selves. Respect, Childress explains in a related article, is both an attitude and "an act of refraining from interfering with, or attempting to interfere with the autonomous choices and actions of others, through subjecting them to controlling influence . . . or manipulation of information."[7] Its implementation, he contends, entails autonomy-related rights such as liberty, privacy, confidentiality, and claims to positive assistance. It is compatible, though, with individuals yielding decision-making power if they *choose* to subordinate themselves to authorities like physicians or religious institutions.

Feminist criticisms of the conception that he and Beauchamp advanced in earlier editions of their *Principles* pointed to its tendency to underestimate the importance of intimate and personal relationships and to rely on a misleading image of an independent self.[8] But in their most recent edition, Beauchamp and Childress respond that theirs is not the "stark, individualistic conception of autonomy" that feminists fault.[9] They offer what I call *weak relational autonomy*, for they do not deny that communal life and human relationships provide the matrix for the development of self. Values and beliefs shared with others may still be fully chosen as one's own. However, their cautious acknowledgement that personal relations play a role in self-development joins social ties only contingently to agents' self-understandings. Bonds that link individuals can seemingly be detached at will. Individuals' beliefs and values are assumed to be transparently self-evident and, barring coercive influences, voluntarily chosen. Their account is weakly relational because it does not acknowledge that social relations are often at least partially constitutive of self-conceptions or that social relations are often not voluntarily chosen by agents. I argue later that in genetic contexts, many affected relations are biologically linked and hence not voluntarily chosen. Moreover, Beauchamp and Childress overlook the impact of the self's social situation in two respects. First, in their model, respect for autonomy is compatible with a contract model of the physician-patient relationship; second, their model ignores macro-level (societal) influences on the autonomy of individual patients. I consider each of these problems in turn.

Despite Beauchamp and Childress's insistence that their conception is neutral with respect to other theoretical perspectives, it fits most comfortably within theoretical accounts that envisage physician and patient as comparably situated independent contractors. First, social position is largely irrelevant to transactions between them. A physician-contractor can fully discharge her responsibilities by satisfying the requisite formal conditions for securing informed consent, so there is no requirement that she enter into an interpersonal relationship with her patient.[10] This independent contractor model fails to capture significant dimensions of relations between physician and patient, for sick people are vulnerable and dependent on the skill and sensitivity of their caregivers.[11] Therefore, respecting such patients' autonomy typically requires attention to details of their life experience and surroundings. Often patients do not fully recognize their own beliefs and values, so reaching an autonomous decision about their care may require extended exploration of their histories and motivational structures. Then, too, patients' self-understandings may be so confused with others' perceptions of them (particularly in hospitals) that no decision can be disentangled from their influence. Respecting autonomy would require recognizing patients' struggles to break free of oppressive authoritative influences and assisting them to sustain relationships essential to their self-identity and well-being. In attending members of marginalized groups, providers would need to transcend group stereotypes that jeopardize effective and equitable care without ignoring group identities integral to patients' self-understanding.

Second, in Beauchamp and Childress's account, respect for autonomy is constructed around micro-level considerations and isolated both from macro-level, societal issues (which principlist accounts categorize under justice) and middle-level concerns. Susan Wolf rightly faults principlist schemes for making no structural provision for ethical problems that arise in relation to middle-level groupings such as family, race, and gender.[12] She points out that these shortcomings are looked on largely as aberrations rather than problems endemic to the bioethical enterprise. To illustrate: in a recent issue of a major medical journal, the authors of "Ethnicity and Attitudes toward Patient Autonomy" surveyed members of several ethnic groups to study attitudes toward end-of-life decision making. They found that some groups were more likely to believe that the patient's family should be the primary decision makers regarding end-of-life care. Whereas the Beauchamp and Childress account of personal autonomy allows only for explicit individual delegation of authority, the survey calls attention to an implicit group value structure that subordinates individual decision making. Harmonious family functioning was more central to the values of the research subjects than the autonomy in decision making of individual members.[13] In light of these findings, procedures for securing informed consent that bypass value differences and rely on an identical set of formal standards are morally suspect. Adequate respect for autonomy requires attention to the specifics of physician-patient interactions, as well as to class, race, and other middle- and macro-level influences that structure these relationships.

My own understanding of autonomy incorporates features of the weak relational conception insofar as it recognizes that social relations provide the ground for the development of autonomy capacities and stresses the respect providers owe their patients. But I move beyond this to a stronger conception that encompasses Jennifer Nedelsky's central idea: that there is a social component built into the very meaning of autonomy.[14] That is, the subject-centered activities of reflecting, planning, choosing, and deciding that enter into self-determination are social activities in both a subjective and an objective sense. Subjectively, material for reflection is built on the foundation of a shared past and future expectations that involve others' participation. Objectively, the alternatives actually available for decision making depend on background norms, practices, social structures, and institutions that configure and limit options. As Martha Minow has noticed, it is true in varying degrees of all of us that how we function depends on circumstances within our social and physical environment.[15] In the balance of this section, I accordingly develop the components of what I call *strong relational autonomy*.

Autonomy in the strong relational sense is both reciprocal and collaborative. It is reciprocal in that it is not solely an individual enterprise but involves a dynamic balance among interdependent people tied to overlapping projects. Moreover, the self-determining self is continually remaking itself in response to relationships that are seldom static. The experience of trauma, so common among hospitalized patients, suggests that the self is affected, and perhaps partially constituted, by the changing circumstances to which it is exposed. For, as Susan Brison explains, it is the loss of connection experienced by trauma survivors that most imperils their autonomous selfhood.[16] I share her conviction that the self exists *fundamentally* in relation to others. Interconnections continue to shape and define us throughout our lifetime, so that patterns through which we construct (and reconstruct) our self-identity and infuse it with meanings are bound up with meanings given in the social world external to us.[17] The threat of serious illness or trauma both endangers these interconnections and thwarts autonomous pursuits. The body one has trusted to pursue one's plans and projects is shown to be vulnerable, fragile, and unprotected.

The other feature of the conception of strong relational autonomy that I advocate is the collaborative component. An appropriate respect for personal autonomy will require helping professionals to respond sensitively to the meanings illness has for those in their care; to deploy their power and influence to restore and strengthen autonomy competencies[18]; and to support patients' struggles to create new personal meanings out of the experience of disease, disorder, or disability. Any tenable conception of personal autonomy is subject-centered; but a *social* conception that is relational in this stronger sense will take into account the network of relationships that bears on individual efforts to be self-determining, responsible agents. In decision-making contexts prevalent in health-care settings, this conception encompasses providers of care, affected family members, and other individuals and groups to whom a subject's identity is bound. The context that configures care, the ramifications of decisions for the life projects of patients and their families, and structures of family power and authority that impinge on decision making are all integral to one's capacity for autonomous self-determination.

My account is also feminist in several senses beyond the features of feminism to which Beauchamp and Childress respond. First, it applies the resources of feminist scholarship to a set of issues that have previously disregarded gender hierarchies. Second, it envisages autonomy from *within* structures of power and authority rather than assuming that pursuit of personal goals can be isolated from social aims and involvements. Third, it is sensitive to structural inequities in the position of differently situated women and members of social groups whose opportunities to shape their lives in self-determining directions are often meager and inadequate. Thus it addresses the micro- and macro-level concerns they ignore. In these respects, my account is sensitive to Susan Sherwin's ambivalence about feminist proposals that prioritize personal autonomy.[19] I aim to steer a path between two risks: that individual self-determination will be overwhelmed by more encompassing social aims and that self-determination will be afforded so much importance that power imbalances are allowed to persist under the guise of autonomous self-determination.

Empirical Support for a Strong Relational Conception of Autonomy

Genetics and Biological Ties

The need for a strong relational conception of autonomy can be most readily shown by examining practical problems that arise within families that are bound together by biological connections. Genetic-related decision making, particularly, brings clearly into focus underlying tensions between prevailing accounts of personal autonomy dominant in bioethics (both individualistic and weakly relational ones) and the interpersonal dependencies so prevalent in families with inherited genetic disorders. Concerns easily overlooked in other medical contexts become more prominent here, for genetic information carries more personal, familial, and social risks and burdens than virtually any other kind of medical information. Practitioners who rely on a standard conception of autonomy may inadvertently exacerbate patients' tensions. Policymakers accustomed to weighing only individual and societal interests when considering the claims of third parties to genetic information may overlook the bearing this information has on the autonomy of patients' families and racial and ethnic groups to which they are linked.

I realize, however, that in focusing on situations in which social families are tied together by biological connection, I risk being misread by feminists who view biological families as reactionary and repressive vestiges of patriarchal social arrangements that should be supplanted by deliberately chosen voluntary relationships. Surely, traditional families organized around biological connections do often replicate and reproduce from other social domains hierarchical gender relations that reinforce the continuing subjugation of women, sanction violence and abuse, and inhibit the development of an autonomous sense of self.[20] But contrary to the presumptions of Beauchamp and Childress and some feminists who presume that social ties can be severed at will, biological grounding inevitably influences social connection, so that our most significant relations will often not actually be voluntary. Short of embarking on radical social reform that severs biological from social connections,[21] family politics could be reconfigured to rectify power imbalances so that the autonomy of all family members is fully respected. Advancing this aim, however, requires recharacterizing personal autonomy in a way that acknowledges the influence of nonvoluntary biological connections on personal identity and social relationships.

The host of issues surrounding newly developing genetic knowledge vividly illustrates the extent to which a conception of family as a biologically linked social unit is imbedded in social institutions, penetrates individual self-perceptions, and perpetuates (often exacerbating) social injustices. For example, new genetic knowledge imposes social and economic burdens on families that cannot be alleviated without recognizing, at a social level, the injustice of the burdens and taking appropriate steps to remedy them. The acknowledgement of biological ties undermines the conception of the individual implicit in both the individualistic and weakly relational models, namely, the conception in which the individual has voluntary control over the network of social relations in which she is imbedded.

In the following sections, I argue that relational considerations are already implicitly taken into account by medical practitioners who are working in genetic contexts, and I examine one example to develop the components of the strong relational model. I first consider intrafamily problems that arise (1) when a family member needs an organ or tissue donor, (2) when genetic knowledge intrudes on pregnancy and child rearing, and (3) when a genetic disorder is detected in the bloodline. In the final section I return to the gender-specific vulnerabilities of women.

Wresting a Relational Conception from Prevailing Medical Practice

Transplantation and Tissue Donation.   Contrary to much popular rhetoric and to the assumptions presupposed in *The Gift*, genetic quandaries did not suddenly descend on clinical practitioners like a bolt from the blue. Their appearance was antedated by problems arising out of tissue-matching techniques used when a family member needed an organ or tissue donor. New information emerged that frequently threatened social bonds among biological kin. In responding to such situations, practitioners improvised, evolving de facto norms. These reflected a double awareness of family dynamics: tensions between the autonomy-advancing projects of individual family members and their relational bonds and a nascent realization that individuals' autonomy is relational. I cite several instances of individual and family interests that butt up against one another, one that involves balancing family interests when children are too young to play a significant role in deliberations themselves and others that involve the deployment of sensitive family information.

The first instance concerns a minor child who risked dying from leukemia that could be treated only by a bone marrow transplant. Only her mentally handicapped sister was a good match. Since the parents had conflicting interests in the well-being of both children, a judicial opinion was sought. The court in this case concluded that the physical risk involved in surgery to retrieve the marrow from the handicapped sister was outweighed by the psychological benefits conferred on her. If the sister with leukemia died, not only would her sibling be denied her companionship, but the grief-stricken mother would find it difficult to provide the retarded sister with the maternal attention she had grown accustomed to.[22] Similar cases have come before the courts in several countries. The courts have commonly used variants of this balancing strategy, weighing actual physical burdens against hypothetical psychological benefits to the donor. Where the children have had a social, as well as biological, relationship, the court has almost always ruled in favor of donation. So the healthy child has been compelled to undergo a nontherapeutic surgical procedure for the sick sibling's benefit.

Implicit in such rulings is a relational ethic that obliges family members to subordinate their individual interests to others' well-being. But there are difficulties in a relational approach that overemphasizes the relations of care and connection between siblings. Thus such rulings satisfy neither individualistic nor relational requirements for autonomy, although for different reasons. Those who lean toward an individualistic discourse fault the courts for not adhering more singlemindedly to a decision-making standard based on the *donor's* best interests. Instead, the calculus of burdens and benefits seems skewed, sacrificing the retarded sister's interests to her "normal" sibling's. Were she a competent, autonomous decision maker herself, she could deliberate with other family members, reflect on the value of her relationship to them, and voluntarily form her own judgment. Those who favor a more relational discourse wonder why courts are so reluctant to recognize that the moral relevance of family connection is not reducible to the interests of discrete individuals. In actual families, children have responsibilities to one another long before they develop capacities to avow them voluntarily. Preparation for autonomous adulthood includes experience in caring for others one cares about and coming to recognize one's own needs by responding to theirs. Adults who lack such grounding are ill-fitted to build enduring voluntary relationships with others on a foundation of mutual reciprocity.[23]

However, the individualistic discourse prevalent in these cases affords protection to the child asked to make the sacrifice that may be lost in a relational account that is inattentive to power relations among family members. Children need protection lest they be treated, Cinderella-like, as mere conveniences to advance others' ends. So even if courts were to set aside the individualistic standard of best interests and adopt a relational model, justice would not be served unless they set constraints on moral sacrifices family members can be expected to make for one another.

An implicit relational approach is even more obvious in two further kinds of situations: in cases in which a family member's blood is tested to determine compatibility for organ or tissue transplantation and in circumstances in which a family is being evaluated to find the most likely transplant donor. In such instances, practitioners may feel obligated to act deceptively, selectively withholding information from a patient who needs bone marrow, a kidney, or a slice of liver. For example, they might withhold from their patient knowledge that a tested family member is a good match but refuses the surgery required to retrieve the tissue. Knowledge of the refusal, these practitioners claim, would have a disruptive effect on family relations at a time when they are already under stress. This practice is sometimes criticized as a kind of quasi-paternalism that elevates the interests of family members who refuse to contribute over the interests of the patient, which should, in the critics' judgment, be paramount.

Practitioners may also act on relational considerations when linkage studies are done to assess risk for a genetic condition. Blood studies may reveal that the social father is not the biological father, as family members believed. When a relationship between the parents is ongoing, the practitioner faces a burdensome quandary. Who should be informed? Is there any general rule that might provide guidance? Should unwelcome information be imposed on people? When this information comes to light in the process of screening for a suitable organ or tissue donor, the medical unit might establish a de facto policy to disclose only information pertinent to the search for a compatible donor. If a family member has already told the transplant team that he will contribute a blood sample to provide a more complete family profile but is unwilling to donate, the sample would be used only to establish linkage and then would be set aside in the continuing search for a suitable donor. But when family linkage studies are undertaken to determine carrier status for a genetic condition, this dodge will not work. So many idiosyncratic aspects of the family situation may have a bearing on the consequences of disclosure that it is difficult to envision a sustainable general rule—apart from adopting truth telling as an absolute requirement. However, all but the most committed deontologist would contend that when intervening in family relations, practitioners should aim to minimize foreseeable adverse consequences.[24]

Pregnancy and Child Rearing.   The need to frame autonomy relationally, if it is to be respected at all, becomes starkly evident when a women who is genetically at risk becomes pregnant. A spouse may never have considered the full impact of marriage to the carrier of a dominant genetic condition until the couple considers children. Dominant carriers are bound to know about affected people within their own families, but recessive carriers may have no advance knowledge of the condition. Often a woman is already pregnant before genetic testing for carrier status is recommended to her. But by then, her options are already diminished. Pregnancy imposes pressures on decision making that would not exist under less constraining conditions. If the couple is willing to consider termination, they may have to decide very quickly. Seldom do they know much about the particular genetic condition, prognosis for the child, social support services, or how their own lives will be affected by a disabled child. Test results compound these uncertainties since their degree of accuracy varies. So suddenly a happy, untroubled pregnancy is transformed into a stressful experience, upsetting everyone's prior expectations.

So determined are many parents to learn the genetic susceptibilities of their children that when a genetic disorder is not identified prenatally or evident at birth, they often request that their child be tested. Here providers have squarely confronted their obligation to consider the impact of their intervention on family relations. Several medical associations have established policies that limit parents' power to demand that their child be tested. To safeguard the children's future autonomy and protect confidentiality, it is recommended that practitioners refuse to test children for genetic disorders unless there is a therapy available to treat them or a medical benefit to be derived from monitoring their condition. Some parents object, charging "paternalistic intervention" that infringes on their own autonomy. Although many parents are reluctant to discuss their own risk with their children, they are often so eager to learn their child's risk that they pressure practitioners to make exceptions to the policy against testing children.[25] But when testing affords no therapeutic benefit to the child, it is difficult to build a case that parents' wishes should prevail.

I turn now to examine more fully quandaries that arise when a genetic anomaly is detected in the bloodline. I show why no simple formula can solve the problems the new genetics thrust before us or shortcut the task of rethinking and renegotiating our relation to this new knowledge. Only a strong relational understanding of autonomy will do here.

Disorders Detected in the Bloodline.   A third example of a relational approach implicit in genetic practice is offered by cases in which a genetic disorder is detected in the bloodline. Trained and experienced counselors will tell people who consider testing for a severe dominant disorder that regardless of the results, their futures will be changed. The news will not be all good or all bad for anyone.[26] Learning that one belongs to an affected family is bound to have a profound impact on all family members, both individually and collectively. The circumstances of testing magnify this effect. First, for many genetic conditions the judgment that one is at high risk involves pooling information among those who share the same bloodline. So the medical risks will be compounded by psychological, familial, and social complexities. An individual who resists testing may not be able to avoid knowing if she is at risk when other family members discuss their test results. Second, when a direct gene test is available to the individual who is seeking diagnosis, the results may still have striking implications for the future of others, so much so that even those who test negative for the disorder may need to reconstruct their autobiographies and reconfigure their family relationships. Some, for instance, may feel a heightened sense of family responsibility, believing (falsely) that their negative result will increase the likelihood that other family members will test positive. Others may have trouble reconciling ambivalent feelings for their family members with this new information. Thus any decision an individual makes about testing will penetrate both the biological and the social family.

Individuals within the same family may use very different strategies to cope with their sense of powerlessness in the face of a wholly random event. Some deny the condition; others undertake a compulsive search for knowledge.[27] Following definitive testing, the more fortunate members may experience "survivor guilt." The unfortunate ones may blame parents and hold them accountable for their disability. If the disorder is X-linked, a mother may bear the brunt of resentment since it has almost certainly been transmitted through her. Parents who undertake prenatal diagnosis and already have a similarly affected child sometimes feel deeply ambivalent about aborting an affected fetus, fearing that their living child may later interpret the abortion as a personal rejection. Brothers, sisters, and parents will all be drawn into a tangled web, laden with tension and conflict. The strain will extend to others in intimate committed relationships with those at risk, thus threatening relationships beyond the biological family as well.[28]

Test results may disrupt family expectations, impelling members to reshape their self-identities and renegotiate family positioning. Then "family scripts," preexisting systems of beliefs about family relations, are shattered. The self-conception one has comfortably developed within a given constellation of relationships is destabilized. All family members are compelled to rethink their personal histories and recast their stories about how they want to live their lives.[29] Although family scripts influence everyone's self-development, in families with inherited genetic disease they may be far more difficult to renegotiate. Such families sometimes cope with uncertainties about which member might inherit a familial condition by preselecting one they believe is affected. Then they interpret the behavior of that individual in ways that fulfill their prophesy. The individual who subsequently tests negative for the condition may be even more severely ostracized by the family than if the result had been positive.[30]

The vagaries of insurance and employment practices will intensify psychological stresses. Unless medical confidentiality can be assured, even a family member who has not been tested herself might lose her job or insurance if the test results of others in the family leak out. In one case, a woman in her fifties requested a direct gene test for Huntington disease (HD). Her son and daughter-in-law protested, claiming they should have a voice in the woman's decision, too. According to standard accounts of autonomy, their interference would surely be unwelcome. But the son had good reason to fear the effects of the test. His employer had been seeking just this kind of information. If his mother tested positive, his own job would be threatened.[31]

Among genetic conditions, HD intrudes particularly forcefully into the lives of individuals and families and imposes complex demands on those who counsel affected families. When families are reluctant to inform other kin who may be at risk, practitioners may be tempted to intervene by passing on this information. A curious spin on this theme is illustrated by the case of a twenty-nine-year-old woman who came to the genetics clinic for counseling because her mother had told her that she (the mother) had tested positive for HD. The mother, the counselor learned, had a long psychiatric history, involving drug and alcohol abuse. The daughter was an only child whose father left home early in her life. The mother and stepfather both abused her. The counselor gained access to the mother's records and found that she had actually tested negative for HD. But the mother, when asked, refused to let her tell the daughter that she did not have the disease.

Within a principlist bioethics framework, a practitioner's moral responsibilities would be articulated in terms of two guiding principles: respect for the daughter's right to make autonomous decisions and for the mother's right to confidentiality. Geneticists and trained counselors who regard confidentiality as sacrosanct would disregard the daughter's interests rather than breach confidential information. The tested individual, they often argue, has a stronger claim to the information than other family members, so she ought not to be compelled to disclose the information.[32] In this view the counselor who overrides the mother's refusal is guilty of "clinical imperialism."[33] Philosophers and legal theorists are more likely to resolve the dilemma by stressing the importance of accurate information for the daughter's future plans. They would argue that the geneticist is obligated to share her knowledge of the deception so that the daughter can free herself from the influence of her overcontrolling mother. For those who follow this line of reasoning, the daughter's claim to information so vital to autonomous pursuit of her own goals would trump the mother's claim to confidentiality.

But as long as the daughter is deprived of this information, she has no compelling reason either to strengthen or sever her relational ties. Unlike the clear-cut personal histories Marilyn Friedman appeals to in her account of relational autonomy,[34] the relevance of a genetically burdened relationship to personal autonomy remains ambiguous in the absence of pertinent information. This case of misinformation illustrates that reflection alone may not be an adequate guide for an agent who is seeking to expand autonomy that relates to her personal relationships. Even in the absence of confounding misinformation, an adequate account of relational autonomy would still need to provide criteria for distinguishing between autonomy-fostering and autonomy-inhibiting aspects of social relationships. In this regard, any account that preserves even minimally Kantian features will recognize that what we *want* for ourselves may not enhance our autonomy if it can be attained only by dodging responsibilities toward others who depend on us. Respect for their interests and their autonomy may require us to relationalize our own autonomy in the course of advancing our plans and goals.[35] Indeed, as a general rule, following one's own sense of the good life usually binds one to schemes of social cooperation over which one may have little direct influence or control. Some of these may be only instrumentally relevant to one's own pursuits, but others will inevitably be substantively bound to one's projects, so that what one desires for oneself is inextricably intertwined with others' desires. Thus, outright disregard of other morally significant values is possible only in certain very limited contexts.

In all these instances, practitioners seem to be operating from not an individualistic conception of autonomy but an implicitly relational model that appraises family interests collectively. In so doing, they expose two fissures in the dominant structure. First, they point to specific inadequacies in a framework that operates from a noncontextual set of primary principles that may have significantly different implications as contexts vary. Second, they address the possibility (not always the case) that disclosure will exacerbate tensions rather than relieve them. Here, too, like the cases of incompetent donors, further protections are needed to ensure equitable treatment for all family members affected by a medical intervention. Respect for autonomy would seem to require respect for both communal matrices and individual decision-making capacities.

Thus there is good reason not to abandon a rule-based approach altogether because the individual who is most vulnerable and has the most riding on the decision deserves the protection that an adequately formulated principle of autonomy can afford. Competing claims of other family members ought not to be allowed to trump hers. Nor should her interests be reduced to the kind of balancing act we saw at work in the judge's deliberations about the incompetent transplant donor. The protection of young children's future interests calls for an approach that gives less weight to the immediate concerns of parents and more to the children's futures, understood broadly to encompass not only physical well-being but also capacities for autonomous self-determination.

An Example of Reciprocal and Collaborative Components of Relational Autonomy

In this section, I return to the example of the daughter who is seeking genetic information to articulate in detail my conception of strong relational autonomy and to show how collaborative and reciprocal components are often intertwined. Since autonomy is not solely an individual enterprise and the self-determining self is continually remaking itself in response to relationships that are seldom static, personal autonomy is not incompatible with adapting one's personal projects to the needs or preferences of others as long as no one's autonomy is trampled on. Respect for everyone's autonomy, however, requires long-term reciprocity and the equitable balancing of power relations. These conditions limit an individual's freedom to opt out of a relationship, but they might possibly *require* opting out if they cannot be met even minimally. Mindful here of the tension Friedman alludes to, I focus on several features of the relationship between the daughter who is seeking information pertinent to her future plans and the mother who is withholding that information. I also consider the counselor's responsibilities insofar as they bear on her professional relationship to mother and daughter.

Insofar as the counselor is obliged to respect the autonomy of both parties, she must decide how to manage the information the mother has withheld that is pertinent to the daughter's decision making. If the counselor is not, herself, to contribute to severing their ties, she will explore possible resolutions to the dilemma. To bring this about, though, she needs a decision strategy that is more open to the complexity of genetic knowledge than the language of competing claims, one that recognizes the interlocking relevance of genetic knowledge for the entire biological family. In this one significant respect, at least, mother and daughter are not free to sever their relationship.

It is important to note that a rigid respect for personal privacy would inevitably be confounded in such situations. The awareness that genetic information is shared among kin is implicit in both the mother's deception and the daughter's quest for further information about her own risk. Both know that their fates are interlinked. If the mother is affected, the daughter has a 50% risk of acquiring the disease too. If the mother does not have the gene, the daughter's risk is reduced to nil (assuming the father is unaffected). Thus a determination of moral responsibility that slights the daughter's request for knowledge about her own susceptibility exaggerates the mother's control over the information. It thereby impedes the daughter's capacity to shape her own future autonomously and disregards the harms a family member in a position of power can exert over vulnerable others.

Nonrelational accounts of autonomy may also distort the actual dynamics of family relationships in a further respect, for an analysis focused on competing claims presupposes that people are normally at odds with one another. On some occasions, they surely are, but a discourse framed around individual rights and interests is bound to neglect other significant features of family bonds. Shifting attention to the relational situation that frames the conflict opens possible routes to further strategies for resolving tensions, reducing injustices, and reconfiguring self-understandings. Mother and daughter could possibly be reconciled on a new level informed by the backward- and forward-looking meanings that this new knowledge has for their conception of self and other. And if reconciliation is not possible on terms acceptable to both, the counselor's empathetic support can nonetheless contribute to integration of this new knowledge into their individual self-understandings.

Pertinent to these observations is Susan Brison's evocative account of her own experience as a trauma survivor, for it reveals the deeply social nature of the self and the limits of an individual's capacity to control her own self-definition.[36] To reconstitute a unified self out of the disintegration that followed violent assault, she needed empathetic and responsive listeners. Disclosure of vulnerability to genetic disease can precipitate a similar crisis. In the face of a threat that one can neither fight nor flee, which damages one's trust in the integrity of mind and body, connections between self and others are needed to combat defenselessness in the face of life-threatening forces and anxiety about a foreshortened future.[37]

Collaboration among family members is necessary to preserve autonomy in families plagued by disabling genetic disorders. Connections to family and other intimates, Brison points out, provide not only nurturing support but also a repository for collective memories and rituals that sustain the sense of a unitary self able to persist through crises. Family narratives about those who coped courageously with the threat of disease and withstood its withering assaults not only serve many of the functions of support groups but also intensify other family members' sense of their reciprocal interdependence. Professional counselors encourage affected families to seek out groups that can offer survival strategies, but recognition of the family's centrality in sustaining the sense of bodily integrity of the affected member is less common.

For example, John Hardwig's concerns about how prevalent norms of medical decision making tend to slight family interests convey a sense of family as a group of disparate individuals with a common pool of material resources and perhaps reciprocal obligations to provide care in times of need. When a family will be affected by a decision, fairness requires, he insists, that the family have a role in reaching it.

In some situations, he believes, the interests of other family members might even outweigh the patient's own.[38] His is an upsetting and radical claim, say Hilde and James Nelson, both because it runs counter to the priority given to individual autonomy and because it ignores the fact that the patient has a greater stake in the decision than anyone else. Certainly, family should have input to deliberation, but family motives and concerns, they stress, are better aired in the open, where the intricate network of their relationships can be protected from breakdown. Practitioners who cast people in a conflictual relationship increase the likelihood that they will, in fact, see one another as adversaries.[39]

The disagreement between the Nelsons and Hardwig runs deeper than the decision-making scenario on which it is focused. Hardwig's formulation of the issue takes family conflict as static, a function of each individual's separate material interests, which are unaffected by the physician's intervention. Insofar as the Nelsons' approach holds providers responsible for fostering family communication and seeking reorientation of the perspectives of interested parties, it is founded on an understanding of the family as a dynamic, interlocking structure that is not reducible to its separate parts. Of the two, only the Nelsons' perspective is compatible with both the collaborative and reciprocal senses of relational autonomy—collaborative insofar as family members recognize their dependence on one another for the achievement of personal plans and projects, and reciprocal in that recollections of their shared history, overlapping memories, and rituals are directed to maintaining and restoring the psychic integrity of their individual members.

Genetics and Gender

Any contemporary account of personal autonomy ought to be responsive to feminist ambivalence about autonomy as a personal ideal that many still associate with a distinctively masculine ideal of self-development. Relational accounts typically aim for a transvaluation that frees the conception from such associations. But unless that account is responsive to structural inequalities in the position of differently situated women, it risks reinstituting some of the most reprehensible features of the masculine ideal, overvaluing individual self-determination so grossly that power imbalances among the more and less advantageously situated are disregarded. Thus an adequate relational account needs to connect personal self-development with more inclusive social aims, emphasizing women's particular vulnerabilities to unjust treatment, namely, their reproductive capacities and social positioning within families. In health-care settings, providers and counselors need to be attentive to such vulnerabilities as they intervene in the deliberations of a family member under treatment and her kin, who share genetic characteristics and participate in a common social network. Providers, I argue, need to consider not only particular circumstances but also rule-based principles if they are to guard against unjust treatment of family members who, by virtue of gender or social position, bear a disproportionate share of family responsibility. Family interests are doubly implicated when there is genetic disability, both because of the care-giving and support functions likely to fall predominantly on women and because of the vulnerability of other family members who are potential victims of the same biological incapacity.[40] First, I note the major respects in which women's lives are likely to be more disturbed by new genetic knowledge than men's. Second, I identify the responsibilities this vulnerability imposes on providers who disseminate this knowledge and advise women and their families of their options. Once again, I emphasize how genetic knowledge can thwart or advance autonomy, depending on how it is imbedded in a clinical relationship.

Genetic information enters into family relations and affects family life along gender-specific paths. It is primarily women who are the central focus of the family-based problems that genetic diseases create.[41] By virtue of both reproductive capacity and social positioning, the role of family caregivers has traditionally fallen to women. Clinical arrangements tend to reinforce this delegation of family responsibilities. How burdensome such duties will be for any particular woman, of course, will depend on her material circumstances and support networks.[42] Women bear more of the responsibility for monitoring health issues in families than men. They are the "kin-keepers" who do the family's genetic housekeeping. They tend to know more about the obstetrical history of the man's family than he—how many pregnancies his mother had, how many ended in miscarriage, and so on. Since only about one in four women is accompanied to a counseling session by a spouse or partner, prudent women may have no choice but to arm themselves with all the information they can muster.

By virtue of reproductive capacity, too, genetic knowledge is likely to influence women's lives far more pervasively than men's. First, only women undergo prenatal testing, which is increasingly becoming a part of the customary prenatal care package. Not only women over thirty-five, but also younger women are increasingly being urged to submit to preliminary genetic screening procedures and follow-up diagnosis, even when there is no prior knowledge of genetic disorders in their family medical histories. Prenatal diagnosis is already available for hundreds of conditions.[43] As DNA technology advances, laboratory procedures are automated, and a skin prick replaces more intrusive procedures, far more screening tests are likely to be included in routine prenatal care, further complicating prenatal decision making.

Second, women endure more of the psychological stress generated by testing than male family members. Since therapies to treat genetic impairments following prenatal diagnosis are virtually nonexistent, a woman whose fetus tests positive for a genetic abnormality must assume primary responsibility for a difficult decision about terminating a wanted pregnancy, often on the basis of incomplete information. For their partners, prenatal diagnosis is often a less immediate worry, more easily postponed or denied.[44] Genetic "therapies" now under development might eventually provide an alternative to abortion following diagnosis of fetal anomaly, but these interventions will also be accomplished through the bodies of women. They carry their own risks, which the pregnant woman will need to weigh in the light of her own values and priorities.

Preimplantation diagnostic techniques (PID) further complicate decision-making options. This procedure (utilized in *The Gift*) minimizes recourse to abortion as a way to avoid the birth of a genetically impaired child. Here too, however, the mother's body must be invaded to facilitate laboratory inspection and selection of embryos.[45] No longer a futuristic technique, PID is already being marketed by diagnostic laboratories for a fast-growing array of single gene disorders.[46] Only adequately informed women can evaluate whether the risk, disruption, and anxiety entailed by PID are worth it to them.

Many genetic anomalies are not discovered until after birth. Since women are the primary caregivers for infants (as well as for disabled people of all ages), they are often the first to notice that their infant is not developing properly, and so they seek out medical advice, battling their way through a health-care system that too often depreciates a mother's observations. Most general practitioners have little or no training in medical genetics. So a concerned mother may need exceptional tenacity and determination to surmount disparaging misinformation ("your baby is just lazy or placid" or "you're a neurotic mother") and reach a consultant qualified to offer an informed diagnosis and the information and support needed to deal effectively with her child's problems.[47]

Compounding the disproportionate burdens imposed on women by virtue of their reproductive capacities are many gender-specific structural arrangements only remotely related to biological differences. Poor women are particularly subject to choice-minimizing health-care policies and practices. Women of color and other underserved populations are doubly disadvantaged and less likely to find their way to trained genetic counselors.[48] For those who do, cultural differences may indirectly hinder the communication and education process.

Class-based differences add a further layer of complexity to the inevitable disparity between lay knowledge about inheritance and scientific accounts.[49] Lay accounts are often tied to cultural and psychological factors that resist scientific explanation. Words like "uncertainty" and "risk" tend to have different meanings for geneticists and lay people. For the professional, risk may mean the probability of a negative outcome; for the patient, it is more likely to connote the severity of the outcome.[50] If such differences are too profound, barriers to a decision responsive to the client's life circumstances and personal goals may be insurmountable.

A woman's ability to make an autonomous decision is determined not only by the amount of information offered but also by the manner in which it is communicated to her. Some providers are more directive in their approaches than others.[51] Obstetricians often offer advice about pregnancy termination rather than options for the patient's determination.[52] Geneticists and genetic counselors are schooled in an ethos of nondirectiveness that pulls in the opposite direction. The counselor is expected to provide the facts a counselee needs to make an autonomous, informed, and rational decision. These facts are to be balanced and given in a nondirective, value-free neutral manner that respects the recipient's "beliefs, cultural tradition, inclination, circumstances, and feelings."[53] Devised to protect patients from eugenicist bias or other paternalistic impositions of the counselor's sense of the other's good, the ideology of nondirectiveness fails to recognize, however, that the context that frames counseling already presupposes the importance of detecting genetic anomalies and interceding.[54] An overly naive commitment to nondirectiveness overlooks at least four problematic moral dimensions of the relationship.

First, a nonselective barrage of information may overwhelm and paralyze a patient. Second, because nondirectiveness promises a degree of neutrality that no provider can possibly fulfill, patients may be caught off guard as they are guided toward a course of action that defeats the primary intention of counseling: to enhance autonomous decision making. Third, judgments about which conditions merit discussion with clients are often value-laden.[55] Unless counselors assume responsibility for the selectivity they exercise, they will inadvertently press their own values, thereby jeopardizing the patient's effective reflection and deliberation. Fourth, insofar as counseling is committed to a traditional scientific model that bifurcates facts and values, emotional dimensions of the client-counselor relationship will be suppressed, isolating the client from the kinds of empathetic support needed to restore a fractured identity or preserve her sense of wholeness in the face of trauma and family conflict. Thus, the illusion that counseling is value-free conceals important moral dimensions of the interaction that if recognized and addressed directly, would clarify everyone's respective goals and empower the client to reorder her own moral priorities and assign them sufficient weight to counterbalance the competing interests of other family members.

In the interest of promoting women's autonomy capacities, then, the nondirective paradigm should give way to a nonhierarchically structured model of genetic counseling that fosters a collaborative relationship and enhances a client's capacities to exercise agency within her own relational context.[56] The client might then make her own determination about the centrality of family relations to her future goals. Ideally, the counselor would not see her role terminating with the decision to abort or continue a pregnancy but would strive to create a basis for a sustained relationship with the client and her family that extends beyond the immediate crisis. Such revisioning would advance genetic counseling beyond the prevailing nondirective model toward a more holistic understanding of family dynamics imbedded in a relational understanding of autonomy that incorporates both its collaborative and reciprocal components.

Conclusion

The individualistic model of autonomy so dominant in medical practice hampers effective medical decision making, gives insufficient attention to the impact of decisions on family members, undermines the agency of those who are excluded from the decision-making process, and often imposes unjust burdens on those affected by others' decisions. Uncritical advocacy of this model by bioethicists fosters what Susan Wolf calls a "bioethics for the privileged," serving the interests of those who have ready access to health-care and an understanding physician who respects them.[57] Medical practitioners who recognize limitations of the dominant model sometimes modify their procedures to draw into discussion other family members who are centrally affected by a decision. But these efforts tend to be fragmentary and ad hoc, often inadvertently polarizing family conflict and jeopardizing the well-being and autonomy of those most centrally affected. They are rarely supported by institutional structures, which are increasingly being centralized. Without major reconfiguration of structural patterns, few will benefit from rearrangement of individual provider-patient relationships. In the context of clinical medicine and practice, then, personal autonomy needs to be understood as involving self-determining individuals who are positioned relationally, both to their families and intimates and to the practitioners who care for them. Two major reorientations are critical in implementing such a model.

First, all parties at risk must be adequately and appropriately identified as individuals within the institutional contexts that circumscribe their options. Such a shift in perspective should bring into focus the disparate distribution of benefits and burdens among family members. Decision-making strategies that attempt only to balance their individual interests risk silencing the voices of some who are immediately affected by the action at issue. Such persons need the principled protection of a carefully nuanced recognition of relational autonomy and an unswerving commitment to honor it.

Second, this acknowledgement needs to be implemented in ways that recognize and respond to injustices in personal relationships, whether they are central or tangential to institutional structures. Strategies that provide occasion for all family members to articulate their own perspectives and air their disagreements before any decision is imposed can help maximize their autonomy, both separately and collectively. But to avoid reinscribing injustice in a new guise, a relational model must also take full account of relevant ways in which individuals and families are differently situated in relation to one another and to health-care resources. Its effectiveness would depend on the sensitivity of providers to family dynamics, recognition of situations in which the voices of the less powerful members are silenced, and intervention to facilitate their active participation in decision-making processes.

Implementation of such a relational model would impose increased demands on health-care systems, which, belatedly casting off their paternalistic legacy, still recognize individual autonomy only minimally. To aim for less, though, would be to acquiesce in social arrangements that perpetuate disparate respect for the privileged and the vulnerable.

Notes

1. I wish to express my gratitude to all those who contributed to my education in clinical genetics: Indiana University Study in a Second Discipline Program, which enabled me to devote an entire semester to the study of clinical genetics, and particularly to Dr. David Weaver's patient mentoring. Thanks are due, too, to Dr. Ellen Solomon and her colleagues in the Division of Medical and Molecular Genetics at Guy's Hospital, University of London, who so generously gave their time to me so that I could compare the delivery of genetic services in the United States and in Britain. My gratitude also to Catriona Mackenzie and Natalie Stoljar for their careful and insightful comments on successive drafts of this article; to Helen Bequaert Holmes, whose deep understanding of genetic issues enriched my own; and to Edmund F. Byrne, whose comments on previous drafts helped me to say what I meant to say. Remaining inadequacies are, of course, my own doing.

2. The project was sponsored by the Wellcome Centre for Medical Science, an initiative of Britain's largest medical research charity, the Wellcome Trust. The play was written by Nicola Baldwin. Further information is available from the Wellcome Centre, 210 Euston Road, London NW1 2BE.

3. National Commission for the Protection of Human Subjects of Biomedical and Behavioral Research, *The Belmont Report: Ethical Principles and Guidelines for the Protection of*

Human Subjects in Research, DHEW Publication no. (OS) 78-0012 (Washington, D.C.: U.S. Government Printing Office, 1978).

4. T. Beauchamp and J. Childress, *Principles of Biomedical Ethics* (New York: Oxford University Press, 1979). Subsequent references refer to the fourth edition, published in 1994.

5. U.S. Congress, Patient Self-Determination Act. Omnibus Budget Reconciliation Act (1990), Pub L no.101-508: 4206, 4751.

6. For a classic critique of principlism, see K. D. Clouser and B. Gert, "A Critique of Principlism," *Journal of Medicine and Philosophy* 15 (1990): 219–237. For more extended discussion, see the series of articles in the *Kennedy Institute of Ethics Journal* 5, no. 3 (1995).

7. James F. Childress, "The Place of Autonomy in Bioethics," *Hastings Center Report* 20 (1990): 13.

8. Beauchamp and Childress themselves cite Susan Sherwin's *No Longer Patient: Feminist Ethics and Health Care* (Philadelphia: Temple University Press, 1992), p. 138. For Sherwin's more recent reflections on principlist conceptions of autonomy, see "Feminism and Bioethics," in *Feminism and Bioethics: Beyond Reproduction*, ed. Susan M. Wolf (New York: Oxford University Press, 1996), pp. 47–66. Also relevant is Wolf's introduction, especially pp. 15–16.

9. Beauchamp and Childress, *Principles of Biomedical Ethics*, pp. 124–125.

10. For a more comprehensive criticism of the inadequacies of contractual accounts of autonomy in health-care contexts, see Lucy M. Candib, *Medicine and the Family* (New York: Basic Books, 1995). Candib draws on both Sherwin's earlier work, *No Longer Patient,* and Virginia Held's critique in "Non-Contractual Society," in *Science, Morality and Feminist Theory*, ed. Marsha Hanen and Kai Nielsen (Calgary: University of Calgary Press, 1987).

11. Laura Purdy (unpublished manuscript) graphically illustrates this phenomenon in her autobiographical account of her own illness: "Even normally articulate and intelligent patients may have been turned to jelly by pain and anxiety and thus be unable to take the lead."

12. Wolf, Introduction, *Feminism and Bioethics.*

13. Leslie J. Blackhall et al., "Ethnicity and Attitudes toward Patient Autonomy," *Journal of the American Medical Association* 274 (1995): 820–825.

14. Jennifer Nedelsky, "Reconceiving Autonomy: Sources, Thoughts and Possibilities," *Yale Journal of Law and Feminism* 1 (1989): 7–36.

15. Martha Minow and Mary L. Shanley, "Relational Rights and Responsibilities: Revisioning the Family in Liberal Political Theory and Law," *Hypatia* 11 (1996): 4–29.

16. Susan J. Brison's remarkably insightful article, "Outliving Oneself: Trauma, Memory, and Personal Identity," is in *Feminists Rethink the Self*, ed. Diana T. Meyers (Boulder, CO: Westview, 1997), pp. 12–39. The passage I refer to here appears on page 28.

17. Ibid., p. 14.

18. I borrow this usage from Diana T. Meyers, *Self, Society, and Personal Choice* (New York: Columbia University Press, 1989).

19. In Sherwin's "Feminist Ethics and Ambivalence about Autonomy" (unpublished 1994 manuscript) and her "A Relational Approach to Autonomy in Health Care," in *The Politics of Women's Health: Exploring Agency and Autonomy*, ed. S. Sherwin (Philadelphia: Temple University Press, 1998), pp. 19–47.

20. For elaboration on this point, see Adrienne Asch and Gail Geller, "Feminism, Bioethics, and Genetics," in Wolf, *Feminism and Bioethics*, pp. 318–350. Note especially pp. 341–342.

21. As some 1970s feminists advocated, such as Shulamith Firestone in *The Dialectic of Sex* (London: Jonathan Cape, 1971).

22. This particular clase was heard in Britain [(Re Y (Mental Incapacity: Bone Marrow Transplant) 1996 2FLR 787], but the U.S. courts have employed similarly contorted reason-

ing in cases that involve incompetents. The most celebrated is *Strunk v. Strunk* (445 S.W. 2d 145, Ky. 1969). James Dwyer and Elizabeth Vig discuss several others in "Rethinking Transplantation between Siblings," *Hastings Center Report* 25 (1995): 7–12. They build a case for a less individualistic decision-making standard and draw analogies between organ donation between siblings and more mundane situations in which children are commonly expected to take responsibility for one another.

23. I have in mind here not only Dwyer and Vig's discussion but also the work of a host of feminists who have been influenced by an ethic of care. An excellent introduction to this literature is *Justice and Care: Essential Readings in Feminist Ethics*, ed. Virginia Held (Boulder, Colo.: Westview Press, 1995). Communitarians also tend to underscore the importance of rearing children to be responsive to others' needs. However, feminists are likely to fault their tendency to reinscribe traditional expectations that women sacrifice their own needs to (more powerful) others. I contrast aspects of these perspectives that pertain to accounts of personal autonomy in "Reworking Autonomy: Toward a Feminist Perspective," *Cambridge Quarterly of Healthcare Ethics* 4 (1995): 44–55.

24. When testing indicates that the father who worried about his carrier status is not a carrier after all, he might be so relieved to learn the truth that the accompanying information about the child's biological paternity would seem insignificant by comparison. Even when the practitioner has reason to believe that the social father would be distressed, the importance of disclosure may clearly override any adverse consequences. In situations in which the study provides little new information about the social father except that the child is not biologically his, the more common practice is to disclose the results to the mother and let her decide whether to inform her husband. Many practitioners believe that at least she should be informed since this information might have considerable impact on future childbearing decisions. When the mother is the primary patient, this strategy maximizes her capacity to make future decisions autonomously. But if the couple were later to split up and the father continued to harbor guilt about an affected child, the same information might have an important bearing on his future decisions, too.

25. Dorothy C. Wertz reports in "Parents' Responses to Predictive Genetic Testing in Their Children," *Journal of Medical Genetics* 33 (1996): 313–318, that 23% of HD clinics tested children under the age of twelve. See also Angus Clarke and Frances Flinter, "The Genetic Testing of Children: A Clinical Perspective," in *The Troubled Helix: Social and Psychological Implications of the New Human Genetics*, ed. T. M. Marteau and M. Richards (Cambridge: Cambridge University Press, 1996), pp. 164–176. Also relevant is David A. Ball, A. Tyler, and P. Harper, "Predictive Testing of Adults and Children," in *Genetic Counselling: Practice and Principles*, ed. Angus Clarke (London: Routledge, 1994), pp. 63–94.

26. This point is made in the Stanford Working Group, "Report on Genetic Testing for Breast Cancer Susceptibility" (Palo Alto, Cal.: Stanford University Center for Biomedical Ethics, 1996), p. 14.

27. Nancy Wexler develops this point in "Clairvoyance and Caution: Repercussions from the Human Genome Project," in *The Code of Codes: Scientific and Social Issues in the Human Genome Project*, ed. Daniel J. Kevles and Leroy Hood (Cambridge, Mass.: Harvard University Press, 1992), pp. 211–243. Among themselves, genetic counselors refer to these people as monitors and blunters. Monitors can't live with uncertainty and want to know everything. Blunters don't welcome any information and cannot be engaged in any substantive discussion at all.

28. For a fuller account of such situations see the fascinating chronicles of personal experience with genetic disease included in Marteau and Richards, *Troubled Helix*.

29. In *Self, Society, and Personal Choice*, Meyers calls this kind of project "programmatic autonomy," and she distinguishes it from "episodic autonomy," which focuses on particular sit-

uations. "Personal autonomy" in her account is a function of these two. My own account of autonomy resembles hers at some junctures but puts less emphasis on the inner psychological states of the individual subject and more on outer social relations that figure in inner representations. Shifting the locus of consideration in this way brings out interconnections between individual strivings to shape an autonomous identity, social structure, and personal history. This shift in emphasis brings patterns of power and authority into clearer focus. For further discussion of their distinction, see Kathryn Addelson, *Impure Thoughts* (Philadelphia: Temple University Press, 1991), especially chap. 11. Later I refer to such rethinking of individual self-conceptions insofar as they depend on shared family history as "reciprocal relational autonomy."

30. This point is stressed by Martin Richards in "Families, Kinship and Genetics," in Marteau and Richards, *Troubled Helix*, pp. 249–273.

31. Personal communication. Unless otherwise indicated, all cases are direct reports of actual cases generously told to me by staffs of genetics clinics.

32. See Angus Clarke's introduction to *Genetic Counselling*, p. 14.

33. According to Martin Richards in "Families, Kinship and Genetics," p. 266.

34. Marilyn Friedman, "Autonomy and Social Relationships: Rethinking the Feminist Critique," in Meyers, *Feminists Rethink the Self.* Note her remarks on pp. 55–56.

35. In "Abortion and Embodiment," *Australasian Journal of Philosophy* 70 (1992): 136–155, Catriona Mackenzie provides a carefully nuanced analysis of the responsibilities of the pregnant woman toward her fetus, which aims to show how abortion is most fundamentally about women's self-determination. The fetus's moral status, she argues, depends not only on its intrinsic properties but also on relational properties it has with others, particularly the woman carrying it. These relational properties are continually in a process of change as the fetus's intrinsic properties develop and the pregnant woman's bodily subjectivity alters. Her analysis of relationships among self-determination, embodiment, and responsibility has far-reaching implications for other contexts, too, some of which I allude to (too briefly) here. Marilyn Friedman offers a somewhat different reading of interconnections between autonomy and responsibility in her appraisal of Gauguin's "moral luck" in this volume.

36. Brison, "Outliving Oneself," p. 30. In her many autobiographical notebooks, May Sarton owns up to comparable limitations in her own capacity to define herself.

37. Ibid., pp. 13–14.

38. John Hardwig, "What about the Family?" *Hastings Center Report* 20 (1990): 5–10.

39. Hilde Lindemann Nelson and James Lindemann Nelson, *The Patient in the Family: An Ethics of Medicine and Families* (New York: Routledge, 1995). Note especially pp. 114–116.

40. See Ann Williams, "Genetic Counselling: A Nurse's Perspective," in Clarke, *Genetic Counselling*, 44–62. Note remarks on p. 48.

41. Note Peter S. Harper's remarks on this point in "Personal Experiences of Genetic Diseases: A Clinical Geneticist's Reaction," in Marteau and Richards, *Troubled Helix*, pp. 54–59.

42. My thinking on this issue has been sparked by many sources, but I owe a particular debt to insights from Mary B. Mahowald et al., "The New Genetics and Women," *Milbank Quarterly* 74 (1996): 239–283.

43. These range from profound mental retardation and early death, in the instance of some trisomies and Tay-Sachs, to disorders that affect daily living and shorten the life span but do not cause serious mental incapacity—cystic fibrosis and hemophilia, for instance. For more details, see Lori B. Andrews, Jane E. Fullarton, Neil A. Holtzman, and Arno G. Motulsky, eds., *Assessing Genetic Risks: Implications for Health and Social Policy* (Washington, D.C.: National Academy Press, 1994), particularly p. 75.

44. Gwen Anderson's 1990 (unpublished) study of a group of couples she followed

through pregnancy illustrates this phenomenon. The women in her study worried considerably more than their husbands about what they would do following prenatal diagnosis if the results were positive. In one case the worry was borne out and the worrier was far better prepared to cope with the news than her nonworrying husband.

45. To make a single cell from the newly developing embryo available for testing, the woman must undergo in vitro fertilization (IVF), a costly procedure that is seldom covered by insurance and that is uncomfortable, time consuming, and subject to failure at several junctures. She must endure the risks inherent in the surgical procedures to retrieve her ova and transfer the embryo to her uterus, and she needs to weigh the probabilities of failure, for often the embryo fails to implant. Success rates from IVF continue to be disappointing, hovering around 15%—higher at the most experienced clinics and lower at those with little experience. Although success is more likely when there is no evidence of infertility and may even approach pregnancy rates achieved through unprotected sexual intercourse, whether the success rate justifies the bodily risk and expense is doubtful. Undertaking IVF for genetic indications intrudes on the woman's life even more extensively than IVF alone because she is pursuing that route out of a desire not just for any child but also for a child of a certain description. For recent figures on IVF success rates in the United States, see "Assisted Reproductive Technology in the United States," *Fertility and Sterility* 71 (1999): 798–807. For British data (which are likely to be more accurate since all clinics are *required* to report), see *Sixth Annual Report,* Human Fertilisation and Embryology Authority, 1997.

46. Currently these include Tay-Sachs disease, muscular dystrophy, hemophilia, fragile X, Down syndrome, HD, and achondroplasia.

47. Misinformation is very common with such conditions as spinal muscular atrophy. For a fuller account, see Harper, "Personal Experiences of Genetic Diseases," in Marteau and Richards, *Troubled Helix,* pp. 54–59.

48. For a sensitive account of their situation, see Lavanya Marfatia, Diana Punales-Morejon, and Rayna Rapp, "Counseling the Underserved: When an Old Reproductive Technology Becomes a New Reproductive Technology," in *Strategies in Genetic Counseling: Reproductive Genetics and New Technologies,* ed. B. A. Fine et al. (March of Dimes Birth Defects Foundation: Birth Defect: Original Article Series, vol. 26, 1990), pp. 109–126.

49. See Richards, "Families, Kinship and Genetics," p. 270.

50. On this point see Shoshana Shiloh, "Decision-Making in the Context of Genetic Risk," in Marteau and Richards, *Troubled Helix,* pp. 82–103. Note especially pp. 90–91.

51. See Clarke's introduction in *Genetic Counselling,* p. 18. He attributes this information to M. Holmes-Seidle et al., "Parental Decisions Regarding Termination of Pregnancy Following Prenatal Determination of Sex Chromosome Abnormality," *Prenatal Diagnosis* 7 (1987): 239–244, and A. Robinson et al., "Decisions Following the Intrauterine Diagnosis of Sex Chromosome Neuploidy," *American Journal of Medical Genetics* 34 (1989): 552–554. T. M. Marteau, H. Drake, and M. Bobrow confirm this observation in "Counseling after Fetal Abnormality: The Differing Approaches of Obstetricians, Clinical Geneticists, and Genetic Nurses," *Journal of Medical Genetics* 31 (1994): 864–867; and Josephine Green and Helen Stratham cite additional sources supporting it in "Psychosocial Aspects of Prenatal Screening and Diagnosis," in Marteau and Richards, *Troubled Helix,* pp. 140–163.

52. A survey that sampled obstetricians in England and Wales showed that over a third would not refer a woman for genetic testing unless she agreed in advance to terminate an affected pregnancy. For elaboration of this point, see Green and Stratham, "Psychosocial Aspects," pp. 150–151.

53. Quoted from the National Society of Genetic Counselors Code, 2.2, 1991. Cited in Fern Brunger and Abby Lippman, "Resistance and Adherence to the Norms of Genetic Counseling," *Journal of Genetic Counseling* 4 (1995): 151–167.

54. For a persuasive account, see Abby Lippman, "Prenatal Genetic Testing and Screening: Constructing Needs and Reinforcing Inequities," *American Journal of Law and Medicine* 17 (1991): 15–50. (Reprinted in Clarke, *Genetic Counselling*, pp. 142–186).

55. See Brunger and Lipmann, "Resistance and Adherence," and Arthur L. Caplan, "Neutrality Is Not Morality: The Ethics of Genetic Counseling," in *Prescribing Our Future: Ethical Challenges in Genetic Counseling*, ed. Diane M. Bartels, B. LeRoy, and A. L. Caplan (New York: Aldine De Gruyter, 1993), pp. 149–165.

56. In "Interviewing Women: A Contradiction in Terms," in *Essays on Women, Medicine, and Health* (Edinburgh: Edinburgh University Press, 1993), Ann Oakley formulates such a model specific to the relationship between a research interviewer and her interviewees. She develops this model more fully in her subsequent book, *Social Support and Motherhood* (Oxford: Blackwell, 1995). The model she proposes, with appropriate modifications, could be transported to the counselor-client relationship.

57. Wolf, *Feminism and Bioethics*, p. 18.

11

RELATIONAL AUTONOMY, SELF-TRUST, AND HEALTH CARE FOR PATIENTS WHO ARE OPPRESSED[1]

Carolyn McLeod
Susan Sherwin

Relational Autonomy and Self-Trust

Traditional autonomy theory, especially as it is deployed in the context of health-care ethics discussions, has focused on specific factors that interfere with autonomy: coercion, internal compulsion, and ignorance.[2] Depending on the circumstances and the severity, the presence of any of these factors may make it impossible, or at least very difficult, for an agent to act autonomously.[3] What traditional accounts tend to overlook, however, is that there is a fourth way in which an agent's autonomy may also be compromised, namely, by the forces of oppression.[4] Oppression may itself involve dimensions of coercion, compulsion, and ignorance, but it functions in complex and often largely invisible ways, affecting whole social groups rather than simply disrupting isolated individuals; as a result, its effects tend to be ignored within the traditional autonomy framework that focuses solely on individuals. Moreover, addressing these features requires changing the broad social conditions that constitute oppression and not merely changing some of the specific circumstances of an individual agent's situation. It is necessary, then, to explore the distinct ways in which oppression may interfere with a person's ability to act autonomously.

To make explicit the role of oppression in autonomy, we appeal to a concept of relational (or contextual) autonomy. We understand relational autonomy to involve explicit recognition of the fact that autonomy is both defined and pursued in a social context and that social context significantly influences the opportunities an agent has to develop or express autonomy skills. In relational autonomy, it is necessary to explore an agent's social location if we hope to evaluate properly and respond appropriately to her ability to exercise autonomy. Whereas traditional accounts concern themselves only with judging the ability of the individual to act autonomously in the situation at hand, relational autonomy asks us to take into account the impact of social and political structures, especially sexism and other forms of oppression, on the lives and opportunities of individuals. By making visible the ways in which autonomy is affected by social forces, especially oppression, relational autonomy challenges assumptions common to much bioethical literature that autonomy be viewed as an achievement of individuals.

We must, therefore, evaluate society and not just the individual when determining the degree to which an individual is able to act autonomously. Insofar as oppression has reduced or undermined an agent's ability to act autonomously in various contexts, relational autonomy seeks politically aware solutions that endeavour to change social conditions and not just expand the options offered to agents. In particular, a relational view of autonomy encourages us to understand that the best way of responding to oppression's restrictive influence on an individual's ability to act autonomously is to change the oppressive conditions of her life, not to try to make her better adapt to (or simply to manage to "overcome") those conditions privately.

We live in a society complicated by many intersecting forces of oppression. Although we may challenge them and work to reduce their influence, we cannot hope to see their disappearance in the near future. Many members of our society have been damaged to varying degrees by these forces of oppression, and many have diminished ability to exercise autonomy as a consequence of their experiences as members of oppressed groups. Unfortunately, the damage done by oppression may be so deep that the effects can never be completely erased,[5] but reducing oppressive circumstances can increase opportunities to repair some of the damage and prevent its occurrence in future generations. Because oppression is always an impediment to autonomy, any society truly committed to promoting autonomy must work to eliminate the forces of oppression that reduce citizens' opportunities to become maximally autonomous.[6]

Of course, this is not to say that every person who belongs to one or more groups that is subject to oppression is incapable of exercising autonomy or that everyone who belongs to a dominating group is fully autonomous. Rather, it is to make clear that oppression tends to interfere with an agent's ability to develop or exercise autonomy effectively in specific ways. Individual members of oppressed groups are affected to varying degrees by the forms of oppression that are endemic to their society; some manage to overcome the oppressive circumstances of their lives largely unscathed. Furthermore, since there are many intersecting forms of oppression, each person belongs to multiple groups with multiple locations on any map of oppression and may well be privileged in some respects even as she or he is oppressed in others, and this complex positioning may have an impact on the agent's opportunity to develop the abilities needed to act autonomously. Also, the features that support the development of some of the skills necessary to exercise autonomy are products not only of large social forces but also of particular personal relationships; the latter vary significantly from one individual to the next even within the same social groups. Membership in one or more oppressed groups is an obstacle, then, but not an insurmountable barrier to the development of relational autonomy.

Here we focus specifically on one particular dimension of oppression that interferes with autonomy, namely, oppression's effect on self-trust. We argue that an agent requires a certain degree of self-trust to be able to act autonomously; because self-trust is undermined by oppression, oppression reduces an agent's ability to act autonomously. To make our argument more concrete, we review some areas of health-care where it is evident that the effects of oppression on self-trust interfere with patients' ability to act autonomously, and we consider some of the options available to health-care providers in such circumstances. We discuss a variety of cases, concentrating particularly on problems associated with caring for women with serious addictions, as this is an area where the links among oppression, self-(dis)trust, and autonomy create especially difficult challenges for health-care providers. We explore how health-care providers ought best to respond to these patients. In our view, there is no single solution to this difficulty but a range of responses that must vary with the health needs and the situation of each patient.

We begin by looking at some of the distinct ways in which oppression can limit an agent's ability to act autonomously in order to appreciate how self-trust fits within this complex matrix. First, oppression may involve explicit or implicit limitations on the options available to members of oppressed groups. An important example is the way in which oppression may limit the options that are reasonable for an agent to choose under various circumstances by placing her in a double bind;[7] in such cases, whatever she does, she will suffer. For example, it is not unusual for women who are living with violent partners to feel trapped in those dangerous relationships. They may feel that they cannot leave the relationship because the danger of such action would be too great: generally, the most serious attacks of domestic violence occur when the battered partner attempts to separate. Moreover, separation may bring not only the heightened risk of attack but also harassment, financial difficulties, the risk of losing custody of her children, and for immigrant women the threat of deportation. On the other hand, remaining with the abusive partner clearly represents a serious danger to the woman and her children. Unless she has access to excellent social services for battered women, there may be no safe option available to her. Less dramatic examples of oppression-related double binds involve the ways in which women are often considered suspect as job candidates if they are single and if they are married, if they have children and if they do not, and if they quit their previous job and if they were fired.

Second, and more deeply, oppression may shape agents' values and desires in ways that undermine their capacity for autonomous choice in certain matters. In fact, women's oppression typically involves circumstances in which the agent's immediate interests appear to support her active participation in practices that actually promote her oppression. For example, part of women's oppression is that they are primarily valued (by themselves, as well as by others) in terms of their instrumental role as mothers. Many women who have difficulty in conceiving or maintaining a pregnancy seek medical interventions to circumvent infertility problems, using powerful fertility-enhancing drugs and often surgical treatments in the pursuit of a baby. In so doing, they reinforce the social norms that proclaim the profound importance of women being able to reproduce. The relentless efforts of so many infertile women to spare no risk or expense to produce a biologically related child help to deepen social expectations about the normalcy of childbearing for all women and to raise questions about the nature of other women who choose childlessness. Whatever their intentions, their participation in practices that take for granted the desirability of biological reproduction helps to further entrench social attitudes about women's fundamental role as mothers.[8]

Our main focus in this article is on two other ways in which oppression can interfere with autonomy. One is that oppression tends to deprive a person of the opportunity to develop some of the very skills that are necessary to exercise autonomy by restricting her opportunity to make meaningful choices and to have the experience of having her choices respected. As Diana Meyers argues, exercising personal autonomy involves certain types of competency that depend on the development of corresponding skills.[9] If an agent is never exposed to an environment that fosters the development of those skills, she will lack the ability to exercise autonomy. Moreover, she will have been deprived of the opportunities to develop the level of self-trust that is necessary for her to gain and use these skills effectively. She may then not be in a position to exercise autonomy even when invited to do so. Hence, it is not sufficient simply to offer a person an uncoerced choice; it is also necessary to ensure that she has had the opportunity to learn to exercise choice responsibly.

Lastly, oppression can lead to the internalization of a sense of social worthlessness and incompetence that is translated into a lack of self-worth and self-trust. When a group is oppressed, the society at large operates as if that group is less worthy and less competent than others and devalues its members. Members of oppressed groups may then internalize these attitudes; many are inclined to accept society's devaluing of their personal worth on at least an unconscious level and to doubt their own worth and ability to make appropriate choices.[10] This lack of self-worth and self-trust may be devastating to agents' autonomy competency, interfering with their ability to act according to their own interests at all.

Many feminists have explored the effect of these various aspects of oppression on autonomy, and several have addressed the necessity of having an adequate sense of self-worth. To date, none have focused explicitly on the effect of oppression-related reductions in self-trust on the agent's autonomy.[11] Our aim here is to bring out the significance of self-trust in discussions of oppression and autonomy. We are interested in exploring the ways in which oppression interferes with the development of self-trust and with the fact that reduced self-trust tends to reduce an agent's ability to act autonomously. And we seek to understand the special challenges health-care providers face in caring for patients with the diminished autonomy that is associated with low levels of self-trust.

Self-trust (and its correlate, self-distrust) must be considered when evaluating or promoting autonomy skills because autonomy is dependent on self-trust.[12] Exercising autonomy involves, in part, reflecting on one's beliefs, values, and desires; making reasonable decisions in light of them; and acting on those decisions. It is essential in developing the capacity to be autonomous that the agent trusts her capacity to make appropriate choices, given her beliefs, desires, and values; that she trusts her ability to act on her decisions; and also that she trusts the judgments she makes that underlie those decisions. These include judgments about the values and motivations that lie behind her decisions and about the efficacy of her own decision-making skills. Without trust in these judgments and trust overall in her ability to exercise choice effectively, any agent would have little motivation to deliberate on alternative courses of action.

In recognizing some degree of self-trust to be a precondition of autonomy, we are offering a substantive view of autonomy that builds on existing theories formulated by Paul Benson and Robin Dillon.[13] Autonomy theories can be either substantive or procedural. Procedural accounts require that the agent subject her beliefs, values, and desires to some procedure or method of evaluation and that she act on whatever beliefs or desires satisfy that procedure. Meyers, for example, offers a procedural account in which the goal of the procedure is to determine what the agent *really* believes or desires, and being successful in this process of self-discovery requires that the agent possess certain competency skills.[14] We accept the procedural dimensions of autonomy and believe that self-trust has a role to play within them, but we also believe that an autonomy theory must be supplemented with a limited substantive demand. What distinguishes substantive accounts from procedural theories is that the latter, unlike the former, are "content-neutral"; the procedure of evaluation does not dictate that the agent must *really* believe anything specific about herself or the world to be autonomous. Substantive theories, on the other hand, put restrictions on the kinds of beliefs, values, and desires an agent must have in order to be autonomous. The restriction Benson and Dillon argue for is to have a positive conception of one's own worth and respect for one's capacities. The requirement that the agent value or respect herself puts a limit (albeit a minimal one) on the sorts of beliefs or feelings that she can have about herself if she is to be autonomous.[15] We propose a different, though similar limit in requiring that the agent trust her own judgment. As we explain below, we believe that self-trust is a criterion for autonomy distinct from that of self-respect or self-worth.

The role of self-trust within the procedural dimensions of autonomy includes the following aspects. First, to be motivated to exercise her own choices, the agent must trust her capacity to choose effectively, a type of self-trust that we refer to as Type I. Having this capacity involves having good decision-making skills and also being situated to choose well, meaning that the agent is adequately informed of alternative courses of action and of whatever facts are relevant to her decisions. For her to trust herself to make good decisions, she must trust her competency skills and the accuracy and adequacy of the information available to her. Distrust in these areas inhibits her autonomy because it makes it very difficult for her to formulate decisions about what she should believe or desire and how she should act. As noted, oppression can cause self-distrust in the agent's decision-making skills by depriving her of sufficient opportunities to develop and exercise those skills. People who believe that she is less competent than others by virtue of being a member of a particular social group will deny her these opportunities. Oppression can also limit her knowledge base for making decisions by ensuring that most of the information circulating throughout her society is about the lives of members of the dominant group and the risks or benefits *they* would incur by making particular decisions, such as those about their own health care.

Second, an agent must trust her ability to act on the decisions she makes, a type of self-trust that we call Type II. She may lack this form of self-trust because she lacks the courage to act on her judgments and consequently distrusts her ability to do so. She may also lack it because of conflicting desires that stand in the way of her acting on her judgments. Such desires are commonplace among people who are oppressed and who are attempting to fight their oppression. Their trust in their ability to act on decisions that oppose their oppression can be compromised by the desire simply to get along with others or the desire to experience the benefits of conforming to dominant stereotypes or interests. For example, some women find it very difficult to stick with a decision not to appear unwise or innocent around men in positions of power, who would not pay much attention to them otherwise.

Third, the substantive demand on autonomy concerned with self-trust is that the agent must trust the judgments she makes that underlie her own choices. We call her trust in her own judgment Type III. Judgments that are relevant to her autonomy are, for example, her judgments about the trustworthiness of her own decision-making skills. Whether she trusts or distrusts her evaluations of her own capacities as an agent will depend on her level of self-knowledge, or the degree to which she feels that she understands her own strengths or weaknesses as an agent. Other autonomy-related judgments concern the values that inform her decisions. She must have some confidence in the appropriateness of her values for her to be motivated to make decisions that reflect them. If her values have been shaped by oppression, it will not be easy for her to trust them because they will encourage her participation in practices and behavior that undermine her moral worth and that may cause her severe suffering.

Each of these three different types of self-trust or distrust can be situational or more general, meaning that they can apply only to specific situations or to most situations in which the agent finds herself.[16] For example, most of us distrust our decision-making capacities in at least some situations, in particular, those in which we know that we lack the knowledge required to make an appropriate choice. People trained only in philosophy probably would (and should) distrust their ability to make good decisions in situations in which training in engineering is called for. Type II self-trust is also often situational; for example, whether we have the courage to act on our decisions usually depends on the context in which we have made them. If we lack that courage in *most* situations, our autonomy will suffer, and that happens whenever any of the three types of self-distrust occur generally rather than only situationally. On the other hand, situational self-distrust of any type may be minor and, hence, trivial if it occurs in an area of little importance to the agent. However, if it occurs in an area that relates to how she defines herself or to what she values most, it will be nontrivial in the sense that it will interfere with her autonomy. For example, if she defines herself as a proud lesbian but lacks trust in her ability to act on judgments that reflect that pride in relevant situations, that situational Type II self-distrust will negatively affect her autonomy.

Just as it is appropriate sometimes to distrust others, it is also appropriate sometimes to distrust oneself. There are situations in which it is justified for an agent to distrust her ability to act on her judgments. The justification lies in a history of failing to act on the relevant judgments in the relevant situations. Often situational self-trust and distrust develops, at least in part, through inductive reasoning about past successes or failures at using or attempting to use our various abilities. Depending on the soundness of this reasoning, the agent's self-trust or distrust will be well formed or ill formed. For example, an alcoholic may reason that she can trust her ability to act on her decision to refrain from drinking, but her reasoning may be unsound, based on her past experience, in which case her trust in her ability to refrain is ill formed.

Clarifying how the different types of self-trust develop and the exact nature of self-trust (that is, what sort of mental attitude it is) is not something we can accomplish here, but we make some preliminary remarks about both. First, regarding the development of self-trust, the fact that oppression and self-distrust are interrelated means that self-trust does not always or merely develop through inductive reasoning by the agent. The level of support that the agent receives within her social environment will have a profound influence on her self-trust. That support can exist on two different levels: (1) the agent can be given opportunities to develop and use her various capacities and, through these opportunities, learn to trust her capacities and, (2) the agent can receive encouragement from others to trust her own capacities. On the first level, the self-trust is relational in a causal sense; supportive social conditions provide the materials for its development. On the second level, self-trust is relational in a constitutive sense; the agent's trust in herself exists in part because others reinforce that trust in their relationships with her. Our self-appreciation is influenced by the opinions that others have of us, particularly when we are young. It is doubtful that anyone could ever avoid the constitutively relational aspect of self-trust and distrust.

The way in which a particular instance of self-trust or distrust develops will determine whether that trust is informed primarily by beliefs or feelings. The primary influence on self-distrust that arises through inductive reasoning about past failures will probably be a belief, whereas the primary influence on self-distrust that exists because of subtle attempts by others to undermine self-trust will probably be a feeling about our own incompetency. Such subtle attempts, which may not be fully conscious on the part of those who make them, are common in relationships that involve oppression.[17] Oppressed people often receive the subtle (and occasionally not so subtle) message from others that their opinions are not as credible or as important as the opinions of the dominant group. Often the message is vague, and so it produces a vague sense or a feeling in the agent, rather than a belief, that her judgment is untrustworthy.

Thus, self-trust, like interpersonal trust, is an attitude that is shaped by beliefs and/or feelings about the trustworthiness of the trusted. This general description of trust is consistent with the view of many trust theorists, such as Annette Baier, Richard Holton, Karen Jones, and Trudy Govier, even though they differ in their elaborations on the view that trust is an attitude.[18] For example, Jones says that trust is an attitude of optimism about the goodwill and competence of the one trusted, and it involves an expectation that that person will be "directly and favorably moved by the thought that we are counting on her."[19] Holton agrees that it is an attitude that entails assumptions about the future motivations of the trusted person, but he disagrees that it is necessarily informed by a belief about the goodwill of that person. We can infer from where the agreement lies about the nature of interpersonal trust that the attitude of self-trust concerns the competence of the self and expectations about how one will be motivated to act in the future.

Thus, we can see how self-trust differs from self-worth and self-respect; it is not interchangeable with either of them, although that is how some authors, such as Benson and Dillon, treat those forms of self-appreciation.[20] Self-trust differs from self-worth in being about our competence rather than our worth. It makes sense, for example, to talk about trusting our competence to judge our worth. Self-respect can also be about our competence, but there is a sense in which the positive evaluation it gives of our competence is grounded in our past behaviour.[21] In trusting ourselves, we are optimistic that we will be able to carry that evaluation forward into the future. Thus, one can trust oneself to act in the future in a way that maintains one's self-respect. However, it is doubtful that one could have that trust in the absence of self-respect, and moreover, that one could acquire self-respect regarding one's competence without some self-trust. Those self-regarding attitudes are distinct, yet they are mutually reinforcing.

Some theorists, particularly Holton, argue that we can decide to develop trusting attitudes, whereas we cannot simply decide to believe. These attitudes are constrained somewhat by evidence that contradicts them and by our current beliefs and feelings; for example, we cannot decide to trust a person whom we believe to be untrustworthy. However, outside of some minimal constraints, we can will ourselves to trust. As Holton explains, willed attitudes of trust that are unreasonable, given the evidence and our relationship with the trusted, are ill founded.[22] Likewise, trusting attitudes toward the self can be ill founded; for example, if I develop a trusting attitude toward my ability to take a bobsled down a mountain without killing myself but I have no evidence of my ability to do so, that attitude is unreasonable.

In conclusion, we have reviewed how different types of self-trust can damage our autonomy and explained how they can be related to oppression. Being fully autonomous in our view requires having all nontrivial forms of the different types of self-trust. We recognize that autonomy exists in degrees and that lacking some instances of nontrivial self-trust does not make an agent completely nonautonomous. However, our interest lies primarily in cases in which the agent's autonomy has been damaged severely by oppression-related reductions in self-trust, and we intend to discuss how health-care providers should respond to such patients. In the next section, we explore the influence on health-care provision of the impact of oppression on self-trust and autonomy. At the end of it, we consider cases in which that impact is severe, specifically, among women with addictions.

Responding to the Effects of Oppression on Self-Trust in Health Care

It is at present widely agreed throughout the biomedical health-care community that patients should make autonomous decisions about their health care to the greatest degree possible. There is no clear consensus, however, on how health-care providers are to proceed when caring for patients who are not fully autonomous. We are concerned, specifically, with the question of determining how health-care providers should respond to patients whose autonomy is diminished as a result of their oppressed status.

Typically, the health-care system has responded to patients with reduced levels of autonomy (as identified by the traditional analysis) by exercising paternalism (making decisions on behalf of patients without their full consent). Indeed, exercising paternalism has been customary throughout the history of medicine, even when dealing with autonomous patients. It is only in the past few decades, paternalism has become widely recognized as a direct threat to autonomy; as a result, health-care providers have been formally discouraged from exercising paternalism when dealing with patients who are capable of making autonomous decisions. Nonetheless, a certain degree of paternalism pervades modern practice. Health-care decisions can be exceedingly complex, requiring understanding of a great deal of technical information and careful weighing of options. Even the most independent and self-reliant patient often feels overwhelmed and is inclined to defer to medical authority when facing serious health matters. In such a context, when health-care professionals are faced with patients whose autonomy is suspect for any reason, it may seem appropriate to exercise paternalism to ensure the best possible care for these patients.

Paternalism on the part of health-care professionals is always questionable, however, for it may involve significant distortion of the patient's real interests. The exercise of paternalism is especially problematic when applied to patients whose autonomy is reduced by virtue of their history of oppression. Oppression involves unjust distributions of power, and health-care settings are sites of very uneven power differentials. If health-care professionals, especially physicians, further consolidate their already disproportionate power in relation to patients, especially those from oppressed groups, they exacerbate a problematic power differential and further reduce the already limited autonomy of their patients. Moreover, they are unlikely to be in a position to know what is ultimately in the best interests of patients whose life experiences are very different from their own; hence, they are unlikely to be in a position to exercise paternalism wisely.[23] Other solutions to the problem of reduced autonomy must be found.[24]

The impact of oppression on patients' ability to exercise autonomy can be felt in many different ways. For example, the ability to exercise autonomous choice requires, among other things, access to appropriate information. Competent health-care providers strive to simplify the relevant information and to ensure that patients appreciate the meaningful choices before them, but most shape the decisions their patients will make by tailoring the information to ensure the selection of what the health-care expert considers the best choice for each patient—an indirect form of paternalism. Patients' autonomy is generally reduced to the exercise of "informed choice" in which the information provided is restricted to that deemed relevant by the health-care provider (and by the health-care system, which has determined what information is even available by pursuing certain sorts of research programs and ignoring others). Even in "ideal" cases in which patients have strong autonomy skills and full access to all the available information, it is important to recognize the influence that oppression may have on the information base and, thereby, on the meaningful options available to patients.

Specifically, oppression tends to restrict the relevant knowledge base that can be called on for making health-care decisions. It may limit the health-care providers' ability to appreciate the type of information the patient might need to know in order to choose wisely in her circumstances. For example, the need to arrange for flexible work hours to adapt to a treatment regime may not seem problematic to a physician but may pose an insurmountable barrier to women in certain types of jobs. Furthermore, oppression may limit the knowledge base itself; for example, although heart disease is the leading cause of death in women, many important studies of heart disease have used only male subjects, so there are insufficient data about the effectiveness of prevention or treatment programs for women (e.g., the value of taking a daily dose of aspirin as a preventive measure). Similarly, research into treatment for AIDS has concentrated on the progress of the disease on men; as a result, women must often choose drug regimens whose effects on women's bodies have not been sufficiently explored.[25] In these sorts of cases, relational autonomy helps us to recognize that circumstances may limit the autonomy of all patients who belong to oppressed groups by creating an inappropriately limited knowledge base on which such patients must rely.

These sorts of gaps in available knowledge are problematic in that they reduce the agent's ability to choose well. They also raise issues of trust and of Type I self-trust. These gaps mean that often patients who are members of oppressed groups have particular reason to distrust the information their health-care providers supply. In addition, they mean that patients are limited in their ability to obtain independent and appropriate information on their own. In such circumstances, patients must lack trust in their own abilities to acquire the necessary knowledge to make well-informed decisions. Even a patient who has managed to develop strong autonomy skills will lack Type I self-trust when she must choose in the face of inadequate or skewed data. She may have complete confidence in her own ability to make such decisions, but if she knows that she is making them without adequate data, she will still not be able to fully trust the outcome. Many menopausal women feel precisely this unease as they grapple with the question of whether or not to begin hormone replacement therapy. Although the self-distrust at issue is quite limited in scope and located around a particular range of choices—and, hence, is a relatively benign form of self-distrust—it is still relevant to the autonomy of the agent. In this case, it is a form of well-founded distrust of the results of her own deliberations because of the limitations inherent in the circumstances in which these decisions are made. Oppression is relevant here because the data needed to make health-care decisions are often particularly limited for members of oppressed groups; as a result, patients from these groups find that they must often distrust the knowledge base they need to rely on and that distrust will affect their confidence in many sorts of health-care decisions they are required to make.

In such circumstances, autonomy is compromised. Paternalism is not any more reliable, however, since health-care providers will face the same limits in knowing what will best meet these patients' needs. Thus health-care providers have a responsibility not to take over decision making from patients but to ensure that patients understand the limits of the knowledge the former can provide. Moreover, health workers should appreciate their collective responsibility to work toward filling in these important knowledge gaps.

Yet more complex questions arise when we consider cases in which patients choose medical procedures that seem inseparable from their oppression. In these cases, patients who are aware of the ways in which socialization may have shaped their values and desires to conform to oppressive stereotypes will again find it difficult to trust their own deliberations. They will lack Type III self-trust insofar as it concerns the values and desires that inform their decisions. For example, the decision about whether or not to use hormone replacement therapy at menopause is further complicated by factors other than inadequate and inconsistent evidence. There is also the fact that women are encouraged to use such treatments to continue to look young; in doing so, they are participating in the norms of a culture that prefers its women young and beautiful. Of course, hormone replacement therapy is seldom a straightforward, single-dimension decision; women are also encouraged to use it to reduce their risk of heart disease and osteoporosis and now, it is suggested, of Alzheimer's disease. The multiple dimensions of such decisions mean that many factors must be taken into account, making such decisions especially difficult and complex for many women. Those who find that maintaining a youthful appearance is an important consideration are in a particularly awkward position. They may well have excellent reasons for wanting to continue to look young for as long as possible: their careers and romantic possibilities may well depend on appearing youthful, and their own aesthetic sensibilities may also be an issue. The problem is that cultural attitudes that consistently value young (looking) women over older women are oppressive to every woman. To devalue women who clearly have reached a certain maturity is to devalue important aspects of all women's lives. It reflects a value system that cares more about women's appearance than their wisdom or experience; in such a system, women are valued more for their ornamental role than for their personhood. Women who are aware of this cultural prejudice against aging women, yet who feel a strong desire to look young, will find themselves uncertain about their own motivations to use hormone replacement therapy. They may also lack a form of Type II self-trust, one relating to their ability to act on their judgment that in making choices that affect themselves, they should be respectful of their own personhood. They may distrust this ability because they are confused about whether choosing hormone replacement therapy is consistent with that judgment.

Similar problems are associated with the use of cosmetic surgery to better meet society's beauty standards. As more women make the effort to fit these norms, the pressure grows on other women to overcome their natural "handicaps" and adapt to the expectations that apply to women. In such ways, the evaluation of women by external standards of appearance becomes ever more normalized, further contributing to the oppression of all women by overshadowing efforts to recognize them in other terms.[26] For women to participate in this value system is to reinforce it rather than challenge it; their compliance helps to perpetuate its oppressive power.

This issue is made especially problematic because it is an area where women have reason to distrust their own value schemes. Some of the operative values are part of a cultural worldview that is oppressive to women in general and tends to be especially oppressive to women who belong to marginalized groups, including disabled women, lesbians, women of color, and poor women (since the norms promoted are those of young, affluent, slim, fit-looking, white women). Women whose positive evaluations of their own bodies are not attached to these exploitative social values may find it very difficult to identify or maintain their own value schemes in light of the availability of "cures" for certain body shapes, such as small breasts and large tummies, which are treated as subjects for invasive medical responses. Their difficulty in maintaining their own value systems suggests a lack of Type II trust in their ability to act on decisions that reflect those systems or a lack of Type III trust in their own evaluations of their values. Cosmetic surgeons effectively reduce many women's body parts to material for surgical manipulation, invoking technologies otherwise reserved for healing serious illness and conveying the sense that such deficiencies are important enough to warrant dramatic solutions. At the same time, they join their medical colleagues in acting as authorities for women on the health of their bodies. The multiple messages involved make it hard for many women to trust their own evaluations of their values regarding body shape and size when those evaluations are at odds with sexist beauty norms.

Health-care providers have a responsibility, then, to refrain from encouraging such use of medical resources and to refrain from promoting the youth and beauty their procedures may engender. They need to reflect on their role in a culture that cares more about the superficial aspects of women's appearance than their characters or talents. If they wish to promote the autonomy of patients who seek these procedures, they should not simply respond to informed requests for surgical "corrections" but, at least, also encourage their patients to consider the forces that lead to these choices, as well as alternative responses.

In other cases, health problems are even more directly related to the patient's oppression. For example, both poverty and stress, two conditions highly correlated with oppression, are associated with countless illnesses and are inevitably aggravating factors in any illness. Moreover, many health problems are far more common in members of oppressed groups than in the rest of the population; for example, AIDS is more common among the poor and lupus is more common among people of African descent in North America than in the population at large. Aboriginal women die of cervical cancer in Canada at many times the rate of white women, and suicide has reached epidemic proportions in some native communities in North America. Although women tend to outlive men in much of the world, their lives are plagued by more chronic and debilitating illnesses. Furthermore, one of the characterizing features of oppression is that members of groups subject to oppression are highly vulnerable to violent attacks; women, for example, suffer disproportionately from the effects of domestic and sexual violence, and disabled women in particular experience an exceptionally high rate of attack. These correlations are inseparable from the oppressive conditions that affect disadvantaged populations. As we have noted, such experiences undermine the autonomy of members of oppressed groups in multiple ways; in particular, systematic abuse often interferes with an agent's sense of self-trust, as we discuss below.

When patients appear in the health-care system with conditions in which their oppression seems to be a contributing factor, then, it is not sufficient simply to try to correct the immediate damage, for that leaves the underlying contributing factors intact. It is important for patients—and others—to understand the social and political dimensions of their condition. To restore their sense of self-trust, those who have been assaulted need to appreciate that this violence is part of an endemic pattern and not a consequence of their own behavior; those suffering from nutrition-related disorders because of their low incomes need to appreciate the role that poverty (and not necessarily incompetence) plays in limiting their access to a nutritious diet; and those with poorly understood illnesses should understand that there has been inadequate research into such conditions as lupus that primarily affect disadvantaged populations. This knowledge should help patients feel validated in their legitimate claims for care and should help them to avoid blaming themselves for the conditions in which they find themselves. It may help strengthen the patients' trust in their ability to recognize their need for help and give them guidance on how to pursue both personal and political strategies to improve their situation. Such guidance may require directing patients toward self-help activist groups that will promote a sense of empowerment and build skills and forms of self-appreciation that are necessary for autonomy, including self-trust.

Identifying ways in which health-care providers can promote the autonomy of patients with certain oppression-induced problems, as well as seriously low levels of autonomy, can be exceedingly difficult, however. We now consider some of these difficulties when dealing with a group whose members have faced especially serious problems in developing the conditions necessary for autonomy— women with serious addictions (i.e., addictions to dangerous quantities of such harmful substances as heroin, crack cocaine, alcohol, and solvents). Most of these women tend to have several problems in exercising autonomy. The first and most obvious is one recognized by all autonomy theories: addictions are a form of compulsion, so by their very nature, they interfere with autonomy. This feature in itself makes treatment of serious addictions a significant problem for those committed to respecting autonomy.

The compulsive nature of addiction may make it very difficult, for example, for an addict to make a voluntary (let alone an autonomous) choice to enter a treatment program. Hence, the question arises, when faced with an addict with a low level of autonomy who does not wish to seek treatment or who denies that she has a drug problem, should providers be permitted to get her into treatment by deceiving her somehow or by simply forcing her? Despite the fact that addicts have low levels of autonomy, methods that involve force or deception to admit them for treatment are problematic for several reasons, most notably because the treatment that follows is likely to be ineffective. The general consensus in the field of addiction treatment is that many of the addict's beliefs and attitudes must change if she is to modify her behavior, and this change will not occur in treatment if she is there unwillingly.[27] Hence, whatever the ethical arguments are about coercion in such cases, there is a strong pragmatic case against coercing any addict into treatment.

Whatever account of autonomy we might choose, then, there are good reasons to doubt that women with serious addictions are fully autonomous and also good reason to refrain from forcing them into treatment. We believe, though, that there is an even deeper concern that emerges when we adopt the perspective of relational autonomy—the fact that the autonomy of women with serious addictions is undermined not only by the compulsive nature of their addiction but also by the ways in which their personal history has inhibited their ability to acquire the conditions necessary for autonomy. Many women with serious addictions have experienced severe violence or abuse. A strong correlation between women's addictions and their abuse has been proven in various studies (most but not all of which focus on alcoholic women). Brenda Miller and her colleagues discovered that compared to nonalcoholic women, it is more common for female alcoholics to have suffered childhood sexual abuse, emotional abuse by their fathers and spouses, and spousal physical abuse.[28] One study found that 74% of alcoholic women have experienced sexual abuse, compared to 50% of nonalcoholic women, and a similar difference in percentages was found for physical and emotional abuse: 52%, compared to 34%, for physical abuse; 72%, compared to 44%, for emotional abuse.[29] Moreover, the experiences of female alcoholics with different forms of abuse tend to be more frequent and more severe than their nonalcoholic counterparts.[30] For illicit drug use, one study found that teenaged girls who reported a history of sexual or physical abuse used drugs more frequently than other girls.[31]

What makes most forms of violence or abuse examples of oppression is that they are so systemic that they could be defined as social practices.[32] This definition is appropriate given that these forms of oppression occur in a social environment that makes them permissible, either explicitly or implicitly.[33] The emotional, physical, and sexual abuse of women are not isolated problems that concern only individual women; they are political issues because they are encouraged by sexist stereotypes of women as inherently more passive and vulnerable than men, as primarily sexual objects, and as caregivers as opposed to care receivers.[34]

Most forms of abuse tend to have a negative impact on the abused person's level of self-appreciation. Different kinds of abuse can prevent the development of or can destroy existing self-trust of all the three main types, resulting in the diminished autonomy of the agent. Emotional abuse during childhood, as well as during adulthood, that involves continual criticism and labeling the victim as worthless and incompetent can damage all types of self-trust. Experiencing frequent criticism for her opinions and choices can cause the agent to seriously distrust her decision-making capacities, to lack the courage to act on her own decisions, and to distrust her judgment overall. Predominantly physical forms of abuse can also damage self-trust, mostly because the victims often blame themselves for the anger or sexual desires of their abuser. Victims of incest often think that they somehow provoked their abuse, either because that is what their abusers tell them or because blaming themselves seems to offer a way of reasserting control by allowing them to believe that the abuse will stop if they behave differently in the future.[35] When the abuse continues, they are likely to begin to profoundly distrust their judgment and decision-making capacities because every decision they made about what they needed to do to avoid the abuse turned out to be wrong. Hence, their self-trust of Types I and III will be damaged as a result of the abuse. Some empirical support for these claims can be found in a small study by Doris Brothers, which shows that the greatest problems relating to trust caused by incest and rape lie in the victim's trust in themselves.[36] These problems may not only relate to Types I and III self-trust; in some cases, they may also concern the agent's trust in her ability to act on her judgments, trust that she may lack because of having been threatened with harm or violence if she were to alter her behavior or report her abuse to anyone.

Rather than blaming themselves for the abuse, some victims alternatively block it out of their minds, sometimes by retreating to a fantasy world. One survivor of incest explains that "I hid myself; I became invisible. I did whatever I could do with my mind to leave the situation."[37] It is not uncommon for incest survivors who used this method to forget about what happened to them until years later. Their trust in their ability to accurately recall memories of their abuse years later may diminish because of disbelief on the part of others who are close to them and because of a societal acceptance of "false memory syndrome."[38] As Sue Campbell argues, those who have encouraged the acceptance of this so-called syndrome, in particular the founders of the False Memory Syndrome Foundation, have succeeded in making it more unlikely than it was in the past that people will believe the testimonies of incest survivors.[39] The so-called syndrome implies that incest survivors, most of whom are women, are "bad rememberers,"[40] and it encourages them to distrust their memory to a degree that could seriously limit their autonomy. Someone who believes that she is a bad rememberer will have difficulty in trusting her capacity to reflect rationally on her beliefs. This capacity is a necessary decision-making skill, and it relies on the memory of the agent. Reflecting on and evaluating our beliefs often involves determining whether our memory of the situation in which we formed them is consistent with the beliefs themselves. Those who are taught to distrust their memory will lack a form of Type I self-trust that is necessary for autonomy.

Not all survivors of incest and other forms of abuse suffer from diminished self-trust and autonomy. Many of them have resisted the label "passive victim," preferring to define themselves as survivors who have succeeded in developing their own coping strategies for abuse.[41] Not all coping strategies lead to survival, however; abused women who cope with their abuse by becoming severely addicted to harmful substances are not yet survivors.[42] Although using these substances may have been the only strategy available to them in the short term, prolonged and severe substance use puts them at risk of serious health problems and may worsen whatever psychological problems they developed as a result of the abuse.[43] Furthermore, prolonged use inhibits their ability to adopt less harmful coping strategies.[44] Before the term "survivor" can be accurately applied to addicted women who suffered abuse, they need to receive treatment for their addiction that addresses not only their addictive behavior but also the abuse and its psychological effects.

Effective women-centered treatment must attend to the fact that many female addicts probably have diminished self-trust and, hence, reduced relational autonomy because of experiences with abuse that typically undermine self-trust. Those who care for these women face the dual tasks of helping them to break free of their addictions, as well as improving their low levels of relational autonomy by helping them to build higher levels of self-trust. These tasks in most cases will be inseparable, which makes the latter essential in addiction treatment for women. Studies have shown that for addicts who lack confidence in their own abilities, increasing that confidence increases their chances of successful recovery from drug or alcohol addiction.[45] One study performed at the Amethyst Women's Addiction Centre in Ottawa, Canada, revealed that women whose self-esteem and assertiveness skills increase during treatment are more likely to curtail their drinking.[46] Being assertive or confident to express your own opinions and feelings has a lot to do with trusting your own judgment about their accuracy and relevance in discussions with others.

Thus, improving assertiveness usually requires improving self-trust; if the former is essential in addiction treatment for women, the latter must be as well. It stands to reason that if an addict continues to have a psychological problem such as low self-trust that diminishes her autonomy, her ability to succeed at the extremely onerous task of quitting a serious drug habit will be inhibited.

Our analysis of the importance of discussing relational autonomy in the context of treatment for women with addictions and histories of abuse provides an additional, and powerful, argument against coercing these women into treatment. Forcing them into treatment that will probably be ineffective (since coerced treatment typically is ineffective) will have the likely consequence of further undermining their already limited autonomy. Imposing treatment will increase the powerlessness of these addicts because all that it achieves is a further reduction in their decision-making power. Taking this power away from them in the context of treatment for their addictions could only be justified if the intent and the most probable consequence of doing so would be to improve their level of autonomy in the long run. Ineffective treatment would not have this consequence, and thus, for addicts with low self-trust, it is especially urgent that means other than coercion be sought to encourage them to escape from the compulsive nature of their addictions.[47]

For health-care providers to have any effect on whether addicts seek treatment, it is important that providers develop trusting relationships with them.[48] In the absence of such relationships, addicts are unlikely to listen to encouragement from providers or will interpret their encouragement as an attempt to harm or humiliate them. Gaining the trust of patients requires that providers honestly display moral concern for their well-being and competence in addressing their health-care needs.[49] Addicts who are members of oppressed groups may have good reasons to doubt that providers will have either of these qualities, reasons that may relate, for example, to the fact that various health-care professions have tended to ignore the health-care needs of members of oppressed groups. It is important for providers to strive to overcome barriers to trust in their relationships with these addicts by showing them that they are morally concerned for their welfare and are committed to providing whatever help they can. Yet, a delicate balance is called for. Providers should not expect or encourage addicts, in particular those with abusive histories, to trust them before the addicts have any evidence of their trustworthiness.[50] The root of many female addicts' problems lie in having trusted someone whom they should have been able to trust but who instead betrayed them severely.

The ability of providers to address the health-care needs of addicts with diminished self-trust and relational autonomy is largely determined by the availability of forms of treatment that are compatible with their needs. Many feminists have argued that traditional forms of addiction treatment, like Alcoholics or Narcotics Anonymous are male-biased,[51] and the American Medical Association (AMA) has agreed with them.[52] Some feminists have argued in favor of approaches to addiction treatment that are feminist or, in other words, that see oppression as a relevant factor in their addictions.[53] We agree with this position and would add to it that feminist approaches should be informed by a theory of self-trust that is feminist or, in other words, that explains how oppression could be relevant to self-distrust.[54] These programs must pay attention to the ways in which different forms of oppression, in particular violence and abuse, can undermine self-trust; more positively, they also must develop ways to promote self-trust.

The environment and some of the group sessions in existing feminist programs seem to promote self-trust to some degree already. Many women who have been through the Amethyst program say that they feel more confident about their own judgment (and therefore have built greater Type III self-trust) because of the "egalitarian" environment at the center. There women are comfortable in expressing their own opinions because they know that others will listen to them and take them seriously, an experience that some Amethyst clients have never had before.[55] Amethyst also conducts a special session on sexual abuse; one woman reports that from this session she learned that having been abused was not her fault and that knowing this has given her "the strength and courage [she needs] to be a survivor."[56] Gaining that strength and courage probably translated into greater Type II and Type III self-trust; learning about the dynamics of abusive relationships can help abused persons realize that what they were led to believe or feel about their own judgment was unfounded and that they should be more confident about acting on their judgments.[57] As well as giving them the opportunity to explore these dynamics, it may also be helpful for women with low self-trust to explore how oppression may have shaped their values and to consider whether adopting nonsexist, nonracist (and other antioppression) values would make them more comfortable with their decisions. Another helpful method for improving self-trust might involve giving women educational and employment opportunities that allow them to develop autonomy skills and prove their competency to themselves. Most female addicts have lacked these opportunities in the past to a greater extent than male addicts.[58]

Because oppression is morally objectionable and its continuing existence threatens to undermine the ability of its victims to develop self-trust, feminist treatment centers should also work along with other groups to try to eliminate oppression in the lives of female addicts. For some addicts, however, oppression may have undermined their self-trust in such a profound way already that removing oppressive forces from their lives would have little effect. As Susan Babbitt argues in *Impossible Dreams*, feelings of incompetence and worthlessness can be so internalized that improvements to one's social environment would do little to change them. One form of self-distrust that may be extremely difficult to dislodge is Type III distrust in the agent's judgments about her own decision-making capacities. Even if she has been very successful in using these capacities in the past, if she distrusts her judgments about them, she will be inclined to interpret each success as a fluke. No matter how hard she reasons about their origin, she could interpret every good decision she makes in this way. When psychological damage caused by oppression is that severe, it may be unreasonable to expect addiction counselors to heal it. Still, it is possible, though certainly not guaranteed, that a supportive and loving environment in group sessions where people trust one another will heal such damage. What addiction counselors can do is figure out what sort of group dynamics can have that effect and try to reproduce them in future group sessions. What they need to do minimally is to understand the depth of the problem, lest they blame the clients for their own sense of frustration from ineffective treatment.

Treating any patient whose autonomy and self-trust are reduced because of her oppression is a complex matter. It must begin with understanding the political nature of oppression and recognizing the importance of finding ways to empower patients by helping to restore their autonomy, in addition to dealing with their physical symptoms. Much of this work is beyond the scope of health-care providers; it requires broadscale social and political change. Health care by itself cannot, of course, correct all of the evils of oppression. It cannot even cure all of the health-related effects of oppression. If health-care providers are to respond effectively to these problems, however, they must understand the impact of oppression on relational autonomy and make what efforts they can to increase the autonomy of their patients and clients. We have argued that this work must include efforts to help patients develop or strengthen their trust in themselves.

Notes

1. We wish to thank the editors, Catriona Mackenzie and Natalie Stoljar, for their very insightful and detailed comments on an earlier draft of this article. Their guidance has been invaluable. Much of our thinking on relational autonomy emerged through Susan's participation in the Feminist Health Care Ethics Research Network, supported by a Strategic Research Network Grant from the Social Sciences and Humanities Research Council of Canada. Carolyn completed her work on this article while on doctoral scholarships from the Social Sciences and Humanities Research Council of Canada and the Izaak Walton Killam Memorial Foundation.

2. We focus specifically on the ways in which autonomy is used in discussions of health-care ethics. We concentrate, particularly, on the approach of Tom L. Beauchamp and James F. Childress, *Principles of Biomedical Ethics*, 4th ed. (New York: Oxford University Press, 1994), because it is widely seen as the most influential account in the discipline.

3. For example, Beauchamp and Childress say: "We analyze autonomous action in terms of normal choosers who act (1) intentionally, (2) with understanding, and (3) without controlling influences that determine their action" (ibid., p. 123). They do not dwell on the nature of such "controlling influences" but cite examples that deal with compulsion and coercion.

4. For analysis of the concept of oppression, see Iris Marion Young's *Justice and the Politics of Difference* (Princeton, N.J.: Princeton University Press, 1991).

5. This is a central issue in Susan Babbitt's *Impossible Dreams: Rationality, Integrity, and Moral Imagination* (Boulder, Colo.: Westview, 1996).

6. For further development of this argument, see Susan Sherwin, "A Relational Approach to Autonomy in Health Care," in *The Politics of Women's Health: Exploring Agency and Autonomy*, The Feminist Health Care Ethics Research Network, coordinator Susan Sherwin (Philadelphia: Temple University Press, 1998).

7. See Marilyn Frye's *The Politics of Reality: Essays in Feminist Theory* (Freedom, Cal.: Crossing Press, 1983).

8. See Susan Sherwin, *No Longer Patient: Feminist Ethics and Health Care* (Philadelphia: Temple University Press, 1992).

9. Diana Tietjens Meyers, *Self, Society, and Personal Choice* (New York: Columbia University Press, 1989).

10. See Paul Benson, "Free Agency and Self-Worth," *The Journal of Philosophy* 91 (1994): 650–668; Robin Dillon, "Toward a Feminist Conception of Self-Respect," *Hypatia* 7 (Winter 1992): 52–69; and Babbitt, *Impossible Dreams*.

11. In "Self-Trust, Autonomy, and Self-Esteem," *Hypatia* 8 (Winter 1993): 99–120, Trudy Govier draws a connection between self-trust and autonomy, but she does not explore the impact of oppression on self-trust, as we do later.

12. The relation works the other way as well: developing self-trust requires some degree of autonomy. If we are not autonomous beings, we cannot know that the reasons we have for believing or feeling that we are competent and that we have good judgment relate to our own successes rather than successes for which we are not responsible. In *Self-Trust: A Study of Reason, Knowledge, and Autonomy* (New York: Oxford University Press, 1997), Keith Lehrer agrees that autonomy is necessary for self-trust, but he fails to see that the opposite is also the case. He argues that trusting ourselves involves knowing that we prefer and accept things that are worth accepting and preferring. He points out that if every evaluation we make is "imposed or fortuitous," we not only do not know that we are the ones preferring and accepting what is valuable or correct but also we cannot even trust our own judgment about what is valuable or correct in the first place (see especially p. 95).

13. Benson, "Free Agency," and Dillon, "Toward a Feminist Conception."

14. See Meyers, *Self, Society, and Personal Choice*, especially part 2.

15. Benson, "Free Agency," p. 664.

16. Govier explains in "Self-Trust, Autonomy" that self-trust can be merely situational. She contrasts situational self-trust with what she calls "core" self-trust (pp. 112–114).

17. For discussions of the subtle workings of oppression, see Sandra Lee Bartky, *Femininity and Domination: Studies in the Phenomenology of Oppression* (New York: Routledge, 1990), especially "Shame and Gender," pp. 83–98, and Robin Dillon's "Self-Respect: Moral, Emotional, Political," *Ethics* 107 (January 1997): 226–249.

18. See Annette Baier, *Moral Prejudices: Essays on Ethics* (Cambridge, Mass.: Harvard University Press, 1995), p. 10; Richard Holton, "Deciding to Trust, Coming to Believe," *Australasian Journal of Philosophy* 72 (March 1994): 63–76; Karen Jones, "Trust as an Affective Attitude," *Ethics* 107 (October 1996): 4–25; Trudy Govier, "Is It a Jungle Out There? Trust, Distrust and the Construction of Social Reality," *Dialogue* 33 (1994): 237–252.

19. Jones, "Trust as an Affective Attitude," p. 4.

20. For example, in "Self-Respect," Dillon argues that an important part of self-respect is "appreciating" (or trusting) our capacity to live up to expectations we have set for ourselves. Benson discusses the feeling free agents have of being "worthy to act," and at least part of what he means here is that they have trust in their "competen[cy] to answer for [their] conduct" ("Free Agency," p. 660).

21. Determining whether in fact self-trust and self-respect are distinct is more complicated than these comments suggest. The issue is complicated because the philosophical literature refers to different forms of self-respect (and they are reviewed by Dillon, "Self-Respect," pp. 228–232). Self-trust would have to be distinguished from each of these forms.

22. Holton, "Deciding to Trust," p. 71.

23. See Sherwin, *No Longer Patient*.

24. Of course, we recognize that some exercise of paternalism will be appropriate on occasion, but only in very limited circumstances. We do not want to deny the need for paternalism in classic cases of emergency care, for example. We do want to insist, though, that oppression should never be taken as license to presume consent that would not be presumed of other patients in comparable emergency situations.

25. See Anna C. Mastroianna, Ruth Faden, and Daniel Federman, eds., *Women and Health Research: Ethical and Legal Issues of Including Women in Clinical Studies*, 2 vols. (Washington, D.C.: National Academy Press, 1994).

26. The use of cosmetic surgery to promote oppressive norms is not restricted to gen-

der norms. Cosmetic surgeons also help transform people of Asian or African origin so that they appear more Caucasian, a more highly valued look in many parts of the world.

27. See James Foulks, "Should the Treatment of Narcotic Addiction be Compulsory?" *Annals of the Royal College of Physicians and Surgeons* 13 (July 1980): 232–239. Theorists about addiction treatment tend to focus now on ways to enhance the motivation of addicts to enter into treatment on their own. See Mark Schuckit, *Drug and Alcohol Abuse: A Clinical Guide to Diagnosis and Treatment*, 3rd ed. (New York: Plenum Medical Book Co., 1989), p. 263, and W. R. Miller, "Increasing Motivation for Change," in *Handbook of Alcoholism Treatment Approaches: Effective Alternatives,* ed. R. K. Hester and W. R. Miller (New York: Pergamon, 1990), pp. 67–80.

28. See B. A. Miller, W. R. Downs, D. M. Gondoli, and A. Keil, "The Role of Childhood Sexual Abuse in the Development of Alcoholism in Women," *Violence and Victims* 2 (1987): 157–172; W. R. Downs, B. A. Miller, and D. M. Gondoli, "Childhood Experiences of Parental Physical Violence for Alcoholic Women as Compared with a Randomly Selected Household Sample of Women," *Violence and Victims* 2 (1987): 225–240; and B. A. Miller, W. R. Downs, and D. M. Gondoli, "Spousal Violence among Alcoholic Women as Compared to a Random Household Sample of Women," *Journal of Studies on Alcohol* 50 (1989): 533–540.

29. S. S. Covinton and J. Kohen, "Women, Alcohol, and Sexuality," *Advances in Alcohol and Substance Abuse* 4 (1984): 41–56.

30. Ibid.; Miller et al., "Spousal Violence."

31. M. Bayatpour, R. D. Wells, and S. Holford, "Physical Violence and Sexual Abuse as Predictors of Substance Use and Suicide among Pregnant Teenagers," *The Journal of Adolescent Health* 13 (March 1992): 128–132.

32. See Young, *Justice and the Politics of Difference*, p. 62.

33. Ibid., p. 61.

34. Abuse or violence experienced by men who are not members of marginalized groups is not inherently political. Although their abuse may cause similar psychological damage as that motivated by oppressive social stereotypes, the underlying causes of the damage in each case differ.

35. See Govier, "Self-Trust, Autonomy"; William May, "The Molested," *Hastings Center Report* (May–June 1991): 9–17; Diane Lepine, "Ending the Cycle of Violence: Overcoming Guilt in Incest Survivors," in *Healing Voices: Feminist Approaches to Therapy with Women,* ed. Toni Ann Laidlaw, Cheryl Malmo, and associates (San Francisco: Jossey-Bass, 1990), pp. 272–287; Lena Dominelli, "Betrayal of Trust: A Feminist Analysis of Power Relationships in Incest Abuse and its Relevance for Social Work Practice," *British Journal of Social Work* 19 (1989): 291–307.

36. See Doris Brothers, "Trust Disturbances in Rape and Incest Victims," Ph.D. dissertation, Yeshiva University, New York, 1982; cited in Govier, "Self-Trust, Autonomy," pp. 99–101.

37. Lepine, "Ending the Cycle of Violence," p. 284.

38. For a definition of this syndrome, see Sue Campbell's "Women, 'False' Memory, and Personal Identity," *Hypatia* 12 (Spring 1997): 51–82, especially pp. 69, 70.

39. Ibid., p. 74.

40. Ibid.

41. See Dominelli, "Betrayal of Trust," p. 303.

42. It is important to point out that it has not been shown that all women who have addictions and have been abused develop their addiction after their abuse. Their addiction may have come first, and it also may have been a factor in their abuse. Female alcoholics, for example, may be more susceptible than other women to sexual abuse because they tend to be seen as "sexually loose" (Miller et al., "Spousal Violence," p. 538).

43. This point is made by Colleen Hood, Colin Mangham, and Don McGuire, "De-

tailed Analysis of Literature Pertaining to Substance Use and Mental Health," draft prepared for *Health Canada* (March 1995), pp. 21, 24.

44. Ibid., p. 59.

45. Stanton Peele, "What Works in Addiction Treatment and What Doesn't: Is the Best Therapy No Therapy?" *International Journal of the Addictions* 25 (1990–1991): 1409–1419; Amethyst Women's Addiction Centre, "Here's to You Sister. Creating a Women's Addiction Service: Amethyst's Story" (Ottawa: Amethyst Centre, 1997).

46. Ibid., p. 26.

47. The connection between autonomy and self-trust may not be relevant to all addicts because not all of them suffer serious problems with autonomy or self-trust. Among those who do not are most coffee drinkers, smokers, and people who have fairly mild addictions. Lack of autonomy is not a serious issue for people whose addictive behavior does not impair their ability to perform daily tasks.

48. See Sissela Bok's reply to a letter to the editor by Dr. Quentin Regestein on Bok's article, "Informed Consent, Deception, and Discovering Drug Abuse," *Journal of the American Medical Association* 268 (12 August 1992): 790, 791.

49. See Caroline Whitbeck, "Trust," *The Encyclopedia of Bioethics*, 2nd ed. (New York: Macmillan, 1995), pp. 2499–2504.

50. See Lepine, "Ending the Cycle of Violence," especially p. 275.

51. This criticism is described in Iris Marion Young, "Punishment, Treatment, Empowerment: Three Approaches to Policy for Pregnant Addicts," in *Expecting Trouble: Surrogacy, Fetal Abuse, and New Reproductive Technologies*, ed. Patricia Ann Poling (Bloomington: Indiana University Press, 1992), pp. 109–134; J. Yaffe, J. M. Jenson, and M. O. Howard, "Women and Substance Abuse: Implications for Treatment," *Alcoholism Treatment Quarterly* 13 (1995): 1–15; and Ann Abbott, "A Feminist Approach to Substance Abuse Treatment and Service Delivery," *Social Work in Health-care* 19 (1994): 67–83.

52. AMA, "Legal Interventions during Pregnancy: Court-Ordered Medical Treatments and Legal Penalties for Potentially Harmful Behavior by Pregnant Women," *Journal of the American Medical Association* 264 (28 November 1990): 2663–2670.

53. Among these feminists are Abbott, "Feminist Approach to Substance Abuse Treatment"; Young, "Punishment, Treatment, Empowerment"; and the authors of Amethyst Centre's "Here's to You Sister."

54. There are already at least two feminist programs in Canada—the Amethyst program in Ottawa and the Matrix program in Halifax. Both offer services for promoting self-esteem and dealing with sexual and other forms of abuse, and as we discuss below, these services may help their participants develop greater self-trust.

55. Amethyst Centre, "Here's to You Sister," pp. 6, 24.

56. Ibid., p. 35.

57. However, some female addicts should not be encouraged to feel more confident about at least certain aspects of their judgment during treatment. Whereas many female addicts were abused themselves, some also participated in abuse, as the following statistics reveal: over 95% of child sexual abusers are men (Dominelli, "Betrayal of Trust," p. 299), but almost 50% of child physical abusers are women, and a relevant factor in a large percentage of child physical abuse cases is alcoholism; see Linda Gordon, *Heroes of Their Own Lives: The Politics and History of Family Violence, Boston 1880–1960* (New York: Viking, 1988), pp. 173–175. Addiction counselors face the challenge of encouraging some women to increase their trust in their own judgment without letting them off the hook for having exercised very bad judgment in the past.

58. Judith Grant, "The Women and Substance Abuse Project: The Invisible Problem," Final Report submitted to Health Canada, Moncton, New Brunswick, February 1997, p. 8.

12

RELATIONAL AUTONOMY AND FREEDOM OF EXPRESSION[1]

Susan J. Brison

Introduction

A currently prevalent defense of the right to freedom of expression maintains that it rests on the right to autonomy.[2] On this account, governmental restrictions on an individual's speech and on a person's access to another's speech violate the person's right to autonomy.[3] In recent years, the autonomy defense of free speech has frequently been invoked in arguments against restrictions on hate speech,[4] although it is rarely made clear in these arguments what is meant by "autonomy." In an earlier article, "The Autonomy Defense of Free Speech,"[5] I examined six accounts of autonomy in the philosophical literature and argued that none yields a satisfactory argument against restrictions on hate speech and that five fail as accounts of autonomy. I suggested that the sixth—a relational account of autonomy—succeeds as an account of autonomy but does not yield the conclusion that an autonomy-based defense of free speech precludes restrictions on hate speech.

In this article I develop and defend such a relational account of autonomy, one based on Amartya Sen's account of capability,[6] and I discuss the ways in which it can, and cannot, be used to defend the right to free speech. I focus particularly on the application of this relational account of autonomy to recent controversies over hate speech, and I argue that although this relational account helps to explain why the right to speak and to receive others' speech is important, it does not yield a de-

280

fense of the view that speech is special, requiring greater justification for its regulation than is needed for the regulation of other conduct.

I define "hate speech" for purposes of this article as speech that vilifies individuals or groups on the basis of such characteristics as race, sex, ethnicity, religion, and sexual orientation and that (1) directly assaults its target(s), (2) creates a hostile environment, or (3) is a kind of group libel.[7] Some forms of pornography are put into the category of hate speech by those who consider it to be, as Susan Brownmiller put it, "the undiluted essence of antifemale propaganda."[8] Certainly not all that is labeled pornographic counts as hate speech against women. But much pornography presently on the market—especially the extremely violent and degrading variety that has been on the rise over the past decade—does count as hate speech when it is used to vilify individuals or groups by means of assaultive speech, the creation of a hostile environment, or group libel.[9]

The disjunctive definition of hate speech used here is based on definitions found in the ordinances of municipalities and on university campuses. The first disjunct, defining hate speech as directly targeted assaultive vilification, uses the so-called "fighting words" doctrine and was employed in the following code adopted by Stanford University:

> Speech or other expression constitutes harassment by vilification if it:
> a) is intended to insult or stigmatize an individual or a small number of individuals on the basis of their sex, race, color, handicap, religion, sexual orientation, or national and ethnic origin; and
> b) is addressed directly to the individual or individuals whom it insults or stigmatizes; and
> c) makes use of "fighting words" or non-verbal symbols [which] are commonly understood to convey direct and visceral hatred or contempt. . . .[10]

The second disjunct, defining hate speech as hostile environment harassment is based on a University of Michigan code regulating "[a]ny behavior, verbal or physical, that stigmatizes or victimizes an individual on the basis of race, ethnicity, religion, sex, sexual orientation, [etc.], and that . . . creates an intimidating, hostile, or demeaning environment. . . ."[11] The preceding is a partial definition taken from the University of Michigan Policy on Discrimination and Discriminatory Harassment, a policy that was ruled unconstitutional in *Doe v. University of Michigan.* This definition was based on existing sexual harassment law, prohibiting "hostile environment" harassment.[12]

The third disjunct, which characterizes hate speech as a kind of group libel, is modeled on criminal libel law, as well as on the tort of defamation. It holds that speech counts as hate speech if it (a) vilifies individuals or groups on the basis of sex, race, color, handicap, religion, sexual orientation, or national and ethnic origin and (b) harms the reputation of individuals or groups because of their sex, race, color, handicap, religion, sexual orientation, or national and ethnic origin. In *Beauharnais v. People of the State of Illinois,* the U.S. Supreme Court upheld an Illinois group libel law making it "unlawful for any person, firm or corporation to manufacture, sell . . . or exhibit . . . any publication [which] portrays depravity, criminality, unchastity, or lack of virtue of a class of citizens, of any race, color, creed or religion [and thereby] exposes [them] to contempt, derision, or obloquy or which is productive of breach of the peace or riots."[13] Although critics of *Beauharnais* consider its ruling on group libel laws to have been implicitly overturned by *New York Times Co. v. Sullivan*,[14] it has never been officially overruled by the Court and some legal theorists still consider it to be good law.[15] Recent court opinions—while conceding that hate speech, including some pornography, can cause considerable harm, for example, by undermining equality of opportunity—have struck down campus and municipal hate speech codes as well as an antipornography ordinance.[16]

Some opinions have claimed that the right to free speech outweighs the right to equality, without providing arguments for this claim. A number of influential liberal political philosophers and legal theorists, however, have argued that hate speech is and ought to be constitutionally protected, and they have defended their view by invoking a fundamental right to autonomy, which restrictions on such speech would violate.

The autonomy defense of free speech is typically presented as a nonconsequentialist defense. A number of consequentialist defenses of free speech have also been given: the argument from truth, the argument from diversity, the argument from democracy, the argument from distrust, the argument from tolerance, the pressure release argument, and the slippery slope argument. Mixed views combining two or more of these defenses have also been defended. I discuss these defenses elsewhere,[17] arguing that none succeeds as a defense of free speech and that none would preclude restrictions on hate speech. The autonomy defense is supposed to have the advantage over consequentialist accounts of showing why the right to free speech is immune to being balanced against other interests, but as I have argued, not all of the versions of the autonomy defense are nonconsequentialist, and even those that are do not show why restrictions on hate speech should be considered impermissible.[18]

A major problem with the legal literature on autonomy and free speech is that it frequently does not define the term "autonomy," with the result that the autonomy defense of free speech, in some of its versions, can be difficult to explicate and to evaluate. There are, however, hints of at least six different philosophical accounts of autonomy in the free speech literature. I have argued that five of these are unsatisfactory as accounts of autonomy and that they also fail to yield a defense of free speech that explains why hate speech should be protected.[19] These accounts are (1) autonomy as negative liberty,[20] (2) autonomy as moral independence,[21] (3) autonomy as a constraint (labeled the Millian principle) on the kinds of justification that can be used for governmental interference,[22](4) autonomy as a good that consists of the actual ability to be rationally self-legislating,[23] and (5) autonomy as self-fulfillment or self-realization.[24] I mentioned a sixth theory of autonomy, a relational account,[25] claiming that, although this is more plausible, it does not explain why speech should be given special protection. In the next two sections of this article, I elaborate on and defend these claims.

Relational Autonomy—A Capability-Based Account

The theory of autonomy I consider the most defensible is one kind of relational account of autonomy that holds that an agent's autonomy is dependent on her having an adequate capability to function, where "capability" is defined, following Sen, as "the various combinations of functionings (beings and doings) that the person can achieve."[26] In Sen's account, "Living may be seen as consisting of a set of interrelated 'functionings,' consisting of beings and doings."[27] The well-being of a person is dependent on functionings that range from "such elementary things as being adequately nourished, being in good health, avoiding escapable morbidity and premature mortality, etc., to more complex achievements such as being happy, having self-respect, taking part in the life of the community, and so on."[28]

I, like Sen, intentionally leave incomplete the specification of a capability set adequate for autonomy since any such specification, at this time, is bound to be too culturally specific. Although Martha Nussbaum has attempted to list the functionings necessary for (1) having a human life and (2) having a good, or flourishing, human life,[29] her lists, with their strong emphasis on the "separateness" of human individuals, are certainly controversial and arguably overly "Western" in orientation. However, I am not yet convinced that the specification of a capability set adequate for autonomy is impossible. Perhaps it could eventually be drawn up, after extensive cross-cultural dialogue, by arriving at an "overlapping consensus" among all cultures.[30] Or, alternatively, there may be no such consensus, and the best we can do is to come up with a cluster concept of an adequate capability set such that possession of a certain number of functionings in the set is sufficient to establish a family resemblance among various culturally contingent capability sets.[31] For the time being, I assume that a noncontroversial, minimal list of functionings specified in a capability set adequate for autonomy includes not only "such elementary things as being adequately nourished, being in good health, avoiding escapable morbidity and premature mortality, etc.," as Sen suggests, but also avoiding such autonomy-hindering, brain-disordering psychological and physiological states as extreme fear or anger, debilitating depression, and shattering pain.[32]

My view is that one has to be capable of achieving *some*—yet to be specified—set of functionings in order to be autonomous (and that one can be more or less autonomous depending upon one's capability set). It is the capability, rather than the achieved functionings, that is necessary for autonomy since one could autonomously choose not to achieve a functioning one is capable of achieving, for example, by choosing to fast when it is an option to eat. From the standpoint of autonomy, this is vastly different from starving. A person's capability set, on this view, is determined in large part by her relations to others and the functionings they enable or prevent her from achieving. On this theory, whether and to what extent we are autonomous depends on our relations to other people. This is so in at least three different senses.

First, we are, in Annette Baier's term, "second persons," dependent on others to enable us to develop and sustain the competencies required for autonomy.[33] Autonomy is thus causally relational—that is, it comes about (or fails to be brought about) as a result of relations with others in society. It can also be seen to be constitutively relational, in that it requires the right sorts of ongoing relations with others for it to be sustained. Second, to make autonomous choices, as I argue below, we need to have a range of significant options to choose from, and so we need to live in a society that makes these possible. Our personal, familial, social, political, and economic relations with others are what enable or inhibit our access to a range of significant options. Third, to perceive the availability of these options and to recognize their achievability *by us*, we need to live in a culture in which the norms and expectations do not preclude such recognition.

This account of autonomy is, thus, more substantive and normative than most in the literature. However, I share with Harry Frankfurt and Gerald Dworkin the view that an autonomous person is (to the extent that she is autonomous) able to govern herself—to choose which desires to act on—and this requires the ability to reflect on and/or endorse her desires. On the Frankfurt-G. Dworkin view, autonomy is an internal relation (between a higher and a lower self or between second-order desires and first-order desires). The relation is one of rational self-legislation.

Frankfurt's account stresses the necessity of the autonomous agent's endorsement of or identification with her action.[34] Since one way of achieving endorsement, however, is simply to modify one's second-order desires in order to bring them into line with one's first-order desires (which may still seem to us, intuitively, to be nonautonomously chosen), a preferable account is that of G. Dworkin, who counts as crucial to autonomy, not the agent's endorsement of the first-order desires acted on, but rather the agent's ability to critically reflect on and revise or reject first-order desires.[35]

However, a problem G. Dworkin's view of autonomy shares with Frankfurt's (and the variant on it defended by Baker and Redish) is that it is ahistorical, requiring us to look only at an internal relation within an agent at the time of choosing or acting to determine whether the choice or act is autonomous. A number of critics have raised objections to this aspect of the Frankfurt-G. Dworkin account of autonomy.[36] The "critical reflection" condition, to have any motivation, requires a historical account of the formation of higher-order desires. Some conditions under which higher-order desires are formed are autonomy undermining and others are autonomy enhancing. So the capacity for higher-order evaluation must be developed in the right way for it to yield autonomous decisions. John Christman attempts to specify this in a content-neutral way (by requiring that the agent be able to later endorse the means by which the capacity was developed), as does Diana T. Meyers (by requiring that the agent have and successfully employ "autonomy competency—the repertory of coordinated skills that makes self-discovery, Self-definition, and self-direction possible").[37]

My account of autonomy is, like Christman's and Meyers's, a historical one, in that it takes into acccount socialization and other forms of conditioning, specifying some conditions on the formation of higher-order desires.[38] If, for example, one has been socialized, in large part as a result of others' speech, to expect very little of herself or to defer to others, she is hardly in a position to make autonomous choices. To determine whether or not someone is autonomous or is choosing autonomously *now*, we need to know how that person came to have her preferences, including those leading her to the present choice. We need to know whether she developed the competencies necessary for autonomous preference formation and ranking.[39]

The historical account of the development of the competencies necessary for the exercising of autonomy provides a helpful elaboration of the first sense in which the capability account of autonomy is relational, that is, the sense in which we are "second persons." We develop the capacity for autonomy only after considerable interaction with others (parents, teachers, etc.) and socialization into the language, norms, and other aspects of a culture. As second persons, we also require for autonomous personhood the right sorts of ongoing relations with others. Since some forms of conditioning, socialization, and ongoing interactions with others are autonomy undermining, whereas others are autonomy enhancing, the degree to which one is able to be autonomous depends on one's past and present relations to others.

The second sense in which the capability account of autonomy is a relational one is that it takes into account not only the ways in which secondary desires get formed but also the range of important options available to people. As Joseph Raz argues, "If having an autonomous life is an ultimate value, then having a sufficient range of acceptable options is of intrinsic value, for it is constitutive of an autonomous life that it is lived in circumstances where acceptable alternatives are present."[40] The ruling idea behind what Raz calls "the ideal of personal autonomy" is "that people should make their own lives."[41] On this view, autonomy admits of degrees, and one is more or less autonomous according to, among other things, the range of goals one is aware of having as real options. As Raz puts it: "The autonomous person is a (part) author of his own life. The ideal of personal autonomy is the vision of people controlling, to some degree, their own destiny, fashioning it through successive decisions throughout their lives."[42] The sheer number of options is not what is relevant here. What matters is that there be a wide enough range of available *significant* options to yield an adequate capability set. To see if there is such a range, one must determine which options count as significant and what range of these options is necessary for autonomy. In this way, the capability account of autonomy is a substantive—and an explicitly normative—one, and thus differs from the purely procedural accounts of Christman and Meyers. If one has an inadequate range of significant options to choose from, one's autonomy is diminished, and the extent to which significant options are available to someone depends on the kind of society she lives in, as well as on her more personal relations with others.

The third sense in which a capability account of autonomy is relational is that it is a person's *ability to recognize* significant options as options *for her* that is crucial, and this also depends on others. For example, the capability theory of autonomy takes into account the phenomenon of adaptive preference formation, discussed by Jon Elster and by Sen, among others.[43] The sour grapes phenomenon (in which choosers eliminate or fail to form preferences that can't be satisfied because their objects are unattainable) is very common, especially among those historically deprived of equality of opportunity.

A capability account of autonomy requires not only a historical approach to studying the process of preference formation but also a normative specification of the capability set essential to autonomy. The two can be seen to be linked if we look at cases in which people's expectations are diminished, relative to what we think they ought to be, because of entrenched inequalities (legitimized by social norms) and long-term deprivations. As Sen observes: "a thoroughly deprived person, leading a very reduced life, might not appear to be badly off in terms of the mental metric of desire and its fulfilment, if the hardship is accepted with non-grumbling resignation."[44] Such resignation can be seen to be a rational response to a situation one cannot change. In such cases, *"prudential reasoning* would suggest that the victims should concentrate their desires on those limited things that they *can* possibly achieve, rather than fruitlessly pining for what is unattainable."[45] As Sen notes, the problem of entrenched deprivation "applies particularly to the differentiation of class, community, caste, and gender."[46] I would add that the processes by which deprivations become entrenched and expectations are lowered are largely ones that involve speech, that is, the social and cultural dissemination and reinforcement of, for example, racial and gender norms.

Relational Autonomy and Hate Speech

What does a capability account of autonomy have to do with freedom of expression in general and hate speech in particular?[47] One needs access to others' speech to know about one's available options. One also needs to be exposed to alternatives to propaganda and indoctrination. In addition, one needs to have some say about cultural norms to achieve the kind of self-definition necessary for autonomy. These considerations might lead one to suppose that unregulated speech is most conducive to autonomy.

However, unregulated speech can also undermine autonomy by diminishing one's capability set in critical ways. As defined at the beginning of this article, hate speech is speech that vilifies individuals or groups on the basis of such characteristics as race, sex, ethnicity, religion, and sexual orientation and that (1) directly assaults its target(s), (2) creates a hostile environment, or (3) is a kind of group libel. Hate speech of each of these three kinds can diminish one's capability set in distinctive ways. I examine each in turn.

1. Hate speech, defined as assaultive speech or "fighting words," can diminish one's capability set by incapacitating certain competencies required for autonomy. Assaultive speech—directed at an individual and made face to face—causes immediate injury in the form of an uncontrollable emotional response akin to the reaction to a slap in the face. It can also short-circuit reason, leading to a fearful "freeze, flight, or fight" response, as well as to responses such as rage, humiliation, and disorientation, all of which can interfere with the ability to reason and, thus, with the ability to think autonomously. I have discussed such effects of hate speech at length elsewhere.[48]

2. Hate speech that creates a hostile environment can diminish someone's capability set by affecting her self-esteem, her views about her options, her beliefs about her abilities, and the formation of her preferences. As Cass Sunstein argues, libertarians and many liberals have failed to give adequate attention to the ways in which social norms (as well as social roles and social meanings) influence preferences and choices. "We should agree," he argues, "that social norms play a part in determining choices; that people's choices are a function of their particular social role; and that the social or expressive meaning of acts is an ingredient in choice."[49] Of particular relevance to debates about hate speech is the observation that "individual agents have little control over social norms, social meanings, and social roles, even when they wish these to be very different from what they are."[50] This should not be taken

to be an argument for the incompatibility of autonomy with the existence of social norms, meanings, and roles since "human beings can live, and human liberty can exist, only within a system of norms, meanings, and roles; but in any particular form, these things can impose severe restrictions on well-being and autonomy."[51] But if the autonomy of private individuals can be threatened or undermined by norms over which they can, individually, have no control, this may provide justification for state intervention to modify the norms.

One form of such intervention—motivated by respect for autonomy—might be regulation of speech that interferes unduly with autonomous preference formation. If one grants the empirical claim conceded by the courts in the hate speech cases mentioned earlier (that *failure* to restrict such speech can impair the ability of individuals in targeted groups to act on *their* choices)—if the absence of restrictions can limit individuals' employment options, their political potential, and even undermine their ability to take advantage of those options that are available to them— then autonomy, in this sense, cannot be invoked to defend such a policy unless one adds the implausible claim that the threat to the would-be speakers' autonomy is even greater.

Preferences are affected not only by one's options but also by one's beliefs about the actual attainability of these options, and these beliefs are typically arrived at by receiving others' speech. First- *and* second-order desires are heavily influenced, if not instilled, by others' speech. Given that some kinds of influence are more more likely than others to interfere, illegitimately, with the formation of desires and volitions, an adequate theory of autonomy should count as autonomous those "decisions reached with a full and vivid awareness of available opportunities, with reference to all relevant information, and without illegitimate or excessive constraints on the process of preference formation."[52] If we are "second persons"—not just in the sense of having been formed by others in childhood, but also in that we continue to be shaped and sustained by others—then others' speech to and about us and ours to and about them are crucially important in the development and endurance of our autonomous selves. To be arbitrarily (or methodically) deprived of the ability to speak or of access to others' speech, when such speech is essential to autonomous selfhood, is to have one's autonomy impeded. But it is not only the government that can put up such impediments. As Owen Fiss, Frank Michelman, Cass Sunstein, and others have argued, private speakers (alone or as contributors to market forces) can interfere with others' speech as much as (or in some cases more than) the state can.[53] And, as Virginia Held and Judith Lichtenberg have argued, the absence of governmental regulation of speech does not always enhance access to informative speech.[54] In any case, it is useful information, not misinformation or excessive (i.e., too costly to process) information, that is needed for autonomy,[55] and it is an empirical question whether speech as unregulated by the government as it is now (of course, it is already regulated) is as "free" and as conducive to autonomy as is would be with more state control. It is not a question that can be decided a priori.

Judith Butler, in *Excitable Speech*,[56] acknowledges that speech can cause harm to individuals and groups, but she argues that this harm can be countered by linguistic intervention alone (and that governmental regulation would be counterproductive). Harmful racist or other epithets can, on her account, be reappropriated by their targets, defused by subversive usage, and turned into terms that empower rather than degrade those so labeled. This reappropriation has occurred, for example, with the term "queer." But this required a massive political and cultural movement, extended over a period of time, during which gays and lesbians continued to suffer because of others' use of the term. Even now, its use during a physical assault that is motivated by homophobia can add to the harm endured by the victim.

Although Butler's discussion of the ways in which hate speech can harm its targets is a sophisticated and welcome addition to the literature, her proposed remedy—reappropriating the terms used in hate speech, in effect, redressing the harms of hate speech with more speech—overestimates the extent to which individual victims can counter verbal assaults by reappropriating the very terms that historically have been used to degrade them. This remedy may be available to those who (1) do not feel isolated in their victimization, (2) are not silenced by the verbal assault, (3) are—and perceive themselves to be—members of powerful political groups, and (4) are—and perceive themselves to be—able to work in concert with others in their group to change the linguistic and cultural norms that gave and continue to give the hate speech the power to harm. There is considerable debate, for example, among African Americans about whether the "n-word" can be recuperated and given a positive spin. Although it is already used among some African Americans as a term of endearment, there are those who claim that it always carries a message of inferiority, no matter who uses it with whom.[57] A further worry about the increasing acceptance of the term is that those who are not African American may begin to consider it acceptable for *them* to use to label blacks, even though in this context the word can still wound in autonomy-undermining ways.

3. Hate speech that constitutes group libel can reduce a person's available options by affecting others' beliefs about her, as well as their behavior toward her. Libel is written (or printed or depicted) defamation, as opposed to slander, which is spoken.[58] Defamation is defined (in Prosser's classic text on torts) as communication that "tends so to harm the reputation of another as to lower him in the estimation of the community or to deter third persons from associating or dealing with him."[59] Prosser goes on to note that "communications are often defamatory because they tend to expose another to hatred, ridicule or contempt."[60] In tort law, however, only those who defame individuals are subject to liability: "One who publishes defamatory matter concerning a group or class of persons is subject to liability to an individual member of it if, but only if, (a) the group or class is so small that the matter can reasonably be understood to refer to the member, or (b) the circumstances of publication reasonably give rise to the conclusion that there is particular reference to the member."[61]

Richard Delgado, in his now classic article "Words That Wound," has called for an independent tort action for racial insults and epithets. Such a tort would, Delgado argues, "protect the interests of personality and equal citizenship that are part of our highest political traditions and moral values, thereby affirming the right of all citizens to lead their lives free from attacks on their dignity and psychological integrity."[62]

There is already, however, a constitutional precedent for considering group libel to be sanctionable as criminal behavior. In 1952, the U.S. Supreme Court upheld the constitutionality of a state law that criminalized group libel, in *Beauharnais v. People of the State of Illinois*.[63] The law in question stated: "It shall be unlawful for any person . . . to manufacture, sell . . . present or exhibit in any public place in this state any [speech that] . . . exposes the citizens of any race, color, creed or religion to contempt, derision, or obloquy or which is productive of breach of the peace or riots."[64] In *Collin v. Smith*,[65] the court considered *Beauharnais* to be no longer authoritative, in light of rulings in such cases as *New York Times Co. v. Sullivan*.[66] However, *Beauharnais* has not been formally overturned, nor has the discussion of libel of a public figure in *New York Times v. Sullivan* been explicitly applied by the courts to the question of group libel. Kenneth Lasson has argued that *Beauharnais* is still good law and has noted that group libel statutes are still in the criminal codes of five states.[67]

Furthermore, there are grounds for rejecting the individualism that underlies the dichotomy between private and group libel. As Isaiah Berlin wrote in his famous essay "Two Concepts of Liberty":

> Even Mill's strenuous effort to mark the distinction between the spheres of private and social life breaks down under examination. Virtually all Mill's critics have pointed out that everything that I do may have results which will harm other human beings. Moreover, I am a social being in a deeper sense than that of interaction with others. For am I not what I am, to some degree, in virtue of what others think and feel me to be?[68]

The view that people can be libeled by hate speech has gotten short shrift in the legal literature, not only because of liberal and libertarian views concerning privacy and individualism, but also because of the dominant focus on audience-centered views of free speech. In First Amendment jurisprudence, as Thomas Scanlon has noted, different interests come to the fore in discussions of the various categories of expression. This has yielded the following set of approaches to free speech: the speaker-centered (or what Scanlon calls "participant-centered") approach, the audience-centered approach, and the bystander-centered approach (in which bystanders are those affected by the speech, although not in the willing audience for it).[69] Political speech, it is argued, lends itself to the first approach, commercial speech more appropriately falls into the second, and libel is in the third. The question remains of whether a speaker-centered, audience-centered, or bystander centered approach to a theory of free speech is the most appropriate in the area of hate speech.

One might be able to use an audience-centered approach to argue for the regulation of hate speech (or at least that variety of it that encourages false views about the groups targeted by it). Such an argument would mirror the defense of restrictions on false or misleading advertising: Those individuals who try to apply these false hate speech–induced beliefs in their relations with real people may be led to make serious, culpable mistakes in judgment. So an audience-centered approach could conceivably lead to arguments for restricting hate speech, as well as false or misleading commercial speech.

A weightier argument for regulation of hate speech is one that takes seriously the question of bystanders' interests, that is, the interests of those who are not in the willing audience for the speech but who are nonetheless affected by it. In discussing libel, as well as hate speech of the group libel variety, I think it is important to divide the category of bystanders into two categories: targets (those the hate speech is directed to or about and who are affected by it) and bystanders (those affected by the speech who are not the targets of it). A speaker may have a very great interest in writing (falsely) that Jones committed some heinous crime (if he wants to frame Jones to get himself off the hook or if he is angry with Jones and feeling vindictive), and a given audience may have a very great interest in reading this bit of libel (perhaps they are predisposed to believe it since they dislike Jones or Jones's race for other reasons and this makes them feel vindicated in their prejudice, or perhaps they are put at ease by the "fact" that the criminal has been pinpointed).

This combination of speaker's and audience's interests is simply not enough to warrant protection for the libelous speech. We have to take the target (Jones) into account, and in this case her interests are overriding. (Joel Feinberg would say this is so even in the case of very damaging *truths* about a private person that the public simply doesn't need to know.[70]) In addition, the bystanders—that is, others not targeted by the speech, not in the willing audience for it, but nonetheless affected by it—may have interests in avoiding exposure (and reducing others' exposure) to it. In this balancing of competing interests, a great deal of weight is given to the target's interests, so much so that it makes sense to call the First Amendment jurisprudence of individual libel (of private figures) "target centered." If one accepts a target-centered account of free speech in the area of (individual) libel, one ought to accept it in the area of group libel, including hate speech that takes that form.[71]

To see why, consider the following example. Suppose you are a black male and someone publishes a newspaper article claiming (falsely, obviously) that black males have a propensity to rape. Why should this not count as libelous material, damaging to your interest in your character and reputation?[72] As the majority stated in *Beauharnais v. Illinois,*

> It would . . . be arrant dogmatism . . . to deny that . . . a man's job and his educational opportunities and the dignity accorded him may depend as much on the reputation of the racial and religious group to which he willy-nilly belongs, as on his own merits. This being so, we are precluded from saying that speech concededly punishable when immediately directed at individuals cannot be outlawed if directed at groups with whose position and esteem in society the affiliated individual may be inextricably involved.[73]

However, although it has to be shown that statements or depictions that defame even large groups can harm individual members of those groups, this is easily done. It is acknowledged, in discussions of affirmative action, for example, that individuals can suffer harms in virtue of being members of stigmatized groups. And few would deny that defamatory statements and depictions contribute to and perpetuate such harmful stigmatization. It has been argued, though, that the harm to an individual member of an attacked group cannot, at any rate, be very great if the targeted group is large. As Feinberg argues: "Racist and porno films do not directly insult specific individuals, but rather large groups, thus diluting the impact of the insult, or at least its directed personal character, proportionately." He compares porno films with an invented genre of popular racist films that cater to secret haters of blacks, the main features of which would be

> stories of uppity blacks put in their place by righteous whites, taunted and hounded, tarred and feathered, tortured and castrated, and in the climactic scenes, hung up on gallows to the general rejoicing of their betters. The aim of the films would be to provide a delicious catharsis of pent-up hatred. It would be prudent, on business grounds, to keep advertisements discreet, and to use euphemistic descriptions like "folk films" (analogous to "adult films").[74]

He goes on to argue that since the degree of insult to an individual varies inversely with the size of the insulted group, "the 'folk films' might be more serious affronts in this respect than the porno films since their target is a much smaller group than half of the human race. . . . A black man might be more likely to feel a *personal* grievance at the folk film he does not witness than a woman would to a porno film she does not witness. . . ."[75] How black women might appropriately react to both genres, especially given the actual proliferation of racist pornography, is not considered.

The flaw in Feinberg's proportionality-of-injury argument is that the ease with which the individual is identified with the group, the social standing of the group, and the history of its treatment are all much more relevant to the degree of harm suffered by individuals in the targeted group than is the relative size of the group. If you are a black woman saxophone player, you are more likely to be harmed by defamatory attacks on blacks and on women than by attacks on saxophone players. And, in any case, as David Riesman pointed out, in an early article on group libel: "It is hard to see why courts should be solicitous of a defendant who has hurt many people rather than a few or one. In many political and social situations, it is likely that the larger the defamed group—if the defamation can actually be made to stick as 'truth'—the more likely that social dangers will ensue."[76] In the case of already stigmatized groups, defamatory attacks all too frequently "stick as 'truth.'" Members of such groups are easily stereotyped, which enables a degrading description or depiction of the group to lead to diminished respect for all its members.[77]

A critic of my position might concede that a *description* of a group, say, women, might well defame them but deny that there could be a *depiction* that defames all the members of a group. For example, it might be denied that *women* as a class could be defamed by a degrading, misleading, pornographic picture, photo, or film that counts as hate speech and targets women.

To reply to this objection, I must first establish that such a defamatory depiction *can* refer to women in general, given that the depiction itself is a particular and is sometimes a depiction *of* a particular woman. Is it possible to depict a group by means of a particular depiction or a depiction of one of its members? We know, from Berkeley's critique of Locke's theory of abstraction,[78] that representing a general category, say, of triangles, is not a matter of constructing an abstract mental image that somehow manages to capture all the features of particular triangles and none of the features that aren't held in common. Rather, having the general idea of triangularity involves being able to use an image of a particular triangle to stand for all triangles. We frequently use pictures in this way, and not only the highly stylized

pictograms found on restroom doors and highway signs. In dictionaries and ency-
clopedias, a photograph of an individual plant or animal is frequently used to refer
to the entire species to which it belongs.

What many degrading symbols or depictions have in common with such pictograms and photographs is their ability to be used as general terms. A photograph
or a caricature of an individual woman can be seen as a depiction of women in general.[79] This is a function of how it is used, and the viewing context plays a large role
in determining the generality of the reference. In this way, depictions, as well as descriptions, can libel groups of individuals.

Group libel, in addition to causing or entrenching harmful stereotypes, can also
undermine the autonomy of individuals by depriving them of a multicultural environment that enhances opportunities for choice. As Raz argues, one needs the options afforded by a multicultural society to be fully autonomous *and* one also needs
to live in a society in which one's culture is not merely tolerated but respected and
encouraged.[80] Hate speech of the group libel variety can undermine multiculturalism, as well as lead to increased disrespect for those in the targeted cultural groups.

It is not only the autonomy of targets that is undermined by group libel. Participant, audience, and bystander autonomy may also be diminished rather than enhanced by unregulated hate speech of this variety. It should be noted that those who
engage in hate speech are as much products of the cultural norms and practices
around them as are their targets. One cannot assume that they are acting autonomously in uttering such speech.[81] Willing audience members, such as the
young, impressionable, and socially vulnerable skinheads recruited by Tom Metz-
ger's Aryan Resistance League, may succumb to autonomy-bypassing indoctrination
techniques. Even those of us bystanders who do not use hate speech, who are not a
willing audience for it, and who strive to rid ourselves of all racist beliefs, for example, can find unbidden and unwelcome racist epithets popping into our minds. Mari
Matsuda reports, for example, that upon seeing a Hindu woman, she found the
word "dot-buster" involuntarily entering her consciousness, instead of something
she would have chosen to think, say, "what a lovely sari."[82]

Thus the extent to which hate speech itself is the result of an autonomously
made choice is not clear. Although those who have given the autonomy defense of
free speech have assumed that the speaker is always speaking autonomously, this
is not always the case. As Kendall Thomas has pointed out, at least some of those
engaged in hate speech, especially young persons, appear to be "channeling" the voices
of others, unthinkingly parroting their speech.[83] On a capability account of autonomy, if one's second-order volitions (to engage in hate speech, for example)
may be formed by indoctrination or brainwashing and not in the right (autonomy-
respecting) way, one's acted-on first-order desires are not necessarily autonomously
chosen.

Speech is nonetheless important to autonomy: it can enhance *and* undermine it.
Freedom of expression, when construed as a positive freedom actually to speak and to
be heard, can at times be seen to be instrumental in the development of autonomous
persons. A capability account of autonomy does *not*, however, yield a distinct principle of freedom of expression. That is, it does not provide a defense of the principle
that the government requires greater reason to regulate speech than it needs to justify

the regulation of other conduct. In particular, unregulated hate speech is not necessarily autonomously chosen speech, and it can sometimes undermine its targets' capacity for autonomy by diminishing, in significant ways, their capability sets. We
need to look at the autonomy-enhancing and the autonomy-undermining effects of
such speech—on the speakers, audience, bystanders, and targets—on a case-by-case
basis, to determine whether regulating it would promote or undercut autonomy.

Notes

1. I am extremely grateful to Catriona Mackenzie and Natalie Stoljar for their encouragement, patience, and extraordinarily helpful comments on an earlier draft. I also thank
them, Sarah Buss, Diana T. Meyers, Yael Tamir, and Thomas Trezise for ongoing discussions
about the nature of autonomy. I am indebted to the School of Social Science at the Institute
for Advanced Study for supporting this work through a fellowship funded by the National
Endowment for the Humanities, during 1997–1998.

2. I use the term "free speech" interchangeably with "freedom of expression," and I use
them both to cover freedom of the press as well. I am drawing primarily on literature by free
speech theorists in the United States who assume the existence of a constitutional right to
free speech, as specified in the First Amendment. Autonomy defenses of free speech can be
found in David A. J. Richards: "Autonomy in Law," in *The Inner Citadel: Essays on Individual
Autonomy*, ed. John Christman (New York: Oxford University Press, 1989); "Free Speech and
Obscenity Law: Toward a Moral Theory of the First Amendment," *University of Pennsylvania
Law Review* 123 (1974): 45–91; "Pornography Commissions and the First Amendment: On
Constitutional Values and Constitutional Facts," *Maine Law Review* 39 (1987): 275–320;
and "Toleration and Free Speech," *Philosophy and Public Affairs* 17 (1988): 323–336; Ronald
Dworkin: *A Matter of Principle* (Cambridge, Mass.: Harvard University Press, 1985), pp.
353–372; "Liberty and Pornography," *New York Review of Books*, 15 August 1991, pp.
12–15; "Women and Pornography," *New York Review of Books*, 21 October 1993, pp.
36–42; and "The Coming Battles over Free Speech," *New York Review of Books*, 11 June
1992, pp. 55–64; Thomas Scanlon, "A Theory of Freedom of Expression," *Philosophy and
Public Affairs* 1 (1972): 204–226, and "Freedom of Expression and Categories of Expression," *University of Pittsburgh Law Review* 40 (1979): 519–550; Charles Fried, "The New
First Amendment Jurisprudence: A Threat to Liberty," *The Bill of Rights in the Modern State*,
ed. Geoffrey R. Stone, Richard A. Epstein, and Cass Sunstein (Chicago: University of
Chicago Press, 1992); David Strauss, "Persuasion, Autonomy, and Freedom of Expression,"
Columbia Law Review 91 (1991): 334–371; Martin H. Redish, *Freedom of Expression: A
Critical Analysis* (Charlottesville, Va.: Michie Company, 1984); C. Edwin Baker, "Scope of
the First Amendment Freedom of Speech," *UCLA Law Review* 25 (1978): 964–990, and
Human Liberty and Freedom of Speech (New York: Oxford University Press, 1989); Diana T.
Meyers, "Rights in Collision: A Non-punitive Compensatory Remedy for Abusive Speech,"
Law and Philosophy 14 (1995): 203–243; Thomas Nagel, "Personal Rights and Public
Space," *Philosophy and Public Affairs* 24 (1995): 83–107. Kent Greenawalt, who criticizes
some attempts to ground free speech in the singular value of autonomy, nonetheless appeals
to autonomy as one of "the subtle plurality of values that does govern the practice of freedom
of speech." See "Free Speech Justifications," *Columbia Law Review* 89 (1989): 119–155, 119.

3. Although not all of those giving the autonomy defense state this explicity, I assume
that they hold that *some* kinds of speech, for example, false advertising, perjury, and insider
trading, may be restricted without anyone's autonomy being violated. If a person shouted

"drop dead," causing everyone within earshot to drop dead, presumably the banning of such speech would not be prohibited by respect for autonomy.

4. See the sources in note 1.

5. Susan J. Brison, "The Autonomy Defense of Free Speech," *Ethics* 108 (January 1998): 312–339.

6. For presentations of Sen's account of equality of capability, see Amartya Sen, "Gender Inequality and Theories of Justice," in *Women, Culture, and Development.* ed. Martha Nussbaum and Jonathan Glover (New York: Oxford University Press, 1995); *Inequality Reexamined* (Cambridge, Mass.: Harvard University Press, 1992); "Well-being, Agency, and Freedom: The Dewey Lectures 1984," *The Journal of Philosophy* 82 (April 1985): 169–220; and "Rights and Agency," *Philosophy and Public Affairs* 11 (Winter 1982): 187–223.

7. The definition that follows is similar to the one given in "Autonomy Defense of Free Speech," pp. 313–315, although some of the terminology has been changed. For a selected list of reported incidents of hate speech on college campuses from 1986 to 1988, see Howard J. Ehrlich, *Campus Ethnoviolence and the Policy Options* (Baltimore: National Institute against Prejudice & Violence, 1990), appendix. For discussions of numerous incidents of hate speech through 1994, see *The Price We Pay: The Case against Racist Speech, Hate Propaganda, and Pornography*, ed. Laura J. Lederer and Richard Delgado (New York: Hill & Wang, 1995).

8. Susan Brownmiller, *Against Our Will: Men, Women and Rape* (New York: Bantam Books, 1975), p. 443.

9. For numerous examples of pornography that could be construed as hate speech under this definition, see the analyses of pornography in Catharine MacKinnon, *Feminism Unmodified: Discourses on Life and Law* (Cambridge, Mass.: Harvard University Press, 1987); *Only Words* (Cambridge, Mass.: Harvard University Press, 1993); and *Toward a Feminist Theory of the State* (Cambridge, Mass.: Harvard University Press, 1993); Attorney General's Commission on Pornography, *Final Report*, U.S. Department of Justice, July 1986; Laura Lederer, ed., *Take Back the Night: Women on Pornography* (New York: William Morrow, 1980); Catherine Itzen, ed., *Pornography: Women, Violence and Civil Liberties* (New York: Oxford University Press, 1992); and Lederer and Delgado, *Price We Pay.*

10. Quoted in Charles R. Lawrence III, "If He Hollers Let Him Go: Regulating Racist Speech on Campus," in Mari J. Matsuda et al., *Words That Wound: Critical Race Theory, Assaultive Speech, and the First Amendment* (Boulder, Colo.: Westview Press, 1993), p. 67. "Fighting words" were originally defined by the U. S. Supreme Court as words or symbols "which by their very utterance inflict injury or tend to incite an immediate breach of the peace." *Chaplinsky v. State of New Hampshire*, 315 U.S. 568 (1942), 572. For a discussion of the fighting words doctrine, see Susan J. Brison, "Speech, Harm, and the Mind-Body Problem in First Amendment Jurisprudence," *Legal Theory* 4 (1998): 39–61. The Stanford code was struck down by the court because of the Leonard law, which requires even private educational institutions in California to abide by the U.S. Constitution. *Corry v. Leland Stanford Junior University*, California Superior Court at Santa Clara, case no. 740309, 27 February 1995.

11. *Doe v. University of Michigan*, 721 F.Supp. 852 (E.D.Mich. 1989), 856.

12. See *Meritor Savings Bank v. Vinson*, 477 U.S. 57 (1986).

13. *Beauharnais v. People of the State of Illinois*, 72 S. Ct. 725 (1952), 728.

14. *New York Times Co. v. Sullivan*, 376 U.S. 254 (1964).

15. See, for example, Kenneth Lasson, "Group Libel versus Free Speech: When Big Brother *Should* Butt In," *Duquesne Law Review* 23 (1984): 77–130. I employ the disjunctive definition of hate speech because it captures most of what has been called hate speech in the legal literature. I do not claim that this is the only or the best definition. I am not arguing that it would pass constitutional muster at a public university or that it would be good

policy at a private one. If used in a hate speech code at a public university and then challenged in the courts, this definition would certainly raise questions about vagueness and overbreadth, and the group libel disjunct would probably be ruled unconstitutional for lack of a clear legal precedent. I am using this definition in an attempt to delimit the class of what counts as hate speech to examine whether the autonomy defense of free speech explains why this speech should be protected.

16. See *Doe v. University of Michigan; UWM Post v. Board of Regents of the University of Wisconsin,* 774 F.Supp. 1163 (E.D. Wis. 1991); *American Booksellers Association v. Hudnut,* 771 F.2d 323 (7th Cir. 1985). Since the courts have made this concession, I am not defending this controversial empirical claim here. I discuss the harms of hate speech in "Speech, Harm, and the Mind-Body Problem" in response to those who deny that speech can harm and to those who attempt to make a sharp, morally and legally relevant distinction between speech-caused harms and other harms. In this article, I discuss the ways in which some of the harms of hate speech undermine autonomy.

17. Susan J. Brison, *Speech, Harm, and Conflicts of Rights* (Princeton, N.J.: Princeton University Press, 2000).

18. Brison, "Autonomy Defense of Free Speech."

19. Ibid.

20. On this view, autonomy is simply freedom from governmental interference in some specified domain. Thus a right to autonomy is a side constraint on governmental action. The term "negative liberty" was defined by Isaiah Berlin and contrasted with "positive liberty" in his "Two Concepts of Liberty," in *Four Essays on Liberty* (New York: Oxford University Press, 1969). Ronald Dworkin employs and defends this account of autonomy in "Liberty and Pornography."

21. In this account, defended by Ronald Dworkin in *Matter of Principle,* to restrict people's speech (or their access to others' speech) out of contempt for their way of life or their view of the good violates their right to moral independence or autonomy. This amounts to an unacceptable failure to treat them with equal respect and concern. Since rights, according to Dworkin, trump considerations of social utility: "if someone has a right to moral independence, this means that it is . . . wrong for officials to act in violation of that right, even if they (correctly) believe that the community as a whole would be better off if they did" (p. 359). Dworkin also uses this approach in two more recent articles: "The Coming Battles over Free Speech" and "Women and Pornography."

22. Thomas Scanlon ("Theory of Freedom of Expression, p. 213) defines the Millian principle as follows:

> There are certain harms which, although they would not occur but for certain acts of expression, nonetheless cannot be taken as part of a justification for legal restrictions on these acts. These harms are: (a) harms to certain individuals which consist in their coming to have false beliefs as a result of those acts of expression; (b) harmful consequences of acts performed as a result of those acts of expression, where the connection between the acts of expression and the subsequent harmful acts consists merely in the fact that the act of expression led the agents to believe (or increased their tendency to believe) these acts to be worth performing.

(Although Scanlon calls this "The Millian Principle," it owes more to Kant than to Mill.)

23. This view is defended by Scanlon in a more recent article, "Freedom of Expression," p. 533. This account of autonomy suggests a view of the self divided against itself—a true, higher, sovereign self and an impulsive, lower self that occasionally needs to be brought into line. An autonomous person is able to control herself—to choose which desires to act on—and this requires the ability to reflect on her desires. Harry Frankfurt has argued that it is this

ability to have second-order desires concerning first-order desires that sets humans apart from the beasts. See "Freedom of the Will and the Concept of a Person," in *The Importance of What We Care About* (New York: Cambridge University Press, 1988), p. 12. Although Scanlon himself does not invoke Frankfurt's account of autonomy, it is the position in the philosophical literature on autonomy that appears to be closest to the view Scanlon invokes in this later article on free speech.

24. Versions of this kind of account are advocated by Baker, "Scope of the First Amendment," and by Redish, *Freedom of Expression*.

25. Influential relational accounts of autonomy include those advocated by Diana T. Meyers, "Personal Autonomy and the Paradox of Feminine Socialization," *Journal of Philosophy* 84 (1987): 619–628, and *Self, Society, and Personal Choice* (New York: Columbia University Press, 1989); Jennifer Nedelsky, "Reconceiving Autonomy: Sources, Thoughts, and Possibilities," *Yale Journal of Law and Feminism* 1 (1989): 7–26; and Marilyn Friedman, "Autonomy and Social Relationships: Rethinking the Feminist Critique," in *Feminists Rethink the Self*, ed. Diana T. Meyers (Boulder, Colo.: Westview, 1997).

26. Sen, *Inequality Reexamined*, p. 40.

27. Ibid., p. 39.

28. Ibid.

29. Martha C. Nussbaum, "Human Capabilities, Female Human Beings," in *Women, Culture, and Development: A Study of Human Capabilities*, ed. Martha C. Nussbaum and Jonathan Glover (Oxford: Clarendon Press, 1995), pp. 61–104.

30. Such an account of a cross-cultural overlapping consensus is given by Charles Taylor, "Conditions of an Unforced Consensus on Human Rights," in *The East Asian Challenge for Human Rights*, ed. Joanne R. Bauer and Daniel A. Bell (New York: Cambridge University Press, 1999), pp. 124–144. I thank Leslye Obiora for drawing my attention to this article.

31. This suggestion is inspired by Natalie Stoljar's work on feminism and essentialism. For her account of "woman" as a cluster concept, see "Essence , Identity and the Concept of Woman," *Philosophical Topics* 23 (1995): 261–294.

32. Sarah Buss defends a similarly normative "human flourishing condition" on autonomy, arguing that it "both reflects and and illuminates the widely shared intuition that autonomy can be undermined by pain, fear, depression, anger, and other 'negative' psychological and physiological conditions." "How to Express Yourself in Your Actions," unpublished manuscript, available from author, p. 17.

33. Annette Baier, *Postures of the Mind: Essays on Mind and Morals* (Minneapolis: University of Minnesota Press, 1985); Lorraine Code, "Second Persons," in *What Can She Know?* (Ithaca, N.Y.: Cornell University Press, 1991), pp. 71–109; and Virginia Held, *Feminist Morality* (Chicago: University of Chicago Press, 1993), pp. 57–64.

34. Frankfurt, "Freedom of the Will." See also "Three Concepts of Free Action," "Identification and Externality," and "Identification and Wholeheartedness," all in *Importance of What We Care About*.

35. Gerald Dworkin, *The Theory and Practice of Autonomy* (New York: Cambridge University Press, 1988); see especially pp.15–17 for his reasons for rejecting the endorsement account.

36. For an excellent summary of discussions of the ab initio and the infinite regress problems in such an account, see Christman, *Inner Citadel*, pp. 6–12.

37. John Christman, "Autonomy and Personal History," *Canadian Journal of Philosophy* 21 (1991): 1–24; Meyers, *Self, Society, and Personal Choice*, p. 76.

38. For other discussions of the role of socialization in the development of the capacity for autonomy, see Joseph Raz, *The Morality of Freedom* (New York: Oxford University

Press, 1986), and Cass Sunstein, "Preferences and Politics," *Philosophy and Public Affairs* 20 (1991): 3–34.

39. For a discussion of these competencies, see Meyers, *Self, Society, and Personal Choice.*

40. Raz, *Morality of Freedom*, p. 205; see also pp. 373–380.

41. Ibid., p. 369.

42. Ibid. Note that being an author does not require making up all of one's own language, literary conventions, character types, plot lines, and so on, although it does require making some choices within (or against) available options.

43. Jon Elster, *Sour Grapes* (New York: Cambridge University Press, 1983); Sen, *Inequality Reexamined*; see especially p. 55, where Sen discusses the effects of entrenched inequalities and deprivations on preferences. See also Meir Dan-Cohen, "Conceptions of Choice and Conceptions of Autonomy," *Ethics* 102 (1992): 221–243.

44. Sen, *Inequality Reexamined*, p. 55.

45. Ibid.

46. Ibid.

47. A capability account of autonomy has not, however, been explicity invoked in the literature in defense of free speech, although Meyers has suggested, in "Rights in Collision," that an appeal to her relational account of autonomy, combined with the argument from democracy, can be used to defend the right to engage in even abusive hate speech.

48. Brison, "Speech, Harm, and the Mind-Body Problem," pp. 48–50. See also Drucilla Cornell's discussion of encounters with unavoidable public displays of pornography as assaults on one's own self conception and on one's imaginary domain: *The Imaginary Domain: Abortion, Pornography and Sexual Harassment* (New York: Routledge, 1995), pp. 147–158.

49. Cass R. Sunstein, "Social Norms and Social Roles," *Columbia Law Review* 96 (1996): 911.

50. Ibid.

51. Ibid.

52. Sunstein, "Preferences and Politics," p. 11.

53. Owen Fiss, "Why the State?" *Harvard Law Review* 100 (1987): 781–794; Frank Michelman, "Conceptions of Democracy in American Constitutional Argument: The Case of Pornography Regulation," *Tennessee Law Review* 56 (1989): 291–319; Cass R. Sunstein, *Democracy and the Problem of Free Speech* (New York: Free Press, 1993).

54. Virginia Held, "Access, Enablement, and the First Amendment," *Philosophical Dimensions of the Constitution,* ed. Diana T. Meyers and Kenneth Kipnis (Boulder, Colo.: Westview, 1988); Judith Lichtenberg, "Foundations and Limits of Freedom of the Press," *Philosophy and Public Affairs* 16 (1987): 329–355.

55. For discussions of the potentially autonomy-undermining effects of too much choice resulting from too much information, see Gerald Dworkin, "Is More Choice Better than Less?" in *Theory and Practice of Autonomy*, pp. 62–81, and Catriona Mackenzie, "Bodily Autonomy," unpublished manuscript.

56. Judith Butler, *Excitable Speech: A Politics of the Performative* (New York: Routledge, 1997).

57. Catherine Williams and thousands of others, including the membership of the NAACP (National Association for the Advancement of Colored People), protested Miriam Webster's dictionary definition of "nigger" as "a black person—usually offensive." They lobbied to substitute a definition that stressed the derogatory and dehumanizing aspects of the term. National Public Radio, "Morning Edition," 16 March 1998.

58. I would apply the following discussion of the autonomy-undermining effects of group libel to group slander as well. However, it is group libel that has been explicitly considered, by the Court, to have the autonomy-undermining aspects I discuss below.

59. Prosser, *Restatement of Torts*, 2nd ed. (1977), §559.

60. Ibid., p. 156.

61. Ibid., §564A, pp. 167–168.

62. Delgado, "Words That Wound: A Tort Action for Racial Insults, Epithets and Name Calling," in *Words That Wound*, p. 110.

63. *Beauharnais*.

64. Ibid.

65. 578 F.2d 1197 (7th Cir. 1978), certiorari denied, 439 U.S. 915 (1978).

66. 376 U.S. 254 (1964).

67. Kennth Lasson, "In Defense of Group-Libel Laws or Why the First Amendment Should Not Protect Nazis," *Human Rights Annual*, vol. 2 (1985), p. 298. Lasson notes that in four of these states (Connecticut, Massachusetts, Montana, and Nevada), "the gravamen of the offense is holding up to ridicule, hatred, or contempt of any group or class of people because of their race, color, or religion. The Illinois statute, changed from that which was upheld in *Beauharnais,* specifically requires that the offensive speech be provocative of a breach of the peace" (p. 298).

68. Berlin, "Two Concepts of Liberty," p. 155. (I recognize the irony of citing Berlin in this context.)

69. "Freedom of Expression."

70. Joel Feinberg, "Limits to the Freedom of Expression," in *Philosophy of Law*, 5th ed., ed. Joel Feinberg and Hyman Gross (Belmont, Cal.: Wadsworth, 1995).

71. Feinberg argues, however, that if we allow the category of group defamation as unprotected speech, we have to ban any vaguely insulting speech about *any* group. But Feinberg, along with other liberals, would presumably not be prepared to run a similar argument against the justness of affirmative action programs. In that case, they are prepared to acknowledge both differences among different discriminated-against minority groups and differences in the degree of discrimination suffered by them. (One must acknowledge these important differences to counter the objection that affirmative action programs are unfair to those minorities, say, Irish males, not favored by them.) But if one has this way of distinguishing among different sorts of discrimination, one surely has ways of distinguishing among different kinds of damaging falsehoods *and* different degrees of damage. Such an enterprise will take into account the present vulnerability of the defamed group, as well as their ability or inability to remedy the damage with more speech.

72. It is important to note the history of stereotyping this claim reinforces. Such sensationalistic stereotyping of, for example, black males as rapists, may be seen to be an instance of irrational belief formation based on what has been called the "availability error." A. Tversky and D. Kahneman, "Availability: A Heuristic for Judging Frequency and Probability," *Cognitive Psychology* 2 (1973): 207–232. See also Antonio R. Damasio's discussion of the availability error in *Descartes' Error: Emotion, Reason, and the Human Brain* (New York: Avon, 1994): 191–192. Damasio considers such failures of rationality to be "not just due to a primary calculation weakness, but also due to the influence of biological drives such as obedience, conformity, the desire to preserve self-esteem, which are often manifest as emotions and feelings" (p. 191).

73. *Beauharnais*.

74. Feinberg, *The Moral Limits of the Criminal Law*. Vol. 2: *Offense to Others* (New York: Oxford University Press, 1985), p. 158.

75. Ibid.

76. "Democracy and Defamation: Control of Group Libel," *Columbia Law Review* 42 (May 1942): 727–780, 772.

77. Ann Garry, "Pornography and Respect for Women," *Social Theory and Practice* 4 (1978): 395–421; see also the articles in *Price We Pay.*

78. John Locke, *An Essay Concerning Human Understanding,* ed. A. D. Woozley (New York: New American Library, 1974), pp. 259–267, 368–369; George Berkeley, *The Principles of Human Knowledge* (London: Collins, 1962), pp. 50–59.

79. Such a picture would more easily be seen by whites in a white-dominant culture as a picture of women in general if it appeared to be a picture of a white woman. The depicted race of the woman would typically not be viewed as salient and, thus, would not be a distraction.

80. Joseph Raz, "Multiculturalism: A Liberal Perspective," *Dissent,* Winter 1994, pp. 67–79.

81. For a discussion of the ways in which expressions of racism can issue from the unconscious and not be the result of conscious, autonomous choice, see Charles R. Lawrence III, "The Id, the Ego, and Equal Protection: Reckoning with Unconscious Racism," *Stanford Law Review* 39 (January 1987): 317–388.

82. Mari J. Matsuda, "Public Response to Racist Speech: Considering the Victim's Story," in Matsuda et al., *Words That Wound,* p. 26.

83. Conversation with Kendall Thomas, 16 March 1998, Berkeley, California. Thomas does not endorse the view that hate speech regulation is categorically forbidden under the U.S. Constitution. He cautions, however, that although regulating hate speech may be constitutionally permissible, it may not be politically desirable. I agree with him that pragmatic considerations may lead us to refrain from regulating even harmful hate speech. For example, in recent years, some violators of campus hate speech codes have been elevated to the status of First Amendment heroes, with the effect that the harms of their speech, as well as those of the environment that fostered it, have not been adequately addressed.

INDEX

312

Index